Theater of a City

Theater of a City

The Places of London Comedy, 1598–1642

JEAN E. HOWARD

PENN

University of Pennsylvania Press

Philadelphia

10   9   8   7   6   5   4   3   2   1

Published by
University of Pennsylvania Press
Philadelphia, Pennsylvania 19104-4112

Library of Congress Cataloging-in-Publication Data

Howard, Jean E. (Jean Elizabeth), 1948–
    Theater of a city : the places of London comedy, 1598–1642 / Jean E. Howard.
       p. cm.
    Includes bibliographical references and index.
    ISBN-13: 978-0-8122-3978-2
    ISBN-10: 0-8122-3978-4 (cloth : alk. paper)
    1. Theater—England—London—History—17th century. 2. Theater—England—London—History—16th century. 3. Theaters—England—London—History—17th century. 4. Theaters—England—London—History—16th century. 5. English drama (Comedy)—History and criticism. I. Title.
PN2596.L6H597 2006
792.09421'09032—dc22

                                                                          2006042197

For Katie and Caleb

Contents

Introduction

London is a large, excellent, and mighty city of business, and the most important in the whole kingdom; most of the inhabitants are employed in buying and selling merchandize [*sic*], and trading in almost every corner of the world, since the river is most useful and convenient for this purpose, considering that ships from France, the Netherlands, Sweden, Denmark, Hamburg, and other kingdoms, come almost up to the city, to which they convey goods and receive and take away others in exchange.[1]

This description of London, written by Frederick, Duke of Wirtemberg, who visited London in 1592, attests to the impressive size and perceptible commercial energy of England's premier metropolis. Although the Duke assumed that London was preeminent among other English towns, what he could not know was just how considerably it outstripped them in population and commercial activity at the end of the sixteenth century. In 1600 the population of London included approximately 200,000 people, up from 55,000 just fifty years before. The next largest English city was Norwich, with a population of 15,000 in 1600, followed by York and Bristol with 12,000 people each. Only twenty towns in all of England had populations of 5,000 or more. With London taken out of the mix, the other nineteen towns contained only 136,000 people in total, considerably less than the population of London alone.[2]

Demographics by themselves, of course, do not explain why London was so impressive to this foreign visitor. But they begin to suggest how unusually beyond scale—how vast and sprawling—the city must have appeared to those hundreds of migrants who streamed into the capital from other parts of England and from the Continent throughout the second half of the sixteenth and then the seventeenth century.[3] Not only did London dwarf other English cities; it also rivaled in size the most expansive cities on the Continent. In 1600, London was the third largest city in Europe, outpaced only by Naples and by Paris. By 1650 it was second only to Paris; by 1700 it was first in terms of size.[4] London's spectacular demographic growth during this period was matched only by its economic development. Frederick, Duke of Wirtemberg, describes London in 1592 as a "mighty city of business," and it was. By

1600 London was the anchor of a rapidly expanding national market and the chief port through which the nation took part in overseas trade with Europe, with the Levant, and—later in the seventeenth century—with the Americas.[5]

These economic and social developments had a direct impact on the cultural life of London, specifically on the public theater that was one of the chief entertainment institutions to emerge from this period of spectacular demographic, economic, and social change. And, I am going to argue, the theater, in turn, was important in shaping how people of the period conceptualized or made sense of this fast-changing urban milieu. My title, *Theater of a City*, foregrounds the intimate synergy I see operating between London and the early modern commercial theater. Not only could that theater not have arisen anywhere in England except in London but the course of its development also remained closely linked to changes taking place within the metropolis right up to the Civil War. Many accounts of early modern theater have stressed the genius of some of its theater practitioners, especially Shakespeare.[6] Others have implied that, alongside her accomplishments in nation building and commercial expansion, Elizabeth I brought England to a new ascendancy in the arts.[7] Both, certainly, were important. However, without a commercial theater in place, Shakespeare would have had little chance to display his genius. London provided the material conditions in which such a theater emerged.[8] Moreover, while the Court played a role in protecting the theater from the harsher restrictions the City aldermen might have imposed upon it and in offering limited patronage to particular theater companies, the commercial theater was not essentially a court theater.[9] Westminster was at times a useful ally and at times a troubling force, but from day to day the commercial theater depended on a public to approve its craft and buy its product. And that public comprised Londoners of various stripes, from apprentices to foreign visitors, who had reasons to come to the city.

At the theater Londoners encountered fictions that directly addressed the conditions of social change and dislocation occurring around them. Whereas this is true, I would suggest, for each of the popular stage genres that flourished over this vibrant sixty-year period, this book will focus on those plays that most directly address the urban milieu, namely, London comedies. Beginning with William Haughton's *Englishmen for My Money* (1598) and ending with William Cavendish's *The Variety* (1640), I explore a succession of comedies that took familiar London places as their setting for stories that addressed some of the most pressing issues facing the city's inhabitants: demographic change and the influx of foreigners and strangers into the city; new ways of making money and of losing it; changing gender roles within the metropolis; and the rise of a distinctive "town culture" in the West End. In creating fictions in which these issues figure prominently and by situating them in particular places such as Gresham's Royal Exchange, the notorious debtors' prisons known as the Counters, or the ubiquitous bawdy houses that not only ringed but permeated the city proper, dramatists gave their stories a local habitation and a name. Consequently, each chapter of this book focuses on a particular place within the city and examines the way in which the stage created significant stories about it. The recurring features of plot and character that structure these stories, and the changes rung on them over time, are crucial evidence of both the social tensions these plays helped to negotiate and the terms in which they made city space socially legible.

Throughout this book I am in part investigating the process by which, to use de Certeau's language, plays helped to transform specific places into significant social spaces, that is, into environments marked by the actions, movements, and daily practices of inhabitants.[10] Stories were central to this transformative process. Through their place-based dramatic narratives, playwrights helped representationally to construct the practices associated with specific urban spaces, directing audiences to the uses to which city spaces could be put and to the privileged modes of conduct and the cultural competencies associated with each. Of course, this was a highly ideological process and not merely a mapping of what "really" happened within the London milieu.[11] Through its fictions drama helped less to transcribe than to construct and interpret the city. In the process playwrights imaginatively transformed urban places into settings for specific kinds of social interaction, whether between a citizen and an alien, a debtor and a creditor, a prostitute and a client, or a dancing master and a country gentleman. As represented on the stage, the places of London thus became a powerful resource in complex and socially significant renditions of urban life.

Place, then, functions in these dramas as the material arena within which urban social relations were regulated and urban problems negotiated. These problems included, for example, foreign encroachment into particular London places, such as the Royal Exchange, or the perilous credit arrangements of an economy in which debt loomed large. In staging the city, dramatists focused on many of the same things that Frederick, Duke of Wirtemberg, had, namely, the demographic expansion and the increasing commercial activity that characterized the metropolis, along with its implication in an international system of trade signified by the foreign ships that the German visitor had noted along London's docks. Through their urban fictions the city's dramatists responded to and spurred these changes, creating a stage whose popularity testified to the playwrights' attentiveness to the urban anxieties and pleasures they so persistently solicited and addressed.

The following introduction focuses on three things. First, I lay out a fuller picture of the city London had become in the late sixteenth and seventeenth centuries, paying special attention to the mixture of old and new practices and established and emergent communities within and without the city walls. A site of government and of trade, London was rapidly becoming what Crystal Bartolovich has termed a "world city," one experiencing the dislocating effects of an influx of alien people, tongues, and goods, as well as the more mundane dislocations of extremely rapid demographic growth.[12] Second, I look briefly at how particular London writers responded to the changing social landscape within which they lived and wrote and then at the specific role of the theater in responding to and shaping those changes. A professional dramatist like Thomas Heywood, for example, had strong views about the place of the stage in the city's history and in its bid for status within the international community. Finally, I turn to the actual places and the particular problems I address in each chapter, outlining the many threads of the argument—about the economy, gender, and foreign–native antagonism—that weave themselves through those ensuing chapters.

A City in Flux

While arguing for the essential social stability of London during the late Elizabethan and early Jacobean periods, historians of the city also take note of the many elements of change—from population growth to the increase in foreign craftsmen operating outside the authorized guilds—that put a strain on London's governing structures and its dominant institutions.[13] I accept the view that city authorities by and large maintained order and governed London with efficiency during this period. I want to shift focus, however, and ask not how well political and social order was maintained in the city but what conceptual challenges were entailed in living in London during this period of growth and change. How did the city come to make sense to its inhabitants, many of them new to London, and what role did the theater play in the complicated ideological process of constructing the city as an imagined entity and of creating fictions that addressed the problems of urban life?

The rapid physical expansion of London that accompanied its demographic growth represented one kind of challenge to inhabitants and to dramatists alike. If the walled city and the immediately adjoining extramural wards once defined the core of the city, by the early seventeenth century suburban growth had begun to spin off new loci of activity and power. Westminster, a separate entity to the west, had always been the seat of monarchical authority, but now the expanse between the city and Westminster began to fill up with fancy shopping streets such as the Strand and by the 1630s with upscale housing developments like the Earl of Bedford's Covent Garden project and with parks and other places of urban leisure. By the third or fourth decade of the seventeenth century, the West End had developed a "town culture" of wit and leisure distinct from the "city culture" to the east or the "court culture" of Westminster.[14] At the same time, urban sprawl was overtaking the northern, eastern, and southern suburban regions.[15] Overcrowding within the walled city and immigration from abroad made the eastern districts along the Thames waterfront, for example, a thriving commercial area both because of activity linked to the shipping trades and also because of crafts that took root there to escape regulation by the city guilds.[16] This rapid physical expansion made the city less easy to know in its entirety—"know" not just in the sense of having familiarity with the streets and buildings of various districts but also in the sense of having a conceptual image of the activities imagined to characterize these new areas and of the kinds of people who inhabited them. Moreover, the physical growth of the city was inseparable from other changes such as overcrowding within the walled city, shoddy buildings thrown up in the suburbs, increased congestion on city streets, and the multiplication of taverns, inns, and places of entertainment in and around the urban area.[17]

Writing about London, as many dramatists did, was one way, of course, discursively to manage change and to provide interpretations and conceptualizations of both new and old aspects of the city. Two works produced near the turn of the century begin to suggest how differently writers, including dramatists, went about the job of textually constructing London and foregrounding particular places within it. John Stow, the city's best-known Elizabethan chronicler, typically equated change with decline and decay and often wrote with nostalgia about what he felt to be a vanishing city. His *Survey of London*, first published in 1598 and then expanded and reprinted in 1603, unearthed both textual and material traces of the city's past in order to preserve them in printed form.[18] Delving into books and written records of the city, Stow also dug deep into the actual dirt of London, visiting excavations and ruins, tracing the paths of streams that were blocked with the debris of an expanding city. For him, the important places of London were its guildhalls, churches, and public endowments such as hospitals because they commemorated the shared achievements of what he saw as the city's privileged actors, its civic leaders. Names of mayors, aldermen, great merchants, and municipal benefactors stud his pages. A monumental text, *The Survey* attempts to give fixity to a city in flux, to recover what the forces of time and change have obliterated, and to give a lasting record of its great edifices and of the great civic figures eminent in its history. Consequently, there is a certain relentlessness to Stow's repetitive ward-by-ward descriptions of guildhalls, churches, and famous citizens. In his commemorative narrative, "the list" is his rhetorical signature.

In the course of his narrative, however, Stow could not help but note what to him were troubling new aspects of London life. These included the desecration of tombs in the city's churches by zealous Protestant reformers, the decline of charity, and the way in which the green fields to the east of the city were being turned into jammed residential areas. In an oft-cited passage, Stow describes how as a boy he fetched milk from farms just to the east of the city walls, an area given over to cramped tenements by 1598. Although Stow loved London's ancient buildings, the deeds of its Lord Mayors and the charitable works of its prominent citizens, he was repelled by aspects of modernity such as the repression of popular pastimes like May Day festivities.[19] Certain parts of contemporary London life he simply elided, such as its thriving theater industry. Although in the 1598 edition of his *Survey* Stow makes two passing references to the Curtain and the Theater as London playhouses, he does not discuss their importance or the many other playing venues within the city. Both passages, brief as they are, are deleted from the 1603 version.[20]

By contrast, some texts about London written about the same time as Stow's focus on an entirely different set of urban places, highlighting all that was new and fashionable within the city, including its theaters. Such is Thomas Dekker's 1609 prose pamphlet, *The Gull's Hornbook*. This delightful satire exists in a different stylistic and conceptual universe from Stow's urban chorography. Cheap, short, and wickedly irreverent, *The Gull's Hornbook* gives tongue-in-cheek advice about how to live like a gallant in London. As the word "hornbook" implies, it is a mock pedagogical manual that makes fun of certain city practices but in doing so reveals the new codes of conduct that the "gull" is forever doomed imperfectly to imitate. If, for example, in Stow's city the highest virtue is charity, in the London of Dekker's pamphlet it is fashionability. All advice to the gull rests on the premise that making a good appearance is in every instance of the utmost importance. That means being seen at the right places in the right clothes and saying the right things. Hence, the gull is advised, for example, to go to the middle isle of St. Paul's to show off his fine clothes.[21] In Dekker's text, as opposed to Stow's, a great building such as St. Paul's is less a monument to the city's rich civic past than a fashion runway. Moreover, places largely unmentioned in Stow's narrative achieve great prominence in Dekker's, namely, the taverns, ordinaries, and playhouses that, along with St. Paul's middle isle, offer rich possibilities for self-display.[22] Describing a visit to the theater, Dekker's narrator instructs an aspiring gallant how to show himself to best advantage during a dramatic performance.

It shall crown you with rich commendation to laugh aloud in the middest of the most serious and saddest scene of the terriblest tragedy and to let that clapper, your tongue, be tossed so high that all the house may ring of it. Your lords use it, your knights are apes to the lords and do so too, your Inn o'Court man is zanny to the knights and—marry, very scurvily—comes likewise limping after it; be thou a beagle to them all and never lin snuffing till you have scented them, for by talking and laughing like a ploughman in a morris you heap Pelion upon Ossa, glory upon glory.[23]

Of course, such outlandish behavior would actually heap ignominy on ignominy, but the fact that the would-be gallant does not really know how to make himself an object of admiration only flatters those who do and points to the importance of "proper" self-display and fashionability as emerging urban values. Because *The Gull's Hornbook* is a satire, it implicitly critiques what it anatomizes: for example, the behavior of penniless gentlemen who live for appearances often with no money in their pockets and no food in their stomachs.[24] But in doing so it strikingly calls attention to a cityscape defined less by churches and guildhalls than by places of consumption and pleasure, and it points to the new practices of display they encourage.

If Stow's text is steeped in nostalgia, Dekker's pamphlet is entirely of the moment. If Stow hardly mentions the theater, Dekker makes it central to the daily life of a London gallant. If Stow seems oblivious to the new products such as tobacco penetrating the expanding London market, tobacco's presence suffuses *The Gull's Hornbook*. And if Stow praises the charitable deeds of London's honorable citizens, Dekker focuses on the fashionable appearance of gallants and aspirants to their sophistication. It is as if everything that Stow despises and pushes to the margins of his text rises to the surface in Dekker's pamphlet. In the bookstalls of London, these divergent visions of the city would have coexisted, each turning the city into a print commodity, but with very different understandings of what were the important places and actors that defined London life. The opposite of a monumental text, *The Gull's Hornbook* presented itself as a cheap and fashionable commodity aimed not at London's solid citizens but at a smart set of urban gallants and would-be gallants who could feel superior to Dekker's gull and yet take pleasure in recognizing the text's landscape of fashionable performance.

That London to a Stow could seem disturbingly in decline and to a Dekker amusingly full of new possibilities resulted in part from their conflicting responses to the demographic and commercial changes to which Frederick, Duke of Wirtemberg's description of the city pointed. Both kinds of change invite further exploration. I have already given numbers indicating the city's explosive rate of population growth in the second half of the sixteenth century. But who was represented by these figures and what was their impact on the city's life? Because of the high death rate in London, much of the population growth had to be the result of in-migration.[25] Many people from other parts of the British Isles moved to London to find employment, swelling the city's population and enhancing its labor force and at the same time creating problems in terms of housing, sanitation, and public order.[26] Technically, those who came to the city and were not made free of its guilds were known as "foreigners," a usage that today we would reserve for those born outside the boundaries of a given nation-state. But while the *OED*, as early as 1413, records that a "foreigner" can refer to "A person born in a foreign country: one from abroad or of another nation; an alien" (1.a), by 1460 the term also meant "One of another county, parish, etc., a stranger, outsider. In early use especially one not a member of any particular guild, a non-freeman" (2). Early modern London was full of this kind of foreigner: those born outside the city and not members of its guilds but who worked in and around the metropolis as manservants, day laborers, chambermaids, and workers in unsanctioned guilds operating in suburban locations. In addition, many young men came to London from the provinces to take up apprenticeships. Part of the guild economy, they nonetheless were new to the city. Moreover, London was periodically visited by "foreigners" who did not mean to settle but to take up temporary residence: gentry up from the country for the law terms, aristocrats in attendance at the court in Westminster, and the women who increasingly accompanied their husbands for shopping and entertainment in London.[27]

These foreigners were joined by a sizable group of those born outside England entirely. In the late sixteenth century the greatest number of these "aliens" or "strangers" (that is, "One who belongs to another country, a foreigner" *OED* 1) were religious refugees seeking a safe haven in London. Stranger merchants had, of course, long been a feature of London life. Flemish merchants were important in London in the thirteenth century; Italian and German or Hanse merchants rose to prominence in the fourteenth and fifteenth centuries; the French became influential in the first half of the sixteenth.[28] In every case, these merchants played a major role in England's overseas trade, both in the export of its wool and cloth and in the import of finished goods to England through entrepots in Venice, Lisbon, or Antwerp. The English crown needed the expertise of these stranger merchants and granted them monopolies and privileges, which, however, it could also revoke when pressure from domestic merchants or antialien feeling became too intense.[29] But by the end of the sixteenth century, while there were still a number of alien merchants at work in the city, the majority of strangers were skilled craftsmen who hailed from the Low Countries and France, driven to England by the push of religious persecution and the pull of economic opportunity. In 1567 the "Dutch" comprised 74.5 percent of the strangers resident in London and Westminster, the French 15.5 percent. Besides merchants, they included "schoolmasters, surgeons, physicians, engineers, musicians, and artists."[30] Collectively, they probably made up 4 to 5 percent of London's total population, though their numbers could seem greater when they clustered in particular residential neighborhoods, calling attention to their cumulative presence. As a result of the high degree of migration to the city, it was inevitable that established citizens would have encounters with new arrivals daily, both from other parts of the British Isles and from abroad. So how were these foreigners and strangers comprehended?

There is no simple answer. For a long time it has been assumed that London was, at the end of the sixteenth century, an insular and xenophobic place. There is evidence for that view in the antialien riots that occasionally broke out in the city, usually motivated by economic anxieties about the ways in which foreign workers might be draining away national resources or horning in on English craft production.[31] Popular xenophobia was undoubtedly present in the period, and while the state realized the benefits that could accrue from the skills and expertise of alien workers and merchants, it indirectly fueled anxiety about strangers by supporting a mercantilist ideology that stressed the importance of accumulating wealth within the nation and not allowing bullion to "bleed out" to foreign countries, especially through alien merchants.[32] However, if there was a xenophobic impulse in English culture during the period, it was countered, especially in London, by a competing cosmopolitanism more tolerant of difference and more inclined to look beyond the boundaries of the nation-state with something other than contempt or fear.

To a certain extent, identification with persecuted Protestants from the Continent could counterbalance anxiety about their possible deleterious effects on the English economy.[33] Perhaps to an even greater extent, trade counterbalanced xenophobic impulses. I do not mean to suggest that commerce among nations automatically eventuates in tolerance and enlightened thinking.[34] That would be uncritically to echo apologists for the benefits of unfettered trade. I mean something more hard-edged altogether, namely, that the expansion of overseas trade mandated a kind of forced cosmopolitanism, a recognition that one had to undertake certain kinds of negotiations with strangers in order to further one's own interests.[35] An example may begin to suggest the complex intermixing of xenophobia and cosmopolitanism that could exist side by side in city institutions and communities. Candidates for employment by the East India Company regularly presented as chief qualifications their skill at foreign languages, not just European languages such as Italian, French, Dutch, or Portuguese (although familiarity with any of these was frequently claimed as an asset) but also Persian, Malacan, and Arabic. Many of these candidates had been sent abroad at a young age specifically to receive language training in Lisbon, Istanbul, or Surat, and they spoke confidently of their knowledge of foreign tongues and of foreign customs.[36] It was just these sorts of qualifications that made particular candidates successful in the highly competitive scramble for jobs in the great trading companies. Such men could get on in distant ports without giving offense and could deal with the complexities of trade in a foreign zone.

The other side of the coin, however, was that a very thin line separated the desirability of such cosmopolitan skills and the danger that having them could make one seem a threat to English interests. Some candidates for jobs were turned away precisely because they had been too long in the employ of the Dutch or the Portuguese, even though that employment had given them experience in the very regions where the East India Company wished to trade, or because it was feared that long stays in Lisbon had led to their conversion to Catholicism or long stays in Istanbul to their conversion to Islam.[37] One could, in a sense, be perceived as *too* cosmopolitan, as having lost one's identification with Englishness and the English national interest.

If London was not a uniformly xenophobic place, then, neither did it embody the Derridean ideal of the city as an exceptional arena of cosmopolitan civility, a safe haven from the passions of nationalism and religious sectarianism.[38] Instead, I would make the more modest claim that the demographic and economic changes overtaking the city made ordinary Londoners confront in a new way both the reality and the idea of strangers in their midst and the necessity of learning to deal with foreign cultures and languages. In the middle ages, overseas merchants had regularly been involved with trade in Europe. In a prenational period, the international merchant class was, in fact, to some extent a pan-European group. But in the sixteenth century, identification with country heightened even as contact with and knowledge about strangers probably intensified for more of the urban population as a result of migration from the Continent, the uptick of overseas trade passing through the docks of

London, and the circulation of printed texts dealing with the voyages of exploration, travelers' reports, and captivity tales. Plays were among the texts that most often represented strangers or the influx of foreign practices or commodities into the metropolis, whether on the main floor or in the upper shops of the Royal Exchange, within the city's bawdy houses or in its sophisticated ballrooms and academies of manners. Consequently, I will deal with the particulars of these representations of strangers and alien ways in nearly all the chapters that follow.

Certainly the city as a whole was a less insular place than it had been fifty years before. London was becoming an increasingly miscegenated space, by which I mean a place of mixing, where foreigners from Lancashire pressed up against established members of the London guilds and against stranger craftsmen. Between foreigners and aliens, London must at time have felt like a city where nearly everyone, to one degree or another, was "new," and where the mixing of different kinds of people was inevitable. In one of his last essays (1642), Henry Peacham wrote about "The Art of Living in London" in which he describes the skills needed to live "in a populous place, where multitudes of people reside."[39] London, of course, is his premier example of such a place, and in depicting the city he stresses the mixture of various kinds of residents that the city attracted:

noble and simple, rich and poor, young and old, from all places and countries, either for pleasure (and let me add besides, to save the charge of housekeeping in the country) or for profit, as lawyers to the terms, countrymen and women to Smithfield and the markets; or for necessity, as poor young men and maids to seek services and places; servingmen, masters; and some others, all manner of employment. (p. 243)

It is to this constant influx of new residents that Peacham directs warnings about the dangers of city life. His language is richly metaphorical. London is like a "vast sea, full of gusts, fearful-dangerous shelves and rocks, ready at every storm to sink and cast the weak and unexperienced bark," (p. 243), "a wood where there is as many briers as people" (p. 244), "a quicksand" (p. 245), and the seat of several "poisons" (p. 245) such as drunkenness, gaming, prostitution, and reckless spending. It is a place where an inexperienced newcomer needs a skillful pilot, "another Columbus or Drake" (p. 244), as guide. Peacham, of course, offers himself in this role.

The language of exploration and the invocation of the names of Columbus and Drake are, I would argue, of special interest because they suggest that the difficulties of negotiating the city are in some sense seen as comparable to the dangers of negotiating the New World or the far Asian ports that Drake visited on his round-the-world navigation. People coming to London from outside the city or from outside the country would know neither its geography, its customs nor, as Peacham stresses, its particular dangers. Aids were necessary: prescriptive tracts such as Peacham's, elaborating the dangers of urban life and offering advice for escaping them; networks of family or friends who could orient one and provide contacts and jobs; and places of resort such as public theaters where the act of common spectatorship could make one feel at one with the anonymous others who paid their pennies for the same entertainment.[40] London was not necessarily transparent to those who lived there. Demographic growth, physical expansion, high death rates, and high in-migration meant that the city was opaque and unfamiliar to many of its inhabitants. The theater helped to make sense of city life. In play after play foreigners and strangers intermingled with London-born citizens; suburbs and walled city were juxtaposed; and city worthies were memorialized even as the seamier side of London life — prostitution, con men, crime — was dramatized. The theater, of course, did not just refer to these aspects of city living; it wove them into stories that interpreted, hierarchized, and distinguished the incompetent from the boorish, the insider from the pariah, in the process figuring new social relations for an expanding metropolis and new solutions to pressing urban problems.

In representing the city, the stage focused with particular intensity on the economic and commercial aspects of the city's expansion. In the early seventeenth century, England, then in the early stages of capitalist development, was undergoing a period of economic change in which London played a major part. First, the city was becoming the hub of an integrated national market linking the countryside and the provincial towns to the capital city, encouraging traffic in goods and people between London and the rest of the British Isles. This process of market integration coincided temporally with the evolving consolidation of administrative and political power in Westminster. London was at once emerging as a powerful capital city and the commercial center of a national market.[41]

Second, as a commercial center London was increasingly linked not just to the rest of the British Isles but to the rest of the world. Its status as a port was crucial in this regard. In *The Perspective of the World*, volume 3 of his *Civilization and Capitalism 15th–18th Century*, Fernand Braudel traces the importance of large commercial cities to the economic life of Europe in the period 1400 to 1800. Always ports, these cities — Venice, Antwerp, Genoa, Amsterdam, and finally London — were at the epicenter of important economic arenas that depended on the central city for concentrations of capital, access to credit, sources of news, and stable laws governing mercantile transactions.[42] In the late sixteenth century, after the fall of Antwerp as the major northern entrepot, London and Amsterdam both began to emerge as such cities. They did so at a time when England was no longer solely dependent on the export of wool and cloth for its financial well-being. With the establishment of the London-based joint stock and regulated trading companies such as the Levant Company and the East India Company (1592 and 1599), English merchants were increasingly engaged in the reexport trade. That is, they were importing luxury goods such as silks and spices and currants from Eastern markets and reexporting them to Europe and the New World for profit.[43]

The consequences of this new kind of trade were multiple. For one thing, the growth of the joint stock companies meant increased contact with inhabitants of the distant port cities to which English ships were now sailing. Englishmen were voyaging to Virginia, certainly, and also to the ports of the eastern Mediterranean. Moreover, because the crews of English ships had to be replenished in these foreign ports, London also contained seamen from every European and Mediterranean country to which English ships ventured. Long distance trade also brought many new goods into London's domestic economy. As F. J. Fisher long ago demonstrated, during the reigns of Elizabeth and James, London was increasingly a center for conspicuous consumption, especially the consumption of luxury goods, though many products such as tobacco, sugar, and currants were bought not just by the wealthy but by ordinary citizens as well.[44] The culture of display highlighted in Dekker's *The Gull's Hornbook* depended on an urban milieu in which people could be judged by what they could buy, even though such acquisitiveness was often morally condemned or subject to satiric treatment.[45]

Moreover, and this has been perhaps the most widely noted aspect of economic change in the period, market exchanges were becoming increasingly abstract and generalized. While England still had many market towns and fairs where trade took place directly between buyers and sellers, in many cases exchange occurred in what Jean-Christophe Agnew has termed "a placeless market" in which participants were unknown to each other and transactions were conducted through middlemen using new financial instruments such as bills of exchange or other forms of credit.[46] With the labor of production increasingly occluded, commodities acquired fetishistic value, floating free from their makers but increasingly defining the subjectivity of their buyers.

I want to stress that many of the consequences of the changes occurring in London's commercial life were understood only in retrospect. By the middle of the eighteenth century England would occupy a commanding role in a world economy centered in London but penetrating to many parts of the globe.[47] This outcome was not imaginable in 1600.

In fact, in 1600, despite the enormous changes that were happening in the city, many Londoners probably still felt peripheral to the rest of Europe and in some ways inferior to the cultures and the commercial and military strength of Mediterranean powers, whether Spanish, Ottoman, or Italian.[48] The long history of England's peripheral position on the rim of Northern Europe was not erased in a few decades. Nor was the growth of the monopolistic joint stock companies universally greeted with enthusiasm. Many small traders were barred entirely from the traffic controlled by these companies and resented the profits they made. And even as the presence of increasing numbers of aliens in London caused some degree of anxiety, so did the emergence of a culture of consumption. My emphasis on a city in flux is meant to highlight not only the many material changes overtaking London but also the discursive changes and struggles necessary to make cognitive and ideological sense of life in the city. And this is where the theater enters the story.

London's Stages

The commercial theater was one of the new institutions—along with such things as the Royal Exchange, joint stock trading companies, and Bridewell workhouse—that had their origins in the special conditions obtaining in London in the second half of the sixteenth century; moreover, the popularity of that theater arose in part because of the work it unconsciously but robustly and imaginatively performed in accommodating Londoners of all stripes to the somewhat bewildering world in which they were living. A popular forum speaking to the full range of London inhabitants, the theater drew its energies from the demographically diverse, commercially vital milieu in which it arose.

It is one of the truisms of theater history that something significant happened when, in 1576, James Burbage erected the Theatre, traditionally regarded as the city's first purpose-built commercial playing space, in Shoreditch.[49] The point is not that before 1576 there had not been troupes of professional players who performed at court, for noblemen, and in various English towns or foreign venues. There had been such troupes.[50] Nor is the point that there had never been buildings, such as inns with open courtyards or inner rooms, where theater had regularly been performed for paying customers within London before 1576. There had been such buildings, including the Boar's Head and the Bel Savage Inns, and they continued to be used after the Theater was built.[51] Rather, the innovation lay in the erection of special buildings permanently dedicated to the commercial production of plays, buildings where professional acting troupes could have a London base. From there they could branch out to act at court during the Christmas

holidays, go to the country when the plague shut their London theaters, or leave the city when for other reasons it made economic sense
to take the troupe on tour.[52]

The erection of these theaters required an extraordinary conver-
gence of factors. As Walter Cohen has argued, in England "no other locale [besides London] provided the economic and demographic conditions necessary for the successful interaction of investor, actor,
dramatist, and audience."[53] Commercial theater was not tied to a ritual
or a liturgical calendar; it was a perpetual theater that made the possibility for commercial, secular recreation an everyday occurrence. It was
part of an entertainment industry that only a rapidly commercializing
culture could sustain. The theater industry, like so much else in the
London of the latter sixteenth century, was a mixed affair, part capitalist venture, part artisanal craft guild. To build a public theater required
amassing significant amounts of capital and expending it to lease land
on which to erect a purpose-built playing space. This a number of entrepreneurial Londoners, including James Burbage and Francis Lang-
ley, were able to do. The day-to-day operations of some of the acting
troupes who occupied these theaters, like Shakespeare's Lord Chamberlain's Men, resembled a miniature version of a joint stock company.
Sharers pooled money to distribute risk and to underwrite expenses, including the hiring of other actors. The sharers then drew equally on
any profits.[54] But within the companies, social relations had a craft
guild cast with young boys serving in apprentice roles to older actors.[55]
The parallel to guilds was limited, however. Unlike guilds, theater companies had no halls, courts, or structures of regulation. The remnants
of guild organization present in these companies existed cheek by jowl
with the investment structures and high risks characteristic of capitalist
undertakings. Legally, these companies were only allowed to exist if
they had the patronage of a nobleman. Otherwise, the actors could be
condemned as rogues and vagabonds. Notionally, they thus existed as
servants to an aristocratic lord; but in actuality they were part of a complex commercial venture.

The building of the early commercial theaters—the Theatre, the
Curtain, the Swan, the Fortune, the Globe—did not, therefore, just
magically happen. It occurred because of a particular conjunction of
events that also produced other changes in the city. If capital was available, so were audiences. The growth in London's population was a
crucial element in this theater's success. Commercial theaters could
function because there were enough people to sustain repertory companies performing fairly continuously throughout the year and a
Court to the West of the city that regularly sought command performances during the holiday seasons. Moreover, the *nature* of the London

population was as important as its size. As I have indicated, London was increasingly a place visited by non-Londoners, men and women who came from the country to do business, shop, or bring an action in the London courts, and by strangers of all sorts—ambassadors, overseas merchants, travelers such as Thomas Platter and Frederick, Duke of Wirtemberg. The theater attracted the custom of just such visitors; it had become an early tourist mecca. Just as importantly, it was, as *The Gull's Hornbook* indicates, a place where the fashionable or the would-be fashionable gentlemen of the town congregated to display themselves, and there were many such in London, either studying at the Inns of Court or "looking about" for court employment or the command of a military unit mustering for Ireland or the Continent. And, of course, there were as far as we can tell just a great many ordinary people who found the commercial theater an important communal pastime.[56]

In addition, the Crown supported the public theaters when the city fathers attempted to shut down playing venues on the grounds of their supposedly ungodly or disorderly effects. Perhaps it did so simply to provide the urban population with the equivalent of bread and circuses, public entertainment that would take attention away from public discontents. In allowing the theaters to operate, the Crown supported an institution that provided a place of common resort for many different kinds of ordinary Londoners, including many new to the city. Offering an alternative to the cycle and liturgical drama that was increasingly being suppressed, if not quite eradicated, throughout the country, it provided occasions for recreation in a culture in which the number of saints days and religious holidays was being restricted. In addition, through its rapidly expanding array of theatrical offerings, it provided Londoners with ways to negotiate—through the mediation of staged fictions—some of the changes overtaking these increasingly cosmopolitan urban dwellers.

Thomas Heywood, that naive and often-scorned champion of the city, was one early modern dramatist who recognized the special nature of the link between London and its theaters. In his *Apology for Actors*, Heywood, of course, was seeking to legitimize the theaters and to protect them from opponents, but he did so by creating a narrative in which the greatness of London was uniquely guaranteed by the greatness of its theaters as, he argues, had been true for all cosmopolitan metropolitan centers from time out of mind. Repeatedly in his treatise, Heywood praised the theaters of ancient Rome, and repeatedly he compared contemporary London to the ancient city. "Rome was a Metropolis, a place whither all the nations knowne under the Sunne, resorted: so is London, and being to receive all Estates, all Princes, all Nations, therefore to affoord them all choyce of pastimes, sports, and recreations: yet were there Theaters in all the greatest Cities of the world, as we will more largely particularize hereafter" (C2).[57] Besides Rome's theater, he also praised the playhouses of ancient Jerusalem, Athens, Thebes, and Carthage, and of modern-day Paris, Madrid, Verona, Florence, and Antwerp.

By thrusting London into such distinguished urban company, Heywood was making the theater central to his chauvinistic account of the city's achievement of a certain international status. Of London theaters he boasted: "Playing is an ornament to the Citty, which strangers of all Nations, repairing hither, report of in their Countries, beholding them here with some admiration: for what variety of entertainment can there be in any Citty of Christendome, more then in London?" (F3). Heywood thought theater valuable in making evident to strangers the magnificence of his northern metropolis and, by extension, the English nation; and he was right about the attractiveness of the theaters to foreign visitors such as Thomas Platter, many of whom found a visit to the theater as noteworthy as a visit to St. Paul's, London Bridge, the Exchange, or Westminster Abbey. Heywood was always aware of the competitive contemporary world in which London was ranked and rated against other cities of Christendom and with some outside that boundary. If Paris and Antwerp had great theaters, so must London.

But at times Heywood stressed something else, namely, the antiquity of London's theaters and their role as conduits for ancient theatrical traditions. In this project he sounds at times like John Stow, digging deep into London's past, linking the contemporary city to a venerated past. For example, in *The Apology* Heywood makes London, through its theaters, not only the rival of contemporary Venice but also the inheritor of the ancient city culture of Greece and Rome. In a famous passage describing the theaters of Rome, the landscapes and institutions of modern London become mixed with elements of the older city. He writes: "I read of a Theater built in the midst of the river Tyber, standing on pillers and arches, the foundation wrought under water like London-bridge, the Nobles and ladyes in their Barges and Gondelayes, landed at the very stayres of the galleryes. After these they composed others, but differing in forme from the Theater, or Ampi-theater, and every such was called Circus, the frame Globe-like, & merely round" (D3v). Here, the foundations of an ancient theater remind Heywood of the foundations of London Bridge, the ladies in their gondolas conjure up the boatmen ferrying theatergoers across the Thames, and the round theaters of Rome morph into the roundish frame of Shakespeare's Globe. One can read, as in a watery mirror, the lineaments of one city in the features of the other.

Elsewhere in his tract, Heywood uses genealogies to suggest the persistence of the past in present cityscapes and institutions. Speaking of the ancient lineage of acting he says: "Thus our Antiquity we have brought from the Grecians in the time of Hercules: from the Macedonians in the age of Alexander: from the Romans long before Julius Caesar, and since him, through the reigns of 23 Emperours succeeding, even to Marcus Aurelius. After him they were supported by the Mantuans, Venetians, Valencians, Neopolitans, the Florentines, and others" (G2v–G3). He traces the lineage of theater further until he comes to England. "But in no Country they are of that eminence that ours are: so our most royall, and ever renouned soveraigne, hath licensed us in London: so did his predecessor, the thrice vertuous virgin, Queene Elizabeth, and before her, her sister, Queene Mary, Edward the sixth, and their father, Henry the eighth: and before these in the tenth yeare of the reigne of Edward the fourth, Anno 1490" (G3). In a simultaneous gesture, Heywood uses the theater to link contemporary London to the cities of ancient Greece, Rome, and Macedonia, and to extend London's own native theater tradition as far into the past as he can find textual traces to authorize the operation. For much of *The Apology*, Heywood thus thinks of cities in terms of *filiation* and *inheritance* as much as in terms of urban and national rivalries. Theater is a sign of insular pride; but it is also a sign of cosmopolitan integration into a community of great cities spanning the contemporary and ancient worlds. Through his narratives, Heywood thus transforms the place of the London theaters into a space in which sophisticated playing and distinguished patrons and visitors attest to the city's international preeminence.

Heywood's account of the dramatic genres that make up London theater's repertoire of forms likewise stresses both what is new and what is ancient in the theater's practices. Heywood highlights tragedy and comedy and their instructive value and ancient lineage. Tragedies, for example, "teach the subjects obedience to their King" (F3v) while comedy shows "others their slovenly and unhansome behaviour, that they may reforme that simplicity in themselves, which others make their sport" (F4). Ancient rulers and their communities learned from these generic templates, and so can the English. But particularly in his account of the workings of "domesticke hystories" (B4), Heywood famously allows his particular pride in Englishness to blossom forth:

what English blood seeing the person of any bold English man presented and doth not hugge his fame, and hunnye at his valor, pursuing him in his enterprise with his best wishes, and as beeing wrapt in contemplation, offers to him in his hart all prosperous performance. . . ? What coward to see his contryman valiant would not bee ashamed of his owne cowardice? What English Prince should hee behold the true portrature of that [f]amous King Edward the third, foraging France, taking so great a King captive in his owne country, quartering the English Lyons with the French Flower-delyce, and would not bee suddenly Inflam'd with so royall a spectacle, being made apt and fit for the like atchievement" (D4).

Here, the London stage, it is suggested, uses particular kinds of fictions to body forth a peculiarly English greatness and to create English subjects uniquely fit for great achievement. National pride and cosmopolitan aspiration for inclusion in a roster of great international cities coalesce in Heywood's tract, starkly revealing the ambition of a northern and insular nation and the role of its greatest urban theaters in adumbrating those ambitions.

London Stories

One kind of play produced in great abundance by the commercial stage after 1598 was London comedy, a subgenre of that kind of play characterized by Heywood as dealing with the "slovenly and unhansome behavior," which spectators must eschew. That I use the term London comedy to describe the kind of play that most interests me deserves further comment. For some years critics have been writing about that group of plays usually referred to as "city comedies." [58] The label has been attached to a number of works written between about 1598 and 1615 that take London (or cities that are screens for London) as their setting and deal in some detail with the geography of that urban setting and with the non-noble characters who people it. Ben Jonson and Thomas Middleton are often singled as the prime writers of city comedy, a genre that in their hands involves a satiric examination of city vices and follies such as greed, lechery, and undeserved pretensions to wit. Typically these plays, which are based on Roman New Comedy, pit gentlemanly "gallants" against artisans and merchants for preeminence within the city milieu, and they pay detailed attention to the topography of the city and to urban culture in terms of its fashions, typical occupations, street slang, and con games. These city plays represent a remarkable break from the conventions of the "higher" genres such as tragedy and the national history play. Seldom dealing with monarchs and rarely with aristocrats, they pitch their social register lower. In part, the historicity of these city comedies consists precisely in the fact that they mark a moment in early modern culture when urban commoners, those below the rank of gentlemen, could become the protagonists in theatrical fictions.

As I have argued elsewhere, genre was a key concept for organizing textual production in the early modern period.[59] A term frequently employed by early modern writers, genre indicated the implicit system that made one kind of text distinguishable from another in a relational field. Practically, tacit knowledge of dramatic kinds helped readers or spectators approach texts with particular sets of expectations; at the same time it helped writers by giving them forms and matter for imitation and starting points for improvisations on and transformations of received material. However, in thinking about the early modern stage, in particular, it is important to stress that the utility of generic categories was less ontological than provisional and productive. Dramatic genres were not and are not essential and immutable kinds of writing. Rather, in the early modern theater, generic differences emerged relationally and were performed into being. The dramatic genre system was constantly in flux in response to a wide range of pressures including the collaborative nature of much dramatic production and the competitive pressures fueling theatrical output. Barbara Mowat, using the work of Alistair Fowler, has argued that genre in general is most usefully understood on the model of "family resemblance" in that works within a generic "family" are related in a variety of ways without necessarily sharing any singular feature in common.[60] Works may in fact exhibit features of more than one family without any principle of exclusivity being violated. Some of the rough and ready vitality of the popular plays of the commercial London theater stems precisely from the way they mix and match, repeat and vary, intermix and alter the many generic templates that persisted from the classical and medieval periods as well as those that have origins within the early modern period itself.

Consequently, I want to suggest that the kind of satiric city plays paradigmatically produced by Jonson and Middleton does not exclusively define the period's production of London-based comedies. There are several subgenres within this larger family of plays which includes, but is not confined to, the satiric plays that have traditionally loomed large in critical discussions of city comedy. Together, all of these subgenres share a number of features: they all use London or a lightly veiled substitute as their setting; all deal primarily with non-noble figures; all create comedy from the stuff of urban life; all in some way negotiate the presence of non-native Londoners and non-native commodities within the space of the city. Yet the various subgenres of what I call London comedy also differ from one another in important details. For example, there are some London chronicle comedies—such as *The Shoemaker's Holiday* (1599) or *If You Know Not Me You Know Nobody, Part II* (1606) — that draw part of their matter from historical sources: either the national chronicles of writers such as Holinshed or Hall or the urban chronicles of Grafton or Stow. In a relational field of dramatic genres, these chronicle London comedies are written in view of and partly as an alternative to the national history play. Although monarchs tend to make an appearance in these works, and they are always acknowledged in the narrative as the most powerful authorities in the play's imagined world, chronicle comedies do *not* tell the monarch's story as does the national history play. Rather, they foreground the stories of prominent London citizens such as Simon Eyre or Thomas Gresham, thus performing the cultural act of subordinating the monarchical to the citizen narrative even while overtly confirming the preeminence of the monarch. In tone, chronicle comedies are celebratory, not satiric, making heroes of London citizens such as Dick Wittington, exuberantly installing civic worthies in the starring roles the history genre had reserved for kings, dukes, and earls. Geographically, chronicle comedies usually take place within the old walled part of London and often focus on monumental civic structures within those walls: Leadenhall in *Shoemaker*, The Royal Exchange in *If You Know Not Me, Part II,* and the Guildhall and Crosby House in a related play, *Edward IV, Parts I and II.* Membership in the London guilds is important to social identity in these plays, and gallants are usually peripheral figures.

By contrast, the satiric city comedies associated with Middleton and Jonson stress satire over celebration, omit kings altogether, and add gallants as primary figures in their fictions. They do not draw from chronicle sources and replace the emphasis on monumental civic edifices with the depiction of ordinary shops, taverns, and, interestingly, prisons. Bridewell, the Clink, the Counter, and various unnamed jails impart a penitentiary feel to a number of these plays so that while urban vice is sometimes simply mocked by satiric laughter, it is also sometimes controlled by the threat of incarceration in satiric comedies as diverse as *The Honest Whore, Eastward Ho, Bartholomew Fair,* and *The Dutch Courtesan.* Geographically, satiric city comedies are typically set in the walled city, though with many mentions of and excursions to the suburbs, while a play such as *Epicoene* takes place mostly near the Strand in the newer and more fashionable part of London between the city and Westminster.

Epicoene, moreover, points to yet another subgenre of London comedy developed primarily in the 1620s and 1630s and including works such as *Hyde Park, Covent Garden,* and *The Asparagus Garden.* These plays focus almost entirely on places of urban leisure, such as the ballrooms of the urban gentry, city parks, or the fashionable piazza at the center of the upscale Covent Garden residential development.[61] The setting of these London "town" comedies is mostly the West End outside the old city walls; gallants dominate the narrative; and neither guildsmen nor places of work are foregrounded. Rather, they showcase the lifestyle of a sophisticated urban elite. Wit and good manners are valued in these comedies, and women often function within them as the arbiters of taste and manners rather than as shoppers or gadding wives.

By this admittedly thumbnail sketch, I want to suggest that the large family grouping I am calling London comedy is a more varied dramatic form that we have sometimes assumed, that it has a shelf-life extending well into the 1630s, and that it negotiated many more urban places than simply the city's shops and more urban issues than just those involving a shift to a placeless market economy, although certainly it also did that. The role of women in the city, the culture of debt as well as of abundance that accompanied commercial change, the presence of foreigners and strangers in urban life, and the development of new forms of cultural capital, including urbane wit and the ability to speak French and to dance the latest dance—all of these were recurring aspects of the London plays in one or another of its incarnations. Moreover, while for some time a number of the satiric London plays were approached primarily in moral terms (what was satirized and what were the standards of value implicitly governing the satire?), I find it more useful to suspend moral judgements and to think of these plays as sometimes confused attempts to come to terms with a complicated and changing city. If, however, we think of them as providing imaginary resolutions to real social problems, then we must also admit that, like the culture in which they were imbedded, plays did not always have coherent solutions, not even imaginary ones, to the bewildering and contested culture of which they were a part. I would argue that the theater was popular in part because it was not a moralizing institution but an opportunistic one, making fictions from the arenas of life—gender and family life, commerce, encounters with foreignness—where change was most immediate and solutions least pre-scripted. What remains interesting, however, is the record these plays afford of the messy struggle to come to terms with issues that continued to provoke repeated attempts at narrative resolution.

One of the notable features of all kinds of London comedy is their attention to the places of the city. Unlike the unlocalized spaces of much Shakespearean tragedy, London comic drama frequently sets the action in particular city districts, buildings, or streets. In *The Roaring Girl*, Moll meets Laxton in Lincoln Inn's Fields; in *Chaste Maid in Cheapside*, points in and around this famous goldsmith district, including the wharfs along the Thames, are carefully enumerated; in *Covent Garden*, Bedford's upscale piazza and the houses and taverns that surround it anchor the action; and in *Every Man Out of His Humour*, we have the first instance of London comedy's preoccupation with St. Paul's Walk as a satiric setting for the display of urban vanity.[62] The list could be extended indefinitely. Nearly every London play to some extent localizes the action by referring to the streets and landmarks of the city and by setting key scenes in recognizable places. As I will discuss at some length in the ensuing chapters, such citations serve complex purposes, not all of which simply aim at giving audiences the pleasure of recognition. Rather, in invoking the places of the city and filling them with action, the plays also *construct* the city and make it intelligible for those *un*familiar with its places or the uses to which they can be put, and they parse the permissible and impermissible actions attendant on those places.

In this book I focus on four city places that the drama turns into significant social spaces by its repeated staging of and discourse about them. My premise is that we can learn something about how the drama engages with issues that drew the attention of London spectators by looking at its iterated use of particular urban locations. Sites, I will argue, become ideologically charged as they were visited and revisited by various dramatists and as they became connected with particular urban actors and with particular kinds of stories. One play with a key scene set in St. Paul's Walk is interesting; a series of such scenes by successive dramatists reveals the collective cultural labor by which a place becomes a vehicle through which particular kinds of social problematics are addressed, visited, and revisited. Consequently, all of the places I address in this book appear in a number of plays; each becomes associated with key social actors, whether they be debtors, whores, international merchants, or French dancing masters; each addresses an associated cluster of issues, whether those be the cultural competencies that allow mastery within certain social milieu, the relationship between native and stranger urban inhabitants, or the changing place of women in London's urban landscape. Collectively, each sequence of plays participates over time in rendering the city ideologically knowable, in regulating conduct within it, and in negotiating the most vexed issues with which Londoners were confronted.

The first chapter deals with one of the truly consequential London buildings to be erected in the city in the second half of the sixteenth century, Thomas Gresham's Royal Exchange. Purpose-built to imitate the great trading bourses on the Continent and to provide a place for international merchants to gather, the Exchange became one of the most celebrated landmarks of Tudor-Stuart London. Mentioned by travelers and depicted by famous engravers and map makers, the Royal Exchange also figured in a number of London comedies, including the first to be written, William Haughton's *Englishmen for My Money* (1598). In this chapter I argue that the Royal Exchange came paradoxically to symbolize London's pride in its growing role as an international entrepot and its simultaneous anxiety about the traffic with strangers that such a role mandated. Several plays, including Haughton's, but also Thomas Heywood's *If You Know Not Me You Know Nobody, Part II*, foreground the Exchange in plots that attempt to come to terms with the changing nature of London's commercial life and with the vexed relationship between native and foreign-born merchants and their relative economic preeminence within the city. But plays featuring the Royal Exchange also reveal something about the insistent gendering of space in representations of London as well as in its material practices.[63] Although the main floor of the Exchange was a male-dominated space, the upper pawn, or retail shopping area, contained a large number of women, both consumers and shop attendants. *The Fair Maid of the Exchange* is one of the many plays of the period that refer to the women who work in the pawn, and in this case they become central figures in a plot that turns on their vulnerabilities and new-found powers within this public space. Collectively, the Exchange plays I examine reveal some of the tensions surrounding London's changing economy, the enforced cosmopolitanism entailed by its new commercial expansiveness, and the gender disequilibrium attendant on new economic practices.

Chapter 2 switches perspective and looks not at the place where big money could be made, that is, the Royal Exchange, but at the dreadful places, the London Counters, where people faced incarceration when money had been lost and credit denied. Once one starts to look, it is truly surprising, at least surprising to me, how many London comedies mention either the Wood Street or the Poultry Street Counter and how many actually set part of the action in one or another of these institutions. Starting with Jonson's early play, *Every Man Out of His Humor* (1600), which concludes with Sir Fastidius Brisk in one of the Counters, London comedies use these prisons to explore the social death that results from losing one's credit, a word that encompasses both one's reputation and one's ability to accrue debt. Playing on the internal structure of the debtors' prison, with its purgatorial descent from the privileges of the Master's Ward to the miseries of the Hole, dramatists construct the prisons as sites of social undoing and material divestiture as prisoners, time and again, shed their clothing in the course of their incarceration, spiraling down to the absolute privations of the Hole. Central as this descent is to narratives about the Counter, London comedies ring surprising changes on their basic tales of prodigality undone. Sometimes a harrowing of hell occurs, and the prodigal steps forth as a new man, liberated by acts of charity. Sometimes the debtor is cast as victim, rather than as guilty prodigal, and Counter narratives become occasions to query the mysterious operations of the market or the venality of creditors. Occasionally, the Counters are transformed from sites of punishment to performative spaces in which the theatrical cleverness of the prodigal, rather than his repentance, garners his release. In each case, however, the Counter becomes a space for negotiating the place of debt in urban life and for constructing and querying the social logics by which one's "credit" is or is not made dependent on financial viability. Interestingly, in the overwhelming majority of Counter narratives, the debtor is male. For reasons I explore in Chapter 2, the Counters are gendered as male spaces, and the basic Counter narrative of the death of social identity is rendered as a male story.

By contrast, the third social place I examine, the London whore-house, while it involves men, tends to give at least equal billing to women. In fact, I argue that whorehouse narratives become a chief site for negotiating the changing nature of women's place within urban culture. A recurring trope found in these comedies, that of the conversion of chaste maids into whores and whores into wives, is especially crucial in foregrounding anxiety about the malleability of women's identities in the new circumstances that pertain in the metropolis and puts in question the comfortingly stable and discrete categories of maid, wife, widow, and whore that characterize much prescriptive literature of the period. While the whorehouse is sometimes represented in London comedy as a moralized space where female guilt is revealed, more often whorehouse narratives are marked by a high-spirited flouting of moralizing discourses. This is even true, I argue, when the whore herself is seen as the bearer of a contaminating foreignness. Ironically, while whore-houses are sometimes constructed as sites of dangerous miscegenation, they are equally likely to be represented in London comedy as sites of a forgiving cosmopolitanism. Like representations of the Royal Exchange, whorehouses, I will show, are spaces where Londoners' relationship to the world beyond its shores is negotiated, though in a refreshingly irreverent fashion. Unlike the Royal Exchange or the Counters, however, the bawdy houses of London comedy are often generic places, though frequently they are given quite specific geographic locations, and occasionally an historical whorehouse, like Holland's Leaguer, is used as the setting in a particular play.

The same thing is true of the final places I will examine in this book, namely, the ballrooms and academies of manners that are so prominently featured in the town comedies of the 1620s and 1630s. A few comedies, such as Brome's *The New Academy*, refer directly to specific London academies such as Francis Kynaston's Museum Minervae, established at the west end of Bedford's Covent Garden piazza in 1635. More often, however, academies of manners are generic places, though they are nearly all located in fashionable West End areas outside the old walled city. Common to all the plays featuring such places, however, is their intense preoccupation with the inculcation of new regimes of manners and bodily discipline. A chief actor in each is the dancing master, the Galliards, Lightfoots, and Frisks who pirouette and bow their way through the plots, dispensing advice about the proper management of foot and hand, the right way to bow, and the wrong way to do a fashionable dance. Plays featuring ballrooms and academies, I suggest, use these places to model new standards of deportment, the acquisition of which becomes both crucial cultural capital in a town setting and a new means to discriminate between those who matter and those who do not. Consequently, the incompetent boor, the person who cannot dance and cannot manage a proper bow, is as necessary to such plots as the dancing master, for it is such a figure who defines what is unacceptable behavior within these emerging spaces of social privilege. Moreover, the relentless emphasis on the French origins of these new bodily regimes raises in a fresh register the enduring preoccupation within London comedy with the relationship between what is native to the city and what is alien or foreign. Almost always, the dancing master who teaches and corrects English bodies is of French origins, and anxiety about the consequences of foreign cultural practices on English bodies is given forceful representation by his ubiquitous presence. An object alternately of scorn and emulation, he is nonetheless omnipresent— simultaneously a reminder of the elegance the English lack and would acquire, and of the effeminacy they scorn.

The gendering of academy spaces is particularly complex. Some fictional academies serve both men and women, but gender identities within these spaces are never secure. As the ambivalence surrounding Frisk suggests, masculinity is at risk in an arena where acquiring new skills in bodily deportment both authorizes gentlemanly status and also threatens to compromise native English manliness. For women, the dangers of ballroom and academy are even greater as the practices of these spaces authorize the intense specularization of the female body and blur, even in these fashionable arenas, the boundaries separating reputable and disreputable women. This book ends with Margaret Cavendish's *The Female Academy* (1662), a withering riposte to the ways in which London comedies of the Caroline period had imagined the participation of women in academy culture.

A number of threads bind together the arguments developed in each of the ensuing chapters. A focus on place anchors each chapter as I explore the dramatic stories through which places become significant social spaces and arenas for negotiating particular urban problems. But the book loosely traces a geographical progress, as well, as the locus of London comedy slowly moves west from the walled city toward the fashionable West End. I begin with the Royal Exchange located in the very heart of the old city and then explore the Counters, far less monumental structures than the Exchange, but still located within its geographical orbit. The chapter on the bawdy houses of London, however, has a much broader geographical reach. Once Henry VIII dissolved the Bankside whorehouses in the 1540s, places of prostitution proliferated both within the city proper and in all the surrounding suburbs. Some, such as Holland's Leaguer, flourished in the traditional Bankside location, but others sprang up within the walls and at every compass point without. Consequently, one of the things I explore in Chapter 3 is the ubiquity of places of prostitution and the connections between this expansion and other kinds of economic and social change that marked the city's growth. The final chapter, on ballrooms and academies, is based firmly in the West End where these places became part of the ensemble of fashionable resorts in which a new regime of manners and bodily deportment was both constructed and displayed. The book, then, is designed to move from the ceremonial and commercial center of the old walled city to the expanding suburbs and the fashionable West End.

Whatever the geographical locations examined in these London plays, however, one thing that remains constant is their preoccupation with gender relations and definitions. The city, as I will demonstrate throughout, was a place where both status and gender relations were constantly being renegotiated. Urban life created new places for women to work, such as the pawn at the top of the Royal Exchange, and new places such as dancing schools and academies of manners to display and refashion their bodies. Even the oldest occupation, prostitution, took on new forms in the post-reformation city as the sanctioned stews were dissolved and the places of prostitution became more varied, some becoming indecipherable from everyday taverns and houses, others, like Holland's Leaguer, becoming landmarks in their own right. Through their stories of brothels, bourses, and ballrooms, London comedies repeatedly, even obsessively, attempt to come to terms with the changing place(s) of women in urban life and to draw and redraw the boundaries of permissible action.

The same is true, though in a different way, for men. Some forms of masculinity, such as those founded on martial skill, are largely peripheral to the genre of London comedy. Rank remained crucial to male identity, but in the urban context it was challenged by money-based forms of status and by a new emphasis on what I call performative masculinity, that is, the ability to master codes of fashionability and to comport oneself with distinction in the city's emerging arenas for mannerly display.[64] Ironically, stories of the Counters, in which masculine social identity could effectively be obliterated, provide some of the most complex narratives about the pressures on masculinity in the urban context and the struggle between old and new ways of achieving and displaying masculine privilege. For both men and women, having money was one way of achieving status, but only one way. In the academy comedies of the Caroline period, for example, the privileges of both birth and wealth are challenged by an emphasis on new kinds of cultural competencies having to do with deportment, manners, and a sophisticated sense of personal and social style.

Identity is never formed except relationally, and hence the emphasis throughout the book on the mutually defining and ever changing relationship of men to women in the London context and on the relationship of native English men and women to those who are strangers to the city. When Frederick, Duke of Wirtemberg, described London, he was struck by the international cast of the ships anchored at its docks, ships from France, the Netherlands, Sweden, Denmark, Hamburg, and beyond. Those ships brought products from distant places into London markets, and they also brought strangers into every corner of the city, including its taverns, whorehouses, theaters, and places of commercial exchange. How London comedy negotiated foreign encroachments is a major theme threading its way throughout my argument. In the Exchange plays, strangers figure prominently as players in London's high-stakes commercial life and put considerable pressure on Englishmen's sense of their own preeminence in their purpose-built bourse. But the proper relationship of Englishman to alien is a topic revisited in the many whore comedies of the Jacobean stage and, in a different way, in Caroline academy comedies in which it is foreign standards of comportment, as much as literal foreigners, that pose the threat and the challenge to English identity.

Thomas Heywood, that tireless apologist for the city and its actors and playwrights, felt that London theater of his time and place was worthy of comparison to the best theater produced by the great cosmopolitan cities of both past and present. I think he was right. Early modern London provided the conditions of possibility that allowed a vigorous commercial theater of marked sophistication to flourish. The plays I examine in this book, taking London places as their setting and urban life as their theme, reveal the remarkable synergy between the city and its entertainment industry and make evident the theater's role in imagining London and the new forms of social life and social identity flourishing within it.

Chapter 1

Staging Commercial London: The Royal Exchange

Almost from the moment of its completion in 1568, Gresham's Bourse, better known as the Royal Exchange, became a significant place in London life. Its founder, Sir Thomas Gresham, modeled it on the great Nieuwe Beurs of Antwerp near which he had lived during his years as a merchant and Royal Agent on the Continent in the 1540s and 1550s.[1] Located at the corner of Threadneedle Street and Cornhill within the walled city of London, the Royal Exchange was designed to give the city a meeting place for merchants that would rival in beauty and scope the great bourses of Venice, Antwerp, and Constantinople. Before it was built, stranger or alien merchants,[2] along with English ones, had had to meet in the open air in Lombard Street, named, as Stow informs us, for the Longobard, or Florentine, merchants who had assembled there from at least the time of Edward II.[3] After 1568, these merchants gathered at the Exchange to do their business, and it quickly became a notable city landmark like St. Paul's Cathedral and rapidly drew the notice of foreign visitors.[4] The first extant visual record of the Exchange is Franz Hogenberg's (1569) engravings of both the exterior facade and the interior courtyard (Figures 1 and 2), the first known topographical engravings of any English building.[5] As early as the late 1560s the Exchange was included in a woodcut map of London ascribed to Ralph Agas, and in 1574 it was incorporated into Hogenberg's map of the city, as well.[6]

By the close of the sixteenth century, the Exchange, firmly established as an important part of the commercial life of London, was also constantly mentioned in discursive productions dealing with the city. Stage comedies featuring London life are a case in point. The first such play, the 1598 *Englishmen for My Money,* by William Haughton, focused on the topography of London and on the lives of its merchant class. It sets one long scene in the Royal Exchange. Dozens of London comedies follow Haughton's play, and while most do not depict the Exchange directly, many allude to it and work it into their depictions of city life. In *Westward Ho* (first performed in 1604), for example, a

Figure 1. The exterior of the Royal Exchange, engraving by Franz Hogenberg, 1569. Copyright the British Museum.

merchant mentions to his wife that he has heard at the Exchange that an Italian merchant, Justiniano, has gone bankrupt.[7] In the same play a group of city wives is directed to include the pawn or retail arcade at the Exchange in a list of London places where they can say they have gone to shop when they in actuality are meeting their gentlemen suitors.[8] In *Chaste Maid in Cheapside* (1613) a husband approvingly recounts how his wife's lover has provided magnificently for her laying in: "A lady lies not in like her; there's her embossings,/ Embroiderings, spanglings, and I know now what,/ As if she lay with all the gaudy shops/ In Gresham's Burse about her" (I.ii.32–35).[9] Ben Jonson's *Staple of News* (1626) highlights the Exchange as one of the four places in London (St. Paul's, Westminster, and Court are the other three) where one must have a news emissary posted at all times. A Dutchman, Buz, gets the Exchange beat.[10] As I will explain below, dramatists had good reasons for mentioning the Exchange in the diverse contexts of merchant

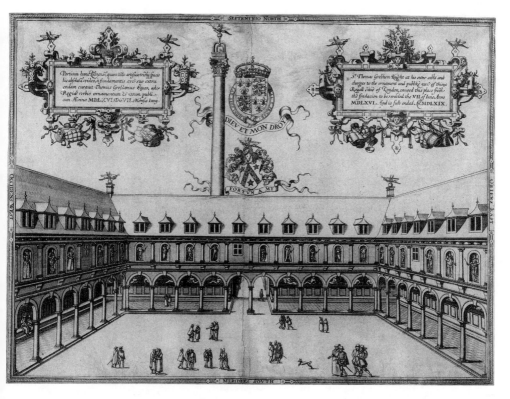

Figure 2. The interior of the Royal Exchange, engraving by Franz Hogenberg, 1569. Copyright the British Museum.

business, women's shopping, and foreign news. This complex place was connected to all three, and all three were interconnected.

In this chapter I am going to argue that the Exchange became one of those ideologically charged sites that writers used to think about the city, to stage its fault lines, and to enter it into discourse in historically significant ways. Connected to older forms of merchant life, the Exchange also facilitated new kinds of commercial and social practices; powerfully identified with the expanding ambitions of England's home-grown merchant class, it was the meeting place for communities of stranger merchants; though its central public space was insistently defined as a masculine arena, various forms of feminine activity and feminine transgression quickly became linked to it. I will be looking at how the public stage, through the emerging genre of the London comedy, took on some of the contradictory associations of this impor-tant city landmark and created fictions that spoke to the cultural and economic changes it came to symbolize. Near the turn of the century, three plays in particular feature the Exchange and collectively they give some indication of how this place figured in the drama's lexicon of London. One is the aforementioned *Englishmen for My Money* (1598), which highlights the family of a Portuguese merchant who does his daily business on the Exchange. Another, by Thomas Heywood, *If You Know Not Me You Know Nobody, Part II*, probably first performed in 1604–5, is an origin tale about the founding of the Exchange with Sir Thomas Gresham as its hero. The third, *The Fair Maid of the Exchange* (1607), probably also by Heywood, draws on a different set of associations and ideologies connected with this place. Its heroine is a shopgirl, Phyllis Flower, who works as a sempstress in the pawn, the second floor shop-ping arcade.

That at least three London comedies written within a decade of the genre's invention should take the Exchange as a principal setting for their action suggests its importance as an imagined space within the genre's fictions of the city. Because this new kind of play makes so many references to actual places, people, and things within London, it is tempting to think of it as a straightforward reflection of social reality. But this of course is a mistake. The London of city comedy is an *imaged* place, as is the Royal Exchange that appears in these plays. While the stage Exchange makes reference to the historical Exchange, what is important is not mimetic fidelity but how the theater *re-presented* this place and made it intelligible to London's theatergoing public. The key questions I will address are these: what kinds of stories did the theater tell about the Exchange? how did these dramatic fictions help to turn the *place* of the Exchange into a significant social *space* by connecting it to certain kinds of narratives and social actors? and how did these dramatizations of the Exchange matter as indications of the anxieties and the ideological struggles accompanying a specific period of social change?[11] In what follows, I will try to answer these questions and to outline the cultural work performed by what I call "Exchange fictions" within the stage genre of the London comedy.

The Royal Exchange as Historical Place

To do that, I want to turn first to the building as understood by social and economic historians. What went on there? What was new about the social practices or the social actors with which it was connected? A return to Hogenberg's engraving of the interior facade is the place to start. It depicts an open courtyard surrounded by a covered walkway. Both open yard and covered walk were designed to facilitate the business negotiations of stranger and native English merchants. When it rained, they could congregate in the covered walk. Otherwise, they mingled in the open yard. Exchange hours, signaled by a bell, lasted from eleven until noon each morning and five to six each afternoon. Importantly, the courtyard was "zoned" by nationality. As the French Protestant L. Grenade observed in 1576: "Each nation has its own quarter, so that those who have business with them can find them more easily. The English occupy about half the Exchange, and the French have their particular station too, as do the Flemish and the Walloons, the Italians and the Spanish. However, they are all at liberty to go hither and thither through the Exchange according to their need. Their letters can reach them there, and letter-carriers deliver [messages] to those to whom they are addressed. Here also one regularly hears the news of other countries and regions, which is a great convenience for those who traffick in merchandise across the seas."[12] Other contemporary accounts of the Exchange also remark on the ubiquity of alien merchants in this space and its function as a center for the exchange of information and gossip dealing with overseas trade. John Eliot's *The Parlement of Pratlers* (1593) contains a fictional dialogue set in the Exchange depicting English, Castillian, Portuguese, Italian, and French merchants discussing news from abroad and the whereabouts of various ships, while nearby a Jew and a merchant haggle over whether particular coins are sound, or clipped and cracked.[13] Finance, trade, and intelligence from abroad were widely assumed to preoccupy those who did business in this place.

Much of what made the Exchange new, then, was simply the existence of a large building dedicated to the needs of the international merchant community. There had, of course, been long-distance trade before the building of the Exchange and places like Lombard Street where merchants congregated, but never before had London had a purpose-built structure to encompass these activities, and hardly one as grand and imposing as Gresham's Bourse. Some of the business practices connected with the Exchange were also new and marked England's soon-to-be altered place in a world economy in the process of shifting its locus of gravity to northern Europe after centuries of Italian and Spanish dominance in Mediterranean Europe.[14] For example, early forms of commercial insurance were brokered at the Exchange in the late sixteenth century, making merchants more willing to venture the enormous sums needed to launch long and dangerous sea voyages.[15] And at the bourse, merchants and their factors regularly drew up and received bills of exchange and other financial instruments that facilitated long-distance business deals without the immediate exchange of money. As Fernand Braudel and other economic historians have demonstrated, the highest level of finance necessary for large-scale capitalist markets to develop depended on the expanded use of instruments of credit such as bills of exchange that could themselves be bought and sold to third parties as well as presented directly for payment to their guarantor. In Italy bills of exchange were in use as early as the thirteenth century but had spread more slowly to northern cities. For a while the high finance of international merchants was conducted primarily at trade fairs that occurred three or four times a year in places like Frankfurt or Cologne. Gradually, permanent bourses developed in Amsterdam, London, and other northern urban centers where such transactions could be daily, rather than semiannual or quarterly, affairs.[16] Whether Londoners consciously realized it or not, then, the Exchange was a material embodiment of England's changing role in international trade, a sign, recognizable primarily in retrospect, of both early capitalist practices and what was to be the increasing prominence of northern Europe on the world stage.

What was more *immediately* perceptible, however, was the cosmopolitanism of the building itself and the striking internationalism of its cast of characters. As the Hogenberg engraving shows, the internal facade had a classical composition unique in the city in 1566 when it was designed, and except for Somerset House it remained one of the few London buildings to show strong Continental influences for some decades.[17] Moreover, Gresham, who had spent a number of years in Antwerp, brought over both workmen and materials from the European mainland. The Antwerp mason Hendryck van Paesschen oversaw the construction of the entire edifice; Gresham's factor, Richard Clough, sent over wainscoting, slate, and other building materials from the Continent; and Gresham employed so many foreign workmen on the construction site that the London bricklayers protested.[18] Ironically, what was quickly to become a leading London landmark was largely built to a foreign model by foreign workers and partly inhabited by alien merchants. When Hogenberg made his two famous engravings, he topped each with two cartouches proclaiming Gresham's role in erecting the building. The inscriptions, all giving Gresham credit for his efforts as founder, were written, respectively, in French, Dutch, Latin, and English, as if to signal that knowledge of this place would be bruited far beyond England's shores and that its proper inhabitants included more than native Londoners. The cosmopolitanism of the place was often a source of pride, an assertion of England's increasing importance in international trade and finance, but as I will discuss below, it could also be a source of anxiety.[19]

Another visual representation of the Exchange, Wenceslas Hollar's (1644) engraving (Figure 3) gives yet another glimpse of what was novel about the site. Again we see the interior courtyard, but this time teeming with people. Focusing on the people and not the place, one gradually realizes that they are almost entirely men. A lone woman appears in the front left of the picture space, and she seems to be selling a newssheet. Everyone else is male, though some of the men are exotically clothed in turbans or in distinctive Dutch slops or Russian fur hats, indicating their status as strangers. Moreover, these men are grouped in conversational units, either strolling side by side while talking or standing in clusters of five or six, heads bent forward, hands gesturing. Hollar constructs/ reveals a public space where London citizens and stranger merchants, all male, gather to talk, hear news, strike deals, and debate the issues of the day. In 1644, there must have been burning issues to discuss, and while the building still is ornamented with royal statues, the actual monarch was at this point no longer able to inhabit the capital with safety. However unintentionally, Hollar has depicted the potential of the Exchange to form part of an emerging public sphere outside the formal control of the crown and visually defined as the domain of men. The age of the coffee house had not yet arrived, but some of its cultural functions were antici- pated by the Exchange. Surrounded by bookshops,[20] long associated with the circulation of gossip and news from abroad, the Exchange also func- tioned physically as a public meeting space where opinion could be formed, debated, and contested.

Of course, while pictures are worth a thousand words, they are also partial renderings of reality, and Hogenberg's engravings are no excep- tion. What he does not show is the activity in the part of the Exchange I have so far neglected: the pawn, the shopping arcade on the second level of the building, accessed, as Grenade informs us, "by 25 or 30 steps which are arranged in flights of seven. That gallery has all around it 150 stalls of rich merchandise, most notably of all sorts of mercery."[21]

Figure 3. Interior of the Royal Exchange thronged with people, engraving by
Wenceslas Hollar, 1644. Copyright the British Museum.

This gallery of shops, which Gresham had impressively furnished for Elizabeth's visit in January 1571, is often mentioned in early modern drama. Its innovation was to bring together all kinds of merchandise in one spot, eliminating the need to move from one part of the city to another to acquire, for example, a ribbon from a haberdasher, a book from a stationer, or a portrait from a painter-stainer. Inventories of the early retailers on the pawn show that it included not only a number of tailors, mercers, haberdashers, girdlers, and drapers—that is, tradesmen associated with the cloth trade and with items of clothing and adornment such as shoes, ribbons, and lace—but also leathersellers, painter stainers, barber surgeons, vintners, goldsmiths, scriveners, notaries, booksellers, ironmongers, among others. The shops themselves were traditional in form. They were narrow and not very well lit, and goods were in most cases probably displayed on a board that was let down at the front of the shop.[22] But the novelty of assembling so many different shops in one location drew customers and helped to consolidate the notion of shopping as a leisure, as well as a necessary, activity.

The pawn was, moreover, the part of the Exchange where women were most plentiful. Ann Saunders has determined that some shops were owned by women, usually widows and spinsters;[23] many more employed women to sell items retail; and those who shopped at the pawn appear to have been both men and women. The architecture of the building thus, in effect, had gendered zones, as well as national zones. The floor of the Exchange was a masculine space where high finance was conducted and news circulated. The pawn was a more feminized arena, though men both worked in and owned the majority of shops and comprised at least some of its customers. Nonetheless, it was the retailing practices of the pawn that helped to construct the increasingly prevalent idea of woman both as a consumer within commodity culture and as herself a commodity to be surveyed and purchased.[24] As we shall see, a number of theatrical references to the Exchange focus on the pawn and concern the important but controversial participation of women in its commercial activities. For women, the public space of the pawn could be a complicated site of gender negotiation.

This was partly because the Exchange never functioned entirely as planned, that is, as a place where merchants met and shoppers shopped. Rather, as Laura Gowing has demonstrated, the Exchange was also quickly connected with forms of disorder, many of them gendered. For example, women fruitsellers were frequently prosecuted for causing annoyance at the entrance to the Exchange; women workers such as sempsters and embroiderers carrying work to the homes of customers brought complaints against men who accosted them on their way in and out of the courtyard; in the evening the place was frequented by prostitutes and their clients; in 1579, just a decade after it opened, three women were tied to a cart's tail and whipped naked through the city for having abandoned three children in the Royal Exchange, presumably their illegitimate offspring.[25] Gowing argues that these records reveal the dangers attendant on women's presence in the public spaces in and around the Exchange. Women selling certain kinds of commodities, like sex, were criminalized, or cited, like the female fruitsellers, as public nuisances. "Honest" women were frequently assumed to be vendible in a venue where illicit and licit economies shared overlapping space and where women were set out at shop fronts to attract custom. As I will show, these are precisely the issues taken up in Heywood's *The Fair Maid of the Exchange*. For women, the Exchange thus offered mixed opportunities. For wealthy city wives it afforded a place to shop, to meet other women, perhaps to meet gallants. For a few female shopowners it offered economic advancement. But for women working at the lower end of the economy—those employed to mind shops or embroider shirts, those who sold fruit at the entry, or who sold themselves after dark—the place could be a constant reminder of the disadvantageous terms, of both class and gender, from which they traversed public space and negotiated the world of paid employment.

The Royal Exchange on the Stage

London comedies that stage the Exchange both reveal and construct the different ways this complex place figured in the symbolic and psychic economies of Londoners. The first Exchange play, *Englishmen for My Money*, also has the distinction, as I have noted, of being the first English stage comedy set specifically in London. Predictably, it depicts the Exchange as the central gathering place for London's merchant community; perhaps less predictably, the chief merchants on the Exchange in *Englishmen for My Money* are not English. In fact, I will argue that the main problem the play has to negotiate is the alien presence at the heart of London's merchant world. Despite its nativist associations, Gresham's Exchange is here constructed partly in terms of the centrality of strangers to its functioning. While the play attempts to draw and enforce distinctions between strangers and English Londoners and to subordinate the former to the latter, it never perfectly succeeds at either task. The attempt, however, strikingly reveals some of the particular anxieties that became associated with this important commercial and social space.

In considering how the play articulates the relationship between strangers and the English, and how it confirms and constructs English identity, I want to begin with the effect of *Englishmen for My Money*'s extensive references to the specific workings of the Exchange. Critics have commented on the "realism" of the play's Exchange scene,[26] and it does indeed refer to many of the actual practices historians have identified as part of the daily life of this institution. It shows, for instance, stranger and English merchants on the floor of the Exchange conversing about what ships have arrived from Spain, which have been lost to pirates, and what bills of exchange must be cashed out. Pisaro, a Portingale and the play's leading merchant, tries to buy some clothes from an Englishman to ship to Stoade, a town at the mouth of the Elbe near Hamburg. A post arrives from abroad, bringing letters to the various merchants. Finally, the Exchange bell rings, ending business and sending everyone home to dine.[27]

It has sometimes been assumed that in watching scenes like this Londoners primarily took pleasure in seeing their familiar world staged and in recognizing particular places, persons, or customs within that world. That is, such scenes are taken to confirm the audience members' knowledge of the city and their status *as* Londoners. That indeed may have been part of what was pleasurable about London comedies, at least for some audience members. But I want to suggest, as well, the genre's role in rendering the *un*familiar intelligible and in *creating* rather than simply calling upon an audience's sense of itself as knowing urban dwellers. For example, how many audience members of *Englishmen for My Money* would have had any direct experience with the practices of international merchants and of the day-to-day working of the Exchange? There is no way to know for sure, but my guess would be: not most of them. Apprentices, city wives, and visitors from abroad would probably have had little first-hand knowledge of international merchant transactions even if they had paid a visit to the Exchange as a tourist site. The function of the Exchange scene, then, can be viewed as an induction into the ways of a monumental, but not intimately known, urban site as much as a confirmation of knowledge already in the viewer's possession. Inviting the audience to peer over the shoulders of English and alien merchants, the scene could function in part as a guide to the *un*familiar, a way to render legible a set of practices *not* directly experienced by most London theatergoers. In doing so, it helped to constitute them *as* Londoners. The play thus constructs as much as it assumes both urban identities and urban literacies. In the rapidly changing city of the 1590s, London comedies were more than a chauvinistic and celebratory exercise in self-recognition, though that might be part of their function; they also helped make discursive sense of the city to inhabitants with differing durations and kinds of experience with it; and by promoting a shared literacy about the city and its ways, they invited those in the audience to see themselves as knowledgeable members of an urban community. In a radical sense, London comedies made London as much as they were made by it, and they made Londoners, as well.[28]

This process of identity formation in which the London comedies participated was, of necessity, a complex and contradictory one. It was fully ideological in the sense of forging interested representations of social relations and categories, and it depended almost inevitably on constructing identities by way of oppositions and triangulations that were at once powerfully evocative and fundamentally incoherent and unstable. The complexities of this process can be glimpsed by considering the implications of *Englishmen for My Money*'s novel and insistent focus on London geography. In this play—as is true in other London comedies—place names abound. In the second scene, for example, three men talk about walking to Pisaro's house in Crutched Friars behind Tower Hill (I.ii.229–34); a little later a clown is sent to the middle walk of St. Paul's Cathedral to hire a tutor for Pisaro's daughters (I.ii.326–30); still later we learn that one of the Dutch merchants lives in Bucklersbury (II.ii.1202). The acme of the play's geographical localism, however, occurs in IV.i, a scene whose humor hinges on the gap in knowledge between those who have an intimate familiarity with London's streets and those who do not. Frisco the clown leads disoriented Italian and Spanish merchants in the dark through London, supposedly taking them to Pisaro's house in Crutched Friars. In reality he is leading them on a wild goosechase and confusing them with the names of places they don't recognize but which a geographically knowledgeable audience would know were impossibly far from one another: London Stone in Candlewick Street, Ivy Bridge in Westminster, Shoreditch in the northern part of the city, the Blue Boar Inn in Queen Hithe in central London (IV.i.1551–1646).

This scene is a sustained place-based joke, which those literate in London geography would most fully appreciate. One might assume that those possessing such literacy would be London's English-speaking inhabitants, while only confused strangers would ignorantly stumble about in the dark. And yet, given the enormous in-migration from the countryside that fueled London's population growth throughout the second half of the sixteenth century,[29] it is quite likely that many "English" theatergoers were as in the dark, so to speak, as the hapless Italian and Spanish merchants before this barrage of place-specific information. The joke seems to depend on what in truth was an unstable distinction between aliens and native Londoners that obscures not only how long many stranger merchants resided within the city and how extensive their knowledge of it could be, but also how many English-speaking Londoners were foreigners, that is, people born elsewhere in England and not officially made free of the city and at least initially having little familiarity with it. These facts simply highlight the ideological work done by this scene. By identifying geographical "ignorance" as a mark of Italian and Spanish strangers, the scene promotes a distinction between those strangers and the more knowing London theater audience who laugh at them, even as, paradoxically, the community of the knowing might well include foreigners, aliens, and native-born Londoners. The actual dramatic event thus creates theatrical communities that cross-cut the rigid binaries of the represented action.

Within that represented action *Englishmen for My Money* repeatedly harps on the presence of strangers, especially stranger merchants, in London, and their ubiquity is crucial to the complex and contradictory ways in which the play highlights and manipulates both urban and national identities. The very title of Haughton's play—*Englishmen for My Money*—aggressively underscores its investment in promoting Englishness. Yet the choice to pivot the play around the family of Pisaro, a nonnative Exchange merchant, suggests that questions of "Englishness" cannot be thought separately from the issue of the alien within the city. Paradoxically, at the inception of a self-consciously London-centered stage genre, a dauntingly wealthy Portingale dominates the narrative. Through Pisaro, I will argue, Haughton both acknowledges the importance of strangers in the life of international trading cities, of which London was rapidly becoming one, and tries to come to terms with the threat they pose to fantasies of English superiority and national purity. The phrase "Englishmen for My Money," after all, articulates a wager as much as certainty, and wagers can be lost.

The themes of *Englishmen for My Money*, written for the Admiral's Men, found a precedent in Shakespeare's *The Merchant of Venice*, which was probably performed by the Chamberlain's Men the previous year. In *Merchant*, an "alien," the Jewish Shylock, threatens to undermine the power of the Venetian merchant community by entrapping one of its chief members, Antonio, in a bond that specifies he must forfeit a pound of flesh if he fails to repay Shylock the money he has borrowed from him. Antonio does not repay on time, and the Venetian state is faced with the uncomfortable prospect of letting Antonio die or of disregarding its own laws, laws that enable alien merchants to trade with confidence and safety on the Venetian Rialto. The play, of course, miraculously allows Antonio to escape Shylock's clutches, while the Jew is forced to convert and forfeit much of his wealth. But the play nonetheless highlights some of the anxieties pervading a cosmopolitan trading center.[30] Native merchants can be upstaged by strangers, whether Jewish usurers or powerful merchants from other nations. Italian families can be exposed to the risks and possibilities of intermarriage. In the *Merchant*'s second plot, Portia, the play's representative of old Venetian landed wealth, is pursued by suitors from around the Mediterranean and northern European world: Spain, Morocco, Germany, France, England, Scotland, and other nations. Fending off strangers, Portia contrives to marry a Venetian gentleman, Bassanio; the one interfaith marriage, between Shylock's daughter and an Italian gentleman, is often read as tension-ridden. Mixed marriages, including marriages across national boundaries, are not resoundingly applauded in Shakespeare's play.

Haughton boldly "Englishes" the themes that Shakespeare had treated from behind the screen of his Venetian setting. The Rialto, daringly, becomes the Royal Exchange. In *Englishmen for My Money* the main merchant figure is the Portingale, Pisaro, who in an opening speech proclaims an economic mastery within the London city space that the play never seriously questions:

How smugge this gray-eyde Morning seemes to bee,
A pleasant sight; but yet more pleasure have I
To thinke upon this moystning Southwest Winde,
That drives my laden Shippes from fertile *Spaine*:
But come what will, no Winde can come amisse,
For two and thirty Windes that rules the Seas,
And blowes about this ayerie Region;
Thirtie two Shippes have I to equall them:
Whose wealthy fraughts doe make *Pisaro* rich:
Thus every Soyle to mee is naturall:
Indeed by birth, I am a *Portingale,*
Who driven by Westerne winds on *English* shore,
Heere liking of the soyle, I maried,
And have Three Daughters: But impartiall Death
Long since, deprivde mee of her dearest life:
Since whose discease, in *London* I have dwelt:
And by the sweete lovde trade of *Usurie,*
Letting for Interest, and on Morgages,
Doe I waxe rich, though many Gentlemen,
By my extortion comes to miserie. (I.i.1–20)

Possessed of at least thirty-two ships, some plying the profitable trade with Spain, and a self-proclaimed usurer snapping up the land of impoverished English gentlemen, Pisaro is a stranger who has successfully made London his base of operation, an obvious acknowledgment of the city's increasing importance as an international commercial center.

That the confident speaker of this remarkable passage is also a threat to English interests is signaled not only by his reference to the misery of the gentlemen whose lands he has acquired, but also by the whole thrust of the plot, which pivots on the question of who will control the marriage choices of Pisaro's daughters. The Portingale wants them to

marry three Continental merchants, the Dutchman Vandal, the Frenchman Delion, and the Italian Alvaro. Were they to do so, all the money
Pisaro makes from his foreign trade and his usurious loans would ultimately flow out of English hands into alien ones. In the mercantilist
logic of the day, such an outcome would drain precious resources out
of the nation, which is what alien merchants were often accused of
doing.[31] To the extent, then, that Pisaro represents a non-English merchant who is buying up English lands and channeling wealth out of the
country, he is presented as an economic threat.

   The vexed status of stranger merchants in London was an issue with
a long history. As Braudel has argued, one sign a nation is in a marginal
or nondominant position in a world economy is when its trade is controlled by foreign merchants.[32] Until the sixteenth century, this was
largely true of England.[33] The Hanseatic merchants (and, at various
times, the French, the Flemish, and especially the Italians) had, from
the thirteenth century, handled much of England's import and export
trade, receiving privileges from the Crown that exempted them from
many custom duties while ensuring their monopoly over traffic in specific goods. As T. H. Lloyd has detailed, it was really only in the early
sixteenth century that the English Merchant Adventurers predomi-
nated over the Hanseatic merchants in control of the English cloth
trade. In 1598, the year of Haughton's play, Elizabeth closed the Steelyard, the long-standing home of the Hanse traders.[34] By the second
half of the sixteenth century, England had also begun to form other
regulated and joint stock companies such as the Levant and East India
Companies that would eventually bring portions of the lucrative trade
with the East under English control. Theodore Rabb has suggested that
it was only in the 1630s that English merchants decisively established
dominance over England's overseas trade.[35] But in 1598 that outcome
did not seem inevitable, and the Crown was struggling, as it had long
done, to balance its need for the innovations, skills, and expertise
brought to England by alien artisans and merchants with the need to
regulate the activities of strangers to allow native interests to flourish
and to mitigate antialien sentiment. Stranger merchants working in the
city, for example, were often charged custom duties double those of
domestic merchants; war subsidies were imposed upon them; and at
times their trading privileges were summarily suspended.[36]

   Englishmen for My Money is not an economic treatise, or a gloss on
Elizabethan policy on aliens, but it does use the stranger merchants of
the Royal Exchange as a way to articulate and deal with popular anxieties about the economic and social consequences of alien merchants
and artisans in the city. Pisaro, as the greatest of the play's stranger merchants, must be foiled in his plan to link his daughters to other alien

merchants and so to keep his accumulated wealth out of English hands. He is. His daughters, claiming allegiance to their English mother, resist. Determined to marry Englishmen, they succeed, insuring that the suitors who have mortgaged their lands to Pisaro get them back and that they also receive the income from both his usurious loans and his fleet of ships. Marriage halts the flow of resources out of the nation, concentrating wealth in the hands of the native-born, however feckless they may appear. In what was to become a stock convention of city plays, a merchant is thus outsmarted by members of the impoverished landed gentry who compensate for shallow pockets with their witty charm.[37] *Englishmen for My Money,* however, is unique in that this contest is given an antialien twist. It is specifically an alien merchant who is outsmarted by a clever English servant, Anthony, a trio of clever gentlemen, and three witty women. Acknowledging the presence and dominance of Pisaro within the Exchange, the play nonetheless stages his defeat within the domestic realm. This is a powerful fantasy of incorporation whereby without overtly demonizing the alien, his bloodline and his wealth are assimilated without remainder into the English body politic. Such an incorporation fantasy is itself, of course, an unmistakable act of imaginative aggression and suggests that Pisaro is indeed the greatest "problem" that the play must negotiate.

The treatment accorded to Pisaro is even more interesting once one realizes that he is also unmistakably coded as a Jew within the text, though he is never explicitly named as such.[38] The connections to *The Merchant of Venice* are thus more complicated than I first indicated. Pisaro's Jewishness is indicated, first, by the fact he practices usury, although he does not do exclusively that. Second, he has a "snoute/ Able to shaddow Powles" (I.ii.243–44); in fact, he is called "signor bottle-nose" (III.iii.1382) by one of the Englishman, a bottlenose being a common stage property of Jewish characters. In addition, he lives in Crutched Friars (I.ii.233), a section of the city where remnants of a Jewish community seem to have survived.[39] He takes interest at 22 percent, 12 percent above the allowed rate (V.i.2322–23).

Despite these unmistakable codings, the play never marginalizes Pisaro in the way Shylock is marginalized, that is, by obvious differences of dress, diet, and mode of speech. He is not overtly constructed as the poisonous anal infiltrator that Jonathan Gil Harris has identified as the prevailing Jewish stereotype in both *The Merchant of Venice* and Marlowe's *Jew of Malta.*[40] Rather, he appears to have some of the privileges of a denizen, that is, an alien merchant who has obtained a limited sort of citizenship by paying a fee and obtaining a patent from the Crown.[41] Pisaro, however, is never called a denizen within the play. Nonetheless, he has a centrality that in historical terms might indicate denizen status. If we think of Pisaro in relation to the characters of *The Merchant of Venice*, he in part conflates in one person the figures of Shylock and Antonio. He is an outsider who to some degree functions as an insider. Pisaro speaks good English, had an English wife, and has produced three very patriotically English daughters. He is shown to be on good terms with his neighbors. One Master Browne arranges to send his daughter to spend the night at Pisaro's house when his own is too full of guests. On the Exchange, Pisaro has a place of great importance. He is a leading figure among the stranger merchants, three of whom he invites to his house to woo his daughters; and he is completely caught up in the exchange of commercial news at the Exchange, including what turns out to be a false report that Spanish pirates have seized some of his ships headed for Turkey. He conducts business on the floor, receiving, for example, a note from one of his factors saying that he had had to borrow money from Master Towerson's factor, a loan that he secured with a bill of exchange he requests Pisaro to pay. By contrast, the three English suitors who come to the Exchange to ask Pisaro for more money are completely at sea there. They have no foreign contacts, no business to conduct but borrowing. Pisaro treats them like gnats, paying attention to them only by fits and starts when he thinks they might be induced to mortgage more of their property.

There are one or two signs in the text that indicate that Pisaro feels himself to be at a disadvantage as an outsider. At one point he acts slightly paranoid when he thinks the Post has failed to deliver letters to him but has brought them to everyone else (I.iii.429–32). At another point he says that he had been driven home by unruly boys who threatened to mar his ruff or poke out his eyes, though it is unclear just why he was threatened in this way and whether other merchants suffered the same treatment (I.iii.550–54). In general, however, the play does not present Pisaro as an isolated, antisocial figure in the manner of Shylock. He remains at the heart of the commercial world of international trade centered at the Exchange. Dealing less in demonizing anti-Semitic stereotypes than does *The Merchant of Venice*, *Englishmen for My Money* comes closer to acknowledging the complicated status of certain Jews, such as Conversos from Spain and Portugal, in late Elizabethan England, and their role in international trade and finance.

Edmund Campos and Alan Stewart, building on the work of James Shapiro, both have recently suggested that Portingales held a unique place in the political and commercial worlds in London in the 1590s. Most Portuguese in London were in fact Jews who had fled the Inquisition but who, outwardly at least, had converted to Christianity. After Spain's annexation of Portugal, they were sometimes mobilized in

English plans against Spain, although they could also be conflated with the Spanish and ironically subjected to anti-Spanish and anti-Catholic persecution.[42] Roderigo Lopez, Elizabeth's Jewish Portuguese doctor, convicted of treason for attempting to poison her, was the most notorious such figure. Portingale merchants in London, however, often had commercial connections to other diasporic Jewish communities in the great trading cities of Europe and the Levant, and they were not subject to the trading embargo that prevented direct trade between England and Spain.[43] Alan Stewart has identified three sisters from the Jewish-Portuguese Freire family whose marriages tied together a London-based commercial network whose tentacles extended to Lisbon, Madrid, and beyond.[44] In *Englishmen for My Money* Pisaro seems to be tapped into just such a network. His first words concern the antic-ipated arrival of his ships from Spain, and his great wealth derives in part from trade with the thirty-two points of the compass to which his vessels have been dispatched. However indirectly, the play seems to reg-ister the centrality of Jewish, or formerly Jewish, merchants to interna-tional trading networks and to connect them, of course, to the Royal Exchange. While never called a Jew in the play, Pisaro nonetheless is tainted by a faint whiff of illegitimacy. He is vulnerable, for example, because others know that he takes interest at 12 percent above the allowed rate. But it is the work of the play's narrative structure to make this powerful alien presence pass—through his daughters' marriages—harmlessly into the national fabric, trailing his wealth behind him. James Shapiro has discussed how Conversos were often feared to be merely passing as Christians while secretly clinging to Jewish beliefs.[45] Haughton's play handles this fear by making Pisaro's daughters active agents for total assimilation. What their father wants is irrelevant, since the girls will have their will, and their will is to be totally and completely English. Moreover, unlike Shylock's Jessica, there is no sign that Pisaro's daughters will be made unhappy by their mar-riages. Already assimilated to Englishness and presumably to Christian-ity, they are simply made more so by their weddings. In this case, Jewish blood functions less as a poison than as a physic, renewing the decayed gentry and then disappearing.[46]

If the play, then, imagines the Exchange as a port of entry for alien difference to permeate the city, in the case of Pisaro it diminishes this threat by subsuming that difference through marriage, in the process incorporating the wealth of the stranger into the English body politic. But the play also finds a way to indulge more anarchic forms of an-tialien sentiment that find their outlet in Haughton's representation of the other three alien merchants, Vandal, Alvaro, and Delion. They are the butt, first, of hilarious but cruel linguistic mockery.[47] All of them speak a dreadfully mangled version of English that is a constant source of merriment and disgust to Pisaro's daughters and, one assumes, to the London audience. Frisco, the play's clown, is the vehicle for much of this linguistic commentary. Sent to St. Paul's middle walk to hire a Frenchman to tutor Pisaro's daughters, he says he will recognize French because "my great Grandfathers Grandmothers sisters coosen told mee, that Pigges and *French-men*, speake one Language, *awee awee*" (I.i.173–75) and boasts that he can speak Dutch when he wants: "I must have my mouth full of Meate first, and then you shall heare me grumble it foorth full mouth, as *Haunce Butterkin slowpin frokin*" (I.i.182–84). It is this same Frisco who urges the English suitors to marry Pisaro's daughters quickly in order that they not permit "a litter of Languages to spring up amongst us" (I.ii.338–39).[48] The girls share this sentiment. As one of them, Laurentia, says to her Dutch suitor Vandal: "If needes you marry with an *English* Lasse,/ Woe her in *English*, or sheele call you Asse" (II.iii.1092–93). This, of course, is precisely what the strangers cannot do. At one point they decide to disguise themselves as the English suitors and woo the girls in that guise. Of course, when they open their mouths, their disguise will be blown. No one in this play can play an Englishman who is not native-born. By contrast, the play does allow the English characters to undertake various kinds of cross-gender and cross-national disguise successfully. Anthony, the English tutor who is the mastermind behind the girls' successful plot to outwit their father, spends much of the play disguised as a French pedagogue, and he arranges for Laurentia to exit Pisaro's house disguised as him and for Walgrave, one of the English suitors, to enter Pisaro's house disguised as Susan Browne, a neighbor woman. In short, playing with identity and disguises is the privilege of the truly English characters, while Vandal, Alvaro, and Delion remain locked in the prison house of language and stereotype.

The Dutchman fares the worst. Tricked into getting into a basket, which the girls say they will use to haul him up to their second-story window, Vandal spends a cold night suspended between heaven and earth when the girls hoist him half way and leave him hanging—a nice visual joke that can be protracted over a good stretch of stage time. Not only do these aliens not know their way around the London streets, but they also do not know how to woo a woman or avoid being made an ass. In the theater, through laughter aimed at the ignorance and linguistic incompetence of strangers, the audience is imaginatively, though not legally, consolidated as true Londoners, even though, as we have seen, this category is an unstable one. If one thinks of the public theater as helping to constitute new forms of subjectivity and points of identification for its audience, in this instance the audience at the Rose was being solicited to recognize its Englishness in contradistinction to the ludicrous strangeness of strangers.

Englishmen for My Money, then, is an important text to begin an inquiry into the way London comedies mobilized the Royal Exchange as part of their fictions. For Haughton the place seemed to represent the site where the global interconnections of advanced mercantile practice were most visible. His Exchange is full of commercially competent, well connected foreign merchants, the most powerful of whom is not only engrossing profits from abroad but also seizing landed wealth from prodigal native-born gentry. This patriotic, even chauvinistic play uses a dual strategy to deal with the acknowledged prominence of alien merchants in the imagined London of the play. Pisaro, the Portingale crypto-Jew, is not so much demonized by denigratory stereotype as subjected to a powerful fantasy of assimilation, his Jewish difference eroded by his decision to marry and settle on English soil and seemingly effaced by his daughters' marriage choices. With the French, Italian and Dutch merchants, the tact is different. Here English superiority is asserted by emphasizing the linguistic incompetence, gullibility, and ignorance of these stranger merchants.

As I have suggested, however, both strategies are vulnerable ones. For example, the play leaves intact the image of Pisaro as master of the thirty-two ships wafting cargo to London from thirty-two points of the globe. In the play no Englishman has his connections or his wealth; the English suitors get the girls, but not Pisaro's dominance at Exchange business. And laughing at the geographical ignorance and nonstandard English of Dutchmen might be dicey business for those audience members recently come to London from Bristol or trailing their own Welsh, Scottish, or North Country accents behind them. Moreover, the play pinpoints an issue that was to persist: that of England's increasing imbrication in a global marketplace and London's emergence, as Crystal Bartolovich has argued, as a world city.[49] Though English merchants might gradually control more and more of England's foreign trade, that was not to mean that stranger merchants and factors would no longer be found at the Royal Exchange, that English ships would not increasingly return from hazardous overseas journeys with seamen taken on board in distant ports in the Mediterranean and the Far East, or that the English marketplace would not increasingly be infiltrated with foodstuffs, fabrics, books, and ways of thinking that originated beyond the British Isles. The very design and contents of the Royal Exchange were proof of that fact. And the English who were invited at the Rose to laugh at stranger merchants speaking with funny accents would themselves have to learn to converse in alien tongues or would find themselves having to rely on the services of Jewish middlemen, dragomen, who peopled the many port cities to which the English were now traveling.

It is perhaps not surprising that the heightened chauvinism of *Englishmen for My Money* should emerge alongside the play's imaginative conjuring of the pervasive hybridity of the city, pointedly given expression in this first London comedy in its representation of Gresham's Bourse. The dream of a clean division between an "us" and a "them" here seems to have been made more urgent by the simultaneous recognition of its impossibility. The other two Exchange plays that followed upon *Englishmen for My Money*, *If You Know Not Me, Part II* and *The Fair Maid of the Exchange*, while elaborating different aspects of the symbolic significance of the Exchange, also take up the anxious mingling of native and alien practices and persons within its walls. Whatever else Gresham's building meant to the city's playwrights, it was indisputably a site that conjured both pride and anxiety about what it meant for London to become a commercial center with ever-increasing international connections, a city where strangers, strange tongues, and strange commodities could not be wished, or laughed, away.

The Exchange as Civic Monument

In 1602 an anonymous play entitled *Alarum for London* appeared in the London bookstalls. Probably first staged in 1599, it is loosely based on George Gascoigne's account of the destruction visited on the city of Antwerp by Spanish soldiers several decades previously.[50] In the 1560s growing Calvinist enthusiasm contributed to a rebellion in the Netherlands against the Spanish Crown; in 1567 the Duke of Alva arrived in Antwerp to stamp out what was left of the rebellion and to punish the offenders. Ruthlessly, he put 12,000 of those involved on trial and executed 1,700, including prominent noblemen. Alva, however, never achieved control of the northern provinces and withdrew from the Low Countries in 1573, though he was often connected in the popular imagination with subsequent events in Antwerp. The Spanish forces there were placed under new command in 1573. Spain's bankruptcy in 1575, however, disrupted its credit relations with the Netherlands, leading to a mutiny of unpaid Spanish soldiers in 1576. These soldiers sacked Antwerp, killing 8,000 people, in an event that became known as the Spanish Fury. This is the "spoil" of Antwerp reported by Gascoigne, and it forms the basis for the events depicted in *Alarum for London*, though the play also features the Duke of Alva and conflates a number of incidents that happened in Antwerp in these tumultuous years. After the 1576 "fury," Spain only gradually reasserted control in the southern provinces, finally regaining Antwerp in 1585.[51] This whole series of events contributed to the collapse of Antwerp as the chief trading center of northern Europe. By 1568 international merchants had moved a good deal of their trade to Hamburg, and in that year Gresham's Exchange opened in London, providing a new venue for international commerce.

Alarum for London is violently anti-Spanish and shows Spanish soldiers engaging in the rape, torture, and murder of innocent Antwerp citizens as well as a hapless English factor. But the play is also disdainful of what it represents as the self-indulgence of the fat Flemish burghers who are in no way prepared to defend their city. The play's title, *Alarum for London*, suggests its didactic purpose. It warns Londoners against the Spaniards and also against the self-indulgence that comes with worldly success. Although the Antwerp Exchange is not directly depicted in the play, it is mentioned several times. At the sack of the city, the Duke of Alva takes the bourse, the statehouse, and the marketplace under his own control, and at the end of the play a valiant Flemish soldier named Stump says that he will go to the Exchange where Spanish soldiers and their whores are playing dice and there he will wager his wooden leg.[52] The famous Antwerp bourse, like the rest of the city, has been taken over by the enemy and its functions debased.

Just a few years later, probably in 1604 or 1605, Thomas Heywood's *If You Know Not Me You Know Nobody, Part II* was also staged in London. But if *Alarum for London* luridly depicted the fall of the great commercial city of Antwerp, Heywood's play celebrated the rise of another commercial power, London. The play's two chief events are the building of the Royal Exchange and the defeat of the Spanish Armada.[53] But the Exchange of Heywood's play is quite different from Haughton's. It is more a triumphalist civic monument than a working institution. A source of pride for all true Londoners, a signifier of the city's grandeur, Heywood's Exchange nonetheless raises a disturbing question: what does the place honor—London's past or its future? time-honored traditions or new practices? More than the other Exchange plays, Heywood's reveals nostalgia for a "lost London" even as it marks its passing. The play's treatment of Gresham, the founder of the Exchange, is equally complex. Taking considerable liberties with historical fact, Heywood simplifies his career, first turning him into a traditional city hero and eliding altogether his important work on the Continent as a Royal Agent for the Crown, and then unhistorically making him the representative of commercial undertakings to North Africa and the Levant. Similarly, drawing on John Stow's nostalgic vision of the city, Heywood first depicts the bourse as a traditional civic benefaction undertaken by a successful city guildsman, but then refashions it as a scene of high-risk speculation on an international scale. Heywood's attempts to model the man and the building on nostalgic and outdated templates falter. He elides but cannot entirely suppress what was new about the Exchange and the sweet scent of big money and high risk that attached to it. The contradictions and anachronisms in Heywood's Exchange drama suggest how powerfully the place could channel anxieties not only about native and alien presences within the city, but also about the potential for new commercial practices and values to push out old. That the play was produced during the initial period of Jacobean nostalgia for Elizabeth, who makes an appearance in the play, only heightens the poignancy of its depiction of a city ambivalent about a future that would entail both a new international visibility and also the loss of familiar practices and time-sanctioned values.

After Haughton's presentation of the Exchange as a bustling place of business full of stranger merchants, factors, and newscarriers, Heywood's bourse is eerily empty of commercial activity. This is partly the result of Heywood's choice to dramatize the day when Elizabeth I visited Gresham's edifice in January of 1571 and gave it the name the Royal Exchange. By focusing on the monarchical visit, the dramatist monumentalizes the building and abstracts it out of the daily merchant routines that so interested Haughton. He suggests that the city has produced a building worthy of a queen's notice and worthy of inclusion in the annals of the city—which is where John Stow had in fact incorporated it. His *Survey of London*, first produced in 1598 (the date of Haughton's *Englishmen for My Money*) and expanded in 1603, throws light on Heywood's decision to portray the Exchange as he does. As I discussed in the last chapter, Stow's vision of London is a static and nostalgic one.[54] Stow's *Survey* offers an encyclopedic ward-by-ward, street-by-street verbal mapping of London in which the topography and history of the city are primarily constructed by detailing its civic buildings, churches, wharves, and waterways and by enumerating the worthy London citizens who erected or repaired them.[55] For Stow, the proper use of wealth is charity and civic endowment. Nearly every page of the *Survey* bristles with lists of the prosperous London men and women who built a fair parish church, repaired its roof, gave unto it sundry ornaments, and so on. In his nostalgia for a London centered on traditional guild and parish life, Stow ignores new developments in city life like the emergence of the joint stock companies and is quick to condemn instances of individual entrepreneurship as signs of selfish denials of the common good.[56] He overlooks indications that the London of 1600 was no longer an insular northern outpost, but increasingly a world city, and that breaks with the medieval past were not pesky anomalies but everyday events. By the time Stow published his *Survey*, the city he described was already a fiction. The Elizabethan Poor Laws were redefining charity as the duty of the state, not the individual; and the traditional guilds that had dominated the city's life were under pressure both from unregulated economic enterprise in the suburbs and from the appearance of crown-sponsored monopolies like the East India Company.[57]

When Stow mentions the Gresham family and its achievements, he characteristically downplays what is new about Thomas's bourse-building venture. Stow sweeps both Richard Gresham, Thomas's father, and Thomas himself (Figure 4) into his catalog of those London citizens who have made the city "glorious in manhoode,"[58] most often by crowning lives of civic service by endowing the city with some notable charitable institutions. Richard, Stow notes, had been Lord Mayor of London in 1548 and had founded a free school at Holt, a market town in Norfolk. Thomas, who is mentioned a number of times, is first said to have "builded the Royall exchange in London, and by his Testament left his dwelling house in Bishops gate streete, to be a place for readings, allowing large stipends to the readers, and certain almes houses for the poore."[59]

True as far as it goes, this account elides certain aspects of the historical record. By representing the building solely as a charitable gift to the city, Stow obscures several facts: first, as he later acknowledges, the city actually purchased the land on which the Exchange was built and tore down a number of dwellings to make way for it; second, Gresham hoped to achieve some commercial gain from this venture from the rents that he retained under his and his wife's control until their deaths. Moreover, Ann Saunders argues that Gresham may have misled city officials in his initial negotiations with them for help in obtaining and clearing the land. Rather than giving the Exchange directly to the city after his and his wife's death, Gresham's will stated that control would be shared by the city and the Mercers' Company. Income from the property was, moreover, encumbered in a number of ways, including yearly provision for the maintenance of Gresham College and its lecturers.[60] Saunders concludes that the charitable "gift" turned out to be more burdensome to the city than anyone at first imagined. These slightly sordid details aside, however, what Stow also elides is precisely what Haughton captures: the varied business dealings, the licit and illicit interactions, and the international cast of characters that made the Exchange more than a monument of civic charity, made it, in fact, a center of new kinds of commercial practice and productive of new kinds of social relations.

To a large extent, in dramatizing the Exchange, Heywood drew on Stow's vision of a unified city dominated by a succession of civic-minded mayors and prosperous guildsmen defined by their charitable acts. For example, at one point the Dean of St. Paul's, Dr. Nowell, draws Sir Thomas Ramsey, Ramsey's wife, and Gresham into a gallery at his home where he has hung the pictures of many charitable citizens. To edify his listeners, Nowells tells the history of each person pictured in his gallery. Of one portrait he says

Figure 4. Portrait of Sir Thomas Gresham by an unknown Flemish artist, 1544.
Mercer's Company Picture Collection Catalogue Number 043.

This Sir *Richard Whittington* three times Mayor,
Sonne to a Knight, and Prentice to a Mercer,
Began the Librarie of Gray-Friars in London;
And his Executors after him did build
Whittington Colledge, thirteene Almes-houses for poore men,
Repair'd St. *Bartholmewes*, in Smithfield,
Glased the Guild-hall, and built Newgate.[61]

Other city worthies receive similar laudatory descriptions and, with
their pictures displayed on the stage, they form a civic honor roll,
introducing playgoers to the great men central to Heywood's, and
Stow's, history of London. It is to this pantheon that Gresham aspires.
He later tells Nowell that the day Nowell showed him his picture
gallery Gresham promised to join this "rancke of charitable men"
(1252) and to the world "leave like memorie" (1255). The Exchange
is his bid to join this fellowship of worthies. This is despite the fact
that, as Vanessa Harding has argued, Thomas Gresham in fact lived
his life somewhat outside the world of public service and public office
characteristic of the most important members of the London guilds.
He was never, for example, an alderman or lord mayor. His patronage
came more directly from the Court especially from Elizabeth and
Cecil.[62] In this regard, it is important to note that Heywood changes
the reason for Gresham's knighthood. In actuality he was knighted in
1559 for his services as a Royal Agent on the Continent looking after
the finances of Edward, Mary, and Elizabeth, successively. Heywood
has Elizabeth knight him for building the Exchange. While in both
cases the honor came from the Queen, Heywood links it to an act that
serves the honor and glory of the city rather than the fiscal stability of
the Crown.

In thus mythologizing Gresham as a civic worthy and charitable
benefactor in ways that recall Stow, Heywood falsifies the historical
record but helps to create another new kind of London play, what I
call the London chronicle comedy.[63] Haughton's place-obsessed,
satiric portrait of city life has the honor of being the first extant play to
take the daily life of London as its subject. With its clever servant, its
urban setting, and its marriage plot in which the young outwit the old,
it owes a debt to Roman New Comedy, although its field of reference,
as I have shown, is very much contemporary London. *If You Know Not
Me, Part II* is a different sort of London play, a kind of history. First of
all, it has a "real" historical figure, Gresham, as its hero. Second, as I
will show, it draws on material found in urban chronicles such as
Stow's. Third, it brings an historical monarch, Elizabeth I, to the stage,
but does so in a way that makes the monarch a subordinate player in
Gresham's story.

At the heart of *If You Know Not Me, Part II*, then, lie several contradictions. While its picture of the Exchange and of Gresham's career is in part a nostalgic, backward-looking one, it nonetheless privileges citizen over monarch in its telling of history. Although the play glorifies the queen, shows her learnedly speaking foreign languages with foreign ambassadors, and grants her the power to rename Gresham's Bourse as the Royal Exchange, Gresham is the play's protagonist and some of his actions challenge a monarch's in magnificence — even extravagance. But these extravagant gestures, which I will discuss further below, also reveal a fissure within the representation of Gresham himself. Heywood constructs his hero partly within the terms laid down by Stow, but pulling against this construction is another that makes Gresham a hyperbolic and exotic figure quite unlike a decorous city worthy. It is the Exchange itself that prompts this second discourse, for Heywood is not quite able to make the place just another example of a charitable bequest like a church or a conduit. Rather, its associations with high finance and international trade invite Heywood to think of Gresham partly in terms of the activities of the new chartered companies seeking monopolies on Mediterranean and Eastern commerce. Paradoxically, Heywood makes Gresham more a member of the traditional London guild oligarchy than he in actuality was, *and also* more of an exotic North African merchant.

An example will help make some of these tensions concrete. When the play opens, Gresham is striking a deal through his factors with the King of Barbary to secure a monopoly on Moroccan sugar during the Moroccan king's life. For this privilege he is to pay 60,000 pounds — as Edward Bonahue Jr. has shown, a staggeringly large sum in Elizabethan times.[64] Historically, Gresham made his money carrying on his father's business in the English cloth trade and as a Royal Agent in the Low Countries where he raised loans for the monarch and helped to stabilize English coinage after the disastrous debasements of the 1550s.[65] He does not ever appear to have been himself a player in the North African sugar trade. In depicting him as such, Heywood anachronistically connects Gresham to events that primarily occurred after his death, namely, the rise of the chartered companies, especially the Turkey Company in 1581, the Barbary Company in 1585, and the Levant Company in 1592. All of them dealt in luxury items from the Mediterranean and the Far East, such as sugar, spices, currants, and wine.[66] If the historical Gresham was not directly connected to this trade, by 1605 Heywood nonetheless is not able to separate the Royal Exchange — and hence its builder — from such associations.

Of course, representing Gresham as a high-risk investor in the Moroccan sugar trade puts pressure on the schema Heywood derived from Stow to represent the elite members of London's guilds. Schizophrenically,

Heywood's Gresham transmutes in the course of the play from a sober civic worthy to an extravagant, hyperbolic, supremely self-confident speculator. In this latter role he is given several highly over-the-top scenes, and I would like to focus on those involving his further dealings with the King of Barbary. When this king dies soon after Gresham has paid him the 60,000 pounds, the new king refuses either to honor the sugar monopoly or to return the money—but he insultingly sends Gresham a pair of slippers and a dagger. Gresham receives these gifts at the dinner he gives to Elizabeth and a group of foreign ambassadors at his home on the very day that Elizabeth is to undertake her visit to his new bourse. Gresham's audience, then, is an august one. He rises to the occasion. In a bravura gesture, taking the King of Barbary's dagger and putting on the slippers, he cries:

then Hoboyes, play,
On slippers ile daunce all my care away:
Fit, fit, he had the just length of my foot.
You may report Lords when you come to Court,
You *Gresham* saw a paire of slippers weare
Cost thirtie thousand pound. (1531–36)

A moment later he tops his gesture with another of equal bravado. Earlier in the scene, Gresham had bought a pearl worth 1,500 pounds, a pearl that the King of France and the Russian ambassador, among others, had refused to buy because the price was too dear. Immediately after his slipper dance, Gresham orders the pearl ground up and drinks it down in a toast to Queen Elizabeth:

In stead of Sugar, *Gresham* drinkes this pearle
Unto his Queene and Mistresse: pledge it Lords,
Who ever saw a *Marchant* bravelier fraught,
In dearer slippers, or a richer draught? (1552–55)

This is a remarkable stage moment. Gresham makes a gesture of such extravagance that it not only separates him from the more sober ethos of public charity familiar from Stow's accounts of merchant virtue, but makes him the rival, even the superior, of the princes before whom he performs this unusual act of conspicuous consumption.[67] After all, neither Russian ambassador nor French King had bought this jewel, much less swallowed it. In quaffing the pearl in honor of Elizabeth, Gresham is appropriating and refunctioning chivalric gestures in a display of sprezzatura that defines him as, indeed, a royal merchant, a knight of commerce, in short, a walking oxymoron, something new and almost unclassifiable.[68]

That it is specifically a pearl Gresham swallows also invites comment. First, this white jewel—broken, mixed with wine, and swallowed— obliquely references the communion service.[69] Rather than the body of Christ, however, the pearl embodies the fruits of commercial venturing. The stage moment is a bizarre consecration of the high-risk financial dealings that the Gresham of Heywood's play at times appears to represent. Moreover, in early modern London pearls were exotic objects, signifiers of the East and of its wealth.[70] Probably the most famous historical pearl-swallower was the Egyptian queen, Cleopatra, who drank off a pearl dissolved in vinegar—just the sort of gesture that got her a bad reputation among reproving Puritans as well as among the Romans who felt she ruined their Mark Antony.[71] By repeating her gesture, Gresham incorporates the foreign, the exotic, and the extravagant into his own hyperbolically English body.[72] This is the second incorporation fantasy encountered in these Exchange plays. But this time it is not the alien Pisaro who through his daughters' marriages must be absorbed into the body politic, but rather a foreign object, a pearl of great price, that is being sluiced down its English buyer's throat. In Heywood's Exchange there are no stranger merchants (though several foreign ambassadors do come to Gresham's house for dinner and surround the Queen at the Exchange). Rather, exotic gifts and precious trifles (daggers, slippers, pearls) represent the influx of foreign matter into England. Tellingly, through his dance and his toast, Gresham subjects these objects to his own ends, rather than being awed or cowed before them. A knight of commerce, this Gresham takes huge risks, deals with foreign monarchs, and emerges unscathed, whatever his temporary losses.[73]

The play's schizophrenic portrayal of Gresham—half public benefactor and half extravagant entrepreneur—makes visible the play's anxieties about how practices associated with the Exchange could alter traditional values and social relations within the city. To what extent is Gresham like the other worthies whose pictures the Dean of St. Paul's has collected, and how much does he represent a break with that past? The question is underscored by the presence of a number of characters who inhabit the play's commercial world in a more traditional way. Chief among these is old Hobson, a city haberdasher who buys many of his wares from France and who fondly remembers his youthful friendship with Gresham:

O *Master Gresham* 'twas a golden world
When we were Boyes, an honest Countrey-yeoman,
Such as our fathers were, God rest their soules,
Would were white Karsie. (266–69)

The historical Gresham's father was not a yeoman, but a merchant. In Hobson's nostalgic reverie, however, both he and Gresham have risen from humble origins, underscoring the theme of upward mobility through honest labor that Hobson, at least, really embodies. Ironically, by stressing their common origins, Hobson also highlights how differently he and Gresham are now situated. Hobson, while sufficiently well off to own a haberdasher's shop and make moderate loans, including one of 100 pounds to the queen, has nowhere near the vast sums of money possessed, ventured, or even swallowed by Gresham. Hobson, after all, is a haberdasher, a traditional merchant who deals in small items of dress and ornament of the sort the peddler Tawnycoat, another character in the play, can put in his pack. Moreover, as with much traditional guild trade, Hobson's chief overseas dealings are with northern Europe, not North Africa. He sends his factor to France to purchase certain items he will resell in the domestic market. While profitable, these commercial dealings are represented as on an entirely different scale from Gresham's attempts to get a corner on the Barbary sugar trade.

Similarly, Hobson's "good deeds" are of a different sort from Gresham's grand gesture of erecting the Royal Exchange. Hobson, for example, is instrumental in getting Gresham and the Lord Mayor to end a foolish quarrel over a piece of property. He particularly objects to their spending money on the case that might better be spent in other ways:

> were *Hobson* in your coate,
> Ere i'de consume a pennie amongst Lawyers,
> Ide giv't poore people, bones a me I wold. (348–50)

The ethos of charity associated with Hobson associates him consistently with Stow's vision of civic virtue.[74] After the scene in which Gresham swallows the pearl on the very day the Royal Exchange is named, Hobson bestows charity on Tawnycoat who has fallen into extreme poverty by attempting to help his neighbors during hard times. Hobson forgives Tawnycoat's debts and gives him 40 pounds to start again in the peddler's trade. This episode seems designed to contrast with Gresham's extravagant feats of Exchange building and pearl swallowing. Through the depiction of the two figures, Heywood, however incoherently, gestures toward old and new ways of being part of the city's commercial and social life.

The play does not entirely idealize Hobson. Portrayed throughout as a worthy man, Hobson is also something of an obsolescent bumbler. Both his apprentices and his factor take advantage of him, and his speech has a jerky, repetitive quality that comes from his exclaiming, every third line or so, "Bones a me" or "Bones a God." For example, when his apprentice says that he has been breakfasting on a dagger pie instead of minding the shop, Hobson responds

A Dagger Pie! Ud's, daggers death, these knaves
Sit cocke a hope, but *Hobson* payes for all.
But bones a me, knaves either mend your manners.
Leave Alehouses, taverns, and the tipling mates,
Your Punkes, and cocatrices, or ile clappe ye
Close up in Bridewell, bones of me ile doo't. (201–6)

He is also given to sententiae and commonplaces, and, tellingly, he gets his own "slipper" scene. Wandering out one morning in his slippers to take the morning air and see his rents and buildings on the south bank of the Thames, he gets lost in the mist. Eventually he meets Tawnycoat, whom he aids, and then his apprentice, who informs him that his factor is playing fast and loose with his business in France. Without changing his shoes, Hobson heads off to France where, still foolishly dressed in his slippers and morning gown, he is tricked by his factor into consorting with a courtesan and profoundly embarrassing himself. In short, Hobson in his slippers is a foolish victim, not the recklessly confident figure that Gresham insists on being when he dances in the King of Morocco's ill-intentioned gift.

Heywood's seemingly simple play about the founding of the Royal Exchange is, in actuality, far from either straightforward or unproblematic. His answer to the place's foreign associations is either to elide them by depicting only one stranger merchant, the Barbary merchant of the first scene, or to make Gresham their embodiment as he becomes a pearl-imbibing Levant merchant. Rather than a Jewish Portingale with thirty-two ships upon the seas, Gresham is the Exchange's only man of wealth. In many ways, the play is as chauvinistic as *Englishmen for My Money* with its more overt anxiety about foreign dominance of both trade and English lands. For Heywood, the Exchange becomes a place where strangers like the Russian ambassador can watch an Englishman perform his unflappable dominance over both monarchs and merchants from other climes. But what Heywood's play registers most forcibly is the ruptures this new place signals in the terms in which civic life was conceived, ruptures that made Stow's template inadequate to the task of delineating civic virtue and heroism. Heywood's chronicle comedy boldly dramatizes a version of history that makes protagonists, not of monarchs, but of exemplary figures from London's citizen classes. But the play points to rents in the social fabric of that citizen group, as well. Robert Brenner has argued that the emergence of the great overseas trading companies at the end of the sixteenth century exacerbated long-standing splits between the great merchants and the smaller artisans, retailers, and small traders who could have no part in joint stock ventures.[75] This gap is signaled in the play by the contrast between the representational strategies used to encompass a Gresham and a Hobson. The danger, the excitement, the dynamism of Gresham's risky ventures find expression in the quaffed pearl, the abrupt announcement that the King of Barbary is dead, the hyperbole surrounding the building of London's bourse. He is a figure of dazzling self-confidence, embodying the ambivalent danger and promise of one vision of the future, a vision where entrepreneurship is only imperfectly sutured to ideals of charity, communal responsibility, and sobriety.

By contrast, the story of Hobson is rendered in ways that are by turns pious and patronizing. He is good in recognizable ways, but also bumbling and naive. His befuddlement in a Parisian brothel, his repetitious tics of speech, his inability to control his apprentices, much less his factor—all these create a certain ironic aura around his acts of unmistakable piety and charity. This is the familiar defamiliarized by various distancing devices and turned into quaintness—the modality of nostalgia, a modality familiar from certain other early modern plays, including *Henry IV, Part II*, in Shakespeare's depiction of the foolish, well meaning country squires, Master Slender and Master Shallow. Through Hobson, Heywood solicits his audience at once to savor and to relinquish a certain understanding of the past. Hobson, significantly, does not have a shop on the Exchange. In Heywood's play the building is all Gresham's—a place that ambivalently links him to his city's traditions of civic benefaction but, more importantly, to its future as a center for long-distance overseas trade and commercial empire. It is a transition that in this play solicits excitement, but also nostalgia and regret.

The Women of the Exchange

The Exchange was, of course, the site for other kinds of commercial transactions besides those represented in *Englishmen for My Money* and *If You Know Not Me*. In the pawn, located above the main floor of the Exchange, were the many retail shops mentioned by early commentators who described the building. It was these shops that Gresham was so careful to have stocked when Elizabeth visited his bourse. But Heywood, in *If You Know Not Me*, did not dramatize them. He was too busy showing Gresham imbibing crushed pearls and dancing in his North African slippers. But in *The Fair Maid of the Exchange*, a play perhaps also by Heywood and probably first performed in 1607, the pawn becomes the focus of a dramatic narrative as complex as the ones we have already encountered. With the change of locale within the building comes a change in the gendering of the dramatic narrative. Now the protagonist is not Gresham, revered city father, but Phyllis Flower, the fair maid of the play's title. Her name, and that of her friend, Moll Berrie, conflate these urban women with the flowers and fruits of the English countryside. Phyllis and Moll's names predict their destinies. Ripe, sweet-smelling, attractive, they are the native produce to be plucked, the sweetest of the wares available on the Exchange. But *Fair Maid* is not an urban idyll in which ripe girls and eager young men outwit stupid fathers to achieve the satisfaction of their own desires. Rather, the setting in the pawn seems to make a simple marriage plot hard to construct as both women and men are endangered by their marketplace practices and lose control over the nature and course of their own desires. There is a decidedly sinister and mysterious quality to this comedy. On one level it simply dramatizes everyday practices in and near the Exchange, but on another it suggests that these practices endanger and compromise those who engage in them and disrupt the successful reproduction of family-based authority and values.

Phyllis and Moll work in the textile trades within the pawn. They are, in a phrase that was to become proverbial, Exchange sempsters. That is, they do sewing; they carry cloth to the drawer's shop where embroidery patterns are stamped on it; they take ruffs to be starched; they deliver finished products to the houses of customers. Not domestic servants who work in people's houses, they are shopgirls who serve a mistress or master within the public setting of the pawn. Phyllis and Moll thus do for money what women of all classes were trained to do as part of their preparation for domestic life, namely, make and adorn clothing and household linens.[76] As a place of work, the pawn incorporated these women into a commercial venue constructed to highlight the aggregation and display of many kinds of commodities. In the 1593 *Parlement of Pratlers*, gallants go to the pawn seeking and having thrust upon them an endless array of fashionable items: ruffs, falling bands, handkerchiefs, socks, coifs, cuffs wrought with gold and silver, fine holland, cambric, Venice glasses, French garters, Spanish gloves, Flanders' knives, Italian silk stockings, hose, hats, feathers, high shoes, and other items. Among the presumed vendibles are the shopgirls themselves who are solicited by the gallants to share a pint of wine with them while a pandar offers to sell one of the "wenches" to a Northern gentleman.[77]

The pawn is represented both in *The Parlement of Pratlers* and in *Fair Maid* as a place that sexualizes the women who work there and makes them seem potentially vendible. Moll, it should be noted, was the most common early modern name for a prostitute, and one of the "fair maids" is assigned it.[78] Throughout the play the two women are assailed by suitors, legitimate and otherwise. Neither actually appears unchaste, yet their site of work constantly threatens to compromise them. The very first scene of the play stages a near rape. Phyllis and her coworker Ursula are taking some finished textile goods to a woman's home in Mile End in the northern suburbs. It is getting dark, and they are set upon by two rogues, Scarlet and Bobbington, who plan to "rifle them of what they carry,/ I mean, both goods, and their virginitie,"[79] the line clearly equating the textiles they carry and their own ripe bodies. The young shopgirls are only rescued by the arrival of a crippled man named, fittingly, Cripple, who chases off the rogues with his crutches and in turn has to be rescued by Frank Golding when the villains circle back around and plot to snatch away Cripple's crutches and so render him harmless.

The pattern of endangerment continues. When Moll takes work to Cripple the drawer, she is noisily approached in his shop by Bowdler, a loudmouthed spendthrift who wants her virginity. When Phyllis is working in her mistress's shop up in the pawn, two gentlemen come in to buy bands and other linen goods, but one of them quickly focuses his full attention on Phyllis's "so rich a beautie" (1219), pleading with her to "let me weare/ This shape of thine, although I buy it deere" (1235–36). There then follows a lengthy dialogue between the two on the relationship between the garments she wears and the body beneath. It ends with Phyllis ordering the two men to "Get you downe the staires, or I protest/Ile make this squared walke too hotte for you./ Had you been as you seemd in out-ward shew,/Honest Gentlemen, such terms of vilde abuse/Had not been proffred to virginitie" (1265–69). While Phyllis here is able to beat back the predatory gallants by herself, the confusion of women and goods that persists throughout the text always puts virginity at risk. While essential to the allure of the pawn, the young women who work there seem imperiled by it. If the floor of the Exchange marked out the world of high finance and spawned fantasies of powerful foreigners who must be contained and huge risks that must be endured, the pawn defined risk differently, locating it in the body of the wage-earning woman.

Fair Maid thus speaks to the plight of a group of female workers represented as especially vulnerable within the sexualized commercial scene of the Exchange's upper floor. Importantly, these women have skills. In the scene in which Phyllis is assailed by the two gentlemen she has been left in charge of the shop in her mistress's absence. It falls to her to supervise the other workers, a young boy who resents her temporary authority, as well as Ursula, who has taken herself off to a shop on the other side of the pawn. Phyllis, in short, is a manager as well as a productive worker who whitens or bleaches cloth, cuts out patterns, and does sewing. She is also in charge of retail operations, giving customers what they legitimately require of her. The play powerfully suggests the paradoxes of her position and that of women like her. Skilled and eminently employable, she is nonetheless not the owner of the shop, and her authority is ultimately limited, partly by her gender. The boy rebels against taking orders from her, saying "I would not be a byword to th'Exchange,/For every one to say (my selfe going by)/Yon goes a vassall to authoritie" (1175–77). Moreover, as we have seen, her position subjects her to constant sexualization. In fact, positioning attractive women at the front of shops to draw in customers is a practice commented on in many plays besides this one and in many sites besides the Royal Exchange, suggesting that beautiful female shopworkers could widely be perceived as vendible commodities like ruffs and ribbons. While women played an active part in market life throughout the city, and often without negative comment, the potential was always at hand to equate their bodies with their goods. In Heywood's play, women's presence above the aggressively masculine space of the Royal Exchange's main floor, and the break with tradition in the Exchange's aggregation of many kinds of shops within one enclosed space, seem to have activated that potential with surprising virulence, leading to the picture of these "Exchange sempsters" as a sexualized and vulnerable group.

While powerfully registering the risk to women of their public positioning within the commodity culture of the pawn, *Fair Maid* also struggles with another danger, however, that posed *by* these very public, multiply skilled women: namely, the danger that they will grow beyond the control of the families who are supposed to supervise their passage into marriage. As Juana Green has convincingly shown, both Moll and Phyllis try to arrange their own marriages to men they appear to have met on the Exchange or at least somewhere outside their parents' homes.[80] Moreover, each uses her knowledge of textiles to design a handkerchief to give to her chosen beloved. Moll chooses a nicely phallic peascod pattern to adorn her love token (151–76). Phyllis designs a more elaborate story picture in which Cupid shoots an arrow into a heart, while disdain languishes in a corner and a laurel tree springs up to crown victorious love with a wreath (869–79). Green's point is that the women use their partial autonomy as workers outside the home to initiate courtship. In the process they turn to their own ends the skills they use as paid workers, designing handkerchiefs they will bestow as gifts on potential lovers.

As Green also points out, neither woman simply gets to choose her mate and so make her desire her destiny. Phyllis wants to marry Cripple, the man who rescued her from rape. She does not get her desire, and in the end weds Frank Golding. Moll goes so far as to pledge herself to a boisterous gentleman, Bowdler, but finally is persuaded to marry a more earnest, but bankrupt fellow, Barnard. At some level the play not only warns of the dangers of public exposure to women in the shops of the Exchange, but also registers anxiety about the willfulness of those women, their potential independence from the control of families.

What interests me, however, is *how* the correction of female desire occurs. Parents, it turns out, are not effective at reasserting control. Phyllis's father is a merchant who lives on Cornhill near the Exchange, but early in the play he is approached by one of the same men, Bobbington, who tried to rape his daughter in the first scene. The con man says his name is Racket and that he is about to depart for Barbary and wants to borrow 10 pounds. He will leave a diamond worth 40 pounds as a pledge against his return. In the last twenty lines of the play, however, officers of the law come on the stage and arrest Master Flower. Bobbington's diamond was a stolen one, and for his greed Flower will be arraigned on charges of receiving stolen property. The play thus ends with the discrediting of patriarchal authority. His daughter barely escaped rape at Bobbington's hands, but Mr. Flower was actually fleeced both of his 10 pounds and of his freedom. Moreover, throughout the play, Mr. and Mrs. Flower quarrel and scheme against one another to choose Phyllis's mate. Mr. Flower wants Ferdinand Golding for a son-in-law; Mrs. Flower wants Anthony Golding. They end up with Frank. The Berrie family is equally unanchored at the top. Mr. Berrie seems to be a moneylender. Several times in the play he gloats over his impending imprisonment of Barnard, whom he has already once jailed for forfeiting payment of a debt and whom he now intends to put in the Counter again. It is this same Barnard his daughter eventually marries, presumably erasing his debt.

This is odd. In a play bent on correcting the independence of shop-girls and rerouting their erotic desire, presumably set loose by their public position in the Exchange, the answer is not the reassertion of the authority of parents or even the superior skill of witty young men. Though the play does have one such character, the young Frank who eventually gets Phyllis, the Fair Maid of the Exchange, only succeeds because he is helped along by the man Charles Lamb called the hero of the play, namely, Cripple.[81] The 1607 title page gives Cripple subtitle billing. The play is called *The Fair Maid of the Exchange: With The Pleasant Humours of the Cripple of Fanchurch.* Supposedly, his story is also told in a ballad by Thomas Dekker called "The Cripple of Cheapside," but it is not extant. As it stands, Cripple's role in the play is something of a mystery. He once was able-bodied for he speaks several times about the "visitation" that has come upon him and driven him to walk with crutches. But what accident or illness caused his lameness remains unspoken. He has a shop where he compulsively works, and his primary trade is as a drawer, that is, someone who transfers patterns onto cloth so that sempsters can stitch or embroider it according to the design he has employed. But he also seems to work as a scrivener. Frank takes a love letter to him, and he supplies Frank with letters of reply, which he says he got from a poet who bequeathed to Cripple his library of writings (1283–1431). His occupation(s) are suited to a location in or near the Exchange. Sempsters working there constantly needed the services of a drawer to make patterns, and the amount of large-scale commercial business conducted on the main floor of the Exchange increased the demand for the services of notaries, scriveners, and stationers.[82] At one level, then, despite the mysterious nature of his disability, Cripple has an understandable place at the Exchange.[83] But this does not explain the unusual amount of influence he wields within the narrative.

This influence is evident in a number of ways. First, everyone knows Cripple and comes to his shop: Frank, Moll, Phyllis, Bowdler, Barnard. Not only do they come, but they surrender utterly to the drawer's advice. His power over the two women is uncanny. Phyllis, of course, wants to marry him despite his disability. Moll Berrie, moreover, is persuaded to marry Barnard, rather than Bowdler to whom she has promised herself, because Cripple persuades her that Bowdler, that "fond humorist" (2205), that "froth of complement" (2215), is not only unworthy, but is also not "really" whom she desires. He tells a tale in which he heard her talk in her sleep about her love for Barnard! In short, Cripple claims knowledge of Moll's true desires, though they are unknown to her conscious mind, and manages to make her believe he is right. His manipulation of Phyllis is, if anything, even more extreme. When he receives the story handkerchief in which she confesses her love for him, in soliloquy he says he "detest(s) the humor of fond love" (887) and that he will not be one of those barred from all joy by marriage (ll. 998–99). He then begins to work to further Frank Golding's aim of pushing aside his two older brothers and seizing Phyllis for himself. A number of tricks accomplish this, but the culminating one involves Frank assuming Cripple's clothes and crutch and wooing Phyllis in the drawer's stead (2002–60). She is made to pledge her troth to a simulacrum of her love, not the thing itself. When it is finally revealed to her that she has been tricked, she accepts Frank, making her desire conform to the wishes of Cripple and of the man who assumed his clothes and crutches.

The prime mover of the plot, then, is Cripple. He is the closest thing to a governing authority that the play allows, certainly more so than either the moneylender Berrie or the swindled merchant, Master

Flower. Yet he is an outsider and somewhat monstrous, even as he is integral to the life that centers around the upper floor of the Exchange. At his first entrance he speaks of himself as a "huge deformitie" (88) borne along on "foure legs" (97). Later, he tells Frank that he is too "unworthy," "foule," and "base" (ll. 1957, 1958, 1958) to match with the beauteous Phyllis, even though he is the object of her desire. More troubling things are said of him, constantly, by Bowdler. In scene vi, their first encounter, Bowdler calls Cripple a "dog" and a "filthy dog" (616, 620), remarks twice on his nose (627), calls him dog again (627), and ends up calling him a "Jew" (637) whose venomous tongue he will cut out. The scene is one of banter; nonetheless, the abusive language codes Cripple as a Jew, however jestingly it is employed. As James Shapiro has shown, Jews were constantly referred to as "dogs" and "curs." Their noses were a constant source of comment, and their—to Christian eyes—antisocial and churlish behavior was proverbial.[84] A few scenes later, Cripple refuses to go with Barnard and Bowdler to see the dancing at a wedding in Gratious (Gracechurch) Street. Again, Bowdler calls Cripple a "dogge" (721) and "dogge of *Israell*" (842), while Cripple refuses to play when he has "businesse" (722 and 841), setting up a dialectic, familiar from *The Merchant of Venice*, between the improvident Christian gentlemen of the town and the provident Jew. It is an opposition again sounded in scene x when Bowdler calls Cripple a cynical "Diogenes" (1580) sick of melancholy and returns to his language of "dogge" (1601, 1609) and "filthy curre" (1607). Cripple, of course, gets his revenge, for it is Bowdler who is made a "*Menelaus*" (2670) in the end, his Moll stolen away by Barnard, the Paris whom Cripple has installed in his place with his tale of Moll's unconscious desires.

What I am suggesting is that Cripple is the ambiguous genius of the Exchange, the spirit of the place, and that spirit is of mixed and vaguely sinister origins. Like Pisaro in *Englishmen for My Money*, Cripple is central to this narrative of Exchange life. Yet like Pisaro he is somewhat mysterious. Pisaro came from beyond the sea and took up residence in London. The origin of his disability unknown, Cripple holds some part of himself in reserve from the life around him. He will not marry; he will not dance; he will not forego business for pleasure. Yet he is powerful in his manipulations, rewriting the desires of the young women and picking winners and losers among the English suitors. The biggest winner, Frank Golding, can only have his prize when he assumes the form of the "huge deformitie," Cripple. The Fair Maid of the Exchange, the English flower, does not wed the cur, the dog, and yet she does, comedy allowing the fantasy of this unlikely coupling to play out in the garment-based doubling of cripple and handsome suitor.

The Fair Maid of the Exchange is finally a darker play than the others I have examined. It begins with a near rape and ends with the imprisonment of Phyllis Flower's father for receiving stolen goods. Moreover, while it ends with two marriages, both have been engineered by the mysterious Cripple. I do not believe that this figure is literally to be read as a Jew, but the Jewish discourse that Bowdler insistently uses about him, his deformity and self-marginalization, cast a shadow over the considerable power he wields. *Fair Maid* suggests that the Exchange endangers the women who work within it, but it also empowers them in novel ways, allowing the troubling exercise of their will. But in placing the power to curb female desire not in the hands of good English parents but in the control of a man at once mysterious, deformed, and all-knowing, the play cannot help making the endings he engineers seem problematic. In this play the novel position in which the pawn places young women manages at once to weaken familial structures and to incite and then frustrate female desire.

All of the Exchange plays capture some of the excitement this new structure generated. Yet in none of these is Gresham's Bourse easily absorbed into seamless fictions. Whether it is the troubling dominance of strangers in Exchange business or the dangers posed to the women who work in its pawn, Exchange dramas inevitably pivot round the problems as well as the possibilities of this imposing building, using it to probe the tensions of a city imagined as claiming an enhanced place in the commercial dealings of Europe. *If You Know Not Me* is probably most ambivalent about this change, clinging nostalgically to a vision of "lost London" even as it celebrates its pearl-quaffing merchant hero. But in each of these plays there are fault lines suggesting the losses that accompanied the new practices of a city becoming "the mart of the world."

Chapter 2

Credit, Incarceration, and Performance: Staging London's Debtors' Prisons

In 1573, Isabella Whitney's second book of verse, *The Sweet Nosegay*, appeared in the London bookstalls near St. Paul's Cathedral.[1] The final poem in this collection, her "Wyll and Testament," takes the form of a poetic will in which the speaker, a fictional version of Whitney herself, leaves various bequests—not to relatives—but to the city of London. The speaker assumes the persona of an unemployed servant who, having lost her position in a London household, has descended into poverty and feels death approaching. Remarkably, though the speaker is writing a will, she is actually so poor that she has nothing of her own to bequeath to anyone. The only thing she can distribute to London is what London already possesses, namely, its shops, streets, prisons, foodstuffs, cloth, luxury items, and its places of physic and entertainment.[2] With high-spirited irony, the speaker thus munificently gives away what is not hers, not only the content of whole shops, but what might be counted the common property of the entire city: its municipal infrastructure of streets and buildings and common meeting places. She positions herself as generous to a city that, she claims, has not been generous to her. "Thou never yet, woldst credit geve/ to boord me for a yeare:/ Nor with Apparell me releve/ except thou payed weare"(32–35).[3] Specifically, the speaker calls attention to the benefits traditionally allowed servants who would receive an allotment of apparel and food, as well as wages, during their time of employment. Having lost her position, the speaker gets none of these benefits.

Besides a poetic will, Whitney's poem is also an urban chorography of sorts[4] in that it describes in some detail specific London streets, buildings, and institutions, mostly within the southwest quadrants of the old walled city.[5] The speaker maps London from a particular vantage point, that of a poor servant girl whose knowledge of the city would have been obtained by walking the streets looking for work, running errands for a mistress, or just gawking at what the shops and market stalls put on display. Several decades later John Stow's *Survey of London* would focus primarily on the public buildings of London, especially on its churches, guildhalls, conduits, and charitable endowments. Whitney, by contrast, says little about the churches of London, other than St. Paul's, and little about the great city monuments, although she does mention the Mint and the Royal Exchange, the latter, however, only in terms of the many shops that line the pawn. About the court she is silent. Instead, Whitney's speaker focuses primarily on two things: where within the city one can buy food, clothing, and luxury goods, and where one can be incarcerated. It is the striking prominence of prisons in "Wyll and Testament," and their relation to London shops, that I want to focus on here.

At line 75, the speaker begins her catalog of bequests. The ensuing 110 lines name street upon street and the kinds of goods and services that could be obtained at each. At the Steelyard, for example, one can buy wine from the German merchants who congregate there; in Watling Street one can buy wool, gold in Cheapside, hose in Birchin Lane, shoes at St. Martin's, books in the yard of St. Paul's, and legal services at the Inns of Court. In essence, the speaker provides a kind of early shopper's guide to London. This section of the poem with its list-like structure overwhelms the reader with the abundance of material things the city affords to those who have money: plate, jewels, hoods, hats, caps, ruffs, gorgets, sleeves, knives, combs, hose, boots, shoes, pantables, fish, linen, silk, swords, bucklers, cloaks, salt, oatmeal, candles, soap, junkets, baths, and on and on. Lines 185 to 242 change course. Suddenly, the speaker thinks of what she can leave to the poor of the city, those for whom the abundance of London's shops is unobtainable. The answer is prisons. They are what London has provided for the poor and what she, in her turn, can bequeath to them. The first prison that comes to mind is the Counter.

And fyrst the Counter they shal have,
   least they should go to wrack:
Some Coggers, and some honest men,
   that Sergantes draw a back.
And such as friends wyl not them bayle,
   whose coyne is very thin:
For them I leave a certayne hole,
   and little ease within. (191–98)

The two Counters, the Wood Street and the Poultry Counters, were important debtors' prisons under city jurisdiction (I will discuss them further below), and the Hole to which Whitney refers was the part of these prisons where those most destitute were held in squalid conditions, dependent on charity for their daily bread. There is dark irony in the speaker's assertion that the existence of such a place keeps the poor from going "to wrack." She then moves on to mention Newgate, the

Fleet, and, finally, Ludgate Prison, another debtors' prison specifically for the free men and women of the City of London.[6]

The stark juxtaposition of shops and prisons goes far to support Ann Rosalind Jones's assertion that the "Wyll" is fundamentally concerned with the opposition and interrelation of abundance and deprivation, with detailing the riches of London and documenting the consequences of exclusion from the privileged circle of those who can partake of such abundance.[7] The speaker presents herself as one who has lived the irony of immersion in streets lined with shops full of things to eat and clothes to wear while herself lacking a job that would bring her board and apparel. The juxtaposition of the two central parts of the poem dealing first with commercial London and then with carceral London suggests there is something fundamentally wrong with the economic life of the city. Consumer goods and services are multiplying at a dizzying rate, and the busy shops imply that there are many who can buy what is on display. As a writer, Whitney herself has benefitted from the market in printed books that the city has fostered. But at the same time, many city dwellers are sinking deeper and deeper into the stinking corners of the city's prisons, unable to buy what the shops afford and dependent on charity for daily food.

The speaker herself teeters on the edge of prison life. Speaking of Ludgate Prison, she says that she at first did not bequeath it to the city because she meant to reserve that legacy for herself "if I my health possest./ And ever came in credit so/ a debtor for to bee" (230–32). This interesting set of lines plays tellingly on the meaning of the word "credit." "Credit" is the reputation for trustworthiness (*OED* 5a and b) that allows one to borrow money.[8] The lines imply that if Whitney were a healthy woman (not sick from poverty as she now presents herself) and "in credit," that is, possessed of enough of a reputation for trustworthiness to secure loans, she might then be in danger of forfeiting on those loans and so needing to take refuge in Ludgate in order to avoid paying money to creditors. However, the speaker now recognizes that she will never be in that position. "Yet cause I feele my selfe so weake/ that none mee credit dare:/I heere revoke: and doo it leave,/some *banckrupts* to his share" (239–42). No one will believe in her creditworthiness; no one therefore will extend her a loan. As a result, she is not in danger of being arrested for debt or needing to take refuge in Ludgate to escape her creditors. Instead, revoking her bequest of Ludgate to herself, she gives it to a bankrupt, someone who once had had enough credit to get a loan. The speaker, however, is placed on a lower rung, among those who do not even have the credit potential to afford them a death in debtors' prison. Rather, she seems to imagine dying in the open streets and receiving at best a pauper's burial (311–22).

In this chapter I argue that Whitney was not the only writer who made prisons, and particularly debtors' prisons, important material and symbolic sites within their London texts; in their London plays, dramatists were particularly obsessed with the Counter as a pivotal place in their imaginative mapping of the city. In considering the role of debtors' prisons in London comedies, I will explore further some of the issues raised by Whitney's rightly famous poem: namely, the relationship in the drama between the burgeoning of the consumer market in the city and the burgeoning of debt; the role of charity as a response to both poverty and debt; and the complexities of various forms of "credit" as a fact of urban commercial life. If the Royal Exchange represents, in monumental form, the increasing participation of city merchants in a global network of commerce, the grubby debtors' prisons represent the not unrelated underside of commercial growth, namely, the expansion of credit relations and with that expansion enhanced possibilities both for default on proliferating debts and also for imprisonment.

In satiric city plays, Counter stories reveal the savage side of commercial growth and frequently foreground debt's destruction of social selfhood or identity. The drama's handling of the debtor's clothing, in particular, materializes that destruction in ways I will discuss below. However, debtors' prison narratives differ considerably from one another, revealing conflicts or contradictions in the way the culture made sense of debt, debtors, and what brought one "credit." Many plays make the male debtor a figure of folly, constructing him as prodigal or fop and the prison as the place of his just humiliation. Other plays, however, make the debtor a pitiable object of benevolence and focus on the amelioration of marketplace disasters either by the action of a just monarch or by the exercise of charity. These I call Hand of God narratives in which the Counter is not the punitive end of the debtor's story, but the place of his redemption. In these narratives, of which *A Woman Never Vext* is perhaps the most interesting example, benevolence wipes away the dangers of debt and obscures its ubiquity. Nostalgic for an imagined past of neighborliness and charitable benefaction, they resist the harsh logic by which imprisonment is seen as a fit ending for those who fail in marketplace endeavors. A third group of Counter plays, my favorites, query the premises of other Counter narratives and offer a performative logic as an alternative to marketplace calculations of "worth," especially creditworthiness. Self-reflexive and impious, these plays—represented here by *Eastward Ho* and *Greene's Tu Quoque*—make the Counter into a performance space where the witty display of theatrical skill queries market logic. In short, while the Counter looms large in the drama's staging of London, not all the stories told about this place are the same, nor, taken collectively, are they necessarily self-consistent. Rather, the contradictions in and between Counter plays suggest that they are part of an implicit and unfinished struggle within urban culture to make sense of a complex market economy in which debt and the acquiring of credit were an increasingly central aspect of daily life and how to deal with them a cultural negotiation not yet concluded.

The London Counters

London plays contain references to and representations of many prisons, only some of them specifically debtors' prisons. Richard III, for example, confines the sons of Edward IV in the Tower in Shakespeare's *Richard III*; Falstaff is banished to the Fleet at the end of *Henry IV, Part II*; Jane Shore visits prisoners at the Marshalsea Prison in the second part of *Edward IV*; some prisoners play at bowls in the Fleet in *Look About You*; the Witch of Edmonton is confined to Newgate in the play bearing her name; whores are incarcerated in the prison-cum-work-house in Bridewell at the end of *The Honest Whore, Part II*. The list could go on.[9] In some plays, such as *Measure for Measure*, the prison seems an amalgam of several "actual" prisons. The one in *Measure* contains sexual offenders one would expect to find in Bridewell; debtors who might be in the Counter; a pirate who would usually be confined at the Marshalsea; and felons such as Barnadine, who might more typically be found in Newgate.

As a group, London playwrights often had personal experience of the prisons that they dramatized. Some of that knowledge was merely that of geographical proximity. The Clink, for example, was located in a liberty in Southwark very close to the Rose, the Fortune, and the Globe Theaters. The Tower literally towered over the East End of the city, a landmark easily viewed from London bridge or from boats on the river, mentioned in many accounts of the city, and figuring on every map. Prisons such as Ludgate or Newgate sat smack beside or athwart two of the five gates giving entry to the old city, which meant they were viewed by many people passing in and out of the city to the west and north. There are accounts of prisoners reaching through the bars of Ludgate Prison to beg alms of those passing by. Yet dramatists did not just walk near or view the city's prisons; some spent time inside them. Thomas Dekker, in particular, wrote very often about London's prisons,[10] and he did so with the vividness of one who had experienced them. In 1616, for example, he added chapters on prisons, prisoners, and creditors to his *Lantern and Candle-light*, originally published in 1608. In *Rod for Runaways* (1625) he wrote movingly of the suffering of destitute prisoners left without any charitable support when the wealthy of the city fled during the plague. And in plays such as *Honest Whore Parts I and II* he depicted with unusual sympathy the plight of those who had been committed to Bridewell, one of the city's first workhouses, and to Bedlam, its madhouse, where many of the inhabitants seem to have lost their wits because of financial disasters.[11] In 1598 Dekker had briefly spent time in the Poultry Counter, and from 1613 to 1620 he was incarcerated for debt in the King's Bench prison. Among the actions entered against him was a bill from his tailor for four pounds, six shillings for a doublet and hose. Not everyone, of course, who wrote about prisons had been in them, but a perhaps surprising number of early modern dramatists had prison stints including Ben Jonson, George Chapman, John Marston, John Lyly, Cyril Tourneur, Henry Chettle, Robert Daborne, and William Haughton, and, as just mentioned, Thomas Dekker.[12] This is not, of course, the only reason that prison scenes turn up in early modern plays, but it does suggest that incarceration or its threat hung like a menacing cloud on the horizon of daily life.

Of all the London prisons, however, in London comedy it is debtors' prisons that are referred to or represented with obsessive repetitiveness. Middleton and Dekker's *The Roaring Girl* is typical. It depicts unruly city sons who do not want to do what their fathers wish. In the plot most often discussed, Sebastian Wengrave desires to marry Mary Fitz-Allard against his father Sir Alexander's wishes. To get his way, Sebastian pretends to want to marry the notorious crossdresser, Moll Cutpurse. Throughout the play, Sir Alexander Wengrave, in a counter-offensive, tries to entrap Moll in actions that will land her in prison. In the end, Sebastian gets his desired bride, and Moll eludes arrest. But there is another man, Sir Davy Dapper, whose son Jack Dapper also fails to follow his father's wishes, and his vices are more properly those of a prodigal. Described by his father as a spendthrift who wastes money on the pleasures of the city including "fiddlers, tobacco, wine, and a whore,/ A mercer that will let him take up more,/ Dice, and a water-spaniel with a duck" (III.iii.58–60),[13] Jack Dapper keeps company with all the roaring boys of London. To cure him of prodigality, his father has entered an action in a false name in the Counter to have his son arrested. Sir Alexander Wengrave and another knight, Sir Adam Appleton, applaud this ploy, making a series of jokes about how the Counter will "break" Jack Dapper, meaning both break his rebellious spirit and also break him financially by calling down all his creditors upon him, and cause him to sing "a counter-tenor sure" (III.iii.75), a reference that suggests both that he will be subdued to the vile conditions of his imprisonment and also that that subjection will colt his manhood, turning him into a shrill-voiced eunuch. These jokes hint at the violence done to the gentlemanly self imprisoned in such a place.

Sir Alexander's subsequent praise of the Counter as a university, however, most vividly suggests both the specificity with which the stage al-
luded to the Counter and also the ease with which it turned the prison
into metaphor. Wengrave says:

Bedlam cures not more madmen in a year
Than one of the counters does: men pay more dear
There for their wit than anywhere; a counter,
Why, 'tis an university, who not sees?
As scholars there, so here men take degrees,
And follow the same studies all alike.
Scholars learn first logic and rhetoric,
So does a prisoner; with fine honey'd speech
At's first coming in he doth persuade, beseech
He may be lodged with one that is not itchy,
To lie in a clean chamber, in sheets not lousy;
But when he has no money, then does he try
By subtle logic and quaint sophistry
To make the keepers trust him.
Sir Adam   Say they do?
Sir Alexander
Then he's a graduate.
Sir Adam   Say they trust him not?
Sir Alexander
Then is he held a freshman and a sot,
And never shall commence, but, being still barred,
Be expulsed from the master's side, to th'twopenny ward,
Or else i'th'Hole beg place.
Sir Adam   When, then, I pray,
Proceeds a prisoner?
Sir Alexander   When, money being the theme,
He can dispute with his hard creditors' hearts.
And get out clear, he's then a Master of Arts.
Sir Davy, send your son to Wood Street College.
A gentleman can nowhere get more knowledge. (III.iii.79–102)

The force of this passage depends on its citation of a well-established discourse of the Counter that uses the internal architecture of the place
(which I will discuss below) to structure narratives of downward mobility,
while at the same time calling attention to the need for specific skills to
fare well within or to win release from this place of confinement. Logic
and rhetoric, the arts of the honeyed tongue, are what might win Jack
Dapper "trust" and leniency from "hard creditors." But above all the passage emphasizes the supposedly pedagogic function of this place. It is a
school for gentleman, a trope used repeatedly in Counter discourse.[14] If
Bridewell became connected with the schooling of vagrants and sexual
offenders, particularly prostitutes, the Counters schooled gallants and
unthrifty citizens. But what exactly were the lessons of the Counters? In

the case of *The Roaring Girl* we never get to see what the Wood Street College might have taught Jack Dapper. When two catchpoles, Sergeant Curtilax and Yeoman Hanger, are summoned to arrest him, Moll Cutpurse beats them off, saying that "If any gentleman be in scrivener's bands,/ Send but for Moll, she'll bail him by these hands" (III.iii.216–17). Part of her folk hero status depends on Moll's capacity to rescue gentlemen from the harsh law of fathers and catchpoles. But as we shall see, in many other plays, dramatists actually take the theatergoer into debtors' prisons to witness the pedagogy of incarceration in action.

Before looking more closely at these plays, however, let me sketch in some of the historical particulars about the Counters to which Sir Alexander's speech refers, including his allusions to lousy sheets, the Hole, the Two-penny ward, and the Master's Side. Of London's many prisons,[15] four were principally given over to debtors, though no prison ever seems to have held exclusively one kind of prisoner only. Of those under Crown control, King's Bench in Southwark was the principal prison for major debtors, many owing money directly to the King or significant members of the Court. Here G. Mynshul, gentleman of Grey's Inn, was imprisoned for debts in 1618 and from which he wrote a stinging critique of the hardheartedness of creditors and the cruel extortions of jailers.[16] Of the four major prisons under city control (Newgate, Ludgate, and the Wood Street and Poultry Counters), only Newgate was for felons. Ludgate mainly housed debtors, but it was reserved for free men and women of London. No foreigners were allowed to be incarcerated in Ludgate, and citizens could demand to be taken there from the Counters. Ludgate in general had lower fees and better accommodations than either Counter.[17] However, the main debtors' prisons mentioned in the London comedies are the Wood Street and Poultry Counters, both under the control of the London sheriffs. (While there was a third Counter in Southwark, little is known about it.) Wood Street runs north of Cheapside just where Paternoster Row and Cheapside converge, and the Wood Street Counter was on the east side of the street behind some houses. The Poultry Counter was the larger of the two, located on the north side of Poultry just a few streets before it turns into Cornhill and thus very near Gresham's Royal Exchange. It, too, was obscured from view by buildings that separated it from Poultry. While these two Counters were thus situated squarely within the center of the walled city, most of the rest of London's prisons were either south of the river (the Clink, the Southwark Counter, the King's Bench, and the Marshalsea), at significant points along London wall (Ludgate, Newgate, and the Tower), or outside the walls altogether (Bridewell and the Fleet immediately to the west and the Gatehouse at Westminster further out). The Counters were thus woven into the fabric of the old city as most of the other prisons were not. Though they both were near the major commercial artery, Cheapside, neither was a conspicuous landmark. Largely concealed from view behind other buildings, they nonetheless were both central to the daily operations of justice in the city and of unusual significance in the drama.

The Counters were open all night, and anyone caught by the watch for any crimes or disturbances would be brought to them and held there until morning.[18] Depending on the crime, the prisoner might then be reassigned to a more appropriate place of incarceration. William Fenner, who in 1616 wrote a description and indictment of life in the Counters, claimed that as many as 5,000 prisoners passed through the Counters, however briefly, each year.[19] The volume is in part explained by the ease of making an arrest for debt. A complaint could be entered against an alleged debtor for four pence; only a shilling was required thereafter to have a sergeant issue a summons and arrest the accused.[20] Though it cost considerably more to bring the case to trial, some lawyers would take such cases on credit, and in most cases the point was to have the debtor simply pay his debts and get released before trial. Such a system was obviously open to abuses; in *The Roaring Girl* Sir Davy Dapper admits to entering an action in a false name against his son, simply to get him committed to the Counter.[21] And while many people who were thus summarily yanked from their lives into the hell of debtors' prison probably managed to settle their debts fairly quickly, some could not. For them, the sergeant's summons ushered them into a world of deprivation from which they could not escape.

In theory, debtors' prisons were not places of punishment, but holding pens; that is, one was not sentenced to a specific term in prison for having failed to pay back one's debts. Rather, people were held there only until they, their families, or their friends could manage to pay their obligations or come to some kind of composition with their creditors. Henslowe, for example, occasionally bailed out dramatists imprisoned for debts. Sometimes prisoners were the lucky beneficiaries of charitable bequests that would help them meet their obligations.[22] At Christmas and Easter, in particular, charitable "legacies" were dispensed to inmates, sometimes at the whim of the keeper of the prison. William Fenner reported that some prisoners abused these legacies in that they got themselves arrested for minor debts just before the Christmas season in order to collect the thirty or forty shillings given to prisoners from the legacies during the holiday season.[23] While the English Poor Laws, especially that of 1572, mandated that every parish pay rates for the relief of prisoners,[24] such support was entirely insufficient to meet the daily needs of inmates, many of whom continued to depend on various forms of charity.[25] For example, alms were often collected in churches for the relief of prisoners, and parishes appointed officials (sometimes called basketmen) who went through the streets soliciting bread, meat, and money to be delivered to the jails. W. K. Jordan has documented the large number of wills, especially those of London merchants, that prior to 1660 left money either for the food and maintenance of poor prisoners or for paying off their creditors.[26] Basically, however, the system was a makeshift and arbitrary one in which some people endured long-term incarceration for small debts and suffered from hunger, cold, and disease in the process. Implicitly, the Counters raised the question: was charity still sufficient, if it had ever been, to maintain the city's debtors?

Especially remarkable to the modern observer is the fact that no early modern prisons, including debtors' prisons, paid for food, clothing, or beds for their inhabitants. Rather, prisoners paid for these things. (It is, however, a horrifying reminder of the precariousness of all social advances that in some U.S. communities prisons are once more billing prisoners for their room and board![27]) If one were already incarcerated for debt, however, a horrible circularity could ensue. Debt caused imprisonment; imprisonment occasioned more debt because of the fees one had to pay for the most basic of services. In all the prison complaints of the time, and there are a number, the unremitting rapaciousness of prisonkeepers and turnkeys is seen as the cruelest and most arbitrary aspect of prison life. The title page of Mynshul's *Essays and Characters of a Prison and Prisoners* (1618) depicts a very large and imposing gaoler, his keys hung at his waist (Figure 5). This image of implacable power gives some idea of how prisonkeepers must have appeared to those over whom they had authority. Keepers of prisons were not paid a salary. They made their money by charging prisoners for services.[28] Prisoners paid fees when they entered the prison and when they exited, but at innumerable other times as well. The Counter, for example, had at least four levels of accommodation. The Master's Ward was the best, but William Fenner recounts that on his first night in the Counter he paid a shilling to enter this Ward and two more to get into a cobwebbed room with poor sheets and a short candle. One paid extra to sleep alone. Most beds were shared. Hence in *The Roaring Girl* Sir Alexander Wengrave asserts that the first thing a new prisoner begs is to "be lodged with one that is not itchy,/ To lie in a clean chamber, in sheets not lousy" (III.iii.88–89). From most accounts, this was not likely to happen.

Further on in his litany of grievances, William Fenner recounts that the day after his nighttime arrival, he had to pay another "garnish" in order to be allowed the "liberty" to walk around the grounds.[29] He discovered that food and drink required fees; and if he wished to leave the prison to try to make composition with creditors, he had to pay for an escort, usually a bailiff of some sort, to accompany him, and to pay

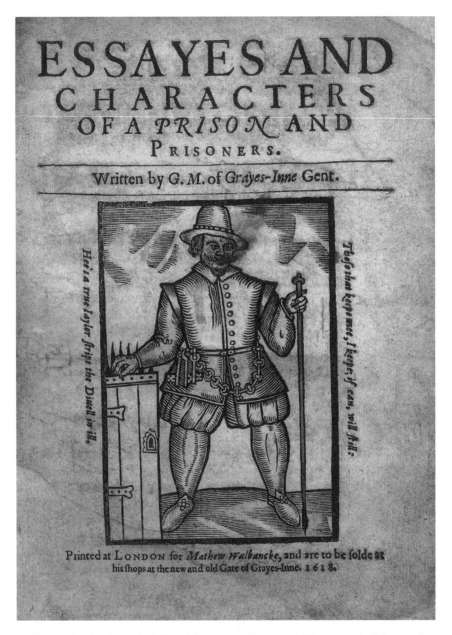

Figure 5. Woodcut of a jailer, title page to *Essays and Characters of a Prison and Prisons* by G. Mynshul, 1618. Reproduced by permission of The Huntington Library, San Marino, California.

for the bailiff's food and drink for the day. If these fees could not be paid, prisoners first had to surrender their cloaks and other articles of clothing; eventually, they had to move down to a less expensive part of the prison. The gradual loss of clothing as prisoners moved into the more squalid parts of the institution became a recurring trope of Counter narratives. Relinquishing cloak, hat, gloves, and shirt, the prisoner also shed his social identity. If the consumer market made men, the Counter unmade them, and the descent into social oblivion could be pitiless. Below the Master's Ward came the Knight's Ward, but the worst conditions were found further down in the Two-penny ward and the dreaded Hole. The lower one went, the more cramped the accommodations became, the more foul the beds and the living conditions. Dekker wrote of debtors' prison as a hell where "sickness, stench, hunger, cold, thirst, penury" dogged the inhabitants.[30] In the infamous Hole, prisoners slept on straw and received their food from an almsbasket, a prop that became important in several Counter plays. Clifford Dobb estimates that the Poultry Counter Hole was twenty feet square and at any one time could hold forty to fifty prisoners, both men and women.[31] The very term, "the Hole," suggested a pit, a gaping gulf, from which one might never emerge, or certainly not emerge unscathed.

The squalor of these prisons and the abuses of the fee system were so notorious that there were a number of attempts at reform. In 1606 the Common Council of London set forth a "Bill for the Ordering of Prisoners in the several Counters of the City."[32] These orders indicate the kinds of abuse the Common Council was attempting to control. They mandate the quick reassignment of foreigners to Newgate and citizens to Ludgate and prevent the keeper and his officers from charging more than a set fee for bread, beer, ale, charcoal, candles, beds, and certain other necessities. They ban all women except wives from visiting the prisoners; discourage keepers from taking excessive fees for cases brought for malicious reasons only; limit exit and entrance fees; and order a table of the ordinances and fees to be hung in a prominent place within both Counters. In 1616 William Fenner complained that it had been five years since the statutes governing the prison had hung in the yard, indicating that the 1606 reform effort, like so many others, had limited efficacy over time.[33] The Orders also made provision for fining or firing keepers who did not enforce the ordinances and set up a regular review process by which members of the Common Council were to hear the complaints of prisoners. In 1606 similar orders were issued for Ludgate, and from time to time for Newgate as well. Despite these efforts, conditions in the cramped city prisons were always difficult and often deadly, especially for poorer inmates who were most likely to be lodged near stinking privies and to suffer from cold and hunger. While aristocratic prisoners at the Fleet or the Tower might set up a fairly comfortable standard of living if they had the money to do so, and might survive in prison for a number of years, it was the truly hardy soul who, lacking friends or family who would pay their debts or make a deal with creditors, could survive six months in the city debtors' prisons.

The Culture of Credit and London Comedy

The centrality of the Counter to London comedies depended in part on the relation the drama forged between this material institution and the larger culture of credit in which it played a role. Not surprisingly, the second half of the sixteenth century saw a vast expansion in the prevalence of debt at all levels of English society. People relied on credit to finance business ventures, to underwrite enhanced consumption, and to facilitate exchanges in a world in which money itself was often in short supply. In his important study, *The Economy of Obligation: The Culture of Credit and Social Relations in Early Modern England,* Craig Muldrew outlines some of the factors involved in this vast enlargement in the use of credit. One was simply the steep increase in consumption of all sorts of goods at every level of society. While the rich obviously could indulge in more luxury goods than those from the middling or laboring classes, enhanced consumption was not confined to the very wealthy. When Isabella Whitney's speaker details the abundance of goods in the London markets, she enumerates many common household items that ordinary citizens would have bought, things such as salt, oatmeal, caps, and candles. Her list also includes more luxurious items such as silk, linen, and jewels.[34] To finance purchases, consumers sometimes relied on credit, and this is one of the practices, as we shall see, to which the drama obsessively turns.

But credit not only fueled consumption; it also fueled production. Setting up a business was expensive. Richard Grassby has estimated, for example, that while some guild regulations allowed journeymen to set up shops for as little as twenty pounds, the average start-up cost in the textile trades was one hundred pounds.[35] Once a shopkeeper was in business, credit was needed to grease the wheels of commerce on a daily basis. As a matter of course shopkeepers regularly gave customers up to six months to pay for purchases, and inventories would frequently be replenished through credit arrangements in anticipation of future payment by customers. The expanding scale of commercial ventures only made the risks involved in business undertakings more acute. A merchant entering into one of the long-distance trading companies needed to be able to lay out initially at least one thousand pounds, often much more, and this capital would be tied up for long periods before it showed a return; it was also subject to enormous risks (pirates could seize cargo, distant warehouses could burn, ships could be lost in storms).[36] Large-scale industries such as shipbuilding, sugar refineries, and glass works required considerable start-up capital, and typically some of that outlay was obtained on credit, often with the backing of family and friends.

Credit practices came to permeate daily life. Muldrew paints a vivid picture of the degree to which by the end of the sixteenth century everyone from small tradesmen to merchants to gentry and peers was typically enmeshed in complicated webs of mutual financial obligation. Shopkeepers would have great numbers of customers in debt to them at any one time, but they themselves would be in debt to suppliers and to an array of local tradesmen, many of whom were simultaneously in debt to them.[37] Often, a casting up of accounts would begin with the mutual cancelling of debts among two parties who each owed money to the other, with only the remainder paid out in cash.[38] In such complicated circumstances, both businesses and households were frequently kept afloat by credit. Some credit arrangements were fairly informal: an oath could be sworn before a witness stating that the borrower would repay his creditor at an appointed time. Neighbors were frequently called to witness these promises. But a host of increasingly complex written instruments also secured loans: bonds, bills obligatory (which set a specific date for repayment), bills of exchange, and mortgages.[39]

Crucially, to secure any of these forms of credit, one had to have a solid reputation for reliability.[40] One had to be perceived as creditworthy, the very quality Isabella Whitney's speaker knew she lacked when she gave over the bequest of Ludgate Prison to a bankrupt. Perceptions and appearances, therefore, became crucial in keeping the merry-go-round of borrowing and repayment spinning. In *Michaelmas Term* Richard Easy, a gentleman of Essex who has come up to London, finds he needs to borrow some money in a hurry.[41] The reason is that he has invited some gentlemen to dinner and it will be "the eternal loss of [his] credit" (II.iii.303) if he fails to entertain them royally.[42] In fact, Easy's obsession with his reputation or credit, to which he returns again and again, is what drives him to sign an ill-advised bond for two hundred pounds with Quomodo, the duplicitous draper who is trying to obtain Easy's country estate. The bond, to which Easy is the first signator, is carefully prepared by Dustbox, the scrivener, in an onstage scene that heightens the sense of legal obligation that Easy is incurring. Of course, Easy has been gulled, persuaded to take the value of his two hundred pounds, not in cash, but in cloth that he will need to sell in order to realize any actual money. Through a middleman, Quomodo then buys back the cloth for a mere sixty pounds, leaving Easy with two hundred pounds of obligation to be paid in one month. Shortyard, a participant in the scam, predicts of Easy: "So his right wing is cut; he will not fly far/ Past the two city hazards, Poultry and Wood Street" (II.iii.370–71).

Although in this particular play Easy does not end up in either of these two "universities," litigation involving debt increased hugely during the period 1580 to 1640, and incarceration was increasingly a possibility for those in whom creditors had lost trust.[43] As in other cities, debt litigation increased markedly in London in the late sixteenth century as market activity increased, and so did imprisonment for debt. Arrests happened when creditors believed debtors would not otherwise appear in court to answer a complaint or if they felt the debtor's credit had become so tenuous that only drastic measures would perhaps prompt friends and relatives to offer relief. Arrest for debt, however, was not only humiliating; it also often had a cascading effect. Maintaining interlocking networks of debt and credit required that one sustain a reputation for making good on one's obligations; incarceration suggested that that reputation had been lost. Consequently, once imprisoned, a debtor was exposed as untrustworthy before all his other creditors, who would then worsen the debtor's plight by calling in their loans as well. To be hauled to the Counter, then, was an ignominious event, and potentially a catastrophic one, even if the prisoner managed to win a fairly swift release. A stay in debtor's prison was often the turning point in a story of downward mobility. Considering the amount of credit circulating in the sixteenth and seventeenth centuries, the debtors' prison was a crude mechanism for addressing the inevitable breakdowns in the system. It made those who were incarcerated *less* able to pay their obligations; it ruined many reputations irrevocably; it taxed the ability of parishes and charitable institutions to provide even basic relief to poor prisoners. Yet it was not until the nineteenth century that the laws governing arrest for debt were significantly altered. Before then, despite the prevalence of codes of neighborliness that promoted out-of-court and informal settlement of financial disputes, incarceration was increasingly the fate awaiting those who could not pay their debts.

Given the growth of the consumer market in early modern London and the expansion of debt and credit relations, it is not surprising that London comedy often involved stories about prodigals, debtors, and long-distance merchants whose ventures failed, or that the Counter became an important social space within these plays' imaginative renderings of the city. In 1599 one of the first London comedies, Ben Jonson's *Every Man Out of His Humor*, was staged at the Globe Theater, and it established a powerful template for representing debtors and their incarceration within the Counter. In this play debt is represented as the result of human folly and pretension, and the Counter as a fit ending for a gallant's giddy course of life. The play was immediately popular both on the stage and as a printed text, with three quarto editions published in 1600.[44] Constructing the city as a site of consumer seduction, Jonson uses the Counter to punish those who give in to those seductions or who try to buy their way up the social ladder. His Counter is a harsh school, but a necessary one, since abuses of credit are aligned in this play with the erosion of the traditional social hierarchy and with the degeneracy of the social elite. The problem posed by spendthrift social climbers is most blatantly thematized in the person of Sogliardo, who comes from the country to the city proclaiming, "I will be a gentleman whatsoever it cost me" (I.ii.7–8). He acquires a coat of arms, hires someone at St. Paul's to teach him to smoke tobacco, buys fancy clothes for his introduction to the court, learns to "pretend alliance with courtiers and great persons" (I.ii.74–75), and plans to dress his men in liveries adorned with gold lace. All of this, he realizes, will "bring a man in debt" (I.ii.106–7). But Carlo Buffone, the tutor to Sogliardo's personal gentrification project, reads him a little lesson on debt and credit.

CARLO.   Debt? Why, that's the more for your credit, sir. It's an excellent policy to owe much in these days, if you note it.

SOGLIARDO.   As how, good signoir? I would fain be a politician.

CARLO.   O, look where you are indebted any great sum: your creditor observes you with no less regard than if he were bound to you for some huge benefit, and will quake to give you the least cause of offence, lest he lose his money. I assure you, in these times, no man has his servant more obsequious and pliant than gentlemen their creditors, to whom, if at any time you pay but a moity or a fourth part, it comes more acceptedly than if you gave 'em a New-Year's gift.

SOGLIARDO.   I perceive you, sir: I will take up, and bring my self in credit, sure.

CARLO.   Marry, this: always beware you commerce not with bankrupts, or poor needy Ludgathians. They are impudent creatures, turbulent spirits. They care not what violent tragedies they stir, nor how they play fast and loose with a poor gentleman's fortunes to get their own. Marry, these rich fellows that ha' the world, or the better part of it,

>sleeping in their counting-houses, they are ten times more placable, they. Either fear, hope, or modesty restrains them from offering any outrages. (I.ii.108–31)

Carlo outlines a certain logic of credit. The more you owe, the more the world will take you for a great man of immense wealth and importance; consequently, the less likely are honest and modest tradesmen to want to offend you by demanding payment in an unmannerly way. Only bankrupts and Ludgathians (that is, those who have been in the Ludgate debtors' prison) are so desperate that they will cause a commotion in seeking repayment of loans. For a good part of the play, the logic seems to hold. Sogliardo makes his way through the thickets of London life, pretending both to wealth and breeding, subject to the relentless critique of the play's choral observers, Cordatus and Mitis, as well as the maliciously envious Macilente, but never being called to account by his creditors, though eventually he has a humiliating social come-uppance at court where his plowman's calloused hands and his poor imitation of elite manners make him an object of scorn.

Sogliardo is the play's most obvious social climber, trying to acquire in the marketplace the manners and accoutrements of a gentleman, and failing miserably. However, it is Fastidious Brisk, a "fresh Frenchified courtier" (II.1.7), who to many in the play seems to have achieved perfect fashionability. A great name-dropper, Brisk loses no occasion to mention his court connections, his new (probably nonexistent) horse, and his supposed court mistress, Saviolina. He is accompanied by a page, Cinedo, whose name (defined by John Florio in 1598 as "a buggring boy, a wanton boy, an ingle") gives a clue to the homoerotic and potentially sodomitical nature of their relationship.[45] As the theatrical signature of Brisk's extravagant pursuit of fashion, he wears, from scene to scene, a succession of dazzling new suits. The extraordinary power of fashion to seduce onlookers and to provoke ruinous emulation receives vivid illustration in Brisk's effects on others. At one point he boasts that in one year he had three suits that made three great ladies fall in love with him, three suits that undid three gentlemen attempting to imitate him, and three suits that, emulated by other men, induced three rich widows to marry (II.ii.249–54). As he tells Macilente,

rich apparel has strange vertues. It makes him that hath it without means esteemed for an excellent wit; he that enjoys it with means puts the world in remembrance of his means. It helps the deformities of nature and gives lustre to her beauties; makes continual holiday where it shines; sets the wits of ladies at work that otherwise would be idle; furnisheth your two-shilling ordinary; takes possession of your stage at your new play; and enricheth your oars, as scorning to go with your scull. (II.ii.264–73)

This paean to rich apparel, however, is quickly countered by Macilente's riposte: "it gives respect to your fools, makes many thieves, as
many strumpets, and no fewer bankrupts" (II.ii.274–76). What the cynic
stresses are the economic consequences of the pursuit of rich clothing.
It can turn men and women into thieves, whores, and bankrupts.

Macilente's jaundiced view is confirmed by the effects of Brisk's appearance on the brother-sister pair of Fungoso and Fallace. The former,
Sogliardo's nephew, has been sent from the country to the Inns of
Court. Striving to be a gentleman, he takes Brisk as his fashion model
and spends much of the play borrowing money to have a suit made that
will be just like Brisk's. Unfortunately, every time Fungoso thinks he has
achieved his goal, Brisk acquires another outfit, prompting Fungoso to
undertake a further round of imitation, a further round of debt. In
what I call "echo dressing," Fungoso typically appears on stage in a suit
modeled exactly on what Brisk last wore. The two actors playing these
characters probably used the same costumes successively, thus graphi-
cally revealing the emulative dynamics of fashion.[46] In a parallel action,
Fungoso's sister, Fallace, married to the uxorious citizen, Deliro, dotes
on Brisk, as well, attracted by the courtier's manner and clothing, so
different from those of her grasping husband. The foolishness of
brother and sister is revealed by their inability to see through the
Frenchified dandy, and his effect on them suggests the rippling consequences of conspicuous consumption as Brisk's appearance incites
Fungoso to ruinous emulation and his sister to adultery. Brisk is thus
the source of a foppish taste for foreign manners and fashions that
spreads like an infection through the city, corrupting country dwellers
as well as citizen households, destabilizing the social order.

Throughout the play Fungoso serves as the poster boy for the dangers of a culture of credit. He is constantly borrowing money—from
his father, his uncle, his sister—in order to pay the haberdasher and
the tailor for his imitations of Brisk's suits. (At one point he even has
the tailor follow him to St. Paul's to take notes on every detail of one of
Brisk's outfits.) Yet Fungoso is never fully able to pay these tradesmen
and fobs off his creditors with promises to pay at "the beginning of the
next term" (IV.iv.39–40). Fungoso, perpetually unable to catch up to
fashion's vanguard, becomes enmeshed in snowballing debt. What
Jonson largely conceals, however, is the indebtedness of the man
Fungoso emulates, Brisk himself. In II.ii. the courtier asks to borrow
sixty to eighty pounds from Deliro, Fallace's husband, who serves as the
"alchemist" who turns Brisk's lands into metal (II.ii.304). This loan,
however, is small potatoes for a man of Brisk's supposed stature. The
catastrophic extent of Brisk's indebtedness must wait until Act IV when
Macilente, who has been at court, tells Deliro that no one there

esteems Brisk, neither the ladies nor the courtiers. They "despise him, for indeed/ He's like a zany to a tumbler,/ That tries tricks after him to make men laugh" (IV.i.85–87). The man whom Fungoso imitates is himself an imitator, aping true courtiers' ways, unconsciously playing the fool. Macilente's account instantaneously alters Brisk's status in the eyes of his chief creditor. Deliro exclaims:

Well, I repent me I e'er credited him so much, but, now I see what he is, and that his masking vizor is off, I'll forbear him no longer. All his lands are mortgaged to me, and forfeited. Besides, I have bonds of his in my hand for the receipt of now twenty pound, now thirty, now twenty-five. Still, as he has had a fan but wagged at him, he would be in a new suit. Well, I'll salute him by a sergeant the next time I see him, I'faith. I'll suit him! (IV.i.97–104)

The pun on suit—apparel and law case—reveals the fatal link between fashion and the debt that now threatens to undo Brisk. All that has kept him afloat is his own self-trumpeted reputation as an esteemed man at court. When that reputation is undermined, he begins a precipitous downward descent. Taken to the Counter for his part in a tavern riot, he becomes suddenly helpless before his creditors. Deliro enters three actions against him: one for three thousand marks and two others amounting to five thousand pounds together (V.iii.553–56). Lesser creditors then pile on: the Knight Puntarvolo demands Brisk repay him a debt of one hundred pounds, and he faces a one hundred ten pound action for a diamond. Earlier, Deliro's wife, coming to the Counter to warn Brisk to win a quick release before her husband enters actions against him, says that Deliro "kept a poor man in Ludgate once twelve year for sixteen shillings" (V.iii.497–98). This history does not bode well for Brisk's speedy release. In fact, the play ends with the broken gallant entombed in the Counter where Macilente censoriously intones that this is the "plague that treads o' the heels of your foppery" (V.iii.568–69) and advises him to get to the Two-penny ward to save charges.

In this early London comedy the Counter itself is not dramatized with much material texture. In the midst of the next-to-last scene, Mitis says: "O, this is to be imagined the Counter, belike?" (V.iii.482). There are no keepers or turnkeys, no almsbasket, and no other prisoners—all features of subsequent Counter dramas—to let the audience know where they are. Moreover, we do not see Brisk stripped of his fashionable attire in the prison, though it is that attire that in retrospect appears to have predicted throughout the play that the Counter will be Brisk's ultimate destination. Nonetheless, though sketchily delineated as a physical space, the Counter in *Every Man Out* begins to assume the symbolic weight it will carry in many later London plays, transformed from mortar and stone into a discursive construct in part by the drama's repeated staging of it. It is the place where gallants pay the wages of debt, their credit lost, their social selves undone by "the flux of apparel" (IV.v.128). This is the understanding of the Counter held by Sir Alexander Wengrave when in *The Roaring Girl* he approves Sir Davy Dapper's plan to have his prodigal son incarcerated there. In Jonson's play it is important that the Counter scene be the end point of the action, the last of the drama's significant social spaces. Prior London scenes have been set in taverns, in St. Paul's, in citizen houses, at a notary's near the Exchange, and at court. As early as 1599 Jonson was thus imaginatively mapping London as a succession of venues where men of fashion and of business conducted their affairs and displayed themselves before the eyes of others. If Act III makes St. Paul's the fashion runway where all the gallants go to see and be seen,[47] Act V uses the Counter to indicate one of the possible endings for a gallant's costly progress through the city, a progress underwritten by credit arrangements he finally cannot sustain. For Jonson, the Counter thus reveals the truth behind appearances, the reality of indebtedness, which the smokescreen of fashion and clever self-promotion have obscured. Though women, especially London women, also went into debt and were committed to the debtors' prisons,[48] for Jonson, as for most of his contemporary dramatists, the story of downward mobility ending in the Counter is imagined as a man's story. The stage thus helps to construct a link between successful middling sort masculinity, in particular, and ideas of financial creditworthiness. As I will argue in the next chapter, however, since women's reputations were conventionally premised more on sexual than on financial probity,[49] the whorehouse, not the Counter, became the significant space not only in which women's social death was typically represented, but also where the conventional ways of viewing female worth were vigorously challenged. But for men, the Counter remained a dominant scene of social death as the credit sustaining an honorable course of life evaporated, leaving the debtor destitute, humiliated, and, often, with barely a shirt on his back.

In *Every Man Out*, Brisk, the Frenchified dandy, models this downward trajectory. He is the hyperbolically rendered scapegoat in a play full of overextended social climbers who float their aspirations on a sea of debt. With his court airs, he arguably has the most lofty social ambitions of anyone in this London world. Flying the highest, he is made to fall the farthest, the Counter the antithesis of the court world in which he aspired to shine. Brisk is so in debt and in the Counter that debt is made so visible to all that he will never again have "the credit" to float himself on the tide of fashionable society. A grim school for this ridiculous gallant, the Counter prompts Brisk's one anguished moment of insight: "O God, I am undone!" (V.iii.557). But with its moralizing

Chorus and insistent commentary from Macilente, this play schools the audience as well, holding up a glass that reveals the time's deformities and, in the Counter, the institution of their correction. Jonson is a harsh reader of the urban world of expanding debt and expanding consumption, excoriating those who borrow to pretend to a status to which they were not born.

Ironically, however, in satirizing social climbers and fashion mongers, Jonson also stages them. The theater could, and I imagine often did, teach its audience quite contradictory lessons. In any performance of Jonson's play, the unusual prominence given to Brisk's succession of new suits makes the stage a fashion runway to rival Paul's middle aisle, undoubtedly creating consumer desire even as it supposedly interdicts it. The theater, in this case the Globe where Jonson's play was first staged, thus becomes part of what Amanda Bailey has called "an irreverent social logic" that promoted conspicuous consumption and self-presentation as spectacle even while satirizing them.[50] At the end of this chapter I will come back to the paradoxes of the theater's staging of the excesses of debt-ridden gallants. I am going to turn now, however, to other playwrights who follow Jonson but mobilize the debtors' prison to tell different stories about the Counter and the culture of credit. Some look to the monarch or to an ideology of charity to redress the excesses of the booming credit market; others, more playful and self-reflexive, wittily use the Counter as a performance space where debtors turn abjection to their own advantage, change the terms through which social "credit" is established, and in the process challenge the punitive logic of Jonson's representation of the resonant social space of the Counter.

The Counter, Good Government, and Charity

In 1604 Samuel Rowley's *When You See Me, You Know Me* was staged, probably by the Admiral's Men at the Fortune Theater.[51] A generically hybrid work, it mixes monarchical history with several "unhistorical" scenes (v, vi, and vii) set in the city of London and depicting characters drawn from "ordinary" London life such as the London watch and members of London's criminal underworld. Some of the London action occurs in the Counter, but in this play that prison is a very different social space than in Jonson's drama. While some of its inmates are debtors or criminals, most are presented as victims rather than as agents of their own destruction. Rather than a site where prodigals justly suffer for their actions, the Counter here comes to symbolize the failures of good government. It is a place where the King himself must be set to school. *When You See Me, You Know Me*, then, is interesting because it shows that dramatic representations of the Counter could focus on the venality or incompetence of those in authority and not only on the folly of debtors and fashion-mongering gallants. In this play the credit of rulers is what the Counter puts in question. Staged in the first year of James I's reign, *When You See Me* implicitly calls on the monarch to attend to the city's problems and to reform the abuses of courtiers and others in power. While it stops short of exposing the structural changes that were making indebtedness a larger and larger part of economic life and not just an indication of individual moral failure, and though it finds redress, not in structural change but in the miraculous goodness of the monarch, nonetheless, it intimates that the social dysfunction symbolized by the Counter needs to be addressed in terms different from those offered by moralized narratives of individual prodigality and individual reform.

On its title page *When You See Me* is described as *The famous Chronicle Historie of king Henry the eight, with the birth and vertuous life of Edward Prince of Wales*. The play resembles other generically hybrid plays produced around 1600 such as Heywood's *Edward IV, Parts I and II*, which intertwine material from chronicle history regarding the reign of Edward with an urban plot involving citizens of London, especially Matthew and Jane Shore.[52] *The Shoemaker's Holiday* and *If You Know Not Me You Know Nobody, Part II*, discussed in the prior chapter, are similar kinds of plays. Each implicitly negotiates between the court and the city material, often foregrounding the citizen plot and "peripheralizing" the monarchical story. This is not the case with *When You See Me* in which the mixture of court-to-city scenes is in inverse proportions to that found in *Shoemaker* and *If You Know Not Me, Part II*. That is, the bulk of the play takes place in Westminster and deals with Henry VIII's foreign policy, several of his marriages, and, above all, with the malevolent presence and eventual fall of Cardinal Wolsey, painted in this very Protestant play as the menacing tool of the Papacy and the enemy of Henry and his virtuous son, Prince Edward.[53] The monarch dominates the play, and the London scenes at its center direct the monarch's attention toward a disordered city and promote a sentimental fantasy of the city's education of the King and his subsequent reform of social ills. The Counter is the site where those ills are most visible; it is a sign of a city in disarray.

In the middle of *When You See Me* Henry abruptly decides to go in disguise, as he says:

To visit *London*, and to walke the round,
Passe through their watches, and observe the care
And speciall diligence to keepe our peace.
They say night-walkers, hourely passe the streets,
Committing theft, and hated sacriliege:

And slightly passe unstaied, or unpunished,
Goe Compton, goe, and get me some disguise,
This night weele see our Cities government. (931–38)

This motif recalls *Measure for Measure*, produced for the King's Men in the same year Rowley produced his play for the Admiral's Men, though there are fewer moral ambiguities in Rowley's treatment of his king than in Shakespeare's representation of the duke. But in each case the disguised ruler sets out to survey the government of his city and the conduct of those charged with providing justice.

Inside London's walls the King learns firsthand about the abuses that trouble the good order of the city. He first encounters a constable and a member of the watch, Prichall the Cobbler, both of whom are masters of the malapropism and neither of whom is an effective apprehender of offenders. Two stranger merchants connected with the Steelyard have, for example, been found murdered and floating in the Thames (a small reminder of the xenophobic violence that could at times be directed at foreign merchants). A notorious criminal, Black Will, admits in soliloquy to having had a hand in the murders and of having left the Southwark stews, from which the violence seems to have emanated, to seek safety in the city (1062–75). The watch lets him pass because of his reputation for being a good fellow and a good fighter. Henry encounters Black Will in the street and eventually challenges him to a sword fight, an event that results in both of them being taken to the Counter for the night since that was the prison where the watch deposited any nighttime offenders.

Within the Counter Henry learns several things, the first concerning abuses within the operation of the prison itself. He says: "in this wretched Counters I perceive,/ Money playes fast and loose, purchaces favour,/ And without that, nought but miserie" (1258–60). He also learns that at least some of the debtors with whom he drinks and talks have been undone because members of his own or Wolsey's households, taking advantage of their high positions, have not paid money for which they were bound, resulting in the financial ruin of poor citizens. These debtors are, in effect, victims of court corruption. Henry also discovers the real criminality of some of those who are merely hiding out in the Counter to escape apprehension for serious crimes. One prisoner confides that he stole one hundred pounds and then deliberately got himself arrested for a trivial debt so that he could stay in the Counter until the first crime was forgotten (1290–99). These are the kinds of abuses delineated repeatedly in accounts of Counter life. Eventually, his disguise removed, the King reveals his fitness to rule by rectifying many of these wrongs. He sends the thief to Newgate; admiring

Black Will's courage, he vows to make him useful in England's wars abroad, channeling his aggression in a socially acceptable direction; and he orders the two prisoners abused by court retainers to petition him for redress. Later, he releases these men from the Counter, dismisses his own corrupt retainer, but orders him to pay "the utmost mite/ Of any debt, default, or hindrance" that he owes his creditors. Boldly, the King declares he will "keepe no man to blurre my credite so" (1695–97).

As with other Counter plays, *When You See Me* is thus concerned with men maintaining—or losing—their social credit. But the stakes are especially high because in this case it is the King's credit that is at risk. Only by righting the wrongs of the Counter can a populist Henry maintain a public reputation for fairness. The Counter scenes echo the play's larger strategy for burnishing Henry's reputation: subordinates commit abuses, and Henry remedies them. Just as injustice in the city is due to incompetent constables and corrupt court retainers who prey on worthy citizens, so the larger problems besetting the state are due to ambitious prelates like Cardinal Wolsey and his accomplices. Eventually, Henry, properly educated, rights all wrongs. On the title page of the 1613 edition of Rowley's play there is a woodcut of the King in a trademark posture: standing with legs slightly apart, face looking straight ahead, plumed hat on head, sword by his side, and rich jewels and rich clothes adorning his person (Figure 6). The woodcut and the play's title, *When You See Me You Know Me*, both seem to point to the transparency of Henry's identity. Even though he is disguised for some of the play, and so literally not "known" by those who see him, in the end his good works drive away the base clouds that might leave his image obscured. He is what he does and emerges as the idealized image of the caring Prince and Protestant hero.

The importance of the Counter scenes in *When You See Me* lies in their construction of the prison as a site of injustice, rather than of justice, and as a school for monarchs, not subjects. They thus tap into an alternative strand of Counter discourse, one that reads debtors at least in part as victims of the sharp practices of their creditors and of the keepers who tyrannize over them. It goes without saying, however, that the play blatantly mystifies the difficult process of institutional reform and of mitigating the devastating consequences of a culture of increasing indebtedness. Historically, complaints about the Counter persisted despite efforts at reform. In 1616 William Fenner was still protesting the cruelty of creditors, the extortion of fees by keepers, and the abuses of those who hid in the Counter to escape prosecution for greater crimes. A King's rebuke of individual offenders could have little effect on the systemic abuses permeating the institution. Moreover, the play

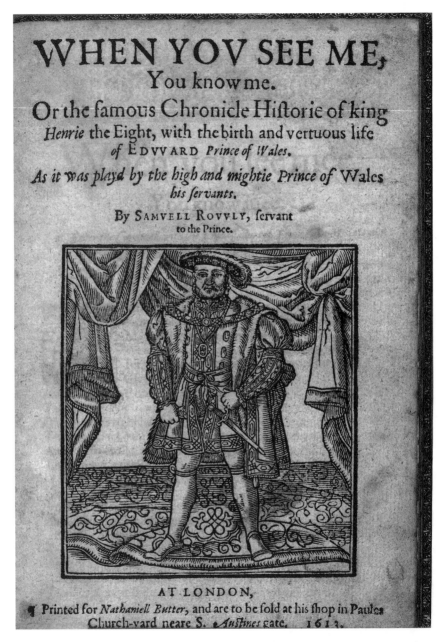

Figure 6. Woodcut of Henry VIII, title page to *When You See Me You Know Me* by Samuel Rowley, 1613. Reproduced by permission of The Huntington Library, San Marino, California.

does not really engage—but merely glances at—the growing culture of debt and consumption that produced the kinds of financial overextension or plain bad luck that resulted in ignominious descents into debtors' prison. Instead, reaching back in time for the image of a powerful ruler, the play indulges in the populist fantasy that under such a monarch justice will somehow prevail and a city in the grip of social ills will be healed. Insufficient as social analysis, this version of nostalgic utopianism nonetheless registers an awareness of a pervasive social problem and calls for reform. First staged in 1604, just at the beginning of James's reign, Rowley's play invented a visit to the Counter for a monarch who wanted to know about "our city's government" and the ills besetting his subjects. For Rowley, this particular prison figured as a symptom of problems needing redress, however inadequate his conception of those problems or of their solution.

A later and more complicated play, *A New Wonder, A Woman Never Vext* (1611–14?),[54] while delineating various paths to the Counter, also focuses on how to remedy the noxious consequences of debt. But the watchword of this play is "charity" and its setting Ludgate, a very particular debtor's prison and one deeply interwoven into the city's long history of charitable benefactions. As I will explore below, *A New Wonder* dramatizes with remarkable energy both the prodigality that leads to debtors' prison and also the high-risk business ventures that can produce the same outcome. And while the play makes those who end up in prison largely responsible for their downfalls, it resists and sharply critiques a punitive logic of perpetual incarceration. Instead, *A New Wonder* endorses an ideology of Christian charity as the antidote both to individual economic folly and to the unpredictable disasters of business life. What makes the play an interesting social text, however, and not a dramatized sermon, is the way many of its elements—such as its schematic formal symmetries and its odd temporal dislocations and slippages—have the effect of undermining its apparent ideological implications. In *A New Wonder* civic endowments and adherence to a doctrine of Christian charity are offered as a solution to the wild fluctuations that mark the financial careers of the play's chief characters, but the implausibilities and contradictions of the narrative allow one to see the inadequacies of this seductive, backward-looking paradigm for addressing the rapidly expanding culture of credit.

Because few know this play, and because it is a very interesting one, let me quickly summarize its plot and unusual features. The play takes its title from a storyline involving two women who are neighbors and gossips. One, known only as the rich widow, is infinitely generous and kind; the other, Mistress Foster, is a grasping shrew, a Xanthippe, who bosses her husband about and is ungenerous to Robert, his son by a former marriage. This plot follows the happy fortunes of the woman never vexed and the sad decline in fortune of her perpetually vexed and vexatious friend. The other plot involves two brothers, Old Foster, married to the shrew, and Stephen Foster, who eventually marries the widow. Marriage choice seems to predict destiny. Old Foster, a successful merchant when the play begins, has disastrous luck with his venturing and ends up in Ludgate prison. His brother, Stephen, a prodigal, begins the play in Ludgate, is released through the charity of Old Foster's son Robert, eventually marries the widow, becomes a reformed man, and eventually rises to be Sheriff of London. The brothers' paths thus cross in the course of the play: the prodigal rises from the debtors' prison, the merchant sinks into it. Their spectacular successes and failures image the mysterious operations of the marketplace, now bringing some into ruinous debt, now blessing others with spectacular good fortune. The play, however, attempts to moralize these market mysteries and to stabilize them through the ideology of charity.

In *A Woman Never Vext* the two things that typically end one in debtors' prison, prodigality and overly ambitious commercial venturing, are vividly anatomized and moralized, and both are "cured" by charity.[55] Stephen, the play's prodigal, is the first beneficiary of charitable ministrations. When the play opens he is in Ludgate Prison, but it does not reform him. He gets out because of the generosity of Robert, his nephew; but after he's released, he immediately goes back to his life of gaming and roistering in a scene (II.i.) that vividly depicts the vices of the prodigal. His real reform comes when the rich widow says he should marry her and spend her money, thinking thereby that she might have the experience of being "vexed" by a husband. But instead, Stephen's good and unexpected fortune reforms him, and with delicious irony he makes himself busy in the widow's counting house, tallying up the debts she is owed and bringing order to her bonds and bills (III.ii.28–45). The charitable "gift" of the widow's fortune redeems him from social death and puts him on a path of honor that ends with his being made Sheriff of London. Charity thus reforms individual subjects, turning a prodigal into a careful business man.

His brother, Old Foster, is similarly rescued from his unnatural and disastrous pursuit of profit purely by acts of charity. His business pursuits are outlined with unusual precision from the play's opening lines, and the degree of realistic and particularized detail in this part of the play sits oddly with the nearly miraculous manner in which he is eventually rescued from financial ruin—a hint of the strain with which the play negotiates its doubled tales of debt and redemption. Early in the play Old Foster and Alderman Bruyne, his partner, with their two factors happily anticipate the return of ships richly laden with commercial goods worth, we later learn, approximately twenty-five thousand pounds. But the response of the two men to their successful "venture" is very different. Bruyne, who is not a greedy man, proclaims that the golden traffic of love is better than gold (I.i.19–21) and thinks about how, when his ships come in, he will endow the city with a charitable benefaction. Old Foster has no such intentions, being focused solely on profit. He disdains his prodigal brother, Stephen, saying that charity is wasted on him (I.i.43–52). Eventually he disowns his own son Robert for helping his distressed uncle in Ludgate. But Old Foster's greed and lack of charity are swiftly punished. Figuring that his joint venture with Bruyne will bring a sixtyfold return on the original investment, he offers to buy out his partner for twenty-five thousand pounds, half to be delivered in cash, half to be secured with a bond to be paid in six months (III.i.266–69). Still later he suggests that in lieu of the bond, Bruyne simply take all of the vendible goods that Old Foster has stored in his warehouses: broadcloths, kerseys, and cutchineal, among others (III.iii.8–21). He will thereby free himself from the bond and also empty his warehouse to receive all the new goods coming in his ships. Momentarily, then, he finds himself without cash, without goods in his warehouse, and with the anticipated replacements still at sea. He has, in a word, risked everything, though in the "respectable" game of commercial venturing, rather than in the disreputable games of dice and cards to which his brother was addicted.[56]

It takes no great predictive power to anticipate that his ships never reach shore. Sailing from Dover to Catharine's Pool at the mouth of the Thames, the ships sink, and all is lost. The merchant, his credit utterly "cracked" (III.iii.186), retreats to Ludgate Prison to escape the writs, arrests, and executions that he anticipates from other creditors (IV.ii.10–16). Though his life in Ludgate is also rendered in some detail, it is, again, acts of unexampled charity that arrest his downward spiral. Eventually Stephen Foster and the widow give Old Foster half of their estate, thus reestablishing him in the community of credit and credibility from which his commercial disasters had severed him. In the economic hydraulics of the play, a disastrous plunge into debt and debtors' prison is answered by the elevating consequences of spectacular deeds of benefaction.

Historically, charity continued to be an important aspect of London's civic life in the sixteenth century and also in the first decades of the seventeenth when this play was written and staged. The city prisoners benefitted from repeated benefactions. Stow, for example, records that Raph Rokeby of Lincoln's Inn in 1596 left two hundred pounds to the prisoners in the Counters, one hundred pounds to those in the Fleet, one hundred pounds to those in Ludgate, one hundred pounds to those in Newgate, another one hundred pounds to those in the Marshalsea, and twenty pounds to prisoners in the White Lion.[57] He was not alone. However, as I have discussed above, these bequests were never adequate to the needs of the prisoners incarcerated in these jails, nor could they begin to address the larger problems to which the play alludes: growth of credit and debt, higher and higher risks on large-scale ventures, the heating up of the London consumer culture, which solicited men to spend their fortunes on marketplace goods.

That *A New Wonder* offers charity as an answer to the problems of debt and marketplace risk results partly from its use of Ludgate as a setting. In *A New Wonder* Ludgate is constructed, in part, just like debtors' prisons in other London comedies, as a place where lives of prodigality or financial misadventure end in eclipse. However, it is *not* the narrative point of closure for the play, as in *Every Man Out*. Stephen is released, and so is Old Foster. Moreover, while it is rendered with some degree of detail, Ludgate functions not only or not primarily as a place that schools prisoners into repentance or at least awareness of their reckless course of life, but as a site for displaying the miraculous virtues of charity. Unlike the two Counters, Ludgate was an ancient prison long associated with the lives of London citizens, and charitable benefaction was very much part of its history. In the 1606 Orders for Ludgate (but lacking in the nearly parallel Orders for the Counters) specific provision is made that "every prisoner shall have his course to cry at the hole one after another; or else he shall appoint another in his stead, at his pleasure." The Order also stated that "every prisoner likewise shall have his course and liberty to walk in the Watch Hall to receive the charity that shall come in at the door."[58] The centrality of charity in the operations of Ludgate is stressed, along with the prisoners' duty to solicit and right to partake of it.

In *A New Wonder* Old Foster as the newest prisoner is told by the keeper he must "beg at the iron grate above, as others doe for your reliefe and theirs" (IV.ii.47–49). He does, crying out for bread money to be put in an alms box described as hanging above from a grate, probably a basket either hanging from the heavens or high on the back wall of the tiring house. Old Foster's son anonymously drops coins in the box, referring to himself as a pelican (IV.ii.101), one of many references to the son's Christ-like nature. The practice of crying out for charity, either as done by the prisoners themselves or by the parish almsman, is recorded in the many illustrated "Cries of London," which were published during the period.[59] In Richard Dering's *Cries of London*, entered for publication in 1599 but existing only in manuscript form, the innumerable popular street cries of London are woven together to form an artful musical piece to be performed by voices and viols. In Dering's work, cries for cherries, mackerel, chimney sweeps, juniper, and garlic are mingled with those soliciting "bread and meat for the poor prisoners of the Marshalsea" or asking "Pitiful gentlemen of the Lord, bestow one penny to buy a loaf of bread, a loaf of bread among a number of poor prisoners."[60] It is this familiar part of the London soundscape of charity that Old Foster, crying at the grate, recalls.

Moreover, the Stephen Foster who appears in the play along with his wife, the rich widow, was an historical figure connected to Ludgate Prison and to the history of charity within the city. Stow records that Stephen and his wife Agnes, who lived in the mid-fifteenth century, had provided many improvements to the prison, including better lodgings, spaces for walking in the fresh air, and the provision of free water. In their honor a copper plaque was hung in the quadrant praising their charity.[61] At the end of A New Wonder Stephen Foster crowns his transformation into a man of charity by undertaking the improvements to Ludgate described in Stow, even as Alderman Bruyne founds St. Mary's Hospital by Shoreditch in order to give lodging and diet to travelers. In Stow, Bruyne's benefaction is mentioned also. Walter Brune, mercer, and Rosia his wife are reported to have laid the first stone for St. Mary's Hospital in 1197,[62] nearly three hundred years before Stephen Foster and his wife improved Ludgate, and more than four hundred years before A New Wonder was performed in London theaters. Within the play, then, Ludgate is connected to charitable acts many times over and to a long history of charitable benefaction of the sort that Stow was particularly prone to record. And it is to honor the charitable benefactions of Alderman Bruyne and his wife, in particular, that King Henry III appears at the end of the play as part of a public ceremony and promised feast.

A New Wonder, while vividly dramatizing contemporary London, thus reaches far back in the city's history for the charitable acts it memorializes. It recalls a tradition of Christian charity that had been part of city life for a very long time and that was particularly honored by the Catholic-leaning Stow. Once noticed, however, the play's temporal dislocations invite skepticism about the adequacy of past solutions to present problems. While it strongly evokes early seventeenth-century London, A New Wonder is supposedly set in the reign of Henry III late in the twelfth century, whereas Stephen Foster's benefaction to Ludgate occurred in the reign of Edward IV. This collapsing of temporalities erases historical distinctions and elides the particularity of early seventeenth-century economic conditions. While charity supposedly unites everyone at all times in a golden chain of love, the disjunction between contemporary economic realities and century-old civic benefactions creates a fissure in the text, intimating that nostalgia fuels its stories of rescue from urban prodigality and dangerous venturing. The feeling of nostalgia is heightened by the fact that when the play was written sometime after 1611 the linking of London comedy and chronicle history, common around 1600, would have seemed more and more old-fashioned. *A New Wonder* is a throwback in both form and ideology, yet one inviting in its sentimental apology for the efficacy of charitable deeds.

Equally striking, and distancing, are the play's remarkable structural and thematic symmetries and miraculous occurrences: brothers rise and fall in perfectly paired opposition; the fates of two gossips diverge as they do or do not display charitable natures; the charitable son, Robert, spurned by his real dad and his uncle when he shows charity to the other, ends up getting three fathers as he is finally honored and claimed by both his uncle and his father as well as by Alderman Bruyne, whose daughter he is to marry. If one of the play's guiding principles seems to be that to the generous much will be given, Robert gets his reward for generosity in the slightly comic form of a surplus of fathers! Even more remarkable, however, is what happens to the rich widow, in addition, that is, to her acquisition of a model husband because of her kindness to a prodigal. Having lost her first husband's wedding ring in the Thames, she has that ring returned to her in the belly of a fish that her maid bought at the market (I.ii.139–58). This is the most obvious of the "miracles" that fuels the play, but it is an emblem of the aura of energetically rendered improbability that marks all of the play's major actions.[63] In this instance something of value lost by a careless act is restored seemingly because the loser is a charitable woman. If only casting one's fortunes upon the sea always led so easily to a full restitution of one's capital!

Both *When You See Me* and *A New Wonder* use the debtors' prisons to stage what I call Hand of God resolutions to the debt and credit problems of contemporary London. In one, the King eradicates abuses simply by going to the Counter and becoming prisoner for a day. By good deeds he shores up his own credit and restores that of those unjustly committed to this secular purgatory. In *A New Wonder* Ludgate Prison becomes the city site where charity is not only exercised and solicited, but embodied. And because of charity, the debts of prodigality and the ruined credit of merchant adventurers evaporate through nostalgic miracle. In Counter plays such as *Every Man Out of His Humour* or *The Roaring Girl* the debtors' prison is a dead end for those who enter it. Fastidious Brisk is, we assume, destroyed by his descent into the Counter. *A New Wonder* in part constructs Ludgate Prison as a place of horrors, where one is forced to cry out at the gate for food and where one is utterly dependent on the good offices of others for one's redemption. But in focusing on Ludgate as a site of miraculous generosity, *A New Wonder* rewrites urban life as a divine comedy and Ludgate Prison as a merely temporary purgatory. In the process it obscures the worst and most immutable consequences of a culture of debt, while offering a powerful, if untenable, fantasy of the power of Christian love to erase the pernicious effects of emerging cultural forces that were making debt a pervasive and often lastingly destructive part of daily life.

In what follows I am going to look at two other plays that contain scenes set in the Counters. Like the first plays I discussed, they focus on prodigals run amuck in the city, and not on the good offices of those who would relieve debtors, but the manner by which these plays resolve their stories of debt and credit is again very different. Both enact or promise the release of the prodigals, and in both plays credit, in the sense of reputation, seems to depend as much on performative skills as on economic viability. These plays, honoring the theatrical medium in which they themselves exist, help to construct new understandings of credit and cultural capital to challenge a social imaginary in which money and a reputation for fiscal probity trump all other values. In this regard, they stand in a supplementary relationship to the dominant culture of economic/moral credit that informed much of urban life.

Cultural Capital, Performance, and Credit

Each of the plays I am going to examine here, *Eastward Ho* and *Greene's Tu Quoque*, assumes a general cultural understanding of the Counters both as the signifiers of debt and loss of credit and as integral to comic dramatizations of the vices of the city. Each drama knowingly plays on these shared assumptions to generate new kinds of cultural narratives. *Eastward Ho*, by Jonson, Chapman, and Marston, was probably staged by the Children of Blackfriars in spring of 1605. It was an "answer" to Dekker and Webster's more genial play, *Westward Ho*, put on by the rival company of boy actors at St. Paul's in 1604. The fact of theatrical competitiveness—of overtopping the rival company—probably has something to do with the way the play incorporates prior stage motifs dealing with Londoners' perceived penchant for ever-increasing amounts of debt, consumption, and high-risk venturing, and then transforms the meaning of those motifs.[64]

Eastward Ho has several spectacular debtors, particularly Francis Quicksilver, apprentice and would-be gallant, and a new-minted knight, Sir Petronel Flash, who has heavily indebted himself, partly to fit out a ship that will be used to seek out "Virginian gold" (III.ii.336). A usurer, Security, urges on the forces of prodigality. In working out the fates of these needy debtors and greedy moneylenders, *Eastward Ho* plays extensively on the geographic motifs introduced by its antecedent [65] and develops much more fully the various economic practices that lead to disastrous loss of credit. Like its predecessor, the play's title draws on the soundscape of London daily life, "Eastward Ho" being the cry used by Thames boatmen heading downriver just as "Westward Ho" advertised a journey up the Thames. In spring of 1605, the court spent several months at Greenwich,[66] so "Eastward Ho" beckons characters East toward the court, the lodestar, in particular, of the play's chief prodigal, Quicksilver. Unfortunately, Quicksilver's perpetual cry of "Eastward Ho" causes his sober master, the goldsmith Touchstone, to opine that "Eastward Ho will make you go Westward Ho" (II.i.112), meaning to Tyburn and the gallows where felons were hung. The threatened reversal of direction remains a distinct possibility throughout the play as Quicksilver's hunger for money involves him in practices that his old master, Touchstone, finds illegal (IV.ii.227–30). East is also the direction toward which Gertrude, the socially ambitious daughter of the goldsmith Touchstone, journeys when, having married Sir Petronel Flash, she goes forth to find his castle. Eastward down the Thames is also, ironically, the direction one must first go if one would later go West to the Americas, which is where Sir Petronel Flash, following the example of Sir Francis Drake, hopes to venture to find his New World treasure.[67] For each of these characters, east is the direction of desire where court, castle, and (a hugely idealized) Virginia are to be found.

This geography of desire, however, is overlaid by an antiutopian geography of London's eastern regions. When the adventurers move out of the city on their eastward paths, they encounter neither court, castle, nor a temperate, fruitful Virginia, but rather a variety of unappealing sites. Quicksilver, thrown overboard into the Thames, fetches up at Wapping Gallows (IV.i.105–12), the eastern counterpart to Tyborn where pirates, in particular, were executed; Security comes ashore at the suggestively named Cuckold's Haven, the usurer having been involved in an elaborate scheme to facilitate the cuckolding of another man while in truth his wife, Winifred, has been sailing off with Petronel; she, in turn, lands at St. Katherine's (IV.i.53–69), an extramural area to the east of the city notorious for its prostitutes; while Sir Petronel Flash finds shore on the Isle of Dogs (IV.i.163), though in a charming instance of his complete incompetence, he believes he is in France. For its effectiveness, the play depends upon and contributes to the collective discursive mapping of city and extramural space and even of the soon-to-be colonized lands across the Atlantic. The Americas are here parodically constructed, via Hakluyt and Sir Thomas More, as an idyllic land blessed with friendly Indians, plentiful food, abundant gold, and few European inhabitants except a "few industrious Scots" (III.iii.38), one of the gibes that famously got the authors of the play imprisoned.[68]

It is in the eastern zone beyond the city that the audience sees the disintegration of ambitious dreams as the darker side of this eastern landscape is revealed. Gertrude is typical. Traveling east in her brand-new coach she discovers that her husband, Petronel, has no castle. Ignominiously, she is reduced to living in her coach and selling her clothing to buy food. In this state, Gertrude hopes for exactly the kind of miracle that will later animate a play such as *A New Wonder or a Woman Never Vext*, for she longs for fairies to come rescue her from her destitution. To her maid she says that fairies can

Do miracles, and bring ladies money. Sure, if we lay in a cleanly house, they would haunt it, Sin? I'll try. I'll sweep the chamber soon at night, and set a dish of water o' the hearth. A fairy may come, and bring a pearl or a diamond. We do not know, Sin? Or, there may be a pot of gold hid o' the backside, if we had tools to dig for't? Why may not we two rise early i' the morning, Sin, afore anybody is up, and find a jewel i' the streets worth a hundred pound? (V.i.77–84)

In this determinedly anti-idealizing play, however, there are no miracles to cure destitution, no fish that leap from the Thames with lost wedding rings in their bellies.

Instead, the economically strapped must encounter the Counter. As in *Every Man Out of His Humor*, the debtors' prison is the end point of the prodigal's course and of the play's narrative. It is also the place where the play's far-flung characters converge. The ambitious and greedy have cast themselves out of the city, but the centrifugal energies of the play reverse themselves in Act IV, as the storm in the Thames precipitates a return to the center of the city, here figured as the Counter rather than as the Royal Exchange, the Guildhall, St. Paul's, or even Cheapside, some of the landmarks on the tourist itinerary of every foreign visitor. In the drama's lexicon of London, the story of greed and prodigality run amuck follows a geographic and moral trajectory that ends in the shabby debtors' prison where the usurer, the prodigal, and the Knight adventurer are all incarcerated.

But if this sounds like *Every Man Out*, in which the play closes with a focus upon the miserable Fastidious Brisk entombed within the Counter, nothing, in fact, could be further from the truth. The latter play certainly depends upon the former (and Jonson was author of one and part-author of the second), but it cites its dramatic predecessor primarily to ring changes on the Counter narrative it inherited. In effect, it elaborates a different standard of worth by which to judge one's credit and so to evaluate success and failure. In this play the Counter does not swallow up its prisoners permanently. Rather, it ends with them stepping forth—a moment to which I will return—as hell yields up her captives. But it is not a miracle that wins their release, nor a Christmas legacy, nor the generous benefaction of a city worthy, nor the operation of the fairies, but rather the performative prowess of Francis Quicksilver, who so successfully manipulates his various Counter audiences—fellow prisoners, keepers and guards, his former master, and the audience in the theater—that they allow him and his companions to be released.[69] If the Counter typically represents social death, in this play it is rewritten as a stage upon which the would-be gentleman is reborn as star cultural performer.

In a very interesting essay entitled "Manhood, Credit and Patriarchy in Early Modern England c. 1580–1640,"[70] Alexandra Shepard argues that while it is clear that economic mastery and a reputation for creditworthiness were extremely important aspects of male identity in the early modern period, not all men could achieve them. She suggests that men of the middling sort were most likely to construct their masculinity in terms of economic credibility, while others, such as impoverished younger sons of the gentry, like Quicksilver, were driven to embrace alternative forms of masculinity premised on such things as drinking prowess, violent behavior, or even extravagant prodigality. In short, a cultural ideal not all could achieve produced alternative norms. The theater, I would argue, functioned as one of the places where such alternatives could be developed, especially, as in *Eastward Ho*, when it slyly queried dominant cultural values and highlighted the spectacular cleverness of its bad boy, the ingenious Quicksilver, whose "credit" depends on his performative skills.

When Quicksilver is brought to bay in the Counter, the audience might well expect it will prove a harsh school in which he will learn repentance and the errors of his past prodigality. But though Quicksilver says he does repent, what the Counter primarily teaches him is the necessity of performing repentance with gusto and a keen eye to the audience if sackcloth and ashes are to lead to forgiveness and, better, to release. At first, Quicksilver sends Touchstone "letters of submission" in which there is a "great deal of humility" (V.ii.8 and 36–37). These letters are entirely ineffective in touching the heart of Touchstone. He will not even read them. Whether or not Quicksilver's repentance is genuine, its written expression is insufficient to affect his chief creditor. What begins to be effective is an account by Wolf, a Counter officer, of how Quicksilver *acts* in prison. In response to this narrative, Touchstone feels the stirring of pity, though he immediately tamps it down. But when, lured to the Counter by a trick, he finally gets to see Quicksilver in full performance mode, he foregoes his desire to punish the prodigal.

Quicksilver in effect treats the Counter as a stage on which he puts to good use the well-known features of the place as props to his performance. Wolf reports, for example, that rather than clinging to the privileges of the Master's Side or the Knight's Ward, Quicksilver attempts to lie in the Hole (V.ii.40–41), the place of greatest discomfort and abjection. Moreover, he has given away all his rich clothes and eats out of the almsbasket provided for the poorest prisoners "for humility" (V.iii.48–50). He has cut his hair (V.ii.50), long hair in men being a sign of luxury and foppishness; and above all he has taken up the singing of psalms and ballads of repentance and telling of stories out of Fox's *Book of Martyrs* and Becon's *Sick Man's Salve*, popular works of Protestant piety (V.ii.42–43, 51–53). As Peter Lake has argued, Quicksilver cites, but hilariously parodies, these repentance narratives, and the fact that Touchstone is eventually moved by this performance merely makes him look foolish as he is revealed as a gullible and undiscriminating consumer of the tritest aspects of the genre.[71] Quicksilver, in short, is making the most of the theatrical potential of the Counter. He seeks out the most degraded part of the prison for his performance, assumes the clothing of a poor man, alters his hairstyle, and calls on the almsbasket as a powerful prop. His script is culled largely from devotional books.

Quicksilver has, moreover, been shown earlier in the play to have the credentials of a performer. Throughout, he has a keen sense of the importance of clothes and props to construct identity. Though an apprentice, Quicksilver first enters wearing a "*hat, pumps, short sword and dagger, and a racket trussed up under his cloak*" (s.d. preceding I.i.), the clothes appropriate for meeting gallants at a tavern. We later learn that during his apprenticeship he has kept a trunk and a punk at Security's, and in the trunk are the silk clothes and the weapons suitable for a gentleman (II.ii.27–30) and which, when cashiered from his indentures, he happily assumes even as he casts off the flat cap that signaled his servitude. Perhaps more importantly, Quicksilver is a constant quoter of theatrical lines and singer of popular ballads. When drunk, he rattles off lines from *Tamburlaine*, Greene's lost play, *Mahomet and the Fair Greek Hiren*, Chapman's *Blind Beggar of Alexandria*, and Kyd's *The Spanish Tragedy* (II.i.82, 100, 102, 122, 124, 126–27). Clearly, among the many things this court-loving, tavern-visiting would-be gallant does is visit the London theaters, listen to the city's street performers, and visit the London bookstalls.

Quicksilver is no Sogliardo in that he does not have to pay someone to teach him how to be a fashionable man about town, nor is he a Fastidious Brisk, imperfectly aping court manners like a Zanni. Rather, a minor gentleman by birth, though a younger son, Quicksilver has acquired on his own the cultural capital that allows him to mingle with gallants and hold his credit among them. Quicksilver repeatedly insists that his tavern-going ways sustain his own credit with the gallants of the town and also draw them to his master's shop for financial underwriting. But Quicksilver's credit with these gallants does not depend so much on his financial standing—his financial creditworthiness—as on his ability to drink, carouse, play tennis, know the most fashionable playhouses and plays, and perform his cultural and social competence effortlessly, a performance that confirms his participation in a circle in which Touchstone, whatever his financial bona fides, will never be welcomed. It is, of course, unrealistic to separate the one form of credit from the other (at the very least, one needs money to buy the props, like tennis rackets, that signal one's place within a certain circle), but the provocation of this play lies in its challenge to the assumption that, at bottom, financial credit is all that matters.

In foregrounding Quicksilver's performative skills and in underscoring their effectiveness the play registers its chief riposte both to the citizen-dominated *Westward Ho* and to the logic of tradesmen like Touchstone, who would keep up his reputation or credit by eschewing all extravagance and performative *elan*. As he tells Quicksilver: "I hired me a little shop, sought low, took small gain, kept no debt-book, garnished my shop for want of plate, with good wholesome thrifty sentences, as, 'Touchstone, keep thy shop, and thy shop will keep thee'. 'Light gains makes heavy purses'. 'Tis good to be merry and wise' " (I.i.45–50). In the face of such a thrifty and calculating regime, Quicksilver's flamboyant theatricality, whether judged morally good or bad, unmistakably registers a difference and unquestionably proves effective. In prison, performing his repentance publically and with gusto, Quicksilver first wins over the notoriously hard-hearted prison officers, here Wolf and Fangs, so often excoriated for their cruelty by writers such as Fenner, Dekker, and Mynshul.[72] He wins over the other prisoners who praise him for his piety and repeatedly call upon him to perform his repentance ballad for them. And in singing that, a wild take-off on prior "confessions" and execution ballads, Quicksilver wins over Touchstone.

Sincerity is hardly an issue in Quicksilver's performance. Parodying through exaggeration the humble repentance that Counter narratives invite (think of Old Foster repenting in Ludgate his uncharitable past), Quicksilver's performance calls forth an appreciation of its bravura qualities, its over-the-top performativity, the appreciation of which makes the audience oh-so-much smarter than the flatfooted Touchstone, the man who cannot imagine irony. Indeed, when Quicksilver, in the Epilogue, steps out of the Counter and out of the frame of the play, he steps into Blackfriars Theater and into the gaze of the audience.

I perceive the multitude are gathered together to view our coming out at the Counter. See, if the streets and the fronts of the houses be not stuck with people, and the windows filled with ladies, as on the solemn day of the

Pageant!
    O may you find in this our pageant, here,
    The same contentment which you came to seek,
    And as that show but draws you once a year,
    May this attract you hither once a week. (Epilogue, 1–9)

The moment merges the fictionalized Londoners supposedly lining Cheapside at Quicksilver's emergence from the Counter and the actual Londoners sitting in the seats at the Blackfriars even as the character of Quicksilver is also being merged with the actor who personated him. Applauding, the audience honors the represented skillfulness of the "reformed" prodigal and the presentational skills of the actual theatrical performer. Together, they define a standard of worth that has little to do with the financial credit by which Touchstone and Security judge their fellow Londoners and, in fact, which Quicksilver's hyperbolic "reformation" not so subtly mocks. Indeed, the actor/gallant's performance is set in direct opposition to the annual Lord Mayor's pageant, which followed a fixed processional route that inevitably took the city officials down Cheapside.[73] Both the Poultry Street and Wood Street Counters were but steps away from Cheapside. Quicksilver, still in the "rug gown" (V.iii.58) he adopted in prison, insists that he will go home "through the streets in these, as a spectacle, or rather an example, to the children of Cheapside" (V.v.190–91). He will, therefore, be traversing the ceremonial route down which the Lord Mayor moved, juxtaposing his histrionic performance of humility with the Mayor's celebration of the power of the London guilds. It is an audaciously bold ending to an audacious play, and one that suggests that the power of London's financial community, embodied in guildsmen such as Touchstone, to define standards of worth and credit may no longer be absolute, at least in the realm of cultural narrative. The play seizes on the Counter, the symbol of broken credit and financial abjection, and uses it to stage the triumphal emergence of a figure who upholds the credit of actors and of the actorly opportunists of London's performative culture. Counterintuitively, the Counter, with its rituals of abjection and repentance, is discursively refigured as the space of a mastery rivaling the Lord Mayor's.

Clowning and Credit

I am going to end this discussion of alternative forms of cultural credit by turning briefly to a final play, John Cooke's *Greene's Tu*

Quoque or The Cittie Gallant, performed by the Queen Anne's Men at court and at the Red Bull in 1611 and printed in 1614.[74] It is in many ways a typical Counter narrative in that it features no less than three prodigal figures and a debtors' prison. *Un*usual, however, are both the bitterness with which the Counter is portrayed and also the presence of Thomas Greene, the famous Queen's Men's clown, in the title role of the city gallant and his image, in full clown's attire, on the title page of the printed version of the play (Figure 7). I wish to suggest that *Greene's Tu Quoque,* appearing after a number of Counter dramas, rewrites narratives of this institution in ways that recall Isabella Whitney's emphasis on the destitution and the suffering that at a material level the prison represented. At the same time, it powerfully critiques the ideology of charity that informs *A New Wonder* and takes in new directions *Eastward Ho*'s emphasis on performative prowess as an alternative to financial credit as a norm for judging masculine social worth.

Briefly put, the play displays three men suddenly put in new social positions because of changes in their financial situations. Spendall, a mercer's apprentice, gets control of the shop and all its finances when his master, Lionel Rash, is knighted and moves to the more fashionable Strand (sc. i, 125–51). Already possessed of a whore and a taste for vice, Spendall quickly jeopardizes the financial integrity of the shop by his prodigality. Simultaneously, a gentleman named Staines finds himself in the clutches of an old usurer and no longer dares to walk abroad lest the officers of the Counter seize him. About to flee to Ireland or Virginia, he receives word that the usurer has died from shock when a butcher asked him for four shillings for mutton (sc. ii, 255–58) and has left all his money to his nephew, Bubble, who has for years been Staines' servant. Now possessed of a fortune, Bubble agrees, in effect, to switch places with Staines whom he employs as his own servant and as his tutor in gentlemanly ways, including the ways of prodigality. This is another play, like *Eastward Ho,* in which sudden reversals of fortune seem to image the operations of an unpredictable marketplace. The play follows the fortunes of Staines, the former prodigal; Bubble, the newly made gentleman; and Spendall, the mercer's apprentice-turned-master.

Spendall, the representative of city guild culture, assiduously pursues the rosy road to the Counter, good-naturedly laying out vast sums on dice and gaming and on clothes and presents for his whore and her bawd. When the sergeants come, as they inevitably do, to take him to the Counter, this same whore denies him the forty shillings it would take to buy off the officers. Ensconced in the prison, this prodigal finds himself without money for fees and threatened with the Two-penny ward or the Hole where he is told he may feed for nothing. In fury

Figure 7. Woodcut of Thomas Greene playing Bubble, title page to *Greenes Tu Quoque* by John Cooke, 1611. Reproduced by permission of The Huntington Library, San Marino, California.

he retorts: "I, out of the Almes-basket, where Charitie appeares/In likenesse of a peece of stinking Fish" (sc. xv, 2066–67). Later, Gatherscrap, the parish basketman, arrives to feed the poorest prisoners, and Spendall refuses to eat, though he knows that

To such a one as these are must I come,
Hunger will draw mee into their fellowship,
To fight and scramble for unsaverie Scraps,
That come from unknowne hands, perhaps unwasht:
And would that were the worst; for I have noted,
That nought goes to the Prisoners, but such food
As either by the weather has been tainted,
Or Children, nay sometimes full paunched Dogges
Have overlickt, as if men had determined
That the worst Sustenance, which is Gods Creatures,
How ever they're abusde, are good enough
For such vild Creatures as abuse themselves. (sc. xv, 2138–49)

Spendall's full degradation here comes home through the image of contaminated food, while the charity that provides it is equated to a stinking fish. Earlier, Staines had asserted that the old usurer had willingly eaten from the prisoners' almsbasket in order to save money (sc. ii, 154–67), which merely confirms Spendall's perception that only those degraded by extreme need or their own vile natures would willingly eat these "charitable" offerings.

Charity continues to be problematically rendered in this play. Though his prison experience leads Spendall to repent of his former folly, he has no money to come to composition with his creditors. He is only rescued by the the "wel-minded Widdow Raysby/Whose hand is still upon the poore mans Box,/Hath in her Charitie remembred you" (sc. xv, 2168–70). She takes care of his creditors, his large prison fees, and provides him with new clothes. But, in an unusual plot twist, once released he shows his "gratitude" for this charity by breaking in upon the widow on the evening she is to marry his old master, Sir Lionel, and at dagger point enjoins her to marry him.[75] Though free of prison, his poverty makes him desperate for her money, in return for which he promises her sexual pleasure, children, and his youth. When she assents to his proposition, he whips out a marriage contract that she must sign. Though she later ties him to a bed, rips up the contract, and voluntarily agrees to his demands, the fact remains that, as Theodore Leinwand has argued, debtors' prison has transformed Spendall into a violent and angry man.[76] He has not become charitable by being given charity. In fact, the stinking fish of charity has first degraded and then hardened him, making him see in a marriage contract that is "Strong and sufficient, and will holde in

Lawe" (sc. xvii, 2587) the only bulwark against ruin. This is a highly cynical riposte to a Counter story such as *A New Wonder or a Woman Never Vext* with its valorization of a golden bond of charity that sweetens all imaginations and repairs ruined credit, ruined lives. Though the date of *A New Wonder* is unclear, it is possible that both plays were written in or around 1611.

By contrast, the other prodigal plot, involving Staines and Bubble, works out an alternative logic of debt and its redress. Staines, the ruined gentleman-turned-servant, recoups his losses by adopting Proteus as his deity (sc. vii, 804) and assuming a series of disguises by which he leads his new master, Bubble, deeper and deeper into debt, all the while craftily using Bubble's own resources to make himself Bubble's chief creditor. Consequently, disguised in silks as a gallant, Staines causes Bubble to spend money on cards and dice (sc. ix, 996–1109); later, dressed as an Italian gentleman, he claims to have traveled, to know Greek, Latin, and Italian, and to be willing to show Bubble how to dress and how to woo Joyce, one of Sir Lionel's daughters. Ironically Staines' rich clothes and his frequent changes of attire—the very things that usually signal a gallant's impending descent to the Counter—are what Staines uses to recapture a prominent social standing and to escape a life of poverty and servitude. In everything Staines does, he undermines his "master, " and in the end he not only reclaims his fortune, but wins Joyce for himself. His recovery does not depend on a Counter stay, nor upon charity, but upon his wit and his performative skills.

Bubble raises the issue of performative credit in another way. The part of Bubble, one of the play's three prodigals, the one who aspires to be "a city gallant," is written as a clown. He was played by Thomas Greene, the distinguished clown who replaced Will Kemp in the Queen Anne's Men Company (formerly Worcester's Men). Within the play's fiction, Bubble is a fool who by a certain logic deserves to end up in the Counter. He cannot perform the part of a gentleman convincingly, and he cannot hang onto his money. He has "credit" in neither arena. At the end of the play, threatened by the Counter, he only escapes by agreeing to again become Staines's servant (sc. xix, 2892–98), a conservative rerighting of a social order disordered by usury and the extreme consequences of Staines' own prior loss of credit. But in the theater Bubble has lots of "credit" in the play's highly touted clown's part. Within the fiction, his incompetent playing of a would-be gentleman not only garners laughs but showcases his actorly skills and highlights the continuing importance of the clown to popular theater. At one highly metatheatrical moment, Geraldine, a gentleman, Bubble, and Bubble's new "friend," Scattergood, discuss going to a play.

SCATT.	if it please you, let's
	goe see a Play at the Gloabe.
BUB.	I care not; any whither, so the Clowne have a part:
	For Ifayth I am no body without a Foole.
GER.	Why then wee'le goe to the Red Bull; they say *Green's* a good
	Clowne.
BUB.	*Greene? Greene's* an Asse.
SCATT.	Wherefore do you say so?
BUB.	Indeed I ha no reason: for they say, hee is
	as like mee as ever hee can looke.
SCATT.	Well then, to the Bull. (sc. xii, 1567–77)

Obviously designed to play on the audience's knowledge that Greene was before them on the stage, talking about "Greene" in the third person, this exchange asserts the value of the particular skills associated with the stage clown. He is so important, in fact, that in the play's title, the actor supplants the character completely. It is not Bubble's "Tu Quoque," but Greene's, the Latin tag being the line that Bubble reflexively uses whenever, in his guise as a gentleman, he can think of nothing else to say. Actor is foregrounded at the expense of the character, an indication, were one needed, of the powerful effects this actor must have had on the audience. In the printed text, not only are there tributes to Greene by Heywood and one W. R. (William Rowley?), but, as I have indicated, an image of him adorns the title page. If *When You See Me* advertises the authority of the King on its title page, *Greene's Tu Quoque* advertises the authority of the clown as actor. Within the fiction, his theatrical skills are echoed by the Protean Staines, a sly indication, perhaps, not only of the way in which credit may be restored through performative skills, but of the influence of the stage on the culture in which it was embedded. In obsessively staging the Counter, and creating stories in which it figured, the city theater not only made its contribution to cultural narratives of debt, charity, and credit, but it rendered itself and its practices part of those narratives.

Coda

Dramatizations of the Counter and of the lives of those who enter there or teeter on the brink of incarceration are central to London comedy because they provide a way to think about the implications of an emerging culture of credit and debt. To be taken to the Counter is often vividly imagined as a kind of social death, a loss of the credit that allows masculine subjects to have a secure place in the commercial and political worlds within the city. Stephen Foster, once a "Ludgathian" and then a Sherif of London, encompasses in one life the extremes of social abjection and social validation that loss and recovery of financial credit made possible. To be hauled off to the Counter is an ignominious social fate, and the stage makes material the loss of social selfhood by stripping debtors of their clothes and subjecting them to the indignities of the stinking fish of the almsbasket. Many Counter plays, from *Every Man Out of His Humour* on, play over and over with the frightening specter of a fall from respectability into the gaping Hole where one is, socially and economically speaking, "undone." This resonant social fantasy probably functioned partly as a disciplinary narrative, warning subjects away from lives of extravagance and overextension. In fact, the course of dishonor ending in the debtors' prison is most often trodden by those who are cast as prodigals, people who eat too well, dress too well, and entertain themselves too freely at taverns and theaters—people, that is, who were very much a part of the city's market economy. The stage did not, by and large, provide a structural analysis of the causes of increasing indebtedness. What it did was to capture the terror of undergoing a social death by debt and so at one level to warn subjects from behavior perceived to lead to such a death.

But the stage was much more than a disciplinary apparatus. A play like *Every Man Out of His Humour* piously enjoins thrift, but impiously stages sartorial extravagance, rendering unstable its obvious ideological thrust. Even at the level of representation, moreover, the stage told more than one kind of Counter story. Some plays, such as *When You See Me You Know Me*, pick up on the complaint tradition that sees the debtors' prison critically, as a site of abuses including the cruelty of prisonkeepers and the potential negligence of kings. Rather than telling the fall into social oblivion as a story about prodigal subjects, it writes debtors primarily as victims of the powerful. More interesting because more complex are the doubled stories of prodigality and business venturing that structure *A New Wonder*. By linking the expected tale of a prodigal with the story of Old Foster, the big merchant, the play begins to make visible the material forces (rather than just the moral weaknesses) that lead to debtors' prison. Old Foster is greedy, and that is presented as bad, but the loss of ships at sea is a real hazard of long-distance trade. But whether the debtor is a prodigal or a merchant, his indebtedness and loss of social credit are remedied by the magical elixir of charity. The fascinating thing about this play is the particularity with which it renders the material forces, from dice playing to treacherous seas, that cause men to "break" financially, even as it relies on entirely fantastic devices to rescue the debtors thus endangered. *A New Wonder* is a play of powerful ideological willfulness—it *wants* the great chain of charitable giving to bind everyone together in Christian fellowship and to erase the marketplace desires that have led prodigals to lust after satin suits and merchants to lust after profits of sixtyfold. Nostalgic and backward looking, it imagines a city of Christian charity in which the speculative and prodigal behavior solicited by the quickening marketplace is simply negated by love.

The theater was itself, of course, part of the marketplace world of debt and credit, which it dramatized. One of the interesting aspects of *Shakespeare in Love* was how vividly it rendered the precarious financial dealings of theater managers like Henslowe and the economic pressures fueling the production of playscripts. Playwrights, actors, and theater managers were also often debtors. The vivid rendering of Counter narratives probably has something to do with how close to home they came. But, perhaps more materially than most institutions, the theater also depended on some of the very things that marked men as prodigals in daily life—above all, on the extravagant display of fashionable apparel and the assumption by actors of stage identities far above their inherited social status. If sartorial excess and rapid changes in status mark the prodigal, they also mark the actor. But if debtors were supposed to lose their apparel as they lost their economic credit, some plays work differently. They present clothes not only as what a debtor loses, but as what can help to refashion him into a man of social standing. This is what happens to Staines in *Greene's Tu Quoque*. Thrust by his prodigality into a life of servitude, he recoups his fortunes by cleverly assuming various sartorial disguises and performing his way back into economic and social respectability. The theater thus elaborates an alternative to the forms of economic credit and reputation that in many contexts defined privileged forms of masculine identity. Fully cognizant of these norms and often recirculating them, the theater nonetheless both embodied and sometimes represented alternatives. In staging men whose reputations depended on performative skills, the theater gestured toward the value of its own forms of cultural capital.

Plays such as *Greene's Tu Quoque* and *Eastward Ho* thus infuse Counter narratives with an antimoralizing performativity that critiques, both directly and indirectly, the pious narratives about bad subjects that are the norm for many Counter tales, and they elaborate alternative standards of social worth. In *Greene's Tu Quoque* the Counter does not so much reform as systematically degrade its inhabitants, and what charity induces is not proper Christian humility but deep and abiding rage. In *Eastward Ho* the prodigal's reform is a purely histrionic affair. In fact, both plays emphasize the performative skills that lead to new forms of social credit. It is not a man's money that makes him valued, but his ability to carry himself well, to act the part of a penitent or a gentleman, or a clown with skill and conviction. These plays, in endorsing a culture of impersonation and self-display, profoundly challenge the assumptions of many debtors' prison stories with their emphasis on the evils of extravagant prodigality and their punitive stance toward sartorial plumage and social climbing. Perhaps more than any other site, the theater was thus able to elaborate a succession of probing and contradictory Counter narratives, ones attuned to both the dominant norms and the alternative social logics possible in the culture of debt and credit in which the theater itself was embedded.

Chapter 3

(W)holesaling: Bawdy Houses and Whore Plots in the Drama's Staging of London

It has become a critical truism that in early modern England, the reputation of middling sort men, in particular, depended largely on their credit in the economic realm, while women's reputations pivoted on their sexual honesty.[1] In the last chapter I argued that London comedies both confirm and challenge this view of male reputation. Plays that use the London debtors' prisons as a setting routinely stage the loss of financial credit as a kind of social death for men; but at the same time London plays such as *Eastward Ho* energetically articulate alternative norms for judging masculine credit or reputation, norms attuned to the increasingly performative possibilities of urban life and to the witty display of cultural, not financial, capital. In what follows I am going to turn to urban women and to use the place of the brothel and the figure of the whore to think again about female reputation in an urban context and about how London comedy used a supposedly abject character, that of the prostitute, to figure the place of women in the changing landscape of the expanding, commercializing, and multinational city that London was becoming.

One might expect that brothels would primarily provide a site for stories of women's social death and abjection. In London comedy, this is not really so. While there are early modern representations of whores and whorehouses that tell moralizing tales of women's loss of reputation and descent into poverty and disease, a great number of London plays do otherwise, putting pressure on the idea that sexual status determines female worth and, with seeming perversity, celebrating women's financial acumen or cultural sophistication over her chastity. In the process these plays undermine strict distinctions between the female-based flesh trade and those forms of "legitimate" business on which men's social reputation supposedly rests. In what follows I will not of course be arguing that the drama's brothel comedies show what London was "really like" for women. Rather, focusing always on the power of stories to confirm or expand social subjects' imaginative parameters and their modes of rendering experience intelligible, I will suggest that through its high-spirited whore plots, the London stage offered power-ful and socially significant alternatives to normative prescriptions not only about prostitutes, but also about women more generally.

A striking fact to register first, however, is just how ubiquitous bawdy houses were in early modern London comedies. The Exchange and the Counter, discussed in prior chapters, were particular places with proper names. Staged directly in a handful of plays and mentioned in many others, they were city landmarks that became rich discursive nodes—sites mobilized for telling certain kinds of stories about urban life. In this chapter and the next I focus, however, on *generic* places: whore-houses in the earlier London comedies and academies of manners in the plays of the 1620s and 1630s. While actual brothels and academies existed in London, certainly, and will be discussed, in neither case is a particular place with a proper name the object of analysis, but rather a particular *kind* of social setting, which, returned to again and again, emerged as a crucial and constitutive element in particular stagings of the city. The bawdy house is such a setting. Within a few short years of the genre's inception, whores and their places of work had become a recurring feature of this new urban drama. For example, *Westward Ho* (1604) depicts the enterprising urban bawd, Birdlime, who runs a busy "hothouse" within the city walls; *Northward Ho* (1605) shows an equally industrious sexual entrepreneur, Doll, moving her place of trade about to suit the season, sometimes working suburban locations and some-times setting up within the city limits; *The Honest Whore, Part I* (1604), set in a Milan with many resemblances to London, features an urban whore who repents her infamous life, while in *Part II* (1605) some unrepentant whores suffer for their sins in Bridewell prison; *The Dutch Courtesan* (1604) stages a high-status alien sex worker who plies her trade in London; *Michaelmas Term* (1606) shows a country wench com-ing to London and setting up as a London courtesan; many other examples could be cited. The various types of whores depicted in these plays reappear in subsequent texts, as do the kinds of plots in which they figure: plots in which sexual innocence is lost, for example, usually by coming to the city, or in which a sinner reforms or has her status changed by the happy event of marriage. In all, the total number of city plays containing a prostitute plot is quite remarkable,[2] and the trend continued even into the 1630s when Shackerley Marmion's play, *Hol-lands Leaguer* (1631), depicted a notorious real-life battle between pros-titutes and constables at one of the Bankside's most upscale brothels.

To some degree this vogue for representing whores and whorehouses is not surprising given the city play's general preoccupation with London as a site of commerce and the whore as a well-established figure for rep-resenting the penetration of a market economy into all areas of life.[3]

Whore plays and other popular texts are quite explicit, and often quite self-consciously funny, in presenting prostitution as a business parallel to other forms of urban commerce, in many of which women legitimately and regularly participated, either as *femes sole* or as partners with their husbands. In Robert Greene's *A Disputation Between a Hee Conny-catcher, and a Shee Conny-catcher* (1592), for example, the whore who is the chief "she conny-catcher" is fittingly named Nan a Traffique. Like others who engage in "the buying or selling or exchange of goods for profit,"[4] Nan is a merchant of sorts, her commodity being her own flesh. She has a million schemes for cozening her clients to increase her profits. But not all whores, or their bawds and pimps, are presented as cheaters or illegitimate "traffickers." In *The Dutch Courtesan* the bawd's trade is said to be the "most worshipful of all the twelve companies" (I.ii.30)[5] (that is, of the twelve major city guilds) because the bawd sells the best commodities on offer in the urban market. Prostitution is equated, however ironically, with legitimate forms of business, including the "most worshipful." The metaphors connecting those employed in the sex trade to other kinds of merchants and tradesmen can be quite elaborate. One text, for example, describing a whore's transformation into a bawd, pithily asserts: "she will no more trust her-selfe on the Surges, but wil traffique by Factours, and according to the wealth of her Wares, so shalbe the encrease or decrease of her Revenues."[6] The rhetoric of long-distance trading practices is appropriated to suggest both the profitability of the prostitution racket and the bawd's position at one remove from the actual exchange of sex for money. No longer launching herself directly on the sea of sex, the bawd employs other women as her "factors" to sell their sexual "wares" for her profit.

How bawds and whores cleverly strategize to enhance the profitability of their commodities is a frequent theme of popular whore texts. Gervase Markham's 1609 poem "The Famous Whore or Noble Cortizan," for example, describes a number of ploys used to keep up the price of sexual goods. The oldest trick is the reselling of maidenheads. In a vivid metaphor, Markham compares such a maidenhead to the Hydra. When one head is lopped, another miraculously grows to takes its place (Bv).[7] But the whore's repertoire of tricks is considerably more extensive than this. It includes her taking three lovers simultaneously, thus making all three jealous so that they will compete with one another to shower her with money and gifts (Cv–C2v); finding a powerful noble patron who can protect her from the fines and loss of income that might result from imprisonment (Dv); and making her house an exclusive venue where as an upscale sex worker she can display all the arts of courtesanship including singing, dancing, and reciting Petrarch, thus raising the price for her services (D4–E). In Markham's poem the whore's business is just that, a business in which wares are set out to best advantage and profits multiplied in whatever way can be found, including providing "free traffique to all Nations."[8] Numerous plays list the wide range of countries from which the whore's clients are imagined to derive.

The matter-of-fact way in which prostitution is described as commercial enterprise in these popular texts makes it difficult consistently to moralize their representations of whores.[9] Overtly, the denigrated prostitute is the low matter that sets off, as against a foil, the legitimate practices of honest guildsmen and merchants. Yet even in the most moralizing contexts, such binaries are hard to sustain. John Taylor's pamphlet *A Common Whore* supposedly exposes and condemns both whore and whoremasters,[10] but putting whores in print both makes them the more notorious and also allows the author to profit from their existence. If the whore sells herself, the writer sells his version of her story. A thoroughly opportunistic publication, *A Common Whore* titillates as much as it edifies. The 1635 title page (Figure 8) is emblazoned with the picture of a well-dressed woman staring out at the reader. Hardly a figure of abjection, this whore bears no marks of poverty or disease. Rather, fashionably and expensively dressed, she solicits the reader's approving gaze, inviting him or her to buy the book in which her story is told. In that book's concluding pages, the imbrication of the worlds of publication and prostitution are outlined with surprising explicitness. Taylor undertakes a sustained comparison between a whore and a book as different yet similar objects of sale. In the doing, the ingenuity of Taylor's comparison creates equivalences where one might have expected oppositions. Both books and whores are loved when new and shunned when old and stale; each must have someone to promote their sale, in one case a stationer, in another a pander; books and whores can both be dedicated to many people; whores often die in hospitals and ditches while books meet similar dismal ends when they serve as bum fodder in privies or as wrapping paper for spices and drugs; books can be treated gently or torn and soiled; so can whores (Taylor, C3–C5). Taylor then concludes his pamphlet by listing the sixty-odd titles he has authored and where they can be found at the local book stalls (C5v). In this way, he pimps for himself or, to put the matter more decorously, engages in an early form of advertising. Whatever the screen of morality behind which he presents his arguments, one consequence of Taylor's pamphlet is to blur the line between legitimate commercial practices, including the sale of books, and supposedly illegitimate ones, such as the sale of sex. Ironically, he renders intelligible his own position within the marketplace by observing the actions and the status of the common whore.

The power of whore discourse to reveal the fragility of the line between legitimate and illegitimate marketplace practices is evident even

A Common Whore

With all thefe graces grac'd,
Shee's very honeft, beauti-
full and chafte.

Writtten By IOHN TAYLOR.

Printed at London for *Henry Goffon.* 1635.

Figure 8. A well-dressed whore, title page to *A Common Whore* by John Taylor, 1635.
Reproduced by permission of The Huntington Library, San Marino, California.

in plays that most strongly press the distinction. Dekker and Middleton's *The Honest Whore, Part I* is a good example. It focuses on a prostitute, Bellafront, who renounces her life of sin when faced with the strong condemnation of it by a gentleman, Hippolito. Subsequently married to her first deflowerer, Bellafront persists in virtue even when tempted by poverty and the abusive ways of her husband to return to the brothel life. In her self-discipline she becomes an emblem of womanly virtue, though she is made to suffer for her prior life by being saddled with a bad husband and grinding poverty. But hers is not the only story the play explores. Its full title is generally printed as *The Honest Whore, With, The Humours of the Patient man, and the Longing Wife.*[11] The patient man is Candido, a linen draper, whose story the play's title subordinates to that of Bellafront. Candido is called a patient man because throughout the play he refuses to be provoked either by the angry and insubordinate behavior of his wife or by the rude and discourteous behavior of his customers. He does not, for example, get angry when his apprentice assumes his clothing and takes his place as master of the shop; or when unreasonable customers demand he ruin a bolt of cloth by selling them a tiny portion cut from the very center of it; or when a customer tries to turn his wife to adultery. Throughout, Candido displays the mentality of the careful shopkeeper whose control over his emotions enables him to be courteously responsive to all his customers, no matter how repugnant. As he says:

We are set heere to please all customers,
Their humours and their fancies:—offend none:
We get by many, if we leese by one.
. . . .
Oh, he that meanes to thrive, with patient eye
Must please the divell, if he come to buy. (I.v.121–23 and 27–28)

This is the common sense of the marketplace, and, in a case of life eerily echoing art, it was repeated in the 1635 treatise by William Scott, *An Essay of Drapery*, in which an actual linen draper speaks of the need to show courtesy to customers, to use honeyed words to everyone, to be thrifty and avoid taverns, to restrain the pride and the tongue of a wife—and all in the pursuit of what he calls "sancta avaritia," holy covetousness.[12]

In his theatrical diary, Henslowe highlighted the role of Candido by calling the play *The Patient Man and the Honest Whore* when he recorded an advance to its authors.[13] In his forthcoming edition of *Part I* Paul Mulholland will use this title. Rather than subordinating the story of Candido to that of Bellafront, it suggests an equivalence between them. As Mulholland argues, Henslowe's title restores a sense of balance to the play and foregrounds its two governing paradoxes. Not only can a whore grow honest, but a man can be patient (patience traditionally was attributed to feminine figures such as the archetypal Griselda).[14] But pointing out the parallels between these two figures tends to call attention to the unflattering ways in which the legitimate shopkeeper both resembles a whore and assumes a feminized subject position. "Oh, he that means to thrive, with patient eye/ Must please the divell, if he come to buy," is the credo of *both* the man of the market and the woman of the brothel. Moreover, if Bellafront's patience, like Griselda's, is represented as heroic, the play presents male patience as both a virtue and also a source of comedy. Everyone makes fun of Candido even as he is held up as the positive middling sort alternative to the sword-waving gallants who otherwise populate the play's cityscape.[15] The market puts subjects in unfamiliar positions, not all of them flattering, and creates equivalences that cut against moral pieties. In the new marketplace, a book may be more like a whore than one had thought, and so may a shopkeeper.

In what follows in this chapter, then, I take for granted that whore plays, while they partly reference the actual social problem of prostitution in early modern London, also use the whorehouse and its central actor, the whore, to examine other troubling or novel aspects of urban life such as the quickening and expansion of the market economy, the feminization of those who became garden variety hucksters in this new market, or the novel positions in which the city places women, complicating their social status. The bawdy house thus becomes a particularly resonant and multifaceted signifier within the genre's discursive construction of an imagined London. To understand how the drama employs this site requires a reading practice that resists unitary interpretation of the sort that assumes that stage prostitution must be either "about" real-life prostitution or about something else, like the market or disease or cosmopolitanism. I want to suggest, instead, that whores and their places of work are capable of bearing several significations at once, or, to put it another way, are simultaneously part of more than one discursive struggle. In what follows I will to some extent artificially separate out different strands of the whore play's cultural import, but my intent is to suggest the overlapping nature of the cultural contexts within which the whore and the bawdy house can be most richly read.

To that end, I will examine several recurring features of London comedy's whore plots, arguing that those conventions offer some of the best evidence of how the genre responded to and shaped the social world of which it was a part. I will focus on three aspects of bawdy house dramas. The first is the distinctive way prostitute plays treat the location and legibility both of bawdy houses and of those who traffic in

illicit sex. While London comedies often evoke the city-suburb opposition, locating bawdy houses in the extramural wards or the suburbs,
they also frequently refuse to assign prostitution its own singular, clearly
legible place. It is a movable feast, and the more anxietyprovoking, I
will suggest, as a result. If the monumental fixity of the Royal Exchange
signals the seeming irreversibility of London's expanding international
commerce, the ubiquity of bawdy houses and their frequent illegibility
register not only the corrosive effects of market forces on cultural
boundaries and distinctions, but also the expansion of illicit sexuality's
terrain and the proliferation of social actors who in some circumstances, at least, become indistinguishable from "a common whore."
Second, I will explore the trope of conversion that animates many
whore plots, a conversion often accompanied by a quasi-ritualized ceremony involving the casting away or the putting on of a new self. I will
argue that these conversion narratives link the prostitute to instabilities
peculiar to the urban gender system, challenging the prescriptive literature's neat categorization of women into maids, wives, widows, and
illicit others and its valorization of sexual chastity as the prime determinant of female worth. Finally, I will turn to one of the most interesting
aspects of early modern prostitute drama, namely, the representation of
the whore as a figure for what I call "perverse cosmopolitanism," the
forced acknowledgement of the hybridity of London culture and of the
inevitable interpenetration of the domestic and the alien. The omnipresence of whores and bawdy houses in early modern London drama is
tied in more complex ways than we previously have recognized not only
to domestic matters, to international ones as well. In this regard,
Hollands' Leaguer, an upscale brothel on the South Bank, and the
Royal Exchange, seemingly so different, are also mirrors of one another
and focal points for the anxieties accompanying a changing city.

Mobile Whorehouses/Illegibile Whores

To understand the immediate social contexts in which London plays
staged prostitution, it is necessary to recount briefly a portion of the profession's history within the city. In the middle ages, the majority of
brothels were concentrated on the south bank of the Thames where
they had existed since Roman times.[16] Cock Lane in Smithfield was the
only allowed area of prostitution north of the Thames, though various
forms of private and clandestine prostitution also occurred in and
around the city. The Bankside brothels were regulated by ordinances
dating from the reign of Henry II in the twelfth century, and they were
under the control of the Bishop of Winchester (one result of which was
that "Winchester geese" became a common slang term for prostitutes[17]).

In 1546 Henry VIII ordered the officially licensed Bankside stews closed, supposedly to check the spread of vice and disease. Like most morality campaigns, this one was unsuccessful. Within a few short years, brothels had sprung up throughout the city and regrouped on the Bankside. John Taylor's *A Common Whore* jauntily records the change.

The Stewes in England bore a beastly sway,
Till the eight Henry banish'd them away
And since those common Whores were quite put downe,
A damned crew of private Whores are growne. (B6v)

Common whores were those who inhabited the licensed and regulated stews; private whores, by contrast, plied their trade anywhere and in a variety of circumstances.

Ian Archer in *The Pursuit of Stability: Social Relations in Elizabethan London* includes a map showing the location of bawdy houses in London in 1575–78, his data largely derived from the Bridewell records that have survived from that period.[18] He does not include the Bankside on his map, and we know that many brothels were still located there. The scatterplot is revealing, however, about the rest of London. Bawdy houses cluster at predictable places outside the city walls: Whitefriars in the west, Clerkenwell and Long Lane in the northwest, Whitecross Street in the north, Shoreditch in the northeast, Aldgate, East Smithfield, and St. Katherine's to the east. In effect, the walled city was ringed by the equivalent of modern red light districts. But there were also a number of brothels inside the walls, as well, especially toward the eastern end of the city. Rather than being confined to one or two areas, places of prostitution permeated the urban landscape.[19]

Nonetheless, suburban regions and the liberties within the walled city became especially associated with prostitution, vice, and vagrancy in the popular imagination. Soon after his ascension to the English throne in 1603 James I ordered the emptying out and pulling down of suburban tenements, which had become the haunt of "excessive numbers of idle, indigent, dissolute and dangerous persons."[20] The immediate purpose of this injunction was to halt the spread of the plague then raging in London, but it formed part of a larger campaign on the new king's part to clean up the city, restrict in-migration, and impose uniform standards on new buildings. Needless to say, these attempts failed. The population of London was growing too explosively to abide for long the ban against the proliferation of low-cost housing, and prostitution and other kinds of suburban (and urban) vice were never successfully quelled. It was James's early attempts to tame the suburbs, however, to which Shakespeare famously refers in *Measure for Measure* (1604) when Pompey laments the proclamation ordering that "All houses in the suburbs of Vienna must be plucked down" (I.ii.78).[21] Incredulously, Mistress Overdone asks: "But shall all our houses of resort in the suburbs be pulled down?" To which Pompey replies: "To the ground, mistress" (I.ii.82–84).

The outpouring of urban plays featuring prostitutes between 1603 and 1606 is undoubtedly related to the notoriety that James's actions brought to what was in truth a recurring preoccupation with controlling the sale of sex in and around the city.[22] Some of these dramas play with the lascivious reputation of suburban locations. *Westward Ho*, like many plays of the period, makes the village of Brainford the destination for the London wives who voyage up the Thames with their gallants to spend the night in a tavern there.[23] And in *Northward Ho* the destination for elicit adventure is Ware with its infamous great bed. In *Eastward Ho* Cuckold's Haven marks one of the spots where husbands' horns begin to sprout. West, north, or east, the suburbs all signify sexual sin. But, so does the city proper. In *Westward Ho* the enterprising bawd Birdlime has her actual brothel, where several scenes are set, inside the city walls. In the play's first speech she claims to keep a "Hot-house in Gunpowder Ally (neere Crouched Fryers),"[24] and at the end of the play she returns to her city establishment, proudly proclaiming that "I scorne the Sinfulnesse of any suburbes in Christendom: tis wel knowne I have up-rizers and downe-lyers within the Citty, night by night" (V.iv.251–53). There is no simple opposition between vice-ridden suburbs and an orderly city.

Northward Ho is especially suggestive in rendering intelligible the mobile nature of prostitution and the commercial and social conditions that fostered its spread. The play opens with two gentlemen discussing, among other things, why a Chamberlain named Innocence has moved from Dunstable to Ware. Innocence serves as a pimp in his spare time, and he is known to the gentlemen because at Dunstable he had twenty times arranged a meeting between one of the gentlemen and "two Butchers Daughters" (I.i.17),[25] a detail significant in itself since the two women are not called whores but were clearly used to provide sexual services to these gentlemen. Innocence, however, left Dunstable when peace broke out in Ireland. Before then, legions of army captains bade farewell to their London wenches in Dunstable; with peace, the place afforded fewer opportunities to barter flesh. Endlessly adaptable, however, Innocence has moved to the tavern in Ware on the York road to the north. As a major stopping point for travelers, Ware is an excellent replacement for Dunstable, a thriving site for pimping and whoring. As Innocence talks to the two gentlemen, two other travelers arrive at the inn. They have been to Sturbridge Fair, near Cambridge. It is immediately clear from their tales that the nearby fair also promotes the trade in human as well as animal flesh. One traveler describes wives busily excusing their husbands' "horns" while freshmen from the university made themselves busy "in the goose market" (that is, the market in whores). Everywhere, sexual and economic transactions are conducted in tandem. The traveler concludes his description of the fair:

Here two in one corner of a shop: Londoners selling their wares, and other Gentlemen courting their wives; where they take up petticoates you shold finde schollers and towns-mens wives crowding togither while their husbands weare in another market busie amongst the Oxen; twas like a campe for in other Countries so many Punks do not follow an army. (I.i.48–54)

Army towns, towns on major travelers' routes, towns near fairs, towns near universities — they all provide the conditions where punks and a man like the slyly named Innocence can thrive. Prostitution follows men and markets. Its sites are multiple and shifting.

Moreover, punks proper are not the only women active in these places. At the fair wives eagerly participate in the sexual free-for-all. They may not be paid for their adventures, but they distinctly and repeatedly defy wifely codes of married chastity, blurring the line between themselves and their explicitly entrepreneurial sisters, the open whores. Mistress Doll, the one prostitute with a face and a name in *Northward Ho*, shows a canny eye for the possibilities made available by the post-1546 decentralization of prostitution and the subsequent uptick in London's population and in its market economy. Doll is a thoroughly mobile whore with an eye to the main chance. Once attached to a young gentleman, Philip Mayberry, who was arrested for debt at the door of a tavern in the play's second scene, Doll immediately thinks about where to find new clients. With term time beginning, she determines to shift house and move to Charing Cross for "we that had warrants to lie without the liberties, come now dropping into the freedome by Owle-light sneakingly" (I.ii.74–76). She will seek out a:

faire house in the Citty: no matter tho it be a Taverne that has blowne up his Maister: it shall be in trade still, for I know diverse Tavernes ith Towne, that have but a Wall betweene them and a hotte-house. It shall then bee given out, that I'me a Gentlewoman of such a birth, such a wealth, have had such a breeding, and so foorth: . . . to set it off the better, old Jack Hornet shall take uppon him to bee my Father. (I.ii.85–92)

In this speech Doll calculates on blurring several lines of distinction. She will pass over from her warranted place outside the city to the "freedom" within (playing, obviously, on the freedom citizens acquire to ply their trades lawfully within a guild structure); she will inhabit a tavern that in truth is barely distinguishable from a hothouse, like the tavern to which Elbow's wife resorts in *Measure for Measure*, and she will make her own behavior mimic the codes of respectable femininity, obscuring her "true" identity. Later, Doll and her fake father and fake servants are shown exulting in the pleasurable theatricality of their game of dress-up and impersonation. Jack Hornet is particularly pleased with the clothing by which the tailor has turned him into a respectable man, though he is a little put out that the chain around his neck is only copper, not silver (II.i.45–46). Money allows a punk to purchase the trappings of rank and respectability, and Doll successfully attracts men of quality to her, including the poet-father of her erstwhile client, the bankrupt Philip.

Northward Ho is simply particularly forthright about depicting what other plays also assume: that London prostitution had become an opportunistic business practice that could not be wiped out and could not be confined to a single locale. There is evidence that the licensed bawdy houses on the Bankside had been painted white to make them readily legible, and Ruth Karras argues that in many medieval towns— though not apparently in Southwark–prostitutes had had to wear distinctive clothing such as a striped hood.[26] Stallybrass and Jones have argued that even in the Renaissance clothing still constituted identity by defining one's social place, occupation, gender, and status.[27] But many popular texts from the late sixteenth century pressure this idea of the automatic or easy legibility of either whores or whorehouses. While women standing in taffeta dresses in the doors of buildings often advertised the whereabouts of suburban brothels, not all whores throve on legibility. Doll depends on the fact that with the right props she cannot be distinguished from a respectable city lady nor a bawdy house from a mere tavern.

Dekker in his prose pamphlet *Lantern and Candle-light* (1608) discusses at length the crisis of legibility that ensues when a suburban whore, who there flaunted herself in silks and taffeta to attract customers, moves her business, as Doll does, into the city proper.

Upon what perch, then, does she sit? What part plays she then? Only the *Puritan*. If before she ruffled in silks, now is she more civilly attired than a Midwife. If before she swaggered in Taverns, now with the Snail she stirs not out of doors. And where must her lodging be taken up but in the house of some citizen whose known reputation she borrows, or rather steals, putting it on as a cloak to cover her deformities. Yet even in that, hath she an art, too, for he shall be of such a profession that all comers may enter, without the danger of any eyes to watch them. As, for example, she will lie in some Scrivener's house, and so under the color of coming to have a *Bond* made, she herself may write *Noverint universi.* And though the law threaten to hit her never so often, yet hath she subtle defences to ward off the blows. For, if Gallants haunt the house, then spreads she these colors; she is a captain's or a lieutenant's wife in the *Low*

[C]ountries, and they come with letters from the soldier her husband. If Merchants resort to her, then hoists she up these sails; she is wife to the Master of a ship and they bring news that her husband's put in the *Straits* or at *Venice,* at *Aleppo, Alexandria,* or *Iskenderum,* etc. If shop-keepers come to her with "What do you lack?" in their mouths, then she takes up such and such commodities to send them to Rye, to Bristol, to York etc., where her husband dwells. But if the stream of her fortunes run low, and that none but Apronmen la[u]nch forth there, then keeps she a politic sempster's shop, or she starches them.[28]

In this fantastic vision of the city, as in *Northward Ho,* every house might be a covert whorehouse, a place where loose women perform versions of respectable femininity in order to conduct their trade. In such a world, the place of prostitution is potentially everywhere.

This fantasy occurs repeatedly in popular pamphlets like Dekker's and in numerous city comedies. As I have suggested, it has an anchor in social reality. As Archer has shown, bawdy houses were widely distributed throughout London, and specific conditions in the city in the late sixteenth century facilitated the spread of prostitution and fostered fears that ordinary women might become involved in it. In the introduction I discussed the nearly fourfold increase in London's population between 1550 and 1600. Much of this increase was due to in-migration from the provinces, and many of those migrants were women. In hard economic times—and the 1590s were just that— many of these women lost or never found jobs in service. They drifted in and out of legitimate employment, in and out of thieving and prostitution,[29] having neither a "fixed" social identity nor a fixed and certain line of work, especially since they were excluded from most forms of labor within the guilds. Clients, by contrast, were plentiful. London had a sex ratio of 113 men to every 100 women.[30] Many of these men were young and unmarried, serving apprenticeships; some were stranger merchants away from their home communities; and some were country gentlemen temporarily in town for term time or some other sort of business. The latter two groups, for example, were the clients for which Doll in *Northward Ho* was angling. As John McMullan has argued, the city at the end of the sixteenth century offered a "structure of illegitimate opportunities,"[31] and sexual disorder represented by the sex trade was a continuing source of concern. The virulence of the plague in 1603 prompted Dekker and others to rail with renewed venom against the disorderly suburbs, and James's proclamation targeting overcrowded tenements simply stirred the pot. The fantasy, then, of a city of whorehouses had a partial basis in reality. Plays about London life highlighted whore plots in part because prostitution in the course of the sixteenth century had taken a new form after the 1546 dissolution of the stews, had spread widely and been nurtured by the very social changes that were making London into a much bigger and more cosmopolitan place. Prostitution was part of London life, and theater practitioners certainly knew it. Theaters on the Bankside and in the northern suburbs, in particular, including Shakespeare's Globe, stood in the middle of well-known brothel districts;[32] the theater manager Philip Henslowe made money from a quartet of Bankside whorehouses; and Edward Alleyn the famous Elizabethan tragic actor also owned brothels.[33]

The omnipresence of bawdy houses in the city drama and their frequent indistinguishability from other kinds of buildings thus speak simultaneously to the changing nature of prostitution in post-Reformation London and to the penetration of commercial exchanges into every corner of life. John Wheeler's 1601 defense of the Merchant Adventurers entitled *A Treatise of Commerce* contains a famous description of a world in which all men "contract, truck, merchandise, and traffic one with another."[34] Wheeler lists all those—children, princes, soldiers, ordinary men and women—who dote upon commerce:

. . . and in a word, all the world choppeth and changeth, runneth and raveth after marts, markets, and merchandising. So that all things come into commerce, and pass into traffice (in a manner) in all times, and in all places: not only that which Nature bringeth forth, as the fruits of the earth, the beasts and living creatures with their spoils, skins, and cases, the metals, minerals, and such like things, but further also, this man maketh merchandise of the works of his own hands, this man of another man's labor, one selleth words, another maketh traffic of the skins and blood of other men; yea there are some found so subtle and cunning merchants that they persuade and induce men to suffer themselves to be bought and sold, and we have seen in our time enow and too many, which have made merchandise of men's souls.[35]

Wheeler progresses from what seems to belong inevitably to the realm of commerce, namely, the riches of the natural world, to what he clearly finds repugnant, a traffic in human bodies and even in their souls. The prostitute goes unmentioned, yet she is among those who "suffer themselves to be bought and sold," not once and for all, but repeatedly, their bodies the merchandise they bring to market. Robert Greene, as I have indicated, named his whore Nan a Traffique. She is the principle of merchandising itself, and in the many London whore plays that pass over the stage after 1598, the ubiquitous prostitute, passing from place to place, taking one guise and then another, figures a market economy that can feel like it knows no boundaries. All men "runneth and raveth after marts, markets, and merchandising." In London city plays, whorehouses are no particular place because they are nearly everywhere: within the walls and without, in Eastcheap and the Bankside, Clerkenwell and St. Katherine's. Potentially, they exist wherever a scrivener, a merchant, or a shopkeeper dwells, his legitimate trade serving as cover for the illegitimate operations of his boarder or his wife. The place of prostitution is sometimes home.

Prostitution, Conversion Plots, and the Urban Gender System

That ordinary dwellings and places of business are often figured in city drama as places of prostitution suggests that whore plots were, among other things, involved in negotiating one of the central social relations of the domestic sphere, that between husbands and wives, as city life was perceived to put new kinds of pressure on that relationship and on gender ideology more generally. As numerous historians have suggested, living in London affected the daily lives of both men and women in numerous ways, heightening and in some ways refiguring anxieties about proper gender roles. Consumption, whether for necessities or luxury items, became, for example, a newly important part of the lives of urban women whether artisan or merchant wives, gentry or aristocratic women.[36] As consumers women were often equated with unregulated desire, including sexual desire.[37] Retail work also grew rapidly for middling sort wives and for unmarried women as the huge surge in London's population at the end of the sixteenth century caused comparable growth in the number of retail shops, inns, taverns, and cookshops within the city,[38] all venues in which women played important roles. Those who sold goods could be suspected of also selling themselves, and the city afforded women numerous opportunities to lead public lives that involved being visible to many people, including strangers.[39] Poorer women came to the city to find work as household servants. As such, they did marketing, accompanied their mistresses on errands, and fetched water from the parish pump or conduit. Wives of shopkeepers not only worked selling goods, but were themselves displayed at shopfronts to draw custom.

Foreign visitors remarked on the freedoms enjoyed by London women who did not seem as strictly kept as the women of Spain and Italy and went about the streets of the city without head coverings, consorting with their gossips and doing their marketing at will.[40] Hugh Alley's *A Caveatt for the Citty of London,* a 1598 series of sketches of London markets, shows many images of London women selling goods or walking freely through the major markets of the city, shopping baskets on their arms.[41] Ian Archer sums up the causes for tension surrounding London women in this way:

Women probably enjoyed more independence in the capital because of the nature of their work, participating at the front of the shop, running an alehouse, buying provisions in the market. But certain demographic peculiarities of the metropolitan scene help to account for the intensity of anxieties about women. High mortality in London meant that many households, no less than 16 percent in Southwark in the 1620s, were headed by women; it also meant that remarriage in the capital was common; no less than 25 percent of the marriages of London tradesmen were to widows, running counter to the recommendations of the moralists that the husband should always be older, and thereby giving women greater leverage within the household. The lack of confinement of women in the capital impressed foreign visitors who commented on their drinking in taverns and engaging in unsupervised sports with members of the opposite sex.[42]

In short, the city as a distinctive kind of social and demographic place could heighten anxieties about women's conduct, chastity, and proper subordination.

The theater's pervasive prostitution plots pick up on such anxieties and give a cultural form for their expression and resolution. The plays repeatedly stage the dangers (and the real pleasures) of women's urban existence, particularly the possibility that in the urban milieu chaste women and whores could swiftly shift places. The many plays that comment on the potentially dangerous practice of placing respectable women at shopfronts to attract customers always, for example, carry a charge of sexual danger. Illicit sex is always a possibility, paving a woman's path into whoredom. In Heywood's *Wise-woman of Hogsdon,* a shopkeeper's daughter, Luce, wishes that her father would not expose her to public view in a shopfront as it violates her modesty.[43] She shows herself a wise girl in this regard, for there are strong semiotic parallels between a chaste woman placed at the door of a shop to attract trade and the equally widely reported practice of positioning whores at the thresholds of brothels for the same purpose. Describing what he saw in the suburbs, Thomas Dekker reports that "the doors of notorious carted bawds like hell-gates stand night and day wide open, with a pair of harlots in taffeta gowns, like two painted posts, garnishing out those doors, being better to the house than a double sign."[44] In London plays, women who keep shops, whether positioned at the door or inside the establishment, are often represented as not so very different from their suburban, taffeta-gowned doubles. Jane Shore, in the London history *Edward IV,* for example, is seduced by the monarch himself while she is on duty in her husband's shop,[45] and in *The Roaring Girl* the gallants who cruise the shops of London are in constant dalliance with the shopkeepers' wives.[46] Most of the time in comic London plays wives do not actually sleep with the gallants who pursue them in their shops, but part of the titillation provided by the genre is the ever-present possibility that they might.

A subset of whore plays, however, makes the threat a reality. They highlight the conversion of chaste women into whores and vice versa. In these plays, narratives in which a possible fall is averted give way to the vertiginous pleasures of watching a seemingly absolute alteration in a woman's sexual status. Either a chaste woman gives in to a life of debauchery or an unchaste woman eschews whoredom for a newly found probity. In the last several years critics have drawn attention to plays, mostly set in the Mediterranean, in which European heroes, nearly always male heroes, "turn Turk," cast off their respectable English and Christian identities and become infidels, renegadoes, lost both to Christianity and to their home countries.[47] The domestic counterpart to such narratives, I would argue, is provided by prostitute plays in which women undergo comparable transformations of identity, particularly as their position in the city is imagined to allow easy passage across the supposedly unbridgeable gap separating chaste wives and maids from unchaste whores. To some extent, London is a woman's foreign land, the place where utter transformations are possible. However, while men's conversions in Turk plays often result in tragedy, as in *Christian Turned Turk* where the converted English pirate, John Ward, takes his own life, women's conversions in city drama are largely shaped by comic conventions, and as I will argue below, this fact works over time to query the conceptual categories of prescriptive literature and to offer imaginative alternatives that stressed the fluid, contingent, and commercially embedded nature of women's urban lives.

A recurring feature of London plays involves women who come to the city from the country, the encounter with urbanity being what precipitates a crisis in identity, much as arriving in Tunis or Malta can precipitate a crisis for the male protagonist of the adventure genre. In narratives about the upscale brothel, Hollands Leaguer, for example, the brothel mistress, given the richly miscegenated name Britannica Hollandia, is said to have begun life as the daughter of a virtuous country gentleman of middling stature. At an early age she begged her indulgent parents to let her go to London. Unwisely complying, they placed her in an "honest Magnifico's service" in a city described as "a Burse of resort where men and their minds were continually trucking for new commodities."[48] The rest of her story is predictable. She married a good man, but growing impudent was seduced by one described as a "Puritane Jesuit" who introduced her to a life of sin from which she never swerved. Soon "Her eares had heard al languages, her purse had received all Coynes."[49] In short, her loss of chastity is described in terms that equate vagina and coinpurse and make the ear the conduit for foreignness to enter her body. From a chaste country maid Britannica Hollandia has been transformed into an oxymoron, an alien native, and a mistress of a brothel.

On stage the transformation of country maiden into city whore could be materially registered by the manipulation of clothing, in particular, to emphasize the utter transformations of the female self under the influence of urban culture.[50] In Middleton's *Michaelmas Term*, for example, a country girl is quickly taught that "Virginity is no city trade;/ You're out o'th' freedom when you're a maid" (I.ii.45–46). Given no name except the generic one of "Country Wench," this young woman is brought to London by a pander, Dick Hellgill. As always, Middleton delights in crafting delicious names for his urban cast of characters, and Country Wench is not only a generic appellation but a sexy one. It is a constant punning reminder that in the city this woman still pursues "cuntry matters," but of a new sort. Hellgill works for Lethe, a villainous and newly knighted Scotsman who has forgotten his simple country background (he was the son of a toothdrawer!) and aspires to marry the daughter of Quomodo, a wealthy London woolen draper. Lethe, however, wants a little action on the side, and so he sends Hellgill to the country to fetch him a woman Hellgill subsequently describes as "Young, beautiful, and plump—a delicate piece of sin" (II.i.151). In I.ii, this girl arrives in London with Hellgill who attempts to persuade her of the benefits of turning whore. He promotes this option as a form of advancement over country life, one that will strip away her "servile habiliments" (I.ii.6) and introduce her to a world of "wires and tires, bents and bums, felts and falls" (15). In her new attire she can "deceive the world that gentlewomen indeed shall not be known from others" (16–17), the others presumably being women of lower rank and women of questionable virtue. The intricacies of fashionable dress elide distinctions between the chaste and the unchaste, common women and merchant wives or gentry ladies. In this regard, the city woman who undergoes a sexual "conversion," embodied in a sartorial conversion, is about as unreadable as the Jewish conversos discussed by James Shapiro whose "true" religion remained an open question in the Christian communities in which they lived.[51] In the period, religious conversion—whether Catholic to Protestant, Jew to Christian, Christian to Turk—invited suspicion regarding its permanence and authenticity and made identity illegible and uncertain.[52] In London comedies, a similar confusion surrounds the identity of a figure such as the sartorially resplendent Country Wench. Such confusion, I am suggesting, works over time to undermine definitions of female worth based solely on a woman's sexual status or her clear position on one side or other of the wife-whore, maid-whore binary.

For the Country Wench, the actual moment of her conversion comes when Hellgill lays before her a satin gown. Rich clothing both solicits her to leave a former identity behind and is the means of effecting her passage into another social milieu. In an aside, Hellgill comments: "So, farewell wholesome weeds where treasure pants,/ And welcome silks where lies disease and wants" (I.ii.53–54), acknowledging the link between a whore's rich dress and her eventual infection with sexual disease and slide into poverty. But with the Country Wench he is less forthright, saying only: "Come, wench, now flow thy fortunes in to bless thee./ I'll bring thee where thou shalt be taught to dress thee" (55–56). As it turns out, the Country Wench does not end up in the spittle house, but as the wife of Lethe, one of the play's gentlemen. The moralizing story of the slide into abjection is thus comically rewritten to make Country Wench's transformation into a whore the means to her eventual good fortune in the marriage mart. In the process a fallen woman is recast as a smart entrepreneur.

The actual scene, III.i., in which the audience observes the Country Wench transformed into a whore is placed in the very center of the play, underscoring its importance. In it, Country Wench is accompanied by a tailor and a and a tirewoman, the agents of her sartorial make-over. The stage directions read: *"Enter* LETHE'*s* Pander, HELLGILL, *the* COUNTRY WENCH *coming in with a new-fashion gown, dressed gentlewoman-like; the* Tailor *points it and* [Mistress COMINGS,] *a* Tirewoman *busy about her head.*" Predictably, the scene is full of sexual innuendo and lewd jokes. Mistress Comings suggests, for example, that the Country Wench adopt a hair style "still like a mock-face behind. 'Tis such an Italian world, many men know not before from behind" (III.i.18–20), alluding knowingly to the supposedly Italian vice of anal intercourse.[53] The Country Wench enters fully into the banter and seems as transformed in manner as in appearance. When Hellgill ribs her about her country origins she roundly replies: "Out, you saucy, pestiferous pander! I scorn that, i'faith," to which he rejoins "Excellent, already the true phrase and style of a strumpet" (III.i.28–31). The passage from country to city has in this case meant the conversion of a maid into a harlot, a simply dressed woman into a fashion plate complete with satin gown, elaborate hair style, and employees hired to maintain her new facade. She is, literally, unrecognizable; the city has made her what she was not. For proof, Middleton has the Country Wench take her own disguised father for a servant, and the father does not recognize his daughter.[54]

Here as in other London comedies the city seems capable of making almost alchemical changes in women's social and sexual status, partly by their entrance into a thoroughly commercial world with its structures of illicit opportunity. *Michaelmas Term* not only foregrounds the spectacle of the Country Wench's transformation, but eventually makes her the spokesperson for a cynical, but not inaccurate, reading of the commercial logic governing the behavior of most of the play's main London characters. Defending her behavior, she asks:

Do not all trades live by their ware and yet called honest livers? Do they not thrive best when they utter most and make it away by the great? Is not wholesale the chiefest merchandise? Do you think some merchants could keep their wives so brave but for their wholesale? You're foully deceived, an you think so. (IV.ii.11–16)

It is hard to say whether the wicked pun on wholesale and holesale does more to discredit merchants or to elevate the whore's trade, here explicitly rendered as a selling of holes, a product much sought after and yet eerily empty, the "no thing" of other Renaissance puns.[55] Moreover, the Country Wench here makes plain that her trade is one that unites the whore and the merchant wife who with her husband's consent adds to the family income by her own acts of (w)holesaling.

With high-spirited irony, Middleton's plot undermines the sanctity of marriage and blurs the line separating prostitutes and honest women. Eventually, Lethe, despite his pretentions to win Quomodo's daughter, is forced by the courts to marry the Country Wench, and she is thus legally, if not morally, transported back across the bar into respectability. There is, however, no corresponding transformation in her dress, no scene in which she eschews her satin garments and returns to the country homespun that was the original sign of female innocence. In the play's final scene, V.iii, the Country Wench is a wife in whore's attire, but she assumed that attire precisely so she could pass as a respectable lady. Clothing constructs social identity, and in the process can erase a subject's social origins and obscure her sexual status. The fluidity of female identity in the urban milieu, though it produces ironic outcomes, is the very premise on which Middleton's comic plots hinge—a fact, not an outrage.

The play is as concerned, therefore, with the possible transformation of city wives as of country maids. Throughout the action, Quomodo's respectable wife, Thomasine, has had her eye on the country gentleman, Easy, whose land her husband is trying treacherously to acquire. When Quomodo pretends to be dead, Thomasine promptly marries Easy (s.d. before V.i.14–15), thus rendering ridiculous Quomodo's self-satisfied prattling about how his wife is so modest and loyal that she will mourn him for many a long month (V.i.64–80). City wives do not mourn anyone long; they choose a new husband and move on. In the end the same court that makes Lethe marry his Country Wench gives Thomasine back to Quomodo. But there is no longer any possibility of his believing that she is the kind of wife who defines herself through marriage solely to him. She returns to Quomodo after having slept, we assume, with her new "husband," Easy. By pretending to be dead, Quomodo in effect gave his wife the opportunity to cuckold him without knowingly committing adultery. The play leaves the audience with the spectacle of a Country Wench who was transformed into a whore being transformed into a wife; while a wife, unwittingly transformed into an adultress, is reconverted to her former status as wife, though now as somewhat shopworn goods. This anti-idealizing play certainly takes the bloom off marriage, and it seems to delight in underscoring the different passages a city woman can make across the line separating the chaste from the unchaste, the wife from the whore, the once-married from the twice-married. In this play there is no formal whorehouse, just the unspecified lodgings where the Country Wench sets herself up to meet Lethe and his friends and Quomodo's house where Thomasine installs Easy in her husband's stead. Illicit sexuality needs no designated brothel; as I've argued, in these urban stories it can occur in common and unremarkable places, a lodging house or a home, wherever wives and maids embrace the chance for illicit sex.

The fantasy of conversion, of course, can move in the other direction. If *Michaelmas Term* makes maids and wives into whores, in Dekker's *The Honest Whore* a prostitute crosses over to respectability but with unsettling results. In her first stage appearance Bellafront, the whore, sits at a dressing table surrounded by the cosmetics, brushes, and articles of clothing that allow her to make herself, with the market's help, into an object of desire. She has a servant, a bawd, and regular clients whom she milks for money. But after she reforms and is married to the man who first slept with her, her life becomes hellish. A rake and a gambler, Matheo is also abusive. In a climactic scene he strips off his wife's one remaining satin dress, the last vestiges of her life as a whore, so he can sell it to buy clothes and rapiers for himself (*Part II.* 3.2.). He also urges his wife to return to her former trade to underwrite his desire for a gentleman's lifestyle.

The scene strongly recalls the stories of Patient Griselda whom Bellafront resembles.[56] When Griselda is first brought to the court of the Duke who marries her, her humble clothes are taken from her, and she is attired in rich robes. When the Duke later sends her away, she is made to resume her cast-off clothing. In *The Honest Whore*, being stripped to her petticoat is, for Bellafront, the equivalent of Griselda's humiliation. Ironically, it associates the conversion from whore to wife with a devastating loss of power. As a virtuous wife who refuses to do any more "(w)holesaling" to support her husband's desired lifestyle, Bellafront nearly starves. The reformed prostitute has put herself so outside the commercial logic of the city that she can only be dramatized as a kind of secular saint, an exception to the culture's common sense. The overt moral of Dekker's plays—that one should leave a life of sin and embrace virtue—is thus powerfully undercut by the terrible things that happen to a woman who does just that. Intentionally or not,

The Honest Whore suggests that in the urban context, a woman who refuses to blur the line between the chaste and the unchaste, the wife and the whore, is a throwback to another time and place, a holy fool, or maybe just a fool.

In the majority of conversion plots, as I have already hinted, the woman's transformation is seldom as absolute or permanent as in *The Honest Whore*. In a number of prostitution plays the movement from chastity to unchastity, from wife to adultress, from maid to whore can happen several times over rather than once and for all. Working from the evidence of social history, rather than as I do from an archive of plays, Faramerz Dabhoiwala argues that historians have taken a too polarized view of sexual behavior in early modern London, and that in actuality there was a fluid spectrum of sexually immoral acts in which a range of women engaged, not simply a subgroup of professional prostitutes. "Whore," he reminds us, was the common term for any unchaste woman;[57] and the research of Laura Gowing suggests with what frequency that term was bandied about by women themselves as well as by men.[58] Gowing argues that many women defamed by being called "whore" were probably not taking money from a man in exchange for sex, but they might be committing adultery or flaunting themselves in public in a way offensive to their neighbors. Moreover, as Dabhoiwala shows, when women did take some form of payment for sex, that did not make them professional or lifelong prostitutes. It may have represented an economically motivated form of casual employment or a one-off opportunity. As with whores, bawdy houses were similarly hard to segment off from homes or legitimate places of business. An illicit rendezvous could happen in "a private home or a tavern or a brothel, of greater or lesser sophistication and expense."[59] The city, with its ever-growing number of places to eat and lodge, made illicit opportunity multivalent. Moreover, the standard practice of having shops in the front rooms of the same houses where the shopkeepers lived further confused and imbricated the realms of commerce and of domestic life.[60] For a long time feminist critics like myself have focused attention on the distinction among maids, wives, widows, and whores so common in the prescriptive literature. But we need to remember that these categories were just that— prescriptive injunctions that did not necessarily fully describe women's social experience, perhaps especially in urban London. City prostitute drama revels in putting pressure on the absolute or fixed nature of these distinctions.

Nowhere is this more true than in the final "conversion" play I want to discuss, Middleton's *A Chaste Maid in Cheapside*. It writes large the difficulty of properly categorizing urban women's sexual status or of

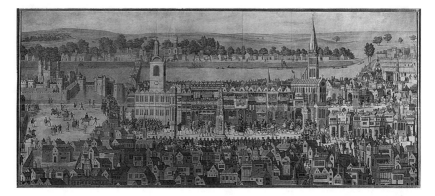

Figure 9a. Eve-of-coronation procession of Edward VI by S. Grimm. The image
includes Goldsmith's Row in Cheapside. By permission of The Society of
Antiquaries of London.

making irrevocable conversions from one state to another. It is no
happenstance that the setting for this work should be the very heart of
one of London's oldest centers of commerce, Cheapside. Stretching
from the Pissing Conduit on the west near St. Paul's to the Great Conduit to the east, Cheapside was in the Tudor-Stuart period one of the
great thoroughfares and commercial centers of London. It formed part
of the ceremonial route used by monarchs in their inaugural proces-
sions and by Lord Mayors in the annual Lord Mayor's day pageants[61]
(see Figure 9a). In 1599 Thomas Platter wrote: "In one very long street
called Cheapside dwell almost only goldsmiths and moneychangers on
either hand so that inexpressibly great treasure and vast amount of
money may be seen here."[62] At the very center of Cheapside between
Cheap Cross to the west and Bread Street to the east was a section
known as Goldsmiths Row, an area famous for the beauty and elegance
of its buildings (Figure 9b). Stow recounts:

Next to be noted, the most beautiful frame of fayre houses and shoppes, that
bee within the Walles of London, or elsewhere in England, commonly called
Goldsmithes Rowe, betwixt Bredstreet end and the Crosse in Cheape, but is
within this Bredstreete warde, the same was builded by *Thomas Wood* Goldsmith,
one of the shiriffes of London, in the yeare 1491. It contayneth in number
tenne fayre dwelling houses, and fourteene shoppes, all in one frame, uni-
formely builded foure stories high, bewtified towards the street with the
Goldsmithes armes and the likenes of woodmen, in memory of his name,
riding on monstrous beasts, all which is cast in lead, richly painted over and
gilt, these he gave to the Goldsmithes with stockes of money to be lent to yong
men, having those shops, etc. This saide Front was againe new painted and
guilt over in the yeare 1594.[63]

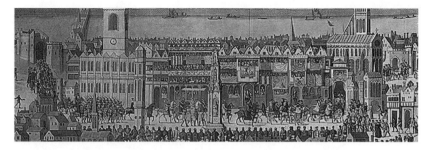

Figure 9b. Detail, showing Goldsmith's Row in Cheapside. By permission of The Society of Antiquaries of London.

This notoriously beautiful and wealthy commercial stretch, refurbished in 1594, centers the action in Middleton's 1613 play, the "chaste maid" of the title being the daughter of a goldsmith named Yellowhammer who has a shop in Goldsmiths Row. The choice of location can hardly be accidental. It invites the audience to locate the play's multiple plots of sex and marriage in what everyone would recognize as a notable center of trade, not far north of the river, squarely between the mighty edifice of St. Paul's to the west and the Royal Exchange just a bit to the east.

By the second decade of the seventeenth century Goldsmiths Row was not quite what it had been in earlier days. In 1619 the Row became the subject of a renovation campaign that was to last for at least twenty-five years. As Paul Griffiths has detailed, in 1619 the Goldsmiths Company spoke before the Court of Aldermen of the need to push out the "mean" traders and stranger merchants diluting the traditional community of goldsmiths who had long inhabited the Row, some of whom were now letting shops in the fashionable West End, instead. The perceived decay of Goldsmiths Row partly signaled the Company's loss of control over the sale of jewels, gold and silver plate within the city due to competition from strangers and the illegal sale of high-priced goods by criminals; it was also part of an almost inexorable drift of fashionable shops to the West End. James and Charles both made the decline of the Row a matter of personal interest and called repeatedly for the return of guild members from the West End to their traditional shops in Cheapside. Most declined, claiming that rents on the Row were too high, and clearly seeing that many of their preferred clients might now have West End addresses.[64]

A Chaste Maid in Cheapside (1613) carries with it the faint whiff of decay, though it is not so concerned with the flight of goldsmiths from the Row as with the astonishing degree to which the commercial values of this center of commerce have percolated through the domestic realm, leading to an impossible confusion of the terms through which both men and women are defined within the traditional gender system.[65] There *is* a designated whore in this play, known simply as the Welsh Gentlewoman, a punk formerly employed by Sir Walter Whorehound who now brings her up to London in order to marry her off, his own marriage to the Chaste Maid of Cheapside, Moll Yellowhammer, being in prospect. This scenario ironically reverses the pattern with which Middleton had experimented in *Michaelmas Term* in which a country wench is inducted into the prostitution trade upon her arrival in London. Here, London also effects an alchemical transformation in a country girl: this time from whore to wife. Whorehound brings the Welsh woman to Cheapside, which he calls the "heart of the city of London" (I.i.92–93), in order to marry her to Tim Yellowhammer, sister of Moll, his own bride. As Whorehound says to the Welsh gentlewoman, "I bring thee up to turn thee into gold, wench, and make thy fortune shine like your bright trade" (I.i.99–100). If he can contrive for her to marry Tim, she will inherit part of Yellowhammer's estate, and he, presumably, the rest. From whore and whoremaster, they will be converted into sister and brother-in-law. But Whorehound's statement does not separate the Welsh woman's marriage from her former trade; rather, he presents it is the perfect culmination of that trade. Tim is simply the most lucrative of all her clients, and one lent permanence through marriage.

This plan only works, of course, because the Yellowhammers are willing to use their children on the marriage market to acquire Whorehound's wealth and the cultural cachet that Mrs. Yellowhammer, in particular, craves. She wants an alliance with a knight and so is quite willing to barter away both her unwilling son and unwilling daughter to Whorehound and his "niece." In the Yellowhammers the spirits of pimp and bawd shine brightly forth. Mr. Yellowhammer does not bat an eye when he learns his daughter is going to marry a whoremaster, being one himself. As he confesses, "I have kept a whore myself, and had a bastard" (IV.i.272); "The knight is rich, he shall be my son-in-law" (IV.i.277). So much for the family values of Cheapside.

The Yellowhammer family is only one of several in the play in which the commercial and the sexual have become so intertwined that fathers and pimps, wives, whores, and bawds are not easily separated. What everyone remembers about *Chaste Maid* is the Allwit family. Their exact address is not given, but they live within easy distance of the

Yellowhammers because there are several scenes in which members of one household are quickly summoned to the other. For the Allwits, the household *is* the place of prostitution. There Mrs. Allwit sells her sexual favors to a "benefactor," Whorehound, who impregnates her repeatedly. In exchange for sex, he supports Mrs. Allwit, her husband, and all their illegitimate children. Mr. Allwit is entirely satisfied with this arrangement because it relieves him of having to work for his living or even to perform sexual labor. One might say that Mrs. Allwit simply engages in an unusual form of household production. Rather than producing a petty commodity like lace, she produces sexual pleasure and children for Sir Walter, using her "hole" rather than her needle as her instrument of labor. For that, she garners all the wealth that has maintained her household for ten profitable years (I.ii.16). No particular scandal surrounds her actions. The "fall" from wife to whore is not represented as a tragedy or even a sin; it is what is expected in a world in which the strong pull of gold is the lodestone governing everyone's actions.

Chaste Maid in Cheapside eschews obvious moralizing.[66] Within the play, the only character seriously punished is Sir Walter Whorehound, who has the audacity to repent of his sinful ways. Ironically, he alone loses everything: Welsh mistress, prospective bride, his land. He ends up in debtors' prison. The finality of the fate assigned him—in effect a social death—contrasts sharply with the way the unrepentant characters fluidly refashion themselves and escape punishment. Improvising, they form alternative social structures and every sort of idiosyncratic, nonnormative family. The Allwits, having lost their benefactor, lovingly gather up their favorite possessions, including a velvet close stool, and set off to open a high-class brothel on the fashionable Strand. Like the smarter goldsmiths, they are following the money to the West End. In another plot, an infertile rich couple (the Kixes) take into their home a fertile poor couple (the Touchwood Seniors), in effect bartering their wealth for Touchwood's sperm. And while Moll Yellowhammer gets to marry the man she loves and not Whorehound, Tim is not so lucky. Married to the Welsh Gentlewoman before anyone discovers her true identity, he makes the best of a bad situation, arguing that "*Uxor non est meretrix*" (V.iv.114) ("A wife is not a whore."). Of course, the lesson of the play seems to be just the opposite. Wives can quite easily be prostitutes. Tim is a boob in love with useless Latin learning; Cheapside demands the vernacular and the street smarts that come with it. Without them, the university man is likely to find that "*Meretrix est uxor*." Yet Middleton, more than most of his contemporaries, refuses the usual alibi of gender whereby women alone bear the blame for the excesses and dangers of a changing economic order. In *Chaste Maid*, the men are as implicated as the women in the sex trade, pandering daughters and wives, making themselves fawning figures like Allwit, who wishes only to avoid displeasing the "benefactor," however unpleasant he may be.

Middleton seems to have decided that the best way to reveal the underlying logic of a commercial city was to treat its blurring of gender norms not as scandal, but as fact. *Chaste Maid in Cheapside* pushes the amoral logic of the market deep into the households of London's famous commercial district, making Cheapside households the site where a wife's "hole" is the chief commodity her husband sells and where children are simply bargaining chips on the way to greater wealth or new forms of cultural capital. In such an environment, the four prescriptive categories supposedly dividing one woman from another — the categories of maid, wife, widow, and whore — become unstable and fungible as the pursuit of gold leads to a whore's conversion into a wife and a wife's conversion into a whore. If the pervasive anxiety of the adventure drama is that a man will "turn Turk," the comparable fantasy of London comedies is that the wife or chaste maid will "turn whore." The city drama restaged variants of this fantasy in ingenious and remarkably obsessive ways. The reasons are multiple, but they have to do, as I have argued, with the growing commercialization of London life and the material conditions that made gender relations in the city a special source of concern. And yet, city drama does not so much moralize the behavior of urban women as turns it into the stuff of comedy. Watching these prostitution plays, the audience sees prescriptions flouted and sexual transgressions normalized by plots in which men marry whores and live to praise the fact and in which women who make calculated decisions about the value of turning tricks still get a husband in the end. If Turk plays imagine the fragmentation of male identity under the pressure of foreign encounters, London comedies most often represent urban women's "conversions" as sometimes reversible, often economically rational, and frequently quite unremarkable. In so doing they lay down discursive templates for a new age and challenge the rigidities of prescriptive literature with the high-spirited flexibilities of the comic stage.

In what follows, I am going to carry this argument further and look at what happens when the whore, on the home ground of London, is imagined either as embodying the alien cultures that Turk plays locate far beyond England's shores or as being the entry point through which alien elements infiltrate the city. In short, I am going to look at how prostitutes allow the drama to tell particular kinds of stories about a multinational city space. In many whore plays there are strong discursive and material connections between prostitutes and strangers, bawdy houses and dangerous foreign matter. Brothels and the whores who inhabit them are thus figured as sites of vulnerability through which strangers and dangerous alien ways find their way into the city. And yet, in many plays, whores are also presented as the embodiments of a perversely attractive cosmopolitanism and of an economic entrepreneurship attuned to the realities of a multinational city.

The Prostitute and the Cosmopolitan Perverse

Recall, for an instant, the sophisticated architecture of hair fashioned for the Country Wench in *Michaelmas Term*. Arranged to resemble a face at the back of the head, this hairdo invited Mistress Comings to remark on the "Italian world" (III.i.19) in which sexual congress could occur from the back as well as the front. Becoming a whore seems to imply being part of these "Italian" practices, either the site where they are acted out or the agent of their inculcation. In *Chaste Maid* the play's only "official" whore is Welsh, her foreignness most marked when she speaks Welsh, which her ridiculous suitor, Tim Yellowhammer, mistakes for Hebrew. Because he has painfully acquired a little Latin, he imagines that he and the Welsh woman are destined to be famous for their learning.

By my faith she's a good scholar, I see that already;
She has the tongues plain, I hold my life she has travelled;
What will folks say? There goes the learned couple;
Faith if the truth were known, she has proceeded. (IV.i.129–32)

Of course, Tim has everything wrong. His is a false cosmopolitanism that leaves him peculiarly vulnerable to deception, including self-deception. He is wooing a cast-off whore, not a lady; the only traveling she has done is to come to London to find a husband; and her Hebrew is in reality her native Welsh tongue. Tim detects none of this. Middleton, however, is playing slyly on the learning and sophistication associated with the high-class Italian courtesan. If Tim had fallen into the hands of such a woman, he might at least be acquiring a certain sophistication with his bride. But his whore is a Welsh one, connected by Walter Whorehound with country assets like the phantasmatic mountains and cattle he promises for her dowry. Her one accomplishment, besides her sexual experience, is her bilinguality, which allows her to pass for English and so to deceive her suitor (I.i.95–99). In marrying her, Tim is bringing a stranger into the heart of the Yellowhammer's Cheapside establishment (remember the Goldsmith Company's anxieties about mean and foreign traders entering Goldsmiths Row) without necessarily acquiring much in return: neither a dowry nor a learned lady.

There are many other London dramas in which whores and whorehouses are connected with strangers or alien matter, though the forms that connection takes are varied. Sometimes the whores themselves are foreign. In Edward Sharpham's *The Fleire* (1607), two newly impoverished Italian women come to London and set up shop as whores in order to repair the family fortunes. They vow: "strangelye mongst strangers let us hold our state, and let our Servants seldome Knowe, how familiar with our friendes wee bee, and though Englands wealth doe now adorne us; lets keepe the fashion still of Florence."[67] Holding the fashion of Florence here seems to imply both hanging onto an identity in a strange place and also carving out a market niche for their trade. What they seek is an upscale clientele and a reputation for selectivity. As part of this strategy, they insist on being called courtesans, not whores, for "your whore is for every rascall but your Curtizan is for your Courtier" (D2v). Eventually, the women find husbands among their clientele and make the passage back to respectability, but in the meantime they have paid the bills by trading on their foreign allure.

The idea that some prostitutes had foreign origins has historical grounding. Stow, giving an account of the brothels on the Bankside, mentioned that some of them were "farmed by Froes of Flaunders,"[68] and there was a long tradition of connecting women from the Low Countries with both the common brothels of the Bankside and more upscale establishments.[69] This tradition is what lies behind the name, Britannica Hollandia, given to the mistress of the toney brothel, Hollands Leaguer. In 1546 when Henry VIII closed the Bankside establishments, the language of his proclamation indicates that some of the brothel owners there were strangers. It ordered both the brothel keepers and the whores to "depart . . . incontinently to their natural countries with their bag and baggage."[70]

While whores were often themselves assumed to be strangers, even more common was the idea that whores *served* strangers. There is no more ubiquitous trope in London drama than that of the whore who sells herself to men of all nations. This is such a cliché, in fact, that when in *Northward Ho* a young serving boy wishes to protest that he is not a bawd to his master's wife, he says:

> . . . my breath does not stinke, I smell not of Garlick or *Aqua-vitae*. I use not to bee drunk with Sack and Sugar: I swear not God dam me, if I know where the party is, when 'tis a lye and I doe know: I was never Carted (but in harvest) never whipt but at Schoole: never had the Grincoms: never sold one Maidenhead ten severall times, first to an Englishman, then to a Welshman, then to a Dutchman, then to a pockie Frenchman, I hope Sir I am no Bawd then. (I.iii.7–14)

By the boy's account, one of the true marks of a London bawd is that she resells her whore's maidenhead to men of many nations, successively. In

Robert Greene's *A Disputation Between a Hee Conny-catcher, and a Shee Conny-catcher,* Nan a Traffique tells of a mother who prostituted her daughter to "Dutch and French, Italian, and Spaniard, as well as English" (C4) until her daughter got pregnant, temporarily putting an end to the game. The trope of a multinational client list is susceptible to endless variation. In *The Honest Whore, Part I* Hippolito, trying to convert Bellafront to virtue, says that as a whore she will "let a Jewe get you with christian:/ Be he a Moore, a Tartar, tho his face/ Looke uglier then a dead mans scull,/ Could the devil put on a humane shape,/ If his purse shake out crownes, up then he gets,/ Whores will be rid to hell with golden bits" (II.i.338–43). Here it is not just European nationals who are the imagined clients but a much more varied field of exotic difference including Jews, Moors, and even the devil himself.[71] The whore is the gateway for them all to enter the city where she plies her trade. Through this trope the multinational nature of the city is implicitly attributed to the whores who solicit strangers as clients, while those strangers are demeaningly represented as indistinguishable dupes of the whore's greed.

In post-1600 London, strangers were in fact an important source of business for the city's prostitutes. As Ian Archer and Paul Griffiths have shown, there is ample evidence that staffs of embassies and members of the stranger merchant community formed part of the clientele of many of London's better bawdy houses, some of which specialized in providing services for one national community or other, such as the Steelyard merchants.[72] Part of the difficulty of successfully prosecuting whores, brothelers, and clients in such places lay in the fact that many patrons of the better establishments were wellconnected and socially prominent. They included not just important members of the international merchant community but also courtiers, Inns of Court gentlemen, and gentry from the country.[73] The Royal Exchange, gathering place for international merchants, was one of the regular sites where pimps solicited strangers to come with them to particular brothels. Ian Archer has found in the Bridewell records, for example, one Melcher Pelse "a broker whoe is every day upon thexchange . . . a notable bawde and doeth bringe strangers iiij at ones to lewde wemen."[74] Bringing four men at once implies that Pelse was taking them to a fairly well-established and well-stocked bawdy house, perhaps one of those specializing in foreign clients. But downmarket whores could also serve strangers. The Bankside brothels had always served travelers arriving from the Continent. Whitefriars, a big brothel area in the west of the city, had a large population of migrant mariners, as did the dockland district around St. Katharine's to the east.[75]

Serving a stranger clientele, English whores were sometimes imagined to themselves be contaminated with foreignness, though that suggestion could take a number of forms. Their clothing, for example, is often described as foreign. Stephen Gosson's *Pleasant Quippes for Upstart Newfangled Gentlewomen* rants against "the Fantastical Forreigne Toyes, daylie used in Women's Apparell."[76] The speaker wonders why fashions from strange countries so delight English heads (p. 5), and as a warning he speaks of the allure of "Holland smockes so white as snow,/ and gorgets brave with brave work wrought" (p. 7). Drawn in by these gorgeous foreign linens, young men learn to shun them only after discovering that the smocks have hidden a whore's diseases and that they themselves have caught both "poxe and pyles" (p. 7). In this tract, the dangerous whores are not necessarily foreign, but their clothes are. Similarly, in *Westward Ho* when Birdlime, a bawd, wants to seduce a merchant's wife into becoming the mistress of an Italian earl, she offers her first a velvet gown, appropriately carried on stage by a tailor. Later, when this same Birdlime is stoking the old Earl's desire for the merchant's wife, she says of her: "youl find the sweetest, sweetest bedfellow of her. Oh! She looks so sugredly, so simpringly, so gingerly, so amarously, so amiably. Such a redde lippe, such a White foreheade, such a blacke eie, such a full cheeke, and such a goodly little nose, nowe shees in that French gowne, Scotch fals, Scotch bum, and Italian head-tire you sent her, and is such an intycing shee-witch, carrying the charmes of your Jewels about her! Oh!" (II.ii.31–38). The city wife, about to embark on a life of sin, is here described as a sartorial United Nations, foreign fashion thoroughly hybridizing her body. Such fashions are both the sign of her fall—writing it on the body—and also the means of seducing her client, the old Earl. Such representations of the sartorial hybridity of whores draw both on longstanding attacks on luxury and emergent discourses of national purity.[77] The foreign fashions and rich clothing adopted by the prostitute suggest both that luxury and lechery are near kin and that the English body politic has been infected with something both foreign and immoral. At the same time, by acknowledging that foreign fashion *is* attractive, such texts register and to some extent promote the appeal of a transnational sartorial and sexual sophistication.

The most xenophobic aspect of whore discourse frequently involves the charge that the whore brings foreign diseases, especially the pox, into the body politic. In Greene's *A Disputation Betweene a Hee Conny-catcher, and a Shee Conny-catcher*, the inimitable Nan a Traffique reports that some say the pox came from Naples, Spain, or France, but it has now become so rooted in England that it should be called "Morbus Anglicus" not "Morbus Gallicus."[78] Prostitution has converted a foreign disease into a domestic one, bearing foreign infection into the body politic. Others see the process working slightly differently, changing

Englishmen into foreigners. As the author of an early modern satire puts it, an Englishman is "Frenchifide" by catching the "Gallicus morbus" in such dangerous brothel districts as Picthatch or Turnboll Street.[79] An Englishman Frenchified in this way is hardly an attractive figure. Just as prostitution can convert chaste wives and maids into their supposed antithesis, it can convert foreign diseases into English ones and make infected Englishmen no better than Frenchmen. Some of the vilest denunciations of whores emerge when the sodden body of the diseased prostitute becomes discursively linked to plague, infection, and waste.[80] In all the moralizing accounts of a whore's life, the inevitable end is disease and poverty, the taffeta days replaced by incarceration, carting, or starvation. In the rant against the prostitute as source of bodily infection, she is castigated as worse than a "common Shore, or Jakes," a "sinke of sinne," "a mire."[81] The body of the whore, conceived as a meeting place for all the world's filth, becomes in such discourses the abjected image of perilous miscegenation.

Plays with foreign courtesans or that stress an English whore's contacts with strangers almost always raise the issue of how Londoners do/should/ could interact with strangers or with alien practices. They offer a range of responses. Many of these dramas suggest that mingling with strangers is simply an economic necessity. They promote, one could say, the inevitability of a certain kind of internationalism. Others go further, suggesting that contact with alien knowledges and customs is a positive good, a way to acquire sophistication and overcome uncivil or rude ways. A few condemn such intermingling as a source of contamination. This is true of *The Honest Whore*, which melodramatically vilifies the whore as a polluted meeting place for many men and many nations. When he tries to reform Bellafront, Hippolyto describes the horror of her body as a "common shoare, that still receives/ All the townes filth" (II.i.325–26) and underscores both the destruction she has brought to her clients and her own inevitable decline in the clutches of "diseases" that will have "suckt her marrow" (II.i.382).

In *Northward Ho*, however, Doll, the whore who shifts her place of business so cleverly and so often, is not destroyed by her contact with foreignness. In fact, she is enriched by it, and she comes to embody a wily English commercial cosmopolitanism. When Doll first imagines setting up shop in Charing-crosse, it is partly with a view to Dutch clients: "if some Dutch-man would come from the States! oh! These Flemmings pay soundly for what they take" (I.ii.58–60). Installed in her new establishment, she describes her client list to her false father and her servants: "I have a Clothiers Factor or two; a Grocer that would faine Pepper me, a Welsh Captaine that laies hard seege, a Dutch Marchant, that would spend al that he's able to make ith' low countries, but to take measure of my Holland sheetes when I lye in 'em: I heare trampling: 'tis my Flemish Hoy" (II.i.55–59). Her clients are of mixed national origin—English, Welsh, and Dutch—but, as befits her aspirations to make money, they are all more well-off than her former client, Phillip, the poet's son, dragged off to the Counter for debt.

Doll's encounters with these "suitors" are thoroughly mercenary. When the Dutchman Hans van Belch comes in, he enters dispensing coins to Doll's servants and bragging about his big ship that has just arrived at the Wapping docks and of his father's house and cattle in Ausburgh. Because of business regarding this ship, van Belch is in a rush and pays Doll for twelve hours though only briefly in her company. He is given a thick Dutch stage accent predictably used, as in *Englishmen for My Money*, to garner laughs as when he proclaims his father "de groetest fooker in all Ausbourgh" (II.i.98), a position that contrary to English assumptions means alderman, not fornicator. Interestingly, Doll can mimic his speech. Her first words to him are: "Ick vare well God danke you: Nay Ime an apt scholler and can take" (II.i.64–65). Her attractiveness to van Belch seems partly to rest on her eagerness to learn his language. She is not herself a Dutch frow, but she can talk like one, and she has her Holland sheets. Throughout the scene, Doll understands van Belch though her entourage seems mystified. At one point she even corrects Hornet, posing as her father, who has misunderstood part of van Belch's speech. Her cosmopolitan openness to learning new languages extends to the Welshman, Captain Jynkins, as well. When he enters, she says: "Pree thee good Captaine Jynkins, teach mee to speak some welch, mee thinkes a Welchmans tongue is the neatest tongue!" (II.i.200–201). After he conducts a little Welsh lesson on stage, and she proves an apt pupil, Jynkins promises to buy Doll a coach and two white mares so that she can go to Wales with him. From her third suitor, Allom the grocer, Doll also extracts fifty pounds, supposedly to pay off a bond, and four or five loaves of sugar to make quince jam, though with him she just speaks English. What's clear is that among her other skills, Doll's intentional interest in and proficiency with languages help her manage an international clientele to produce the greatest profits for herself. In her small way, Doll is like those who trade on the floor of the Royal Exchange. Like them, her contact with strangers is part of her business, and a little sophistication about their tongues and customs greases the wheels of their "commerce."

Deliciously, in the same play, the other character who plays with languages is Bellamont, the poet, long considered to be a satirical portrait of Chapman, who was well known for writing a series of tragedies set in the French court. In IV.i. Captain Jynkins comes to Bellamont for a "witty

ditty" (IV.i.89) to give to Doll. Bellamont takes the occasion to boast to
Captain Jynkins about how he is writing a new tragedy, *The Tragedy of
Astianax*, son of Hector. Jynkins gets the allusions all wrong, insisting that
"Stianax" was a Monmouth man related to Cadwallader. But Bellamont
has another audience in mind, not Jynkins, but the court of France. He
fantasizes standing at the edge of a stage hung in black velvet while his
play is performed. At some point the Duke of Biron or "some other
cheefe minion or so" (IV.i.54–55) will "step to the French King, and say,
*Sire, voyla, il et votre treshumble serviteur, le plu sage, è divine espirit, monsieur
Bellamont*, all in French thus poynting at me, or yon is the learned old
English Gentleman Maister *Bellamont*, a very worthie man, to bee one of
your privy Chamber, or Poet Lawreat" (IV.i.56–60). The cosmopolitanism
of the whore, aspiring to learn the languages of her clients, finds an echo
in the aspirations of Bellamont who longs to receive the largess of the
French king. But exactly to what ends does the juxtaposition work?

Throughout the play Bellamont is represented as a kindly but slightly
comic and pretentious figure. At one point he is tricked into visiting Doll
who is posing as a grand lady seeking a sonnet from him (III.i.1–136).
At another point he is the butt of a joke that has him temporarily incarcerated in Bedlam (IV.iii.127–99).[82] The learned poet who speaks several languages and knows Continental literature often has his head in
the clouds; Doll's cosmopolitanism has a more directly commercial and
opportunistic cast. She belongs to the thoroughly commercial world of
trade; he aspires to the international community of letters. For both,
knowledge of languages, however debased, is essential, and the insistent juxtaposition of her crude but effective entrepreneurship with Bellamont's more refined, but frustrated, aspirations to be a poet laureate
does not necessarily work to his advantage. It simply underscores how
grand his pretensions and how unrealistic his pursuit of them. Moreover, the playwrights eventually have Doll fall in love with the horrified
Bellamont (IV.i.123–200), again taking the lofty poet down a notch or
two since Doll seems to recognize an affinity between prostitute and
poet that Bellafront himself will not, of course, acknowledge. Though
Bellamont eventually helps to expose Doll's chicanery toward her many
clients, she ends the play the beneficiary of citizens' anger at the gentlemen who have tried to cuckold them. The gallant Featherstone is
tricked into marrying her, and when he finds out she has been a whore,
he opines: "Gentlemen, this is my opinion, it's better to shoote in a Bow
that has beene shot in before, and will never start, than to draw a faire
new one, that for every Arrow will bee warping: Come wench wee are
joynd, and all the Dogs in France shall not part us; I have some lands,
those Ile turne into money, to pay you, and you, and any [the men Doll
has scammed for money]; Ile pay all that I can for thee, for Ime sure

thou hast paid me" (V.i.505–11). Doll has been converted from whore to wife, and her husband claims to see advantages in her sexually experienced state. Having been "shot in before," she will not draw back or turn aside no matter what arrow her husband may fit to her string. Her commerce with other men, including strangers, has not made her a common shore or a privy; it has made her a partner who will not shrink from any encounters in the marital bed.

Doll is a frankly commercial London punk whose Charing Cross establishment draws in a good class of men: international merchants, army officers, a poet's son, an English grocer with access to sugar. Other prostitutes in London comedies strive for an even more exalted clientele and either are or model themselves on Continental courtesans. Their cosmopolitanism is expressed not only in an openness to foreign clients and a receptiveness to their languages, but in their acquisition of the refined skills of upscale sex workers, many of them Italian in origin. They bring the dangerous but perversely attractive cosmopolitanism of the Continent onto the London stage. Thomas Coryat's 1611 report of his travels, *Coryat's Crudities*, contains a famously ambivalent account of his visit to a Venetian courtesan. Anxious to present himself as an observer interested only in describing what other authors have neglected,[83] Coryat nervously tries to distance himself from charges of "luxury and wantonnesse" for having inserted "so lascivious a matter into this Treatise of Venice" (p. 402). Consequently, at the end of his description he appends an "Apologie" for himself in which he asserts that he went to a courtesan only so that he could accurately describe to others the danger she represents and also to convert her to a virtuous life. But the overheated rhetoric of his actual description suggests she inspired an interest neither merely pious nor anthropological. Calling the courtesans "amorous Calypsoes," Coryat details the "variety of delicious objects they minister to their lovers, that they want nothing tending to delight" (p. 403). These include palaces fitted with tapestries and gilded leatherwork, portraits of the courtesan "decked like the Queene and Goddesse of love" (p. 403), beautiful garments, jewels, perfumes, lute music, fragrant bedding, and a thousand other delights. As he admits, "the ornaments of her body are so rich, that except thou dost even geld thy affections (a thing hardly to be done) or carry with thee Ulysses hearbe called Moly which is mentioned by Homer, that is, some antidote against those Venereous titillations, shee wil very neare benumme and captivate thy senses, and make reason vale bonnet to affection" (p. 404). A picture included with the text shows a wary Coryat, hat in hand, stepping toward a richly costumed woman who with her right arm embraces his body and with her left signals him to come closer (Figure 10). Her breasts are bare,

Gl Signior Tomaso Odcombiano

Margarita Emiliana bella
Cortesana di Venetia

Gu: Hole sculp

Figure 10. Thomas Coryat meeting a Venetian courtesan, from *Coryate's Crudities,* 1611. Reproduced by permission of The Huntington Library, San Marino, California.

her hair elaborately curled, and her neck festooned with jewels. Coryat confesses he did not convert this woman, but he also insists he was "nothing contaminated therewith, nor corrupted in maner" (p. 409), the protestation attesting to the danger he felt her to represent. The Venetians, he reports, tolerate the innumerable courtesans in their city both because these women pay goodly revenues to the state and because they protect the chastity of Venetian wives, saving their husbands from being "capricornified" (p. 403).

A few years earlier, in 1609, Gervase Markham in *The Famous Whore or Noble Cortizan* had detailed the life of a famous Roman prostitute named Paulina who had accomplishments to match Coryat's Venetian courtesans. She could recite Petrarch, create beautiful needlework, dance, ride horses, sing, play the lute, and on occasion go abroad in men's apparel.[84] Especially interesting is Markham's description of her house and the kind of meeting place it represented.

> My house was like a Princes royall court,
> Whether the noblest spirits doe resort,
> Where strangers meete and in comercement stand,
> *French, English, Spanish, Dane and Netherland,*
> Striving with mirth to spend the time away,
> And each as other with conceit to play.
> The finest spirits there did shew their wit,
> Whilst vast uplandish rudenes learnt by it,
> To make their knowledge civill. (D4v-E)

The house was a meeting place for men of many nations, a rather less crude representation of intermingling than the trope of the whore's *body* (rather than her *house*) as a sink or common shore. Moreover, in that space civil knowledge is acquired and uplandish rudeness banished. The courtesan and her arts are agents of civilization, the mirror of the Italian courts that for Castiglione were the places of true courtesy. The odd word *comercement* suggests the mixture of motives and effects of this site. It is a place of commerce in the sense of trade, and shortly after describing her palace, Paulina boasts about how much gold she made in this, her golden age. Over her gate was painted a picture of Jove stealing to Danae in a shower of gold (E). But it is also a place of commerce in the sense of conversation and interchange, a meeting place where strangers mingled and were educated away from their rude ways. Such a text expresses an anxiety about English cultural sophistication vis-a-vis Continental rivals.[85] In *Englishmen for My Money*, the most successful merchant at the Royal Exchange was a Portuguese Jew; in Markham's poem and Coryat's travel account, no one is quite as cultured as the Italian courtesan.

Marston's *Dutch Courtesan* (1604) engages with this anxiety about English cultural inferiority in a highly complex way. It features a foreign prostitute, Franceschina, who, like Paulina, is mistress of all the arts of courtesanship, though in Marston's play she displays them in a fully realized London milieu. Alluring and dangerous, this courtesan is ambivalently presented, but she is the reference point for the play's wide-ranging investigation of how Londoners stack up against their Continental counterparts and of how they can shed their rude ways without being colonized or overwritten by alien practices. *The Dutch Courtesan* was written for the Children of the Queen's Revels by John Marston, a dramatist associated with the cosmopolitan Inns of Court milieu,[86] an association that helps explain some of the play's features. It has two plots. In the main one, a virtuous gentleman, Freevill, ends his attachment to Franceschina, the Dutch courtesan, to marry a virtuous woman named Beatrice. Though firm in his approbation of marriage, Freevill defends prostitution as a way of relieving men's sexual desires and as a bulwark to marriage. Anticipating Coryat's description of Venetian justifications for marriage, Freevill says: "I would have married men love the stews as Englishmen lov'd the Low Countries: wish war should be maintain'd there lest it should come home to their own doors" (I.i.62–65). Englishness is here associated with a defensive or manipulative stance toward other nations. Freevill positions the Dutch not as fellow allies in a Protestant cause, but as inhabitants of a convenient buffer zone keeping Spanish troops from attacking England. By analogy, prostitution offers a similar buffer zone keeping sexual assaults on women confined to the brothel and away from English homes. That in this play the prostitute is "Dutch" further underscores a gender binary established through a language of national difference. Wives are English; the prostitute is a stranger.

In this main plot, as Freevill separates from Franceschina, he introduces her to his friend, Malheureux, who, though he has spoken strongly against prostitution, falls helplessly in love with the courtesan. In one reading the absolutist Malheureux first has to be redeemed, like Angelo in *Measure for Measure*, from an unrealistic sense that the desires of the flesh can simply be renounced and then also from an obsessive, lustful involvement with the seemingly unmarriagable courtesan.[87] As Marston states in the argument to the play, "*The difference betwixt the love of a courtesan and a wife is the full scope of the play, which, intermixed with the deceits of a witty city jester, fills up the comedy*" (p. 3). In the main plot *The Dutch Courtesan* thus overtly directs its male characters away from involvement with what is foreign and illicit, figured in Franceschina, and toward the purity of a good English marriage well protected from foreign incursions.

But such a reading is too simple. It both underestimates the attractiveness of Franceschina and her power to disrupt the neat ideological binary between wife and whore, and it fails to take account of the subplot in which Cocledemoy, the witty city jester, shares with Franceschina, as with Doll, a cosmopolitan rather than an oppositional approach to foreign difference. Cocledemoy's Englishness is not premised on the xenophobic rebuff of all foreign things. Instead, he absorbs and plays with alien difference, as is perhaps playfully indicated by his French-sounding name. Though set in London, *The Dutch Courtesan* contains many characters with foreign names. Caqueteur, for example, is French for one who talks nonsense, and Malheureux is French for one who is unhappy or unfortunate. While these names indicate character traits, their presence in a London drama adds to the general sense that the city is full of people not born in England or that names, in this place of mixing, are no longer a reliable guide to origin and national identity.

Franceschina, the play's title character, is the person most obviously marked as a stranger, and through her the special characteristics of Cocledemoy are most clearly discernible. That she is called "Dutch" pays homage to the long-standing centrality of Dutch frows to London's illicit sexual economy. Yet she is herself a mixture of nationalities. Her names comes from a figure in the *commedia dell'arte*,[88] and in many ways she is more Italian than Dutch, partly because of the artful way she plies her trade and partly because she acts like an avenging fury from an Italian revenge drama when Freevill leaves her. Her artfulness is everywhere evident. When Malheureux and Freevill come to see her, she plays for them, one time on the lute, another time on the cittern, and sings and dances. When Malheureux tries to lead her precipitously to bed, she reads him a telling lecture on the joys of slow sex.

No, no, not yet, mine seetest, soft-lipped love:
You sall not gulp down all delight at once.
Be min trat, dis all-fles-lovers, dis ravenous wenches
Dat sallow all down whole, vill have all at one bit!
Fie, fie, fie! Be min fait, dey do eat comfits vid spoons.
No, no, I'll make you chew your pleasure vit love;
De more degrees and steps, de more delight,
De more endeared is de pleasure height. (V.i.24–31)

To which he answers flatfootedly, "What, you're a learned wanton, and proceed/ By art!" (V.i.32–33).

The point is that Franceschina does, indeed, proceed by art. She has perfumed sheets, knows when to let down her hair, and can sing, dance, and play instruments. She is, as Malheureux initially nominated her, a "money-creature" (I.i.90), but for that money she has perfected an artful product to offer upon the market, and she is in the business of rooting out "uplandish rudeness." Her effect on Malheureux, at least for a time, is overwhelming. The scorner of prostitutes finds himself obsessed with this artful creature, and in the heat of passion, he expresses his willingness to kill his friend to satisfy her desire for revenge. In her liveliness, Franceschina makes Beatrice, the good woman, look positively inert. Proclaiming her artlessness, Beatrice is the passive object to whom men sing Petrarchan love complaints (II.i.1–27). Franceschina, by contrast, is a creature with life, agency, and a craft. As a "money-creature," she and her bawd, Mary Faugh, are thoroughly implicated in the commercial culture of London. By contrast, the virtuous Beatrice stands outside it in the supposedly protected space of the household, a space that many other London plays reveal as itself susceptible to penetration both by commerce and by sexual predators. Even though Franceschina is later exposed for plotting murder and sent to prison, her initiative and her artfulness present an energizing alternative to the inert heroine.[89]

Moreover, Franceschina is cosmopolitan in the sense of serving, like Doll of *Northward Ho*, an international clientele. In Mary Faugh's words, Franceschina has been acquainted with "the Spaniard, don Skirtoll; with the Italian, Master Beieroane; with the Irish lord, Sir Patrick; with the Dutch merchant, Haunce Herkin Glukin Skellam Flapdragon; and specially with the greatest French, and now lastly with this English (yet, in my conscience) an honest gentleman" (II.ii.13–18). Faugh's words serve as a reminder of the mixture of nationalities present in the city. Franceschina has found a way to make money from them all. Yet despite her artfulness and ingenuity, the courtesan is ultimately an abjected figure in *The Dutch Courtesan*—the only one sent to "severest prison" (V.iii.55) at the end of the play. The treatment of her speech is one indication of the play's deep ambivalence toward her. Her artfulness does not extend to linguistic mastery. As the Regents editor, M. L. Wine, impatiently notes, her language is "a helter-skelter of Germanic, French, Italian, as well as pure English, pronunciation, added to somewhat conventional grammatical errors" (p. xix, note 15). Her mistakes are not, as in so many other plays, primarily adduced for comic effect. Rather, they seem to signal that at some level she is a figure rendered monstrous by her trade and by her traffic with the men of many nations. While she can dance, play the lute, sing a pre-scripted song, scatter her hair, and prolong amorous pleasure, when she talks she shows herself a hybrid creature who masters no one tongue but roils about in a mixture of many. In her Marston manages a doubled representation, at once alluring and monstrous, of the figure whose artful trade allows her to negotiate across national boundaries and to dispel uplandish rudeness in her clients, but who at some level is not fully in control of her passions or her language. Hers is a cosmopolitanism rendered attractive and then monstrous.

The Dutch Courtesan offers two alternatives to Franceschina's broken speech and dangerous cosmopolitanism, Cocledemoy and the London vintners, Mr. and Mrs. Mulligrub, the latter, I will argue, a debased version of cultural intermixing, and the former the play's privileged alternative to the prostitute's dangerous, but sophisticated, allure. In effect, Marston makes Franceschina part of a larger and quite complex investigation of the "proper" relationship of Englishness to what is construed as alien to it. I will begin with the Mulligrubs whose name comes from the expression "to have the mulligrubs," or the griping of the intestines, and, by extension, a fit of depression. Interestingly, the Mulligrubs are connected with a discourse of Dutchness, even though they are English. Both Mr. Mulligrub and his wife, along with the bawd, Mary Faugh, are members of the Family of Love, a dissenting sect with origins in the Low Countries and connected in the English imagination with sensuality, free love, communism, and moral hypocrisy.[90] They also represent the burgher sensuality already in this period one aspect of the English construction of the Dutch. The Dutch were represented as great drinkers; the Mulligrubs run a tavern.[91] The Family of Love was associated with free love; Cocledemoy meets his bawd in their tavern; Mistress Mulligrub intimates that she draws trade to her inn by giving favors to the squires, knights, and gentlemen who diet at her table while receiving from them "very good words, and a piece of flesh when time of year serves" (III.iii.23–24).

Both Mulligrub and his wife are obsessed with possessions. In the first lines of the play Malheureux none-too-respectfully urges Mulligrub not to weep onto his expensive Spanish leather jerkin after Cocledemoy has run off with his goblets. "Advance thy snout; do not suffer thy sorrowful nose to drop on thy Spanish leather jerkin, most hardly-honest Mulligrub" (I.i.2–3). Later the vintner and his wife appear on stage with a replacement goblet, then a huge piece of salmon, patterned napkins, a bag containing fifteen pounds, a cloak, a purse, and other things. Mrs. Mulligrub even collects words as trophy objects, writing down or mentally noting the fine phrases used by Cocledemoy (III.iii.30–31) and her suitors. At one point the word *methodically* swims into her head. "Methodically! I wonder where I got that word. Oh! Sir Aminadab Ruth bade me kiss him methodically! I had it somewhere, and I had it indeed" (III.iii.53–56). This member of the Family of Love is sensualist, a materialist, and a social climber.

Together, the Mulligrubs represent a slow-witted, money-grubbing, thing-loving version of the English guild housesehold filtered through a comic stereotype of the Dutch burgher. They are sensual hypocrites who cheat when they score up the cost of wines, hate tobacco but have a dining room that reeks of it, and substitute for "the true ancient British and Troyan drinks" (such as ale and cider) "Popish wines, Spanish wines, French wines, *tam Marti quam Mercurio*, both muscadine and malmsey, to the subversion, staggering, and sometimes overthrow of many a good Christian" (V.iii.105–10). They represent a debased form of cosmopolitanism, the pitiful "Dutchification" of the English guildsman, wallowing in his sensuality and his material goods without a trace of enlivening wit and certainly untouched by any attempt to banish uplandish rudeness. As an Inns of Court man, Marston was probably playing to the prejudices of his children's company audience. Contact with Dutch ways and foreign trade has simply rendered the vintner repulsive. He has adulterated British traditions of drink and offers nothing to compensate but a hateful obsession with garnering more "things." He offers an object lesson in how not to engage with what is alien.

By contrast, Cocledemoy, who shares more with Franceschina than with the Mulligrubs, his bitter enemies, emerges as a figure of attractive cosmopolitanism. He is, of course, thoroughly money loving. His name suggests cuckoldry, or poaching in other men's nests, and he poaches on the Mulligrubs quite successfully, gradually absorbing to himself all the goods so carefully acquired by this obsessive pair. Cocledemoy starts by crawling out the tavern window with Mulligrub's goblets in tow, and gradually he filches Mulligrub's replacement goblet, his salmon, his fifteen pounds, his purse, his cloak, and finally, when Mulligrub is about to hang, he moves in on Mulligrub's wife. While thoroughly acquisitive, Cocledemoy gathers the goods that give him pleasure not by traditional forms of work, but largely by his wit, his verbal dexterity, and his extraordinary skills at impersonation. He is the shrewd dealer, the artful trader whose success depends on reading well the strangers he encounters, not on the dogged labor of production. In this regard he is more than a witty jester pleasing to the clever Inns of Court gentlemen. He is also a man suited for dealing with the differences central to urban life.

Rhetorically, Cocledemoy glides masterfully from one linguistic register to another. With Freevill he drops Latin tags as he becomes a man of learning; with Mary Faugh he indulges in gutter talk, letting into the play the graphic sexual language found in Marston's verse satire;[92] speaking when disguised, with Mulligrub, he can ape the conversational tones of a barber or the addled repetitions of a simple night watchman. "Nay, and it be such a trifle, Lord, I could weep to see your good worship in this taking. Your worship has been a good friend to me; and, though you have forgot me, yet I knew your wife before she was married; and since, I have found your worship's door open, and I have knock'd, and God knows what I have saved. And do I live to see your worship stock'd" (IV.v.86–92). He is a verbal chameleon who apes strange tongues with ease.

Cocledemoy's verbal dexterity is useful as he slips from one disguise to another, sometimes appearing as a belman or night watchman, sometimes as a French pedlar, sometimes as a "Northern" or Scottish barber. In these roles, he crosses not just class boundaries, but national ones as well. His performative skill rivals that of Quicksilver in *Eastward Ho*, but as matter for his performances he traffics in the linguistic and national differences to be found within the city space. In this he shares ground with Franceschina, but he is more in control than she is of both his language and his passions. Consider his impersonation of the Scottish barber, Andrew Shark. When Cocledemoy plots to trick Mulligrub out of his fifteen pounds, he says: "My scurvy tongue will discover me; must dissemble, must disguise. For my beard, my false hair; for my tongue— Spanish, Dutch, or Welsh—no, a Northern barber! Very good" (II.i.201–4). He later makes a series of sly jokes about how he will shave and poll the English Mulligrub, a jab at the many Scotsmen whom James had brought to London and who were seen as "shaving" the English of their good and rightful honors. Marston treads on dangerous ground here, having just gotten in trouble for anti-Scots satire in *Eastward Ho*.[93] In *The Dutch Courtesan* he does not give the audience a broad satire of an actual, buffoonish Scotsman. Rather, he shows how, by impersonating one Andrew Shark, Cocledemoy can turn the invasion of London by northern strangers to his own benefit, while retaining his own identity. While Cocledemoy disguises himself with false beard and with the furniture and the professional jargon of a northern barber, he is not assigned a Scottish accent such as that given Jamy in *Henry V*. Rather, Marston chooses to show Cocledemoy successfully passing as a foreigner without sounding like one. The important contrast is with Franceschina. She, like the city jester, is a successful entrepreneur, but her entry into the international marketplace has left her a linguistic mess: called a Dutch courtesan, textually coded as partly Italian, and speaking like a one-woman Tower of Babel or as if all the tongues of Pentecost had visited her at once. Cocledemoy remains linguistically coherent whatever his disguise. A chameleon, slipping from register to register, he always emerges as himself, with his distinctive expression, "Hang toasts," intact.

I have argued that the prostitute often functions in the London drama to raise the question of cosmopolitanism, in what way and degree Englishness will open itself to acceptance of and civil interchange with the nations beyond its borders, whether the nearby nations of Wales and Scotland or the more distant ones of Holland, Spain, and Italy. In *The Dutch Courtesan* Franceschina is a powerful figure for the allure of what is alien and sophisticated, what might, in some circumstances, tame the uplandish rudeness of the English. But she is also subject to denigration, her speech a sign of the monstrous hybridity resulting from the wrong kind of cultural mixing, and her murderous passions a sign of the dangers she poses. By contrast, however, the representatives of London guild culture, the Mulligrubs, have picked up the worst traits of the Dutch without having become the least bit alluring or less rude in the process.

Only through Cocledemoy does Marston find an alternative to both the monstrous and debased cosmopolitanism of the courtesan and the vintner. Freevill is the structural protagonist of *The Dutch Courtesan*, but stage history has made it clear that Cocledemoy is the most engaging character.[94] And, I would argue, that through him Marston most fully stakes out a distinctive position in the ongoing cultural negotiations concerning how the English will manage the new realities of a Scottish king, a multinational city, and a burgeoning global economy. In Cocledemoy Marston offers an alternative to the defensive repudiation of foreignness signaled by Franceschina's imprisonment and the mindless absorption of less desirable forms of foreign culture represented by the Mulligrubs. Not only can he impersonate French pedlars and northern barbers while retaining his own distinct persona, thus revealing both playfulness and flexibility, but he also refuses to valorize marriage. His ongoing relationship is with Mary Faugh, herself a member of the Family of Love. If Freevill embraces both the symbolic purity of marriage and a defensive view of Englishness, Cocledemoy represents an Englishness dependent on quick wits, libertine sexuality, and the cosmopolitan ability to observe and master otherness without being destroyed by it. Cocledemoy, like Doll in *Northward Ho*, displays flexibility in the moral arena and adaptability in dealing with various sorts of social difference. Like hers, his skills are aimed not at a political, but at a commercial arena, the increasingly cosmopolitan world of trade and the traffic in goods. In that arena, the interchange with strangers is inevitable. The only question is whether in dealing with difference one becomes a feminized figure of deformity, a Dutchified materialist, or an embodiment of the mastery of tongues and personae apparent in the clever-witted, thoroughly cosmopolitan Cocledemoy.

Coda

In the winter of 1631/32 a strange event erupted in London that provides an interesting glimpse at how a hybridized English prostitute could be represented as a folk hero some twenty to thirty years after most of the plays I have discussed in this chapter were first performed. Around Christmas of 1631 London authorities attempted to enter and perhaps to shut down an upscale brothel located in Old Paris Garden, a liberty south of the River, which also contained the Swan Theater and was very near the Globe, the Rose, and the Hope. Many of the details of what happened that Christmas and why are obscure, but the events produced several interesting texts dealing with the attempt to overrun the bawdy house. The brothel itself seems to have been headed by an experienced madam named Elizabeth Holland.[95] In employing the Manor House for her place of business, she had shrewdly chosen a location in a liberty, making it difficult to police. It was also surrounded by a moat, effectively shutting the brothel off from near neighbors and making it possible easily to control access to the premises by a narrow isthmus. One theory is that someone else had purchased the lease to the premises in 1631, and the siege may have represented an attempt to install the new owner. The name Hollands Leaguer (a leaguer is a military camp) may not actually have attached itself to the property until the events of 1631–32 when the attempt by constables to overrun the establishment was repulsed. A siege of sorts ensued, and on January 26, 1632 Elizabeth Holland was called before the Star Chamber, but did not appear. A petition by residents of Paris Garden on February 9 for help in protecting Hollands Leaguer and twenty other nearby brothels from Shrove Tuesday apprentice riots claimed that Elizabeth Holland had left the premises six weeks ago. She then fades from the historical record.[96]

She did not, however, fade from the popular imagination. Three texts were quickly printed that represented aspects of the 1631–32 events. In December of 1631 Shackerley Marmion's play, *Hollands Leaguer,* was played at Salisbury Court by Prince Charles's Men. On January 20 a pamphlet by one Nicholas Goodman, which may have been an alias, was entered in the Stationers' Register. It was called *Hollands Leaguer: or an historicall discourse of the life and actions of Donna BRITANNICA HOLANDI-AZA the Archmistris of the wicked women of Eutopia, wherein is detected the notorious sinne of Pandarisme and the execrable life of the Luxurious Impudent.* Six days later Marmion's play was also entered. On May 24, 1632 a ballad, "Newes from Hollands Leaguer," was published.

Goodman's pamphlet, adorned with a woodcut showing the moated brothel, makes the whore-turned-bawd a heroic embodiment of the entrepreneurial spirit. She is, Goodman says, "without parallel in her profession" (p. 56). He tells her life's story, beginning with her arrival in London, her marriage, seduction, life as a whore, decision to turn bawd, her imprisonment in Newgate, her escape, and finally her crowning achievement: the establishment of Hollands Leaguer. The place is described in detail. A ruffian named Cerberus guards the door, and the woodcut shows him standing with folded arms at the entrance (Figure 11). Four whores, each named and described in some detail,

Figure 11. Frontispiece to *Hollands Leaguer* by Nicholas Goodman, 1632. Reproduced by permission of The Huntington Library, San Marino, California.

provide the main attraction, and to tend to them Britannica Hollandia has hired a surgeon, a tyre woman, a sempster, and a tailor, suggesting again the importance of clothing in the construction of the whore's identity and her allure. Entertainment, food, and drink are lavish, and the woodcut pictures a man and a woman in an arbor in back of the brothel, another couple in a garden, while an elaborately dressed prostitute looks out a window at the front of the building. The impression is of people experiencing refined forms of pleasure.

The genre of the pamphlet is interesting. It presents itself as a cautionary tale meant to warn the reader from sin, and to some extent it follows the conventional narrative of the fall of innocence. But it lacks the spittle house ending in which the whore, having fallen from former glory, grows diseased and dies in poverty. Instead, Britannica Hollandia's story ends in the midst of her heroic battle with the constables. Like the Amazonian Long Meg to whom she is compared, Britannica is a fighter and a successful entrepreneur; and she is presented as a hero as much as a sinner, one of the worthies of London. In her youth the man who seduced her told her tales of the glories of the famous Roman whore Paulina, the protagonist of Gervase Markham's 1609 poem. But in her maturity Goodman boasts that Britannica herself could write annals to teach Rome, Venice, Florence, and the Turk's Seralio about the arts of courtesanship (p. 80). The flow of influence has been reversed. Her name indicates the perverse national pride she embodies. Punning not only on Elizabeth Holland's name but also on the long tradition of Flemish frows as heads of London brothels, Britannica Hollandia has Englished the trade. The successful incorporation of foreign sophistication is now presented as a form of heroism, rather than as contamination. Not the abjected detritus of the city, Britannica is a folk icon, a theme echoed in the ballad, which, written several months later, claims that her brothel has relocated to "Bewdly." The woman warrior/brothelkeeper has emerged victorious from her battles. In a hyperbolic way, she embodies the spirit of all of those ordinary women, *femes sole* and wives of tradesmen, who participated in the market economy of London and without apology made such activity part of their daily lives.

Marmion's play, though a wretched piece of playmaking nonetheless rings a final change on the place of the whorehouse in London's dramatization of itself. It is a play about the varieties of self-love, conceit, and false cosmopolitanism that have overtaken London's men. Its protagonist is Philautus, a Narcissus who neglects his wife because he is so in love with himself; and it is peopled by men who cannot fight and who spend their time boasting of their foreign travels and their attractiveness to women. The agents of correction in this text are all women:

the virtuous Faustina who turns Philautus from a fop into a soldier; Millicent, a young woman of loose virtue who cleverly entraps the vain Trimalchio into a marriage; and, crucially, the whores of Hollands Leaguer. In the fourth act, a quartet of city fops, fools, and hypocrites goes to the brothel to prove their valor. The whores, who vociferously complain that constables meddle in the vending of their commodities, strip several of the men of swords, money, hats, and cloaks and send them limping home (I). While Philautus is learning to be a man in the wars abroad, the citydwellers are being disciplined by another kind of warfare at home. Rather than a sinkhole of female vice, the whorehouse is rewritten as a place of masculine correction, where a triumphant bawd, pander, and whores shame weak men and themselves escape reproof.

In their many incarnations, the bawdy houses and whores of London comedy nearly always exceed their predictable function as the site and emblems of urban vice and abjection. Rather, they are key to the genre's innovative examination of the effects on social relations of the city's expanding market economy, of the special pressures put on gender relations in the metropolis, and of the necessary, if sometimes fear-provoking, cosmopolitanism of urban life. Collectively, whore plays negotiate the changing place of women and strangers in the city. If they sometimes denigrate prostitutes, they also use them to pressure outmoded or inadequate conceptions of normative femininity and to acknowledge the increasingly hybridized life in an international commercial center. In *Hollands Leaguer* and in Goodman's pamphlet about the brothel, whores emerge as heroic figures precisely because they can run an upscale business, correct masculine folly, and incorporate foreign ways and foreign clients without losing their own distinctive place as emblems of a triumphant Englishness. In fact, their Englishness is premised on their sophisticated cosmopolitanism. Ironically, the brothel becomes the site, every bit as much as the Royal Exchange, for narratives that attempt to come to terms with the entrepreneurial and multinational place that London was fast becoming. And in the city these plays stage, women's place is a question, not a given, her protean transformations a delicious riposte to outmoded pieties about who the good women are and for what they are to be valued.

Chapter 4

Ballrooms and Academies: Producing the Cosmopolitan Body in West End London

In the last chapter I explored the link in London comedy between cosmopolitan sophistication and foreign prostitutes, especially Italian courtesans. Through an *ars erotica* encompassing a knowledge of music, languages, and conversation, foreign whores, or domestic prostitutes who mimicked them, could inculcate civility and banish boorish rudeness in their clients. Whores were thus often represented in surprisingly upbeat ways in London comedies—not only as wily and successful commercial entrepreneurs, but also as instructors in the arts of civility. In this chapter I turn to another agent of cultural instruction—namely, the French dancing master—and to another scene of such instruction—the academy of manners. Academies of manners or schools of complement[1] are important places in London comedy of the 1620s and 1630s, their prevalence suggesting some of the cultural and social consequences of the vast economic expansion that in the prior three quarters of a century had turned London into a world city and had produced social groups eager to legitimate (and sometimes to mask) their commercial wealth by the acquisition of new forms of cultural capital.

As London expanded geographically westward, so did the drama in the sense that plays began to be set in sites in the emerging West End such as Hyde Park, Tottenham Court, and Covent Garden. In staging these places, the theater helped to turn them into significant social spaces associated with a defined set of privileged behaviors and social actors. Caroline drama was thus central to the articulation of the fashionable norms that would define a distinctive West End culture marked by an emphasis on manners and new norms of bodily deportment.[2] I am going to argue that for all its apparent superficiality, this discourse of manners and deportment was an important means for negotiating stresses within the social fabric whether those involved attempts to carve out—or beat back—new ways of marking social distinction or whether they touched on anxieties about women's participation in polite society. The new regime of manners did not, moreover, emerge without significant social struggle evident everywhere in the plays I am going to examine. If new codes of deportment and civil behavior were lauded by some, to many they were associated with what was foreign, courtly, or effeminate and were thought decidedly inferior to other systems of assigning social worth and value. In what follows I will show how ballrooms and academies of manners became places central both to Caroline comedy's articulation of new norms of mannerly behavior and to its revelation of the social struggles attendant on the fashioning of cosmopolitan bodies.

A good place to start is with James Shirley's *The Ball*,[3] staged for Queen Henrietta's Company at the Phoenix in 1632. In this play a French dancing master named Frisk asserts that he will teach the cynic, Barker, to "dance with all de grace of de body for your good, and my profit" (III.i.45–46).[4] A moment later, struggling to teach the novice dancer the basic five-step cinquepace, Frisk enjoins Barker to "stand upright" and to observe the proper "posture of de body," later reproving him: "hah, you go too fast! You be at Dover, begar, and me be at Greenwish" (III.i.52, 56, 62–63). Eventually, his legs proving recalcitrant, Barker storms away, swearing to be revenged on his friend, Lord Rainbow, who has urged him to submit to the dancing master's instruction. Much of this chapter will be devoted to unpacking the complicated social meanings encoded in this exchange and replayed, with variations, in a number of other Caroline comedies. Why, exactly, is it a *French* dancing master who is instructing Barker and other Londoners on the art of dancing? Why is Frisk so insistent that Barker stand upright, strike a proper posture, and not dance too fast? Why is the cynic so reluctant to engage in dancing lessons, and why does he feel so humiliated by his brief stint as Frisk's tutee? In exploring answers to these questions, I will show how Caroline versions of London comedy helped to construct, and through performance to embody, standards of civil conduct and bodily deportment often associated with Continental norms and practices.

Those antagonistic to these new practices sometimes attributed their prominence to the influence of Charles's French Queen, Henrietta Maria, a woman whose love for dancing, theater, and French refinement generated opposition, including William Prynne's famous attack on women actors as "notorious whores." Prynne's outburst was aimed at the Catholic Queen's participation in the rehearsals and performance of Walter Montague's eight-hour court entertainment, *The Shepherd's Paradise*, in January of 1633.[5] Prynne was equally hard on dancing, finding it "scandalous" and delight in dancing "a badge of lewde lascivious women and strumpets."[6] In Shirley's *The Ball*, performed in 1632 *before* the Prynne firestorm hit but well *after* the Queen's fondness for dancing and masquing had become known, the French dancing master functions, I will argue, not only as a general reference to courtly fashions, but as a crucial figure through whom to consider the consequences of foreign cultural practices for English bodies and, by extension, for English identity.

In Shirley's play, dance instruction takes place in private residences, but in other Caroline comedies it occurs in academies that, besides dancing, teach an array of social skills from the proper "postures" of the body to the elegant exchange of complements to instruction in French. However exclusive, such academies were at bottom commercial undertakings. They not only made the arts of bodily deportment a product to be sold to anyone with money to buy, thus rendering radically unstable the link between elegance and rank, but also moved education in manners and bodily decorum from the household or private residence to a public venue where the process of rendering common the practices of an elite was easy to observe and the social ambitions of its members easy to satirize. In the second part of this chapter I will turn to Richard Brome's town comedies, which, I will argue, are particularly rich texts for exploring the paradoxes surrounding both commercial academies of manners and the plays that made fun of them. I will end by turning to two plays that constitute particularly interesting examples of how the dancing master and the academy of manners could be used, as well, to comment on political issues both at the level of monarchical policies and also at the level of society's most basic gender arrangements. In 1640 in *The Variety* William Cavendish dramatized a French dancing master and a female academy of manners to mark the degeneration of English culture in the waning years of Charles I's troubled reign. In 1662 his wife, Margaret, revisited, in *The Female Academy*, the idea of a school for ladies that, ignoring the language of postures, complements, and dancing so prominent in town comedies of the 1630s, attempted to make the education of women an intellectual endeavor and the academy of women a site of virtue. In what follows, then, I will trace the fortunes of the ballroom and the academy on the Caroline stage, and slightly beyond, to demonstrate the continuing centrality of the theater to the making and remaking of an increasingly cosmopolitan London, one in which neither the having of land nor of money could by itself insure social legitimacy or prominence.

Dancing and the Town Culture of 1630s West End London

As several critics have suggested, Caroline comedies, of which Shirley's *The Ball* is just one example, were linked to the development of what has been called "town culture" in West End London in the 1620s and 1630s, a culture to which the dancing master and the academy of manners were integral. As historians have used the term, "the town" was a relational concept distinct both from court and city though never entirely separable from either. Putative membership in town culture depended primarily on certain cultural markers such as wit and taste.[7] Leisured, fashionable, and monied, those imagined to belong to the town were as dependent on manners as bloodlines for their cultural distinction. Unlike the stereotype of the city merchant, they were not primarily devoted to making money but to displaying the civilized life made possible through its possession. If one had to translate "the town" into crudely demographic terms, it would have been composed primarily of sophisticated gentlemen such as those who frequented the Inns of Court, country gentry in town for the season, wealthy merchants bent on acquiring cultural as well as financial capital, and cultured professionals; its geographical center was the West End, that is, the area north of the Thames and south of Holborn and stretching from Westminster in the west to the Inns of Court in the east.[8]

By the 1630s this area was becoming one of the most fashionable districts in greater London, and Caroline town comedies, spurred in part by the development of exclusive hall theaters such as The Cockpit and Salisbury Court, refer constantly to the parks and important new social spaces within this emerging West End world. If many of the early London comedies were set within the walled city to the East, by the 1630s the geographical fulcrum of these plays had moved decidedly westward.[9] One readily associates West End settings with the Restoration London comedies of Congreve, Wycherley, and Etherege; but as Julie Sanders and others have noted, Caroline comedies often take place there too.[10] With the geographical move westward came changes in the way London was dramatized. Business activites such as making and selling shoes, dealing on the Royal Exchange, or buying feathers in shops ceased to be in the representational foreground. Instead, attention focused on sites of leisure where people who had money were shown displaying the civilized life it enabled in an increasingly fashion-conscious urban milieu. Rather than financial capital, the drama focused at least in part on the acquisition, display, and dissipation of something more intangible but no less important to West End life: cultural capital, the skills that allowed one to belong to the aristocracy of the tasteful.[11]

A notable feature of the town culture emerging in the West End was its cultural cosmopolitanism. Many of the fashionable places around which the town constituted itself had complex mixtures of homegrown and foreign elements. A bellwether of things to come, Salisbury's upscale shopping arcade, the New Exchange (opened in 1609 on the south side of the Strand) specialized in upscale consumer goods, many of them foreign in origin. For example, among the goods on display in the China shop that Salisbury had especially fitted out for the official opening of the Exchange were a range of exotica including many kinds of porcelain chinaware, glassware, and ostrich eggs.[12] By the 1630s ambitious housing projects were undertaken in the area, the most famous being the Earl of Bedford's Covent Garden venture. Around a piazza laid out in the Italian manner, Bedford built a planned and uniform series of residences with an Inigo Jones church gracing the west side of the square.[13] Continental fashions in architecture thus found an English home within the West End. When not promenading in the piazza at Covent Garden, West Enders could visit other sites of fashionability including Hyde Park, the Spring Gardens, and the Mulberry Gardens, the latter two both being part of what was to become St. James Park and partially open to the public. Among the attractions of the Spring Garden were orchards, lawns, bowling greens, a bathing pond, a butt for archery practice, part of James I's menagerie of exotic beasts, and an ordinary.[14] In the Mulberry Gardens James tried to establish a silk-growing industry. Hence the planting of the hundreds of mulberry trees from which the place took its name. Parts of the West End were thus versions of the *Wunderkammer* writ large, places where English eyes confronted what was new, exotic, and strange, but in settings woven into the fabric of daily life.

To be part of West End town culture required certain skills, many of which had to be learned, some of which were themselves regarded as foreign in origin. Without these skills, people lacked the all-important cultural capital that allowed them to move with ease and assurance through its privileged spaces. In Shirley's 1635 play, *The Lady of Pleasure*, a young scholar, Frederick, is brought to London by his demanding aunt, Lady Aretina, who is appalled by his clothes, his manners, and even the way he holds his hat (II.i.42–110). She wants him to forget Latin and Greek, the languages of the university, and learn French, the proper tongue for a gentleman about town. More importantly, he is to have a French tailor make him new clothes and teach him how to wear them, and he is to employ masters to instruct him in fencing, singing, dancing, and riding, as well as in French (IV.ii.46–47).[15] Only under the tutelage of all of these has he any hope of becoming a gentleman fit for fashionable company.

Of all these officers of cultural instruction, the French dancing master has a particular prominence within Caroline comedy. In many West End plays, and not just in *The Ball*, dancing is one of the quintessential skills by which fashionable status is judged, and the dancing master the crucial agent through whom this skill is acquired. In *The Ball* the dancing master is Frisk; in Brome's *The City Wit* it is Footwell, an identity assumed by a failed-merchant-turned-dancing master; in Brome's *The New Academy* (1635) it is Lightfoot, the persona taken on by the poor brother of a wealthy merchant; in Newcastle's *The Variety* (1640), it is Galliard, a Frenchman like Frisk. The popularity of the figure continued after the Restoration. In 1662 Samuel Pepys saw a play he called *The French Dancing Master*, which critics have thought might be a reference to *The Ball*. Pepys praised the dancing master's part as "the best in the world."[16]

Dancing masters such as those found in the drama seem to have existed in some numbers within the actual social world of the West End. Records left by those who attended the Inns of Court suggest that gentlemen who enrolled there often spent as much time in the courtly trivium of fencing, dancing, and music as in learning law. Wilfrid R. Prest argues that many acquired private tutors to teach them these arts while others attended schools of dancing, fencing, and music scattered near the Inns.[17] In the late 1620s and 1630s Shirley lived near the Inns of Court and was officially admitted to Gray's Inn in 1634. Many of his friends and patrons had connections with the Inns, and he would have been familiar with their practices.[18] Dancing masters were also an important feature of court society. Buckingham, for example, prided himself on his skillful dancing, which he first learned in France. When in England, he kept several French dancing masters in his employ, along with a French barber, a French fencing master, and a French musician to give him singing lessons.[19] One of his dancing masters, Barthelemy de Montagut, dedicated a dance treatise to him and went on to become in 1630 a groom in Henrietta Maria's Privy Chamber. Montagut is the model for the figure of Galliard in Newcastle's *The Variety*.[20] But while an aristocratic or courtly elite might be assumed to have a monopoly on elegant deportment, what the plays record is the constant assault on this prerogative by people somewhat less exalted in social status, but whose money lets them buy instruction in the very arts in which a Buckingham was trained. The social tensions revealed in these plays thus rang new changes on the old story of the battle between the prerogatives of old rank and new wealth, but played out in indirect and varied ways.

In the drama, the dancing master is always male, though his masculinity and that of his clients is sometimes disputed; he is usually French; and that alien status could make him either silly or attractive. Frisk's comic French accent, for example, does nothing for his dignity, but that does not make him any the less in demand. What he offers is a skill regarded as the cosmopolitan acquisition of men and women of fashion, one that in the words of John Playford makes "the body active and strong, gracefull in deportment, and a quality very much beseeming a Gentleman."[21] The gentleperson who obtained the services of a French dancing master was electing to embrace fashionable practices associated with Continental sophistication and to submit his or her body to new regimes of discipline. Whether the dancing master was associated with the Court or the commercial schools of the West End, his purpose was to inculcate what both Jorge Arditi and Anna Bryson have identified as modes of civility that became increasingly important in regulating elite conduct as the seventeenth century progressed.[22]

A pan-European ideal, civility was nonetheless inflected differently in various national contexts. Concerned with propriety of behavior, civility involved techniques of self-presentation, including the mannerly control of the body, as well as regard for the sensibilities of others. As an ideal, it was linked to the courtesy tradition that had sprung up to regulate the behavior of courtiers, but civility had a slightly different social meaning. Especially in the English context, it did not necessarily refer to the behavior governing courtiers, but to the codes of conduct governing social interactions within "good" society, however variously defined.[23] Bryson has argued that in the seventeenth century, civility became an ideal within urbane London culture, the West End equally with the Court.[24] Of course, the norms of civility were not established overnight; rather, their growing importance was the consequence of considerable cultural labor, some of it undertaken at the site of the stage. A play such as Shirley's *The Ball*, then, should not so much be read as an illustration of ideas about civil behavior, but rather as a performance text through which those ideas were constructed and given physical expression.

The Ball and the Molding of Fashionable Bodies

The *OED* lists Shirley's *The Ball* as the first recorded use of the word "ball" to mean "a social assembly for the purpose of dancing" (p. 2). The play's commitment to the vanguard of fashion is thus blazoned in its title; it boldly introduces a new social practice and focuses on those who participate in it. In fact, much of *The Ball* is taken up with "training exercises" as the men and women of the West End get themselves ready for this event, which takes place in the house of a city merchant (location unspecified), which Lord Rainbow, the ball's organizer, has rented for the occasion (V.i.1–5). So what happened at a ball? As depicted in Act V of Shirley's play, the main activity was the dancing undertaken by the fashionable people who were Rainbow's guests. There were, however, some preliminaries. First a golden ball descended from the ceiling, and this signaled the beginning of a short masque in which Venus and Diana struggled for control of Cupid (V.i.247–302). This was followed by an antimasque danced by one of the characters dressed like a satyr. Then the golden ball was tossed into the assemblage. The import of catching the ball is not entirely clear, but probably it determined a temporary "king" or "queen" of the night's revels or entitled the catcher to lead the first general dance.[25] After this dancing, there was a banquet, and then more dancing.

"The ball," then, has two meanings. It refers both to the event at which the dancing and the masque occur and to the decorative ball that descended to signal the beginning of the festivities. That golden ball, in turn, suggests the fatal object that Paris famously gave to Venus rather than to Diana or Juno, a choice that eventually precipitated the Trojan War. The masque alludes to this event when Venus says to the assembled gentlefolk: "These are all/ Met in honour of my Ball,/ Which Paris gave [on] Ida hill" (V.i.255–57). The reference underscores the competitive relationships that the ball incites—who is the fairest? who the most graceful dancer? who the favorite of Lord Rainbow, the ball's patron?—as well as the possibility that the ball is a destructive or disreputable event. Moreover, the fact that the ball as an event includes a masque, but with no royalty in attendance, suggests that while the Court serves as a point of reference throughout the play, its practices are being incorporated into a social milieu of "gentlepersons" whose orbit is particular to itself.

A use of the word "bal," which the *OED* does not record, suggests something further both about the origins of this institution and the controversy it could occasion. In Robert Dallington's "Method for Travell" (1605), which formed the preliminary to his *View of France*, he warned of some of the dangers of travel in that country. French wines, he asserted, might not agree with English constitutions; the French obsession for tennis could be dangerous for the bodies and purses of Englishmen; and French dancing, while much in request with the English, should be pursued sparingly. As a cautionary tale, he tells of:

A countriman of ours, well seene in arts and language, well stricken in years, a mourner for his second wife, a father of marriageable children, who with other his booke studies abroad, joyned also the exercise of dancing; it was his hap in an honorable *Bal* (as they call it) to take a fall, which in mine opinion was not so disgracefull as the dancing it selfe, to a man of his stuffe.[26]

It is not clear exactly in what this "Bal" consisted. Maybe it was simply the generic name for a dance or dancing, or perhaps it referred to some kind of assembly for that purpose. In any case, the fact that it involved a fall suggests that Dallington's countryman may have been engaging in dancing that required acrobatic leaps, such as the capriole, which some dancing masters warned against attempting in public, lest bad execution make one stumble or look ridiculous.[27] Most striking in this account, however, is Dallington's outraged reaction to his countryman's participation in such a frivolous pastime. While an "honorable ball" might be appropriate for a young man, a man of years and affairs should not be engaged in such an activity, whether or not he falls down doing it. Moreover, Dallington's outrage is couched in the context of a more general diatribe about the dangers of French practices on English bodies, whether those practices involve drinking too much wine, playing too much tennis, or falling down while dancing.

In Shirley's play the ball is coded as a French practice. It is said to have been "transported hither by some ladies/ That affect tennis" (IV.iii.121–22), a sport long been associated with France, in Dallington's report and elsewhere.[28] In Shirley's play the "Frenchness" of the ball is heightened by the fact that all the preparations for it are overseen by the officious Frisk. He not only teaches everyone the dance steps they will need to know, but, taking "much trouble in my little head" (V.i.13), arranges for perfuming the room where the dancing will occur and at Lord Rainbow's direction devises the masque for the ladies in which he himself takes the part of Cupid (IV.ii.104–34). While the "Frenchness" of the ball, as I will discuss below, contributes to suspicions that it might be a scandalous or frivolous event, this same quality also enhances its fashionable cachet. Those who plan to attend the ball know they have to acquire some new and difficult skills and that only the French dancing master can impart them. Building toward the final ballroom scene, incidents of dancing and dance instruction punctuate the play, revealing the effort necessary to school bodies into proper dancing postures and serving to separate those who can attain mastery of these skills from those who cannot.

These scenes also permit the stage itself to become a showcase for displaying both properly and improperly educated bodies. Martin Butler has argued of 1630s "town" drama that it "was providing this [fashionable Caroline] society with models for its behavior. Plays by Brome, Shirley and Davenant offered the audience images of themselves in parks, squares, taverns and gaming houses, supplying standards against which forms and codes of behavior could be established, scrutinized and adjusted, and that these comedies of manners are among the best plays of the period is a measure of the importance of this function for the theaters."[29] I agree, but wish to underscore the importance of physical performance to the way in which the stage addressed the issue of the mannerly body. While the theater may not have been well equipped to showcase a gentleman's skills at horsemanship, it *was* suited for the display of dancing bodies. In fact, as scholars have long known, dancing was an integral part of the practices of the early modern stage.[30] Jigs followed plays; dances occurred between acts in the hall theaters; and dances were incorporated into any number of dramas. In *Antony and Cleopatra*, for example, Antony and Enobarbus lead a drunken dance aboard Pompey's ship; in *Midsummer Night's Dream* rustics dance a Bergomask at the wedding of Theseus and Hippolyta; in *More Dissemblers Besides Women* a pregnant woman disguised as a male page goes into labor as the result of overvigorous dance instruction. In every case, stage dancing displays the physical skills of the trained actor whether he is flawlessly executing a stately measure or parodying dancing competence by deliberately ungainly displays.

The dancing in *The Ball* is different from early instances of stage dancing in several ways. First, the value of dancing is the conscious object of discussion from the play's first scene when Monsieur Frisk makes his initial appearance and is characterized by a contemptuous bystander as "the Court dancing weasel" (I.i.129). This description suggests that even though his skills are much in demand, there is something a little contemptible or a little ridiculous about him and about his art. Throughout the play a subtle tension persists between embracing and denigrating the dance and the dancing master. Second, privileged forms of dancing are associated in the play, not with what is traditional, but with what is new and what must be learned, both in terms of steps and in terms of fashionable execution. In II.ii, during his first scene of instruction, Frisk repeatedly reproves the three assembled ladies for their graceless ways, saying that they "trot, trot, trot" (II.ii.9) and will "be laughed when you come to de ball" (II.ii.12–13), associating the graceless, unschooled body with social humiliation. Interjecting his instruction with a healthy dollop of French phrases (*plaît-il; pourquoy; par ma foy; Allez, allez; fort bon*), Frisk repeatedly emphasizes the necessity of having erect posture. To Lucina he says: "look up your countenance, your English man spoil you, he no teach you look up" (II.ii.29–30), while he castigates men who "dance lop, lop, with de lame leg as they want crushes, begore, and look for *argent* in the ground, pshaw!" (II.ii.38–40). The elegant body is the erect body;[31] moreover, it is a body committed to graceful movement. Frisk dislikes women who trot and men who lop when they dance, activities suggesting jerky movement and, in the man's case, deformity. By contrast, Lucina is enjoined to "carry your body in the swimming fashion" (II.ii.30–31), gliding, not trotting.

What they dance is also important. Rosamond wants to practice the coranto, a rapidly executed courtly dance that had outpaced the galliard in fashionability by the second decade of the seventeenth century. It involved sets of couples who together circled the dancing hall with ever-quickening steps.[32] It required skill and teamwork. Lucina, however, calls for a country dance, and it is "a new country dance" that the group eventually sets to practicing. Country dancing, often performed to popular tunes, typically was opposed to forms of courtly dancing because it emphasized rougher movements, groups of dancers rather than couples, and often involved bodies that bent parallel to the ground rather than being held elegantly erect.[33] Fashion, however, can refunction popular practices for its own ends, and that is clearly what is happening here. The "new" country dances are obviously ones that alter received materials, making country dances into fashionable ones. In 1651 John Playford published the first dancing manual in English to transcribe actual dance steps. His treatise was entitled *The English Dancing Master: or, Plaine and Easie Rules for the Dancing of Country Dances, with the Tune to each Dance.* While most of the dances are traditional in nature, he includes at least one courtly dance, the pavane, and the title page to the treatise visually places the scene of dancing in a fairly elegant hall or ballroom, rather than outdoors or in the midst of a rustic festival (Figure 12). The woodcut foregrounds a fashionably dressed man and woman gesturing decorously with their hands as they prepare to dance. Between them stands a naked Cupid, his bow and arrow stowed in a quiver on his back, and in his hands a stringed instrument

Figure 12. Title page to *The English Dancing Master* by John Playford, 1651. Reproduced by permission of The Huntington Library, San Marino, California.

like a fiddle or violin. Clearly, this Cupid is not promoting lascivious desire, but the meeting of man and woman in patterned, decorous movement. Around the edges of the room, other couples seem poised to join the dance. Whatever the origins of the dances Playford has transcribed, the title page shows a scene of restrained fashionability. So, I assume, it is with the "new" country dances of *The Ball.* They may have country origins, but they are being inserted into a new performance context that elides their rustic origins.

The play's other scenes of dance instruction also emphasize grace and the difference between refined movements and crude. When Frisk attempts to instruct Barker, he tries to elicit "grace" from him (III.i.40), castigating his rude movements as "horse-play, begar, for de stable, not de chamber" (III.i.41), stressing the desired distance of the dancing hall from the low matter of the stable. Later he says that Barker's legs "have de poc, or something dat make 'em no vell, and frisk" (III.i.78–79). They are diseased legs, and decidedly not "frisk" like the dancing master's own, nor like Lord Rainbow's, who, once Barker departs in a huff, exits the stage dancing with Frisk as the dancing master also fiddles and cries "Allez, ha! Bon!" (III.i.92). This virtuoso performance is clearly meant to underscore both the skills of the highest ranking man in the play, Lord Rainbow, and those of his frisky footed, fiddling instructor. It also suggests that a man's properly schooled leg might be an object of erotic desire. At one point, playing a trick on a knight named Lamont, Lucina says that "I had a dream last night; methought I saw you/ Dance so exceeding rarely, that I fell/ In love—," to which Lamont interjects, "In love with me?" And she replies, "With your legs, sir" (II.ii.149–51). The leg becomes a fetishized body part, opening the possibility that the skill of the dancing man may translate into erotic desirability and enhanced status.

The scenes of dance instruction are among the most interesting in *The Ball* because they reveal the importance of a properly disciplined body to the acquiring of fashionable standing. Everyone wants to be at the ball and to have the dancing skills to acquit himself or herself with honor. But these scenes also raise the important question of just who can acquire such a body. The availability of a dancing master who gives lessons seems to promise that anyone can learn the skill of dancing.[34] However, it is culturally and politically important that some cannot learn lest the art of elegant dancing become common and lose its function as a mark of cultural distinction. Barker is singled out, for example, as someone apparently uneducable in the terpsichorean domain. In his first dancing lesson he storms off the stage. Later, urged to learn to dance by Honoria, he apparently agrees to take part in the ball by dancing in the antimasque that was part of the evening's entertainment. Unfortunately, he plays a satyr whose rough, animalistic movements merely accentuate the refinement of the other dancers. Though he vows to "do better shortly" (V.i.316), he becomes the butt of everyone's laughter. Disdaining to love him, Honaria cruelly says:

I am not mad to love a satyr,
For that's thy best condition. Judgment all!
How scurvily this civility shows in him.
Faith, rail, and keep your humour still; it shows excellent.
Does he not become the beast? (V.i.319–23)

There is a brutishness about Bostock that is revealed rather than overcome through his rough mode of dancing. Failing at civility, he rushes off vowing to revenge himself on his tormentors.

These scenes of dancing and dance instruction are especially important, moreover, in underscoring the reliance of all the would-be dancers upon the skills of the French dancing master. To be part of sophisticated town culture, English bodies must meet French standards, assume French postures. Many in the play spend a good deal of time trying to master the skills Frisk teaches, no matter how comic his accent or how foreign his origins. To dance in the French fashion and to avoid English rudeness is represented as a good thing—who, after all, would be Barker, the man who cannot dance properly, if he could be Rainbow, Frisk's best pupil? In fact, Lord Rainbow's exalted rank—he is the play's only titled character—seems to be confirmed by the fact that he dances so well. Perfect control of the body is thus "naturally" made to coincide with traditional forms of status. Nonetheless, Barker's initial dismay at being forced to learn fashionable dances, along with the comic aspects of Frisk's representation and the derogatory description of him as the "court dancing weasel," all raise subtle questions about the consequences of Frisk's cultural centrality. Might perhaps a passion for the foreign import, "the ball," and wholehearted submission to the Frenchman's tutelage do something undesirable to the ball's enthusiasts— make the men less manly, the women more frivolous, and all of them less "English"? Is the "court weasel" perhaps bringing unwholesome influences into "the town" from Henrietta Maria's courtly and Catholic ambit? These are the slightly scandalous questions the play cautiously invites and, especially in Act V, delicately negotiates.

Shirley, of course, was no enemy of the court. Before he went to Ireland in the 1630s all of his plays but one were performed at the Phoenix in Salisbury Court by Henrietta Maria's Company. In 1633 in the dedication to *Bird in a Cage* he was to make fun of Prynne, her sworn opponent; in the same year he was appointed Valet to the Chamber of Queen Henrietta Maria; in 1634 he helped to write the important masque, *The Triumph of Peace*, which Gray's Inn presented at court. None of this suggests an inclination to affront the Queen. In fact, Shirley has usually been considered a devoted Royalist,[35] though as Martin Butler has suggested, Royalist politics did not necessarily preclude criticism of the court.[36]

At some point, however, *The Ball* ran into trouble with the censor. Henry Herbert, Master of the Revels, wrote:

In the play of *The Ball* written by Sherley, and acted by the Queens players, ther were divers personated so naturally, both of lords and others of the court, that I took it ill, and would have forbidden the play, but that Biston [Beeston] promiste many things which I found fault withall, should be left out, and that he would not suffer it to be done by the poett any more, who deserves to be punisht; and the first that offends in this kind, of poets or players, shall be sure of publique punishment.[37]

Despite the effort of many critics, it is not clear what court figures were "pesonated so naturally," nor which characters in the play were supposed to represent them. Probably Rainbow was one, his rank as a Lord making him fit Herbert's description most closely.[38] As I will argue below, it is likely that Shirley was calling attention to the libertine ways of a particular lord or court group and making them objects of gossip. What interests me more, however, is what the incident suggests about Shirley's relationship to his audience. By in effect including recognizable court personages in his play, he flatters his audience at the Phoenix by including them in the circle of those familiar enough with court doings to understand the allusions. *The Ball* establishes its claims to fashionability precisely by promoting knowledge both about court figures and also about new institutions such as the ball itself. Given that "the town" was a concept under construction, and not a given, the play skillfully situates members of the town in a knowing, emulative, yet potentially critical relationship to the court, a delicate feat that in this instance got Shirley into momentary trouble with Henry Herbert.

No less complex is the play's relationship to the foreign influences that clearly lie behind the culture of the ball. If ambivalence to foreign ways is hinted in the slightly ridiculous figure Frisk always cuts—that ambivalence is intensified by the introduction of another character—the putative traveler, Freshwater, who in his embrace of all things foreign underscores what is problematic about uncritical emulation of foreign ways. In I.i. Freshwater arrives in London with tales of his travels. These might seem to give him a privileged relationship to continental sophistication. Rather than turning to a French dancing master who lives in London, Freshwater purports to have had direct access to all the cultural resources of France, Italy, and beyond. But as is quickly clear, he cannot really make the cut in fashionable society. Unlike those who truly achieve French standards of sophistication, I will argue below that Freshwater's is a bastard and fraudulent cosmopolitanism, a warning of how not to approach Continental culture.

Freshwater's depiction connects to an established tradition of representing travel abroad as a source of contamination as well as a possible benefit to the English who undertook it.[39] Dallington, for example, warned Englishmen who ventured to foreign shores not to grow corrupt in mind or manners (Bv) or to lose their religious faith (B2v). He represented the traveler as permeable, apt improperly to take the imprint of new surroundings. Consequently, he urged them to shed the clothing and manners of foreign lands when they arrive home since to do otherwise was a sign that the traveler's essential Englishness had been compromised. If the traveler's proper objective was "his ripening in knowledge, and the end of his knowledge is the service of his countrie" (B), then learning languages while abroad could serve that end, as could acquiring gentlemanly skills such as riding and fencing (B2v, C). Nonetheless, nearly every commentator makes clear that, improperly performed, travel could also corrupt and effeminate those who undertook it.

From its beginnings London comedy seized on the comic potential of the traveler. In Jonson's *Every Man Out of His Humour* (1599), the bad traveler—in that case the ridiculous Puntavarlo—demonstrated the folly of those whose encounter with the foreign was a matter of self-aggrandizement and not of useful knowledge. In *The Ball* Freshwater underscores by negative example the tact required to imbibe foreign ways without becoming ridiculous. His name, moreover, hints at a truth he wants to hide, namely, that he has not actually crossed any salt water. In fact, he has been no further than Gravesend and is a total pretender to foreign knowledge. That does not stop him, however, from attempting to impress his stay-at-home countrymen with the sophistication he has supposedly acquired abroad and the new inventions he has encountered. In a parody of travelers' narratives, he tells hearing in Venice of:

> chopinos made with such rare art,
> That, worn by a lady when she means to dance,
> Shall, with their very motion, sound forth music,
> And, by a secret sympathy, with their tread
> Strike any tune that, without other instrument,
> Their feet both dance and play. (I.i.141–46)

These fantastic magical shoes that both dance and play music would, of course, obviate the need for the wearer to learn the arts of either dancing or of fiddling since the shoes would do both. Freshwater's attraction to such a rare device is understandable, since he, too, would reap the benefits of travel without actually doing it and without learning the languages that would make it profitable or engaging in the rigorous dance instruction that would make magical chopinos unnecessary.

Through Freshwater, the play mocks not only the short-cut approach to cosmopolitan accomplishments, but also an *over* investment in foreign ways and a merely reflexive contempt for all things English. Coming to Lady Rosamond after an English painter has been doing her portrait, Freshwater reproves her judgement "to let an Englishman draw your picture,/ And such rare monsieurs in town" (III.iii.35–36). In the 1630s Mytens, Van Dyck, and Hollar were all at work in London, and Freshwater may be imagining them as the proper standard of artistic reference.[40] Elaborating further his desire to have a Dutchman paint her face, he says: "You must encourage strangers, while you live;/ It is the character of our nation, we are famous/For dejecting our own countrymen" (III.iii.39–41). "Dejecting" his countrymen, Freshwater has lost himself in the vacuous adulation of all things foreign even while lying about his exposure to them. His specious cosmopolitanism is most hilariously unmasked when, in the last act, he tries to impress several ladies by a farcically jumbled, but interminably lengthy account of European sites. Of Paris he says it is "a pretty hamlet, and much in the situation like Dunstable; 'tis in the province of Alcantara, some three leagues distant from Seville, from whence we have our oranges" (V.i.40–42). Brushing aside the suggestion that Seville is in Spain, not in France, he continues: "Do not I know Paris? It was built by the youngest son of King Priam, and was called by his name; yet some call it Lutetia, because the gentlewomen there play so well upon the lute" (V.i.50–53). Overheard by Lord Rainbow, this remarkable rant reveals Freshwater for the charlatan he is, as does the fact that when addressed directly in French, he cannot reply (II.i.91–92), apparently since he knows nothing of the language. His function in *The Ball* is as a limit case, an example of how not to engage, or pretend to engage, with fashionable foreign ways. If acquaintance with Continental arts can in theory raise one's status, a faked, slavish, or unskilled relationship to them renders one foolish.

Manners, Civility, and Social Status

In *The Ball*, many of the questions about how most appropriately to incorporate foreign and courtly practices into town culture are brought to a head in the plot in which four men of the town seek the hand of Lucina, the rich widow they all desire. This plot also reveals that manners and civil deportment can rival rank and also wealth as forms of cultural distinction. Elegant dancing, a signature of the well-disciplined body, is but part of a larger complex of behaviors distinguishing the truly civil from those whose high birth is their chief endowment. In this plot, birth and manners, new and old forms of status, vie for supremacy, chiefly in the persons of Bostock, a cousin of Lord Rainbow who is excessively proud of this connection, and Winfield, a man of moderate fortune who is a colonel in the army. These two men, along with several others, compete for Lucina's hand. Wishing to winnow her suitors, Lucina plays a trick on all four of them, making each think he is her choice. When the trick is revealed, Bostock's response is telling, and tellingly different from Winfield's. Going to Lucina's house, Bostock rails against her, braying away until he admits to exhaustion (III.iv.50–51). This provides the opportunity for Winfield to step forward and strike Bostock. Although he too has been tricked and mocked by this witty widow, and although he urged the rest of the jilted suitors to come and rail against the cruelty of their beloved, he uses the moment he has carefully orchestrated to separate himself off from the pack. After striking Bostock, he rushes to defend Lucina, denouncing the "impudence" of the railers, bewailing the "dishonor" done the lady (III.iv.61, 65), and ending with the following declaration:

Was ever civil lady so abus'd
In her own house by ingrateful horse-leeches?
Could your corrupted natures find no way
But this to recompense her noble favours,
Her courteous entertainments? Would any heathens
[Have] done like to you? Admit she was
So just to say she could see nothing in you
Worthy her dearer thoughts (as, to say truth,
How could a creature of her wit and judgment
Not see how poor and miserable things
You are at best?) must you, impudent,
In such a loud and peremptory manner,
Disturb the quiet of her thoughts and dwelling?
Gentlemen? Rather hinds, scarce fit to mix,
Unless you mend your [manners], with her drudges. (III.iv.80–94)

The terms of Winfield's self-serving speech are important. Praising the wit and judgment of this "civil lady," he derides his competitors as dishonorable hinds, horseleeches, and heathens, terms designed to emphasis their "low" qualities and lack of manners. Their railing at a lady in her own house proves his point. The striking contrast between Winfield's behavior, however calculated, and that of the other three suitors immediately leads Lucina to say to her attendant: "This shows a nobleness, does't not, Scutilla?" (III.iv.95). Manners win the day.

The consequences of this encounter for Bostock are dire. His status has depended entirely on his claim to be Lord Rainbow's relation, but his blood connection to nobility is not enough to insure his social status if he cannot also comport himself like an honorable man. Struck before witnesses by Winfield, he should retaliate, but does not, though he boasts to Lord Rainbow of having wounded Winfield. When his lie is discovered, Lord Rainbow denounces him for having besmirched the honor of an ancient family. Rainbow proclaims: "we inherit nothing truly/ But what our actions make us worthy of./ And are you not a precious gentleman?/ Thou art not worth my steel" (IV.i.216–19). In short, a gentleman is as a gentleman does, and Bostock is forced to carry a letter to Lucina in which Rainbow disassociates himself from his cousin's dishonorable actions. Bostock thus fails on two fronts. He is unmannerly to a lady and inattentive to the necessity of redressing affronts to his honor by other men. His noble blood alone is not sufficient to make him an object of desire or a winner in the competition for social supremacy.

Shirley uses Winfield, by contrast, to define the contours of proper masculinity. Stung by Lucina's trick, he nonetheless restrained his anger and channeled it into the chastisement of his rival and an elaborate defense of the lady's honor. In Winfield Shirley delineates a mode of civil behavior that differs not only from that of the satyr-like cynic, Barker, the ignoble Bostock, and the false cosmopolitan, Freshwater, but from that of the play's most privileged figure, Lord Rainbow, patron of the ball and agile, avid dancer. Through the juxtaposition of Rainbow and Winfield, Shirley poses the most complex questions concerning the town's proper relationship to the court and its fashionable foreign practices. Rainbow is the play's only lord and the only figure (other than the court "weasel," Frisk) who has an undeniable claim to be part of court society. Though scrupulous about certain points of honor and behavior (such as redressing the insult done to Lucina by his cousin Bostock), Rainbow is not so scrupulous in sexual matters. He is a libertine and one whose bodily health is subtly called in question. When two women, Honaria and Rosamond, reveal their interest in him, Rainbow insists that he cannot possibly choose between them and that they must decide which of them is the "fairest, wisest, sweetest" (I.ii.162). That one will have his allegiance. In essence, he leads on both but refuses to commit to either. At the ball, the women correct his presumption by having him draw lots for them, but present him with two blank papers, signifying their mutual withdrawal from his flirtatious advances. Chastened, he vows temperance and gives each a jewel saying that "hereafter I shall pay/ To your true virtues better service than/ So unnecessary trials" (V.i.228–30). The fact remains, however, that he shows no interest in marriage at any time in the play, and he needs to be rebuked into "temperance" by Honaria and Rosamund's trick. Though Henrietta Maria and Charles presented themselves as a pattern of chaste love,[41] Shirley's presentation of Rainbow hints that not all courtiers were equally circumspect in sexual matters. And Rainbow's may, indeed, be the portrait for which *The Ball* was originally censored.

Equally problematic are Barker's hints that Rainbow's body is also marked by a life of sexual liberty. Barker declares he will not flatter men like Rainbow "Whose bodies are so rotten they'll scarce keep/ Their souls from breaking out" (IV.i.37–38). Elsewhere, warning Honoria away from Rainbow, Barker says that she would not be attracted to his person if, as he had, she had "been acquainted with his body,/ Ha' known his baths and physic" (III.iii.101–2). Barker, of course, is not entirely to be trusted, since he himself wants Honoria, but the suggestion lingers that Lord Rainbow is not entirely "clean." While Freshwater's stench is easily discernible (he is accused of having foul breath by Barker in II.i), the implied venereal imperfections of Rainbow are more hidden. The competing discourses surrounding this Lord point to part of what is at issue in the "town's" incorporation of fashionable court practices. Lord Rainbow is at once the epitome of fashionability and a libertine whose behavior subtly calls into question his social pre-eminence. He both is and is not a proper model for West End emulation. Moreover, because he is the ball's chief promoter, suggestions of sexual impropriety persist around that institution, as well. While early in the play Rosamond proclaims that she "need not blush" (I.ii.20–21) for staying all night in Lord Rainbow's company if they are at a ball, her need to assert the innocence of a blushless face suggests that others might read such nocturnal adventures less charitably.

In contrast, Winfield is suspicious of the ball and firm in his pursuit of marriage, not sexual dalliance. Through him the play articulates a standard of sexual conduct that embraces worldly sophistication and yet is distinct from Rainbow's bantering and indiscriminate pursuits. When Lucina says she will marry Winfield if he will swear that he is "honest," meaning sexually chaste, he refuses, saying that his age, nearly thirty, and his profession, that of a soldier, militate against his chastity. In fact, he takes offense at her question, challenging her thus:

Why, look upon me, lady, and consider,
With some discretion, what part about me
Does look so tame you should suspect me honest? (IV.iii.87–89)

He offers his robust body as proof of sexual desirability and sexual experience. And he draws on the language of fashion to justify his behavior.

We vow no chastity till we marry, lady;
'Tis out of fashion, indeed, with gentlemen
To be honest and of age together; 'tis sufficient
We can provide to take our pleasures, too,
Without infection: a sound body is
A treasure, I can tell you; yet if that
Would satisfy you, I should make no scruple
To swear; but otherwise you must pardon us,
As we must pardon you. (IV.iii.103–11)

Sexual experience, for men of mature age, is "in fashion," with the proviso that in taking their pleasure, the gentlemen in question retain sound bodies. That he is, indeed, sound of body, Winfield is prepared to swear, providing a nice contrast to the reputedly corrupt body of Lord Rainbow. Winfield is marking out a sphere of conduct in which manliness is defined in part by (hetero)sexual prowess, but where regard for the self and for others demands that sexuality be conducted in such a way that the body not become diseased. He disciplines the body, not to chastity, but to health. Moreover, in refusing to swear that he is "honest" in the sense of "chaste," Winfield explicitly distinguishes himself from "Some silkworm o'the City, or the Court" (IV.iii.138) who for Lucina's estate would swear away his soul and vow a chastity he did not have. Not of court or city, Winfield represents the space between, the space of the town, and he claims the status of a gentleman and a soldier (the terms by which he swears when pledging sexual fidelity to Lucina after marriage [IV.iii.154–55]). More truly mannerly than Bostock and less sexually irresponsible than Rainbow, Winfield also has direct experience of foreign ways, having been abroad as a soldier. But while he can speak French, as he demonstrates when exposing Freshwater's linguistic insufficiencies (II.1.91–96), he lacks Freshwater's indiscriminate passion for foreign practices and Monsieur Frisk's slightly foppish dedication to the fashionable display of the body. Manly, experienced, and mannerly, Winfield emerges as a kind of ideal image of civil masculinity and a subtle challenger to the preeminence of Lord Rainbow.

It is therefore crucial what stance Winfield takes toward the ball. Will he become part of this crucial social space and the activities that define it, or hold himself aloof? Importantly, Winfield's attitudes toward the ball are expressed and shaped through interchanges with Lucina, the witty woman whose hand in marriage he has successfully won. His conversation with her signals the importance of women in emerging town culture. Witty, wealthy, and strong in her opinions, Lucina banters with Winfield in a way that presages the wit combat between the Millamants and Mirabells of Restoration comedy. When Lucina, for example, tries to hold him to a standard of sexual behavior he finds ridiculous for an unmarried man of nearly thirty, Winfield counters by implying that women of mature age and robust constitution also engage in pastimes that might make them suspect and for which they might require "pardon."

As if you ladies had not your figaries [vagaries],
And martial discipline, as well as we,
Your outworks and redoubts, your court of guard,
Your sentries and perdus, sallies, retreats,
[Parleys], and stratagems; women are all honest,
Yes, yes, exceeding honest! Let me ask you
One question–I'll not put you to your oath;
I do allow you Hyde Park and Spring Garden,—
You have a recreation call'd The BALL,
A device transported hither by some ladies
That affect tennis; what d'ye play a set?
There's a foul racket kept under the line,
Strange words are bandied, and strange revels, madam. (IV.iii.112–24)

Winfield here claims that women are amatory warriors, just like men, and that their "honesty" may be in question as much as men's. He names fashionable places, such as Hyde Park and the Spring Gardens, where women's honesty might be endangered, but he does not quarrel with women's attendance there. Rather, it is the institution of the ball that receives his greatest scrutiny. Drawing on the fact that it had been brought to London by tennis-loving ladies, he uses the language of tennis play to suggest the ball's sexual disreputableness. According to Gordon Williams, "to play a set" was to have a sexual encounter and a "racket" had phallic connotations.[42] Winfield thus suggests that the ball, with its foreign origins and potentially sexualized practices, is perhaps not entirely "honest," nor are the women who affect it.

Similar charges against the ball were to be even more explicitly rendered in Shirley's *The Lady of Pleasure* (1635), in which Sir Thomas Bornwell, who loves the country, castigates the extravagances of his city-loving wife, Aretina. Her name, of course, is the feminine version of Aretino, a figure already notorious in English culture for sexual licentiousness.[43] It is not surprising, therefore, that Bornwell is not only upset that his wife spends too much money. Worse is her prodigality with her reputation. Her fame is most put at risk, he claims, by:

your revels in the night,
Your meetings called the ball, to which appear,
As to the court of pleasure, all your gallants
And ladies thither bound by a subpoena
Of Venus, and small Cupid's high displeasure.
'Tis but the family of love translated

Into more costly sin. There was a play on't,
And had the poet not been bribed to a modest
Expression of your antic gambols in't,
Some darks had been discovered, and the deeds too;
In time he may repent and make some blush
To see the second part danced on the stage. (I.i.113–24)

Shirley here is clearly commenting on his own prior play and hinting that it whitewashed the sexual "gambols" associated with balls. In a muted form, with his mention of the notorious Family of Love, he seems momentarily to be siding with Prynne and assuming that dancing incites lewdness and that women who love it might be whores.

Winfield ultimately does not hold to this position, however, as Lucina sets about to redeem the ball from his censure. Crucial to his change of heart is the masque that precedes the general dancing. The masque sets Venus and Diana in competition. Venus, with Cupid in attendance, claims that the golden ball belongs to her (as in the story of Paris on Mount Ida) and that at Rainbow's ball "wanton glances fly" and "Lords and ladies of the game" have breasts full of Venus's flames (V.i.252–54). In a reversal of the Paris story, however, Diana emerges as queen of this assembly, casting out Venus's "lascivious fire" and installing "modest thoughts" in all who participate (V.i.263, 266). Cupid finds that his bow is frozen in his hand. Very like the little Cupid displayed on the title page to Playford's dance manual, this Cupid is not a very dangerous fellow. Diana even allows him to stay at the dance, provided that he "Throw [his] licentious shafts away" (V.i.298). That Cupid is played by Frisk, with his dark complexion and little beard (IV.ii.111–26), only heightens the nonthreatening aspect of the love god. The French dancing master is here reduced to a shaftless cherub. The role undermines Frisk's masculinity and diminishes the threat he might pose to the members of West End society. In the end, Winfield is forced to concede that the ball is "an innocent and generous recreation" (V.i.371). And indeed, it is the space in which a clarifying social sorting occurs. At the ball Freshwater is revealed as a pretender; Barker is laughed away as an antisocial "satyr"; and Rainbow is chastened by the two women he was simultaneously pursuing. Rather than a source of scandal, the ball turns out to be a site of moral education as much as a place for showing off one's dancing skill.

Shirley's final act perhaps protests a bit too much about the innocence of the ball, a surmise that his remarks in *The Lady of Pleasure* might support. Neither the impact of French fashions on town culture nor the relative value of manners in determining social worth was an issue with easy resolutions, and *The Ball* makes visible some of the social struggles that accompanied the emergence of these new modes of fashionable behavior. The play advertises the emerging cult of the ball and the offices of the French dancing master whose skills it requires; yet it renders Frisk comic and acknowledges that the ball could be read as frivolous and even salacious should Venus gain the upper hand. With the complex shadings of which Shirley's drama is fully capable, *The Ball* ranges its fashionable lovers across a spectrum that extends from the vacuous Freshwater to the witty Lucina to the vaguely promiscuous Rainbow, leaving the audience to construct its own understanding of what constitutes a desirable model of behavior for West End society. In this process, the initial reluctance of Winfield to embrace the ball only makes his ultimate endorsement the more important. As one whose origins are not courtly, and whose manners and wit win him the play's marital prize, Winfield suggests that the town can embrace courtly and foreign fashions without losing its own particularity or its Englishness. For at least some of the Drury Lane audience, this must have been a powerful solicitation to eschew lopping and trotting and to embrace the new forms of bodily discipline and mannerly conduct through which town culture was being performed into being.

The Museum Minervae and Academies of Manners on the Caroline Stage

In Shirley's play, dancing is taught in private homes, and no one talks about paying Monsieur Frisk, though one assumes he has had his fees. In a number of town comedies, however, dance instruction takes place in a very particular and important social space, that of the "academy." Whether called New Academies, Schools of Complement, or Schools for Ladies, these stage academies all are represented as places where Londoners purchase instruction in manners, deportment, and dancing. Often presented satirically, stage academies mock the quest for new forms of cultural legitimation and social mobility, turning a critical eye on unskilled members of city or country who attempt to master the refinements of emerging town culture and an equally critical eye on the instructors—often imposters—who teach them. However, academy plays are marked by contradiction. Making fun of the world of cringes, complements, and postures, the drama nonetheless obsessively stages just those things. Revealing and satirizing the commercial nature of instruction in deportment, the plays nonetheless occur in a commercial theater that itself has powerful if indirect pedagogic functions.

In the early seventeenth century the idea of academies as elite places of instruction in civil arts had its deepest roots in French culture. There, where the power and centrality of the court were far greater than in England, academies functioned to help the traditional nobility adapt to the new standards of bodily deportment and graceful conduct required by the French court. Beginning to be established at the end of the sixteenth century, these academies provided poorer or provincial noblemen, in particular, with the training in horsemanship, dancing, fencing, and military mathematics that would allow them to be integrated into the upper reaches of the military professions and to assume a place at court.[44] Though concentrated in Paris, elite academies spread to provincial cities as well. Antoine de Pluvinel ran the most famous of the Paris academies, which, after opening in 1594, attracted gentlemen from all over Europe as well as from France. As early as 1610, for example, the Englishman Lord Clifford was in attendance at Pluvinel's academy, where he learned to ride, fence, dance, and play the lute, as well as imbibing a bit of mathematics and philosophy.[45] The main emphasis in these academies was on the careful management of the body. Typically, riding was taught from 7 A.M. to noon each day while dancing occupied one to two hours each afternoon, as did fencing. Emphasizing the new, the fencing methods taught in the academies stressed fluid movements and mastering graceful "postures" of the body, rather than exotic thrusts and parries; dance instruction equally aimed at inculcating grace and perfect bodily control.[46]

In England there were no exclusive, court-oriented academies of the sort run by Pluvinel. But the idea of a school or academy where one learned manners clearly did drift across the Channel as is evident in many plays of the 1620s and 1630s. As early as 1616 in Jonson's *The Devil Is an Ass* a foolish Londoner named Fitzdottrel wants his wife to get instruction in manners in anticipation of his acquisition of a dukedom (The Dukedom of Drowned Lands!). He asks:

Are there any schools for ladies? Is there
An academy for women? I do know
For men there was; I learned in it myself
To make my legs, and do my postures.[47] (II.viii.19–22)

This reference, besides being early, is important because it associates such schools with foolish and upstart figures such as Fitzdottrel, connects them to instruction in the management of the body (making legs and doing postures), and raises the interesting question of whether or not they are open to women. In *Devil Is an Ass* Mistress Fitzdottrel is eventually enrolled in a school run by an Englishwoman (actually a clever male character out to dupe Fitzdottrel) who is called "The Spaniard" since she continues to wear Spanish clothes after her travels there. A "mistress of behavior" (II.viii.37), this "woman" teaches her pupils how to make a good fucus, carry their trains, and manage their chopines or high shoes.

A character disguised as a Master of the Complement School likewise appears in Shirley's 1625 play *The School of Complement.* This figure, with the lovely name of Criticomaster, is actually a jilted lover, Gasparo, who puts up bills advertising his enterprise and quickly attracts to his school a variety of Londoners, both male and female, who wish to learn how to engage in polite conversation (that is, to make complements) and how to manage their bodies in fashionable society. His pupils include a chambermaid who comes for lessons before her mistress gets up in the morning, a widow from the country, a yeoman's son in love with a farmer's daughter, and, above all, Bubulcus, a rich gull who wants to woo a usurious merchant's daughter. The scene in which they are all "schooled" in complement lets every character display social ineptitude and crass ambition in equal proportions. Perhaps only Gasparo as schoolmaster really benefits, since he purges his melancholy by laughing at their absurd imitations of elite behavior. Bubulcus, for example, set to practicing complements appropriate for courting a lady, vows fervently that: "I desire to suck below your waist" (III.i.p.49).[48] From its first appearances in London comedy, therefore, academies of manners were constructed as spaces where instructors operated under false pretenses and where students' desires for upward mobility were matched only by their ineptitude in performing the codes of gentility.

There was at least one historical academy within London, however, that attempted to fulfill some of the same social functions as did the aristocratic French academies, though the differences between them are as telling as the similarities. This academy, pretentiously named the Museum Minervae, was established in the mid-1630s in a pivotal West End site, the newly erected Covent Garden complex, and was the brainchild of Francis Kynaston, a gentleman who held court office under both James and Charles and sometimes served as a member of Parliament from Shropshire. In 1633 or 1634 Kynaston first proposed the creation of an academy to train up the nobility and gentry of England in arms and arts. He received patronage and monetary support from Charles who granted him letters patent in June of 1635. In 1636 he published a constitution for the academy, which operated for several years at a site on Bedford Street just to the west of the Inigo Jones church that had been erected at the western end of the Covent Garden piazza. This was a very good address because it put the Academy within the orbit of all those who lived around the piazza or who came there to stroll and take in the sights. The academy was closed, however, by 1639, the victim of the plague of 1637 and acute shortage of money.[49]

The 1636 *Constitutions of the Museum Minervae* is a fascinating document for what it reveals about what Kynaston hoped his academy would do. First, it was to bring London into line with "other great transmarine Cities,"[50] such as Rome, Padua, Wittenberg, and Paris, that already had such academies. At once chauvinistic and somewhat defensive, Kynaston wants England to be as well equipped to educate its gentlemen as any nation in Europe, but he admits that up to this point London has both overvalued and overrelied upon foreign teachers. Consequently, the *Constitutions* bans any foreigner or alien from being either Regent or Professor at the academy (p. 8); moreover, in his Preface Kynaston asserts that once his academy is established, Englishmen will neither have to travel abroad for instruction in arms and arts nor have to take lessons from foreigners in London, many of whom have, according to Kynaston, proved ignorant instructors. This is not unlike the praise James Shirley gave the Beaumont and Fletcher folio of 1647 in which he claimed that their authentic wit had "made Blackfriers an Academy, where the three howers spectacle while Beaumont and Fletcher were presented, were usually of more advantage to the hopefull young Heire, than a costly, dangerous, forraigne Travell."[51] The academy and the stage are both presented as providing a service for which Englishmen had formerly had to travel abroad. They were institutions through which England was playing a kind of cultural catch-up. If plays such as *The Ball* seem anxious about the effects of French dancing masters on English bodies, Kynaston's academy negotiates that threat by having the instruction done by Englishman, though the academy itself and much of the instruction it offered were resolutely modeled on French prototypes.

The document also reveals something of the difficulty Kynaston had in defining the exact market niche for which he was aiming his academy. Clearly afraid of being seen to encroach on the territory of other institutions, he claimed he did not wish to compete either with the universities (which would continue to teach such subjects as divinity and physic) or with the Inns of Court (which would continue instruction in the law). Instead, his academy was to focus on teaching the accomplishments befitting a gentleman wishing to be at ease either at court or in the urbane culture of the West End where the academy was located. The curriculum included instruction in languages, heraldry, coins, medals, physic, astronomy, navigation, fortification, architecture, music, languages, riding, dancing, behavior, painting, sculpture, and writing (pp. 4–5). Each enrollee was to pursue two sciences simultaneously, one intellectual and one corporal. These "sciences" included many of the skills that formed the informal or parallel curriculum already pursued by many members of the Inns of Court who took lessons in fencing, dancing, and languages somewhere in London outside the Inns. Kynaston's innovation was to gather the teaching of these fashionable accomplishments under one roof and to staff his academy with English

instructors. Kynaston's list of skills to be taught echoes those Henry
Peacham had urged the complete English gentlemen to acquire,
though to do so Peacham told his readers "first of all to see France."[52]
Kynaston, by contrast, would confine the grand tour to the West End.

This fact alone made it possible for clients of his new academy to be
of a more varied social background than much of Kynaston's rhetoric
might suggest. He insisted that those admitted to the Museum Minervae had to show proof of their gentility, but he made an exception for
the sons of benefactors. Though I found no records of who financed
Kynaston's academy, the implication is that some of the benefactors did
not have the requisite coat of arms or other marks of elite status
through which their sons would have won automatic admission to the
academy. For these benefactors, money, not status, would propel their
sons up the social ladder and into the select company for which the
Museum Minervae had been formed. While the *Constitutions*, imitating
French academies, thus speaks repeatedly about training the gentry
and nobility in arms and arts, in actuality the fashionable accomplishments taught at the Museum could as easily appeal to those below the
rank of gentleman who hoped to follow a course of upward mobility or
move with ease in town society. A system of fees, moreover, starting with
a five pound admission fee (p. 9) and persisting for three and a half
years (p. 2), provided evidence of the quasi-commercial nature of an
enterprise that advertised itself as a noble-minded contribution to the
national good, backed by the King and secured by letters patent.

The Museum Minervae's physical location and its prominent back-
ers must have brought it considerable notoriety. One of the great
undervalued playwrights of the 1630s, Richard Brome, found a way to
capitalize on that notoriety for his own purposes. His *The New Academy*,
probably written in 1635,[53] takes devastating aim at Kynaston's undertaking, probing its contradictions and mocking the pretensions of
those infected with the itch to learn postures and complements. In this
complicated play, Brome's satire moves in many directions at once. Directly mocking Kynaston, Brome also mocks court-driven modes of
fashionability and tellingly exposes the commercial logic and the sexual implications of schemes to teach manners, complements, and postures to aspiring members of town culture. In Brome's play the value
and respectability of the "new Academy" are from the outset called in
question because its founder, Strigood, the wastrel half brother of a
merchant, sets it up purely to make money when other sources of income fail. He is, moreover, not a dancing master, though he pretends
to be one, assuming the name Lightfoot. His masquerade casts a cloud
of fraudulence over his "new Academy"[54] and the instruction given
there in "Musick, Dancing, Fashion, Complement" (III.i.p.55). In an

unmistakable reference to Kynaston, Strigood claims for himself the title of Regent and proclaims his assistants are all "Professors of Court-discipline,/ By the most accurate, yet more familiar/ Rules, then have ever yet been taught by any,/ For quick instruction both of young and old" (IV.ii.p.79). While Kynaston had hoped that his pupils might en-roll for up to seven years, Strigood intimates that the main allure of such a school might be the promise of quick-time instruction in man-ners for those hurrying to the top of the social heap. In fact, most of the clients for the New Academy appear to drop by for instruction of an hour or so in French dances, curtsies, and complements. Brome therefore manages to imply not only that Kynaston's teachers are frauds, but also that nothing more serious than a patina of fashionable behavior is on offer in any case.

Strigood is also presented as a Catholic, one who, "adverse in Reli-gion," is suspected of having abducted two young women and carried them beyond the seas to a nunnery (II.i.p.31). He says he learned how to disguise himself as a dancing master from a Jesuit (III.i.p.57), play-ing on the equation of Jesuits and dissemblers. These details connect the counterfeit dancing master to the court of Henrietta Maria by reli-gion as surely as by his espousal of French dancing and complements. By linking Strigood to Kynaston and the court, and by burlesquing court attainments, Brome satirizes the pretensions not only of the Mu-seum Minervae but also of the Queen's entourage, suggesting that in truth their refinement is not much better than the down-market accom-plishments on sale by the hour in Strigood's academy.

But the heart of the play does not lie, I think, in its indirect satire of the court or even of Kynaston, but in its investigation of the destabiliz-ing social consequences of making instruction in manners a commer-cial enterprise and of placing too high a value on purely mannerly accomplishments. One of the characters who longs to visit Strigood's New Academy is Rachel, once a maid for, but now the wife of, Matchil. She exclaims with pleasure that her "friend will carry me to a what-deecall, a new Academy, where I shall see the rarest musick and danc-ing, he sayes, and learn the finest Complements, and other courtly qualities that are to be had for money, and such instruction for the newest fashions" (III.i.p.50). Raw enough not even quite to know the name for this new place of instruction, Rachel nonetheless hones in on a key feature of the academy. It is where "courtly qualities" are to be had for money and where a former chambermaid can be taught to imi-tate courtly ways. More blatantly than Shirley's *The Ball*, Brome's *New Academy* underscores the raw social climbing that lies behind the craze for instruction in manners and also, by implication, behind the found-ing of Kynaston's high-brow academy.

The alternate title for *The New Academy* was *The New Exchange*, and the resonances of that choice are multiple. As I have indicated, the New Exchange was the upscale shopping arcade built on the Strand in 1609, the West End answer to Gresham's Royal Exchange in the heart of the old walled city. When Strigood establishes his new academy, he puts it in the house of a mercer named Camelion who lives very near to the New Exchange (II.i.p.23). The location weaves the academy directly into the culture of buying and selling from which Kynaston's upscale Museum attempted to distance itself. The overlay of the mercer's shop by the academy of manners throws into relief their similarities. At the mercer's shop Camelion's wife sells cut-work bands, shirts, waistcoats, and nightcaps (II.i.p.27), items of personal adornment that proclaim one's social place and, because they are commodities, make social place as much the effect of marketplace negotiations as something innate or immutable. The academy does the same thing, but the adornments it sells are the reverences, bows, curtsies, postures, dances, and complements that structure the body's positioning in space and the nature of its vocalizations. Because these can be taught (or sometimes taught), they too can destabilize inherited social hierarchies. Ironically, if deportment and manners are becoming new markers of social distinctions, making them vendible goods erodes their viability as indications of much besides relative buying power. Strigood's school suggests that by buying a few hours of instruction in dancing, an oaf might be transformed into a gallant or a maid into a lady, "new exchanges" of a socially consequential sort. Of course, most of the scholars fail to perform gentility well, and so the fiction can be maintained that some people have innate gracefulness beyond what the schools can teach. Nonetheless, Brome's play reveals the potentially destabilizing consequences of marketing manners and of shaping and reshaping bodies into fashionable and hence socially powerful forms.

But the relentless emphasis on molding and displaying the body in Brome's and in other academy plays is also powerfully linked with the body's sexualization and sometimes with its deformation. When *The New Academy*'s most foolish gentleman, Nehemiah Nestlecock, desires to learn French, Galliard, a Frenchman temporarily in residence in the academy, says:

Yes, I shall bring his Mout to it. But his Mout is yet a leetel too wide. But he shall have some of de water dat de woman use for anoder ting, to bring it better together; and he shall speak like de Fransh Lady. (V.ii.p.86)

Here a body part must be molded anew, the mouth puckered in some way, to allow French sounds to issue from an English body. I do not know exactly what kind of "water" is to be applied to Nehemiah's face to effect the desired change, but its slightly salacious connection to women's unnamed practices, and the fact that it will cause Nehemiah to speak like a French *woman*, suggests that under the tutelage of his foreign instructor, Nehemiah's body will metamorphose in ways threatening to his masculinity. In the market of manners, not every bodily alteration is predictable or desirable, especially to the unskilled consumer. Brome implies that in this instance following fashion will feminize Nehemiah and make him look silly.

In Brome's play, however, it is the bodies of women that are the most endangered by the changes and exchanges brought about by the New Academy. When Strigood set up his school, he brought with him his niece and a French woman who was her bosom friend. Both had been the unjust victims of Matchil's anger. Chased from his house where they had lived for many years, the women help Strigood instruct customers in dancing and complements. This way of earning a living, however, puts them, they realize, in danger of being perceived as sex workers.

Here we are view'd and review'd by all comers.
Courted and tempted too, and though w'are safe
In our chaste thoughts, the impious world may say,
We are set out to common sale. (III.i.p.60)

This is the common complaint of shopkeepers' wives throughout London comedy, and in this play is it echoed by Camelion, the mercer's wife, who hates to be set to public view in the shop (II.i.p.23). The difference is that in the school of manners the women must purposefully use their bodies to model correct form in dancing, in bowing, in kissing the hand and holding the handkerchief. Their profession requires them to be "viewed" and then "reviewed," and the viewing of their persons in the commercial context of the academy easily leads to the assumption that their bodies are vendible. When two men from France arrive at the academy, drawn by its reputation for French sophistication, they immediately view the girls, salute them with a kiss, dance with them, and eventually pay Strigood a fee to sleep with them. The play thus forges a discursive connection Prynne would have applauded between Frenchness, women who dance, and prostitution. This outcome is averted, however, when the women tell the men they are not whores. Honorably, the men request their hands in marriage. The fact remains, however, that the play overlays the mercer's shop with the academy of manners, the academy of manners with the brothel. They are all implicated in one another in Brome's multilayered satire. The market, which renders common and fungible all it touches, has now simply claimed manners and bodily deportment as its new domain.

Caroline comedies featuring ballrooms and academies place the represented body (and the actor's body) under intense scrutiny. In *The Ball* Monsieur Frisk demands that we notice the difference between the body that stoops and the body held erect, between the body that lops and hops and the body that swimmingly glides. In *The New Academy* there is a monstrously long speech in which Galliard, one of the gentlemen from France, demonstrates the chief arts the school imparts. The first is "the due carriage of the body,/ The proper motion of the head, hand, leg,/ To every several degree of person,/ From the peasant unto the Potentate" (IV.ii.p.85). He goes on and on, suggesting ways that by a movement of eye, hand, knee, or arm or by the depth of one's bow subtle gradations of respect can be shown to various social players. To judge how deeply to bow, of course, depends on accurately viewing the body of the person addressed. How important do her bearing, her clothing, and the set of her chin indicate she is? And, in turn, the bower's own status must be read off the depth of his bow and his carriage of his own body. Just how far must a person of a certain quality stoop in the presence of another person of a certain quality? Galliard evokes a world in which an accurate viewing of a body's deportment and postures is crucial to any meaningful social interaction, and in fact is the ground upon which it is constituted.

I call this a hyperbolization of the body within the emerging regime of manners. A new social language is being developed, but it has not yet been widely learned or fully accepted. Hence the nervous anxiety in ballroom and academy plays about learning to handle the body properly and the neurotic obsession with laughing at those who cannot. Hence also the salacious overtone to the many scenes of instruction in these plays. It is as if there is something slightly indecent about scrutinizing so minutely the "The exactest, newest, and familiar motions/ Of eye, of hand, of knee, of arme and shoulder" (IV.ii.p.85) or the "many exact postures and dimensions,/ Fit to be us'd by way of Salutation,/ Of courtesie, of honour, of obeisance,/ To all degrees of man or womankind" (IV.ii.p.83). What is being created is a scopic regime focused on the minutest details of the well-disciplined body, a body whose parts can easily be sexualized, as was apparent in *The Ball* when Lucina dreamed of the dancing legs of her suitor Lamont. Such sexualization can be a source of power or the opposite as when the young women who offer dance instruction in Strigood's academy find themselves viewed, reviewed, and propositioned.

In many of the academy plays the word "posture" appears as in Fitzdottrel's comment that he learned his "postures" at an academy or Strigood's contention that he teaches the many "exact postures" to be used in greeting others. A 1650 text entitled *The Academy of Complements* gives an indication of what such postures entail (see Figure 13). In the left foreground we see a man bowing as he greets a lady. Each part of

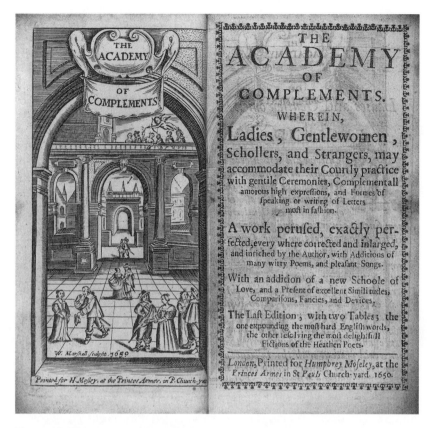

Figure 13. Title page and frontispiece to *The Academy of Complements*, 1650. By permission of the Folger Shakespeare Library.

his body is carefully positioned in space. With his left hand he has removed his hat from his head, and that he holds turned toward the lady. Simultaneously his right hand is raised toward his face in preparation for being swept back as he completes his bow. His torso is supported by a right leg stretched backward while the left points forward, toes gracefully turned out to the side. Prominently placed in the foreground of the woodcut, the gentleman exemplifies the graceful postures one learns from a stint at the Academy of Complement.[55] But in the period the word "posture" did not always occur in the context of mannerly sophistication. The first definition given for "posture" in the *OED* is "the relative disposition of the various parts of anything; esp. the position and carriage of the limbs and the body as a whole; attitude, pose." The first example (1606) is taken from *Antony and Cleopatra* when the Queen says she does not wish to see "some squeaking Cleopatra boy my greatness/ I'th'posture of a whore" (V.ii.216–17), that is, in the bodily pose associated with prostitutes, an idea to which I will return in a moment. Often, however, the term is used to indicate the proper position of a weapon used in drill or warfare (*OED* 2b). For example, a 1623 manual printed in London and entitled *The Military Discipline wherein is mo[st] martially shone the order of Drilling for y[e] Musket and Pike* is composed almost entirely of illustrations showing the proper postures of the musket and the pike (see Figures 14 and 15). In these illustrations, the martial body is a thoroughly disciplined body, arms, legs, and weapons moving together in perfect synchrony.

In the domain of manners, however, "postures" are not about disciplining the body to manage weapons effectively, but about positioning bodies in ways that invite scrutiny for indications of one's command of a new language of fashion and social distinction. For some, the substitution of the "postures" of the pike for the "postures" of the dancing academy traces a decline in English masculinity. In Shirley's *The Ball*, it is no surprise that the soldier Winfield is one of the last to be convinced of the propriety of this new social phenomenon. Used to "winning fields" in a military sense, he is reluctant to submit his body to the complemental postures of the dancing floor, the new field of social action and differentiation. It is, however, the bodies of women that appear most endangered by the intense corporal scrutiny that attends the new regime of manners. So scrutinized, women's bodies can solicit prurient or lascivious interest. In William Cavendish's *The Variety*, a French dancing master named Galliard scrutinizes the "reverence" performed by a young woman and proclaims it unacceptable. "Dis reverence displease a me very mush, because you go back, back vid your buttock, as if some vod take you by dat, to vat me vil give a no name."[56] Intently observing her bowing body, Galliard gages the jut of the young woman's buttock; its angle suggests to him that someone has grabbed hold of an unmentionable body part and pulled the woman's rear end into an unfashionable position. His remark, of course, conjures up a verbal image of what was in this case not physically mimed on the stage, namely, a male character grabbing a woman's pudendum from behind as she bows forward "in a reverence." The lines, once spoken, cannot help but eroticize the young woman's "posture," creating a ghostly mental image of an imagined action. Cleopatra feared being involuntarily displayed "in the posture of a whore," yet this is exactly what happens to Galliard's pupil and what happened to Strigood's nieces, viewed and reviewed within the scopic and commercial context of the dancing academy.

To twenty-first century critics, appropriately enough, the most famous of Renaissance "postures" are those associated with Aretino's "sonetti lussuriosi," a series of sexually explicit poems written to accompany

Figure 14. Postures of the musket from *The Military Discipline*, 1623. By permission of the Folger Shakespeare Library.

Figure 15. Postures of the pike from *The Military Discipline*, 1623. By permission of the Folger Shakespeare Library.

Marcantonio Raimondi's engravings of Giulio Romano's drawings of men and women energetically engaging in intercourse from a variety of inventive "postures"[57] (see Figure 16). Pornography, which from its linguistic roots means "whore-painting," depends on the graphic rendering of the body displayed and observed. As Ian Moulton has argued, its

O 'L mettcrete uoi? di tel di gratia,
  Dietro, o dinanzi? io lo uorei fapere.
Perche farotti io forfe difpiacere,
Se nc'l cul me lo caccio per difgratia?

Figure 16. An erotic posture, Giulio Romano, *I Modi*. Fototeca Berenson, Villa I Tatti, Florence.

primary reference is to visual, rather than literary, artifacts.[58] In Jasper Mayne's 1639 comedy, *The Citye Match*, two footmen carry to an outspoken new wife's bedroom the frame of two great pictures covered with a curtain. Her old and jealous husband sarcastically opines that:

It should be *Mars* and *Venus* in a Net,
Aretines postures, or a naked *Nymph*
Laying asleep, and some lascivious *Satyr*
Taking her lineaments. These are pictures which
Delight my wife.[59]

As it turns out, the curtain does not conceal erotic pictures, but rather two Inns of Court gallants; nonetheless, the reference in this context to "Aretines postures" suggests that they were commonly understood as signifiers of explicit eroticism.

In many Caroline comedies of manners, complemental postures and erotic postures merge, overlap, and intersect sometimes, as in Brome's *New Academy*, as a way of underscoring the purely instrumental use being made of the body in the scramble to acquire new forms of cultural capital and by so doing to snare a rich spouse or acquire a reputation for sexual sophistication. In another Brome play, *The City Wit*, a married woman who intends to cheat on her husband employs the services of a dancing master, Footwell. She implores: "teach me some tricks. Who would care for a female, that moves after the plain pace? No: Give me the woman of tricks. Teach me some tricks I prethee" (IV.i.p.335).[60] The "tricks" she wants to learn implicitly carry a double, sexualized meaning, underscored when she later tells her mother that Footwell "teacheth Gentlewomen to doe all things Courtly, to dance Courtly, to love their husbands Courtly" (IV.i.p.336). The erotics of the scene are further enhanced because Footwell is in actuality her husband in disguise who has found out about his wife's extramarital sexual longings and in the guise of a dancer both furthers her desires for courtly erotic instruction and ultimately thwarts her adulterous designs. To her desire to learn "tricks," he replies:

Tricks of twenty: Your traverses, Slidings, Falling back, Jumps, Closings, Openings, Shorts, Turns, Pacings, Gracings—As for—Corantoes, Levaltoes, Jigs, Measures, Pavins, Brawls, Galliards, or Canaries. (IV.i. p.335)

The moves required for fashionable dancing can easily be read as erotic choreography marked by traverses, slides, closings and openings, pacings and fallings back. As represented in these plays, the dancing master, the agent of civility, is never entirely separable from the whoremaster, teaching "tricks" of a less than reputable sort. That he should be represented in this way suggests not only the nervousness with which the period approached what was widely perceived as a French influence upon English culture, but also the hesitations accompanying the emergence of new ways of determining social worth. If many shared the enthusiasm for learning complements, French dances, and graceful postures, to some these new practices were little more than a form of prostitution.

Brome's *New Academy*, then, uses the overlay of brothel and academy to lay bare the uglier side of hyperbolizing the body in new regimes of physical self-fashioning, even as it comments on the bankruptcy of the court that authorized the craze for complements and postures and the rapid commodification of instruction in graceful deportment. Yet this play, like the others depicting dancing masters, ballrooms, and schools of complement, ultimately spurred the craze for the very practices they often critiqued. *The New Academy*, for example, is full of dances, and for all the fun that is made of those who want to learn the "Tres Bon" or the "Les tous ensembles," these French frolics are exactly what get staged. Moreover, at a much more profound level Brome seems to resist a "little islander" mentality. He may not like courtly affectation as it filters into town and city, but his play begins and ends with emphasis on English and French exchanges of the most intimate sort. Matchil, the English merchant, had sent his son to France as a mere boy to be raised by LaFoy, a French gentleman, with LaFoy's own son. Matchil, in turn, had taken in LaFoy's daughter to be raised with his own. Through a complicated series of mistakes, tricks and mishaps, these are the two girls who end up in Strigood's academy, while the two sons are the visitors from France who also come there where they try to proposition and then to marry the girls. With the promised double marriages at the end of the play, French man will marry English woman and English man French woman. The drama lays down no taboo against an Englishman being educated in France or marrying a French woman, provided that, in the end, he proves himself a worthy gentleman, as Matchil's son does when he refuses to take advantage of the women Strigood has presented to him as whores. Even at the level of comic detail, the play plants reminders that there is no way for England to cordon itself off from French influence. Camelion, the mercer whose house becomes the setting for the academy, is constantly reciting the only French words he knows: *"Honi soit qui maly pense"* (II.i.p.22 and ff.), the French motto of the English Order of the Garter. In this phrase, the long intertwined history of England and France is evoked, just as Matchil's son's French education signals the advisability of a seventeenth-century merchant's son learning the French language. Caroline town comedies are thus once more shown to have a complicated relationship to the

Continental practices they evoke, represent, and criticize. Satirizing the world of complements and reverences, *The New Academy* is nonetheless premised on its evocation and circulates knowledge of its practices.

The Cavendishes, Male and Female

In 1640 William Cavendish wrote *The Variety*, a play that draws liberally on the conventions and motifs of the dancing and academy dramas I have been examining, but gives them an overtly political spin. In this play dancing becomes a complex means of expressing factional differences and of commenting on the condition of England in the period leading up to the Civil War. Like earlier plays *The Variety* focuses on the social consequences of the craze for fashionable conduct and gives a prominent role to Galliard, a French dancing master who resembles Monsieur Frisk in Shirley's *The Ball*. *The Variety* however, multiplies the agents of fashionable instruction to include Mistress Voluble who, part cunning woman, part bawd, and part knowledgeable woman of the town, runs a Female Academy and Nice, a clever maid who can teach the skills of "Fashion, Garbe, and Language" (III.i.p.30) that will make a lady out of a common woman. The play, like other similar Caroline comedies, contains one figure—the aptly named Simpleton—who simply cannot learn fashionable ways no matter how much money he spends on dancing masters or how much he tries to ape the manners of his betters. But at the same time, the easy availability of fashionable instruction in this play, as in others, leads to the disruption of the traditional social order. Most notably, Simpleton's mother, a quicker study than her son, comes to London for the precise purpose of becoming "ladified" and marrying a knight (p. 6). The clever maid, Nice, teaches her everything she needs to know, and in the end the mother successfully passes as a rich and fashionable widow and marries Sir William, her knight.

The persistence of these elements from earlier Caroline town comedies is clear evidence that *The Variety* is knowingly using and commenting on the issues addressed in these plays concerning the acquisition of a new kind of cultural capital centered on the proper deportment of the body and mastery of the language of complement. But more forthrightly than any other dramatist of the period, Cavendish condemns the new fashions in dance and decorum as emasculating the English and making them unfit to defend their King. Cavendish was not primarily a playwright, but, as Earl of Newcastle, an important figure in the Court and, eventually, in the Royalist army fighting for Charles in the looming Civil War. In the 1630s, though loyal to Charles, Cavendish had become increasingly critical of what he perceived as the frivolity of the Court and the way in which Charles was surrounding himself with new men of slight value and pushing aside the traditional nobility. Sardonically commenting on the centrality of dance at the English court, Cavendish complained that those who "did nott make le bon Reverance & could nott dance a Sereban" had no standing with the King.[61] Appropriately, given his views, in *The Variety* the French dancing master is a more pernicious figure by far than in *The Ball*. He is presented as an agent of emasculation, someone who makes Englishmen unfit to fight, to govern cities, or to administer the law.

The model for Cavendish's dancing master, Galliard, was probably Barthelemy de Montagut, the French dancer first employed by Buckingham and later a groom in Henrietta Maria's Privy Chamber. He dedicated a dance treatise, *Louange de la Danse*, to Buckingham in which he argued that nobles needed dance instruction in order to improve their carriage, make proper bows, and join grace to action.[62] He is best known in the history of dance for promoting a less athletic style of dancing than had previously prevailed when Italian dancing masters were in fashion at court. Rather than leaps and lifts, Montagut emphasized bending, rising on the toe of the foot, and gliding. He also introduced the fashion of turning out the toes as one of the basic "postures" of the dance and synchronized the movement of arms with feet. In short, his style emphasized grace rather than athleticism, elegance over vigor.[63] In *The Variety* Galliard teaches dances pointedly named the Montague (II.i.p.18) and the Buckingham (p. 38), and he boasts that a relative of his has taught Englishmen who at one time "vent in vid deir toes" to "valk vid deir toes out" (II.i.p.20). Apparently, he is busy making the English into a splay-footed race.

Cavendish lights into Galliard with all the vigor the dancer himself is portrayed as lacking. One can get some idea of the impression Galliard made on the stage by looking at the woodcut (Figure 17) in which he is represented. In 1662 Francis Kirkman printed *The Wits, or, Sport upon Sport*, which was a compendium of scenes popular from the pre-Restoration stage. These included "The Humours of Monsieur Galliard," a scene lifted straight from *The Variety*. On the title page Galliard appears, along with Falstaff and other figures famous from the earlier drama. Fiddling as he dances and poised on one toe, beribboned and befeathered, long hair flowing down his shoulders, the French dancing master cuts a ridiculous figure, which is just as Cavendish would have wanted. In his play Galliard is the epitome of French mindlessness. His chief desire is to make all of the King and Queen's courtiers perform a perfect reverence, and after that to teach the same to the city's grave aldermen and all the lawyers. Queried by a scornful character named Newman as to whether Caesar or most of

Figure 17. The dancing master from Francis Kirkman's *The Wits*, 1662.
Reproduced by permission of The Huntington Library, San Marino, California.

"the worthies of the world, studied the liberall science of the foot, or puissant toe" (II.i.p.17), Galliard answers: "No, but begar dat make dem dye all unfortunate, for if dey had tinke of noting but de reverence, dey might ha live a great a while" (p. 17). In other words, better for Caesar to have lived a dancer than to have died a mighty public leader. For his heroic work in teaching proper reverences, Galliard wants: "a statur of de brasse, in de pallace yard, ven me goe out of dis varle" (II.i.p.19), thus imagining himself in the place of commemoration usually reserved for warriors and monarchs.

Cavendish certainly satirizes the self-centered and frivolous dancing master, but he most fully shows what is at stake in his centrality in the court and the town by juxtaposing Galliard to a character named, fittingly, Master Manley, an epitome of a deliberately old-fashioned Englishness. Manley's defining stage characteristic is that he likes to dress up as the Earl of Leicester from Queen Elizabeth's court, and his chief attribute is his opposition to the decadence of contemporary life as epitomized by Galliard.[64] Tricked into wearing his Leicester outfit into a fashionable West End house where Galliard is busy teaching Mrs. Beaufield, a rich widow, and Lucy, her daughter, how to do fashionable dances, Manley orders Galliard to pack his fiddle and depart (which he does) and launches into praise of the manly fashions and the warlike achievements of Elizabeth's reign: "these things were worne when men of honor flourish'd, that tam'd the wealth of Spaine, set up the States, help'd the French King, and brought Rebellion to reason" (III.i.p.39). In the context of events in 1640, including the rebellion of the King's Scottish subjects against the use of the Prayer Book, Manley's recollection of the military successes of an earlier era has considerable urgency as a comment on the King's own unreadiness to squash this rebellion. Galliard, earlier in the scene, had argued that teaching everyone to dance would have a positive effect on present disturbances. "Me tell you, ven dey are so bissey to learne a de dance, dey vil never tinke of de Rebellion, and den de reverence is obedience to Monarchy, and begar obedience is ale de ting in de varle" (III.i.p.36). In short, Galliard's way to deal with the present crisis is to have everyone take dancing lessons. The Manley character, by contrast, blames the sorry state of England precisely on the fact that its gentlemen and courtiers have been doing altogether too many "Montagues" and taking too little care of the state.

Eventually this scene deepens into a sustained contrast between the effeminate culture of the current moment and the vigor of Elizabeth's. Manley, after castigating the degeneracy of current days, breaks into several old-fashioned songs, including one in praise of the great English warrior, Lord Talbot, and begins an all-out attack on the dancing fashions of the 1630s. As morris dances are better than Montagues, lutes

and citterns make better music than fiddles or a French kit (small fiddle) "that looks like a broken fagot stick, at the biggest, and sounds as if
it had got the French disease, when it snivels out a Coranto, or so hoarse
with a cold, as if some great base Fiddle had silenc'd it" (III.i.p.43).
Small, sexually diseased, and vile-sounding, French instruments are ultimately no match for proper English ones. Manley, moreover, who is said
to himself resemble the "famous Cardell the dancing Master in Queen
Elizabeths time" (p. 42), has special praise for one Lord Loftie who used
to dance the athletic galliard with capers and half capers galore and
who especially favored the lavolta, a dance in which the man lifts the
woman high in the air. As Manley describes, Loftie "with wonderful skill,
he put his right arme about her, and took her left hand in his, and then
did he so touze her with his right thigh and legg, and lift her up so high,
and so fast, and so round . . ." (p. 43). (Fittingly, this had been a favorite
dance of Queen Elizabeth.) As opposed to the sliding, gliding, and
bending of Mr. Galliard, the athleticism of Loftie offers more than a
contrast in style. It is also a comment on the emasculating effects of
French fashion on English bodies, bodies that need to be recalled to a
native vigor. Cavendish is thus able to use the evolving conventions of
Caroline dance scenes vividly to embody a contrast in styles of dress,
bodily deportment, and manners that quite unmistakably critiques court
fashions and their effects both on England's political leadership and on
the town culture that imitates those fashions.

The Variety also, however, approaches gender issues from the other
side, not only by a critique of the unmanliness of currently fashionable
culture, but by a complicated representation of women's training for
good society. Manliness is never defined without its opposite, and in
this play there are also two types of femininity on display, but in a
more confused fashion than is true for the men. Some women, like
Simpleton's mother and the clever maid, Nice, throw themselves
wholeheartedly into the learning of manners and fashions, and they
use those new skills to make marriages. The mother marries her
knight; Nice snags Galliard who, despite his exquisite taste, cannot
really tell a maid servant from a well-mannered lady! However, the
most interesting figure is Mrs. Beaufield, a rich widow in whose house
much of the action occurs and who rejects fashionable suitors and
marries Manley, thus endorsing his values and his cultural style.
Throughout, she is a beacon of good sense, reproving one suitor for
engaging in courtship using an exaggerated form of complement not
fit to be understood (I.i.p.11) and at another point calling Galliard a
"foole" (II.i.p.24).

By contrast, Mrs. Beaufield is also presented as participating in some
of the very things she critiques. Both she and her daughter, for example,

take dancing lessons from Galliard, and he thus has access to her house and patronage. Beaufield, moreover, is friends with the not-quite-reputable Voluble, who in Act II addresses an Academy of Ladies who assemble in Beaufield's house and from which men are excluded. As far back as Jonson's *Epicoene*, academies exclusively for women were represented on stage as places of instruction in frivolous or lewd practices. The female sciences Voluble teaches are drawn from the standard antifeminist catalogue. She tells the attendees what kind of makeup to have concocted; where they can buy the best fripperies, such as ribbon and lace; what items must be fetched from abroad, such as gloves from Rome; what kind of underlinen is best; what oaths are out of fashion; and how to use curtains to create the most favorable lighting if you need to hide your age (II.i.pp.13–17). Though not as unrelentingly misogynist as Jonson's representation of female collegians in *Epicoene*,[65] or the Academy of Manners run by "the Spaniard" in *The Devil Is an Ass*, Beaufield's Academy nonetheless teaches skills that connect women with trivial and foreign consumption, with face painting, and with deception.[66] The representation of the Women's Academy in *The Variety* thus reinforces a long-standing dramatic convention of depicting Academies or Colleges of Women in a negative light where women have "secrets" that they wish to hide from men, whether these involve ways to hide the decay of the body, as here, or to end a pregnancy, as in *Epicoene*. When women gather together, the only "sciences" they are assumed to pursue are those of fashion or love.

Speaking of the Academy, Newman says he wishes its lectures could be prevented to which Sir William, the knight, replies: "They are more like to purchase Gresham Colledg, and enlarge it for publick Professors, you may live to see another University built, and only women commence Doctors" (II.i.p.20). But if women did establish their own university, Voluble's scene of instruction suggests that they would primarily learn frivolous and fashionable arts and beauty secrets. This representation of the Female Academy fits in a general way with Cavendish's satiric treatment of contemporary fashion, but oddly with his larger portrait of Mrs. Beaufield and her daughter, both of whom ally themselves with a new, more sensible order of things, a new order, which announces itself through allegiance to an older cultural moment. Lucy, in fact, marries a suitor given the apt name of Newman, a man who joins in Manley's dispraise of Galliard and, though a rake, is eventually reformed and proves himself a fighter and no court fop.

Incoherence in the portrait of Mrs. Beaufield has to do, I think, with the double impulse in Caroline town comedy to continue to link fashionable women to frivolous or disreputable concerns and the impulse to accord them a certain amount of power as social players and as arbiters of manners and morals. Such positive social power is certainly vested in women such as Lucina in *The Ball* or Julietta in *Hyde Park*, who in traversing the fashionable parks and ballrooms of London's West End reveal both wit and good sense. Mrs. Beaufield is an interesting case because she encodes both impulses in one figure more sharply than is true of the majority of women in these late London comedies. A woman of good judgement, she nonetheless patronizes Voluble and Galliard. While the main targets of attack in *The Variety* are the men who are betraying English manhood by their pursuit of affected foreign manners, the play nonetheless also participates in misogynist satire of women who wish to withdraw for a time from the company of men and form their own Academy. But in Cavendish's play, as in Ben Jonson's *Epicoene*, nothing but triviality can be learned or taught in such a place. If Kynaston's Academy at least aspired to train up the youth of the nation in arms, arts, and manners, Mrs. Beaufort's Academy teaches only where to purchase a good fucus.

In 1662 Margaret Cavendish, the wife of William, gave the world her own dramatic version of a female academy in a play of that name, and she issued a profound challenge to the ideologies encoded in prior depictions of female collegians. *The Female Academy* is in many ways not a very winning play, being rhetorical and static in manner, but it is fascinating both for its depiction of a school for women and for the self-consciously "undramatic" style in which Cavendish chose to stage it. Whatever else it is, *The Female Academy* constitutes a clever response to the Caroline town comedies that had depicted the fashionable world of London town culture.[67] Crucial to the play is Cavendish's reconstruction of the space of the Academy. In Cavendish's play, nothing happens there except high-minded talk. No one is taught to dance, to give complements, or to make reverences. Nor is anyone taught how to prepare a fucus or buy lace. Instead, under the watchful eye of "two Grave Matrons,"[68] the female members of the Academy take turns giving lectures on such subjects as whether women have as much wit or wisdom as men, on truth and falsehood, on friendship, on theater, on vanity, vice, and wickedness, on virtuous courtship, and on romance. To deliver their speeches, each woman is seated in a chair with arms. She does not move about, and the speeches are rhetorical set pieces, sometimes interrupted by serious questions from the grave matron who presides over the Academy. The women who join the school must be of honorable birth and rich. No man can enter, though men can stand at a grate to hear the women deliver their discourses. Gradually, in fact, the men who come to listen to the women grow jealous of their Academy and establish an adjoining one of their own where they debate topics such as the evils of women cloistering themselves or the ingratitude of women who will not converse with men when men do everything for women. Though they listen to the men's discourses, the women make no reply. In fact, it is as if they had never heard them. Finally, to get the women's attention and to drown out their voices, the men take trumpets and blow them loudly at the grate of the room where the women assemble.

This is a very witty play, especially when placed in the context of the academy drama that preceded it on the Caroline stage. Cavendish, first, effectively rewrites the meaning of the Female Academy. No longer a place for the circulation of frivolous or salacious information, nor a place where bodily deportment is modeled, it becomes a site for serious discourse on significant topics, making clear that women are capable of the pursuit of wit and wisdom.[69] The stasis of the Academy scenes, then, is part of their point, as is the shift from a scopic to an auditory economy and from polite conversation to serious rhetorical performance. Cavendish's women do not move or employ their bodies in eye-catching curtsies and reverences; instead, they insist on being heard. It is, in fact, the sound of their voices, engaged in acts of persuasion and argument, that so enrages the men, used to as they are to being the ones whose voices are heard and before whose eyes fashionable women display themselves. In fact, the self-sufficiency of the women particularly enrages the male listeners. They speak to one another, not to the audience at the grate, and though they hear the men, they do not care to respond to what they say.[70]

When under the threat of the men's trumpet the matron finally speaks to the male auditors, she explains that the women have not cloistered themselves, but rather have retired from public life to educate themselves and to preserve their reputations (sc. 29, p. 679). This echoes the first explanation given for the academy, namely, that it is a place where women, usually denied good tutors and so consigned to lives of folly (sc. 2, p. 656), have gathered to learn to speak wittily and rationally and to live virtuously (sc. 1, p. 653). Once that aim is attained, they have no objection to marrying men whose merits make them worthy of a learned and virtuous wife (sc. 29, p. 679). The Female Academy is rewritten, not as a School of Complement, but as a place for wisdom and virtue to flourish. Margaret Cavendish thus gives us the equivalent of sensible Mrs. Beaufields without insisting that they also be the patrons of Mrs. Voluble.

The Female Academy is a witty rejoinder to some of the dominant values of 1630s town comedy, but it also points to the power of the codes of fashionability and polite deportment adumbrated—though not without resistance and critique—within those comedies. In the 1630s the stage, partly by constructing social spaces like the ballroom and the academy, helped to create a London quite unlike the London of early city comedy. Replacing the shops and the public buildings of earlier London plays, the fashionable places of Caroline town comedy encompass, instead, the parks, the ballrooms, and the academies central to West End life. These venues are less scenes of work than sites for displaying a tempered cultural cosmopolitanism in which English bodies cautiously adapted themselves to French norms and where old rank and new wealth struggled for dominance on the new terrain of civility. New forms of deportment and speech become the cultural capital necessary for living well in such spaces, for acquiring social status, and for meeting Continental standards of bodily discipline. Lopping and trotting, uncouth speech, or an unfashionable reverence became causes for embarrassment and social exclusion. At the same time, those who performed well in these environments and wore their new sophistication lightly accrued power, women as well as men. Unmistakably, though, the regime of manners and the culture of politeness made the body a new site of visual surveillance and eroticization. Seemingly outside the marketplace, but not really, town culture simply put women and men on display in new ways as they were enjoined to buy instruction in civil arts from such ubiquitous figures as the French dancing master and then to submit themselves to the judging eyes of their peers. For women of the town, this could be particularly trivializing and sexualizing since, excluded from the serious learning to which some academies at least aspired, they were reduced to attending to their appearance, learning their "postures," and disciplining their bodies for the eyes of the gallants whom they would encounter at a ball or in the park. It is these more negative aspects of Caroline town culture to which Cavendish found radical redress in a Female Academy in which there is no dancing, only the sound of the learned female voice lecturing to other women about virtue and wisdom.

Epilogue

Margaret Cavendish's *The Female Academy* lies outside this book's primary temporal frame, but it suggests that there were forms of continuity between pre-War Caroline and post-War Restoration drama—continuities that tend to be obscured by the division between Renaissance and Restoration that has structured traditional accounts of seventeenth-century literary history. The Cavendishes, male and female, were deeply enmeshed in London court and town culture in the 1630s, and, having lived out much of the Interregnum on the Continent, they brought memories of the theatrical culture of the pre-War decade with them when they returned to London in the 1660s. They were not alone. Many Caroline theatrical traditions continued on after the Restoration, perhaps nowhere more vigorously than in the London comedies that continued to be written for the city's reopened public theaters.

In these plays the places of the city still provided settings, generic and specific, for many of the liveliest stage events of the ensuing decades.[1] Congreve's delicious *Way of the World* (1700) opens in a London chocolate house, a new and fashionable venue never glimpsed in pre-War London drama, but the second Act, set in St. James Park, recalls the sexual intrigue and witty conversation that marked the earlier "park plays" such as Shirley's *Hyde Park*. Similarly, Wycherley's *The Country Wife* (1675) rings changes on the story, familiar from the plays of Thomas Middleton, of a young woman's arrival in London and her induction into its sophisticated pleasures, partly by her introduction to specific London places. Anxious to seek out the best fields and woods for walking while in London, the country wife, Margery Pinchwife, is told that she should go to the "Mulberry Garden and St. James's Park; and, for close walks, the New Exchange" (II.ii.3–4).[2] Eventually she does try the pleasures of the New Exchange, but only when dressed by her jealous husband in the clothes of a male servant. This disguise does not, of course, fool the hawk-eyed and predatory city gentleman, Horner, who uses the occasion to kiss the attractive "young man" and to draw "him" off away from the jealous and agitated Mr. Pinchwife and into the walks of the Exchange. The building, meeting place for the

fashionable and center of upscale consumption, is thus also constructed as an erotic space in which the country wife gets her first taste
of the sexual pleasures that beckon city women. Running back to
Pinchwife, her hat full of the oranges and dried fruit Horner has
bought for her, Margery has already begun her conversion from country innocence to city sophistication. Placed in the middle of Act III,
Wycherley's New Exchange scene is the play's fulcrum, the space that
epitomizes the weaving together in town culture of sexual sophistication, urbane manners, and a knowing acquaintance with the most fashionable places for consumption and self-display.

If many of the conventions of Caroline London comedy thus persist,
in changed form, after the Restoration, linking Margaret Cavendish's
academy play to previous London comedies also calls attention to just
how much had altered in the genre between 1598, date of *Englishmen
for My Money*, and the late Caroline academy plays to which Cavendish
made reference in her own idiosyncratic drama. The pre-War Stuart
and Caroline drama does not form a homogeneous canon but one
undergoing rapid transformation even within that body of plays that,
under the rubric of London comedy, bears a family resemblance to one
another. Several stories of change can be told about London comedy
and the significant places and spaces that it dramatized during the four
decades that have been my chief concern in this book. One story
involves a gradual westward movement as the preferred locale for the
settings of city drama moved from places within the old walled city to
the fashionable venues of the West End. This story, accurate in its main
outlines, is, of course, complicated by the number of revivals that make
a performance history of the early modern stage such a rich and fascinating story. In the Caroline period, for example, Shirley wrote a number
of his fashionable London comedies, like *The Ball*, for Queen Henrietta's Men while it was performing at the Cockpit, and this company as
well performed such new London plays as *Covent Garden*, *The School of
Complement*, and *Tottenham Court*. But it also had such "old" city plays as
The Knight of the Burning Pestle in its repertory.[3] The history of London
comedy is not only a linear narrative, moving from one set of places
and concerns to another, but also a circular and spiraling story in which
new elements are added to the genre without cancelling the pleasure to
be gotten from revisiting earlier iterations of its conventions.

A second, related story has to do with the gradual substitution of
cultural capital for more blatantly economic forms of capital in the
plays' repeated representation of the battle for social preeminence in
the urban context—a substitution that required new settings for the
dramatic action. If the early plays tend to be set in East End shops or
commercial sites such as The Royal Exchange or Leadenhall, in

Epicoene (1609) Jonson glimpsed the possibilities of the Strand and the developing West End as a venue for exploring the role of wit and cultural sophistication in defining social worth. In the 1620s and 1630s a spate of London plays eschewed the direct depiction of commercial transactions and commercial spaces to focus instead on the parks, ballrooms, and academies where bodily deportment, mannerly behavior, and witty conversation became major determinants of social place. Of course, here too the narrative of linear progression needs to be complicated, not only because "older" forms of London comedy persisted on the city's stages alongside newer ones, but also because economic and cultural capital were never entirely dissevered in these plays. As Jonson demonstrated in *Epicoene*, cultural sophistication of the sort epitomized by Dauphine was not simply an end in itself; in his case it was deployed against the less sophisticated Morose to capture his fortune. Moreover, as Richard Brome, in particular, was fond of depicting, cultural capital was something that, just like pork pies and satin suits, could sometimes be bought and sold, the having of it being as much a matter of well-lined pockets as innate worth. Money and land never entirely disappear as factors in the scramble for social preeminence, though wit and social skills loom ever larger in successive decades.

The changing conventions of London comedy offer a fascinating perspective on the changing shapes of city life, but my main concern in this book has less to do with temporal change *per se* than with the recurring and purposeful use of specific London places to anchor the urban stories the dramatists of the time chose to tell. As I have attempted to demonstrate, London places, both specific places such as the Counter and generic ones such as the whorehouse, were complex and important elements within these London fictions. Partly, of course, they were discursive constructions produced *by* the drama that represented them, imaginative creations that referenced actual places in the city, but in doing so imbued them with meaning and gave them cultural significance. As such, these plays oriented playgoers to the imagined social uses and the implicit rules governing action within particular quadrants of metropolitan city space. At the same time, in transforming historical places into complexly imagined social spaces, dramatists used them to explore particularly troubling or resonant aspects of urban life.

Among the questions to which dramatists returned again and again was the effect on social life of changes in marketplace practices. The Royal Exchange embodied one form of change and challenge. Triumphantly proclaiming London's emergence as an international entrepot rivaling Antwerp, Marseilles, and Venice, the Exchange was staged in ways that also revealed the darker or more anxious side of commercial growth and expansion including its double-edged consequences for the women who worked on the building's second floor or pawn. International in design and inhabitants, the Royal Exchange was evoked by a writer like Haughton to embody the challenge cosmopolitanism posed to homogeneous notions of Englishness. By contrast, Heywood used it in *If You Know Not Me, Part II* to articulate ambivalent attitudes to the scale and abstract nature of international commerce and to the effect of new economic practices on traditional guild life and on the exercise of charity. On the stage, then, the place entered the culture's imaginative life as a densely coded site speaking to the dangers and pleasures of new kinds of commercial practice, but in complex and contradictory ways that were inevitably intertwined with the changing nature of urban gender roles and the city's increasing indebtedness to and interactions with alien people, goods, and practices.

All the dramatic places explored in this book emerge as equally dense sites of ideological contestation, perhaps nowhere more clearly than in the many stories that stage the Counters, the city's main debtors' prisons. The obverse of The Royal Exchange, the Counter does not reveal where money is made, but the consequences of its loss and the effects of that loss on masculine identity in particular. In an age of ubiquitous credit arrangements, to lose one's reputation for creditworthiness was to court social death, signaled in Counter plays by a relentless descent to the lowest depths of the prison and by a gradual loss of the sartorial markings that defined rank and social being. But what caused such a descent, and whether one's financial credibility was the only valid determinant of social value—upon these matters Counter plays differed considerably. Some, like Rowley's *When You See Me You Know Me*, staged the Counter to reveal the abuses of the poor by the wealthy and powerful, while others, like Jonson's *Every Man Out of His Humour*, made the Counter a place of necessary punishment for those too greedy to control their passion for hyperbolic consumption. The Counter plays as a group struggle to make sense of debt and how much it is caused by individual failures, how much by the corruption of the powerful, and how much by the indifferent operations of a market too complex for ordinary people to understand. In that regard, they speak with unusual relevance to the dilemmas of late as well as early capitalism. Moreover, in their exuberant staging of the avid consumption that leads to ruinous debt, Counter plays embody a further contradiction, inciting consumer desire by their displays of sartorial finery and high-end consumption even as they condemned those displays and that consumption. These plays are a good reminder that even as the theater commented *on* the market and its operations, it was always also *in* the market. Even as it told stories that mobilized the places of the city for particular ends, it, too, was a special kind of urban place, one that invited spectators to enjoy the pleasures of cultural consumption, material spectacle, and virtuoso performances of class privilege by those of mean estate. As a result, the theater could solicit spectators to enjoy the very things against which their fictions apparently warned.

In exploring the economic life of the city, perhaps no site, however, was more complexly rendered than the ubiquitous whorehouses that appear in play after play, sometimes clearly designated as such and sometimes intertwined with and indistinguishable from taverns, homes, and lodging houses. The illegibility of brothels and of whores and bawds in some of these plays is, I have argued, part of their point. Ubiquitous but illdefined, the scene of prostitution was potentially everywhere, a signifier of the market's increasing permeation through every quadrant of the city. And yet, while some whore plays, like *Chaste Maid in Cheapside*, can be said to function as a proleptic critique of the saturation of everyday life by market values, many of these dramas use the brothel, and the passage in and out of prostitution, to narrate the changing place(s) of women in urban life and their roles as entrepreneurs and cultural brokers. With highspirited energy whorehouse dramas often show the impossibility of "fixing" female identities within the prescriptive grid of maids, wives, and widows, and they use the figure of the cosmopolitan whore to explore the advantages as well as the dangers of bringing home alien customs and alien tongues.

As in the Royal Exchange plays, whorehouse dramas thus mediate an unalterable fact of London life, namely, the increasingly visible heterogeneity of its population and of the products and the languages seen and heard in its shops and streets. Whether they were foreigners born outside London or aliens born abroad, the city was full of people who hailed from different places and did not necessarily share language or customs. Many of the places explored in this book become sites through which the stage told stories about how London could accommodate, or fail to accommodate, the aliens in its midst. While *Englishmen for My Money*, like many other plays of the period, stigmatized strangers by making fun of their speech, it also tried to incorporate the powerful Portingale, Pisaro, into the English community by the willing marriage of his daughters to English gentlemen. Whorehouse plays, by contrast, typically represented the alien through images of disease or, conversely, of an attractive cultural sophistication. In *Northward Ho* a whore's skill with languages is presented as a boon to her business and her multinational clientele as a simple fact of urban life. In *Hollands Leaguer* a famous Bankside brothel is dramatized as a site of cultural sophistication rather than of disease or degradation. If xenophobic undertones thread through these whorehouse plays, their dominant impulse is the energetic exploration of ways to incorporate and capitalize on difference, if only as a necessary strategy to increase the profits to be made in the flesh trade.

The academies of manners that emerge at a later point in London comedy's history oddly mirror the whorehouses from which they, at first blush, appear so markedly to differ. But they, too, are concerned with the consequences of alien practices on English bodies, though in this case the foreigner is most often a French dancing master and not a Flemish or Italian whore. At stake is the supposed purity of Englishness, repeatedly revealed to need the supplement supplied by alien money or alien expertise. Academy stories dance round and round the question of whether English bodies are improved or enervated by adopting practices of bodily deportment imported from abroad and whether manners and civil conduct are a true test of social worth or a cheapening of more substantial and longstanding means of determining status. In the cauldron of social change represented by London life in the early seventeenth century, Caroline drama focuses on the academy of manners as a site that offers a fresh perspective on recurring questions concerning the cosmopolitan nature of urban life, the malleability of identity in a market economy, and the dangers and pleasures of new forms of bodily practice.

Throughout this book, gender has figured as an indispensable category of analysis. Places themselves are sometimes gendered, as is true of the Counter. Though historically debtors' prisons incarcerated women as well as men, on the stage the Counter is a masculine space, suggesting the importance of fiscal credit to dominant understandings of masculine identity. Other sites are multiply gendered. In Exchange fictions, the ground floor, the place of big financial transactions, is presented as male space, while the pawn, site of everyday consumption, is insistently connected with women who sell or who buy in its shops. Yet these place-based plays not only suggest how social spaces become associated with men or with women, but also reveal how the way space is used, or "practiced," structures social relations between men and women as surely as between different social classes or between foreigner and native inhabitant. In many Caroline plays, for example, academies subject bodies to intense and detailed scrutiny. While some men suffer under this scopic regime, the less skilled forfeiting social preeminence, women are relentlessly sexualized, their bodies invited to assume "postures" that make deportment indistinguishable from erotic display. It is against such practices that Margaret Cavendish constructed her female academy in which the rational voices of intelligent women substitute for elaborate bodily displays as the focus of audience attention. In this case bodily stasis and women's eloquence redefine the space of the academy entirely, banishing the dancing master and foregrounding instead the grave matron who presides over the scene of learned female performance.

There are, of course, many places that this book does not explore but that were central to London comedy. St. Paul's Cathedral is one, its middle aisle a recurring site for masculine self-display; the parks and pleasure gardens of the West End are another. Instead of providing an exhaustive catalog of the significant places of London comedy, however, my purpose has been to suggest the utility of place as a way to understand the synergy between the city and the theater and the role of plays in constructing the social meanings of place and the ideological implications of the stories that unfold upon its terrain.

It is an ancillary benefit of this project that in exploring some of the resonant places of London comedy I have gotten to write about a number of plays not often examined in recent critical literature. For a long while Shakespeare has dominated the study of Renaissance drama, and I have benefited from a long career spent happily writing about his plays and teaching them to my students. But the focus on Shakespeare changes the understanding we might otherwise have of the period and of the role of the drama in it. Shakespeare did not write any plays that without qualification we can call London comedies, though *Merry Wives of Windsor*, with its sharp-tongued housewife protagonists, its focus on the places of Windsor, and its complicated accommodation of foreigners within its celebration of "English" ways, is a near cousin, as is, in another vein, *Measure for Measure* with its dark exploration of the prison and the cloister as significant places in the urban world of Catholic Vienna. But Shakespeare for whatever reason did not focus up close on the city in which he earned his living.

Other dramatists did, and looking, as this book has done, at a broad sweep of city plays makes evident how the city fed the imagination of its playwrights. It also lays out in the starkest terms the collective nature of theatrical culture in the period. Counter plays echo and ring changes on other Counter plays; successive whorehouse dramas work off a shared set of conventions. This did not so much stifle the creativity of playwrights as release it. This density of cross-reference among city dramas, however, was what in part allowed place to have the importance that it holds within this canon as playwrights imitated one another in anchoring their plots around particular sites. As they did so, the social meanings attributed to those sites grew more complex, their value as counters in complex ideological negotiations more pronounced. Yet the wild card in the deck remains the particular and intense pleasures these plays make available. Not documentary records of the city, and not moralized sermons, either, they remake London as they stage it, and through the seductions of spectacle and word, make the theater a place where people would return, again and again, to experience through fictions the world in which they almost lived.

Notes

Introduction

1. Frederick, Duke of Wirtemberg, "A True and Faithful Narrative" (1602), in *England as Seen by Foreigners*, ed. William Brenchley Rye (London: John Russell Smith, 1865), p. 7.

2. David Harris Sacks and Michael Lynch, "Ports 1540–1700," in *The Cambridge Urban History of Britain*, vol. 2, ed. Peter Clark (Cambridge: Cambridge University Press, 2000), pp. 377–424, at 384.

3. See R. Finlay, *Population and Metropolis: The Demography of London 1580–1650* (Cambridge: Cambridge University Press, 1981), esp. pp. 51–66, and Vanessa Harding, "The Population of London, 1550–1700: A Review of the Published Evidence," *London Journal* 15 (1990): 111–28. Because deaths were so high in the metropolitan area, in-migration from the provinces and from abroad had to be extensive just to maintain the population at a fixed level. It had to be considerably greater to fuel the kind of explosive growth typical after 1550.

4. Jeremy Boulton, "London 1540–1700," in *The Cambridge Urban History of Britain*, vol. 2, ed. Clark, pp. 315–46, at 315.

5. For a broad overview of the importance of London in creating a national market within the British Isles, see Fernand Braudel, "National Markets," in *The Perspective of the World*, vol. 3 of *Civilization and Capitalism, 15th–18th Century*, trans. Sian Reynolds (Berkeley: University of California Press, 1992), pp. 277–385, esp. 352–85. See also Eric Kerridge, *Trade and Banking in Early Modern England* (1979; reprint, Manchester: Manchester University Press, 1988); F. J. Fisher, "London as an Engine of Economic Growth," in *London and the English Economy 1500–1700*, ed. P. J. Corfield and N. B. Harte (London: Hambledon Press, 1990), pp. 185–98; Joan Thirsk, "England's Provinces: Did They Serve or Drive Material London?" in *Material London, ca. 1600*, ed. Lena Orlin (Philadelphia: University of Pennsylvania Press, 2000), pp. 97–108; David Harris Sacks, "London's Dominion: The Metropolis, the Market Economy, and the State," in *Material London, ca. 1600*, pp. 20–54; and A. L. Beier and Roger Finlay, "Introduction: The Significance of the Metropolis," in *London 1500–1700: The Making of the Metropolis*, ed. A. L. Beier and Roger Finlay (London: Longman, 1986), pp. 1–34. On the growth of overseas trade to the Levant and the Americas, see, in particular, Robert Brenner, *Merchants and Revolution: Commercial Change, Political Conflict, and London's Overseas Traders, 1550–1653* (Princeton, N.J.: Princeton University Press, 1993); K. R. Andrews, *Trade, Plunder, and Settlement: Maritime Enterprise and the Genesis of the British Empire, 1480–1630* (Cambridge: Cambridge University Press, 1984); and Brian Dietz, "Overseas Trade and Metropolitan Growth," in *London 1500–1700*, ed. Beier and Finlay, pp. 115–40.

6. Andrew Gurr, for example, signals his allegiance to a Shakespeare-centered view of early modern theater by appending the Bard's name to titles of a number of his major books, for example, *The Shakespearean Stage, 1574–1642*, 3rd ed. (Cambridge: Cambridge University Press, 1992), *Playgoing in Shakespeare's London* (Cambridge: Cambridge University Press, 1987), and *The Shakespearian Playing Companies* (Oxford: Clarendon Press, 1996).

7. For example, D. M. Palliser's *The Age of Elizabeth: England Under the Later Tudors 1547–1603* (London: Longman, 1983) uses the name of the queen to characterize the age in which, among other things, England began its overseas commercial expansion and a commercial theater was established in London.

8. Steven Mullaney's *The Place of the Stage: License, Play, and Power in Renaissance England* (Chicago: University of Chicago Press, 1988) paved the way for this emphasis, focusing as it did on the material placement of the theater in the liberties and suburbs of the city. If we now understand that the suburbs were much more than places of licensed transgression and that Stow's "ceremonial city" was an increasingly vestigal construction, Mullaney's book nonetheless still prompts scholars to consider exactly how the stage and the city were related.

9. Gurr, *The Shakespearean Stage 1574–1642*, pp. 4–12, stresses the metropolitan focus of the London theater and reminds us that even when the commercial companies were called to court to perform, they typically presented the same fare that was on offer in the public playhouses. In short, they did not have a separate court repertory. For the fullest account of the performance conditions at court, both for plays from the public theaters and for masques and other entertainments, see John H. Astington, *English Count Theatre 1558–1642* (Cambridge: Cambridge University Press, 1999). For the patronage contexts for theater in the period, see *Shakespeare and Theatrical Patronage in Early Modern England*, ed. Paul Whitfield White and Suzanne R. Westfall (Cambridge: Cambridge University Press, 2002).

10. Michel de Certeau, *The Practices of Everyday Life*, trans. Steven Rendall (Berkeley: University of California Press, 1984), p. 117.

11. For a discussion of the ideological function of early modern drama, see my *The Stage and Social Struggle in Early Modern England* (London: Routledge, 1994), esp. pp. 1–21.

12. Crystal Bartolovich, "'Baseless Fabric': London as a 'World City,'" *"The Tempest" and Its Travels*, ed. Peter Hulme and William H. Sherman (London: Reaktion Books, 2000), pp. 13–26.

13. The most comprehensive treatment of how order was maintained in the London of the 1590s is Ian Archer's masterful work, *The Pursuit of Stability: Social Relations in Elizabethan London* (Cambridge: Cambridge University Press, 1991). See also Steve Rappaport, *Worlds Within Worlds: Structures of Life in Sixteenth-Century London* (Cambridge: Cambridge University Press, 1989) and Jeremy Boulton, *Neighborhood and Society: A London Suburb in the Seventeenth Century* (Cambridge: Cambridge University Press, 1987).

14. For discussion of the concept of town culture, see Martin Butler, *Theatre and Crisis, 1632–1642* (Cambridge: Cambridge University Press, 1984), pp. 108–09; F. J. Fisher, "The Development of London as a Center of Conspicuous Consumption" in *London and the English Economy, 1500–1700*, ed. P. J. Corfield and N. B. Harte, pp. 105–118; and Lawrence Stone, *The Crisis of the Aristocracy, 1558–1641* (London: Oxford University Press, 1965), esp. pp. 385–98 and 672–724.

15. Roger Finley and Beatrice Shearer, "Population Growth and Suburban Expansion," in *London 1500–1700*, ed. Beier and Finlay, pp. 37–59.

16. A. L. Beier, "Engine of Manufacture: The Trades of London," in *London 1500–1700*, ed. Beier and Finlay, pp. 141–67, esp. 156–59.

17. For a fascinating discussion of the provision of food in London during this period, see Sara Pennell, "'Great Quantities of Gooseberry Pye and Baked Clod of Beef': Victualling and Eating Out in Early Modern London," in *Londinopolis: Essays in the Cultural and Social History of Early Modern London*, ed. Paul Griffiths and Mark S. R. Jenner (Manchester: Manchester University Press, 2000), pp. 228–49. For a discussion of the general difficulties of getting enough food from the countryside to feed London's growing population, see F. J. Fisher, "The Development of the London Food Market, 1540–1640," in *London and the English Economy*, ed. Corfield and Harte, pp. 61–80.

18. For important treatments of Stow's nostalgic vision of London, see Ian Archer, "The Nostalgia of John Stow," in *The Theatrical City: Culture, Theatre and Politics in London, 1576–1649*, ed. David L. Smith, Richard Strier, and David Bevington (Cambridge: Cambridge University Press, 1995), pp. 17–34, and Patrick Collinson's "John Stow and Nostalgic Antiquarianism," in *Imagining Early Modern London: Perceptions and Portrayals of the City from Stow to Strype 1598–1720*, ed. J. F. Merritt (Cambridge: Cambridge University Press, 2001), pp. 27–51. Collinson connects Stow's nostalgia to his putative Catholicism.

19. A famous instance of Stow's nostalgia for disappearing popular pastimes is his disappointment that the great May Pole that had once stood in front of the Church of Saint Andrew Undershaft had been cut up and burned as an "Idol" by zealous Protestants. See John Stow, *Survey of London*, vol. 1, ed. Charles Lethbridge Kingsford (Oxford: Clarendon Press, 1908), pp. 143–44.

20. For a description of the changes from the 1598 to the 1603 editions, see ibid., p. 236 and p. 262.

21. The importance of St. Paul's as a meeting place for every variety of visiting or resident Londoner was captured in John Earle's "Paul's Walk," in *Microcosmography: or, A Piece of the World Discovered in Essays and Characters* (1628; reprint. London: Simpkin, Marshall, Hamilton, Kent and Co., 1897). Earle describes Paul's as "the land's epitome, or you may call it the lesser isle of Great Britain. It is more than this, the whole world's map, which you may here discern in its perfectest motion, justling and turning. It is a heap of stones and men, with a vast confusion of languages; and were the steeple not sanctified, nothing liker Babel" (pp. 103–04).

22. For a general discussion of the city as a place for fashionable self-display and the theater as a venue where it could occur, see Janette Dillon's *Theatre, Court and City 1595–1610: Drama and Social Space in London* (Cambridge: Cambridge University Press, 2000), esp. chap. 3, "From Retreat to Display," pp. 59–78.

23. Thomas Dekker, *The Gull's Hornbook*, in *Thomas Dekker: Selected Writings*, ed. E. D. Pendry (London: Edward Arnold, 1967), p. 100.

24. One of the ironies of the gull's life, as recorded by Dekker, is that it depends on display, which in turn depends on consumption, but the gull lacks substantive resources with which to support this lifestyle. After passing through St. Paul's, the gull is advised to retire as if to an ordinary though he is to return at two in a new outfit, picking his teeth with "some quill or silver instrument" and rubbing his gums with "a wrought handkerchief." His "light turkey grogram," silver toothpick and wrought handerchief are all props through which the gull performs fashionability, though Dekker hints that he has actually not been to an ordinary at all. "It skills not whether you dined or not (that's best known to your stomach) or in what place you dined, though it were with cheese of your own

mother's making in your chamber or study" (p. 89). This comment reveals both the essential emptiness of the gull's performance and hints at the culture of debt and credit, which is, as I will explain in Chapter 2, the underside of a life of conspicuous consumption. Tobacco smoke in many ways epitomizes the void at the heart of the gull's life. Something has been consumed, at considerable expense and to maximum public effect, but it is consumption which cannot substitute—in terms of the maintenance of life—for the bread it often replaces.

25. See note 3 above.

26. Archer, *The Pursuit of Stability*. See also many of the articles included in *London 1500–1700*, ed. Beier and Roger Finlay, esp. pt. 1, "Population and Disease," and pt. 2, "Commerce and Manufacture."

27. For a good account of the increasing number of gentry and gentry women coming to London at the end of the sixteenth century, partly as a result of the increasing availability of coach travel, see Ann Jennalie Cook, *The Privileged Playgoers of Shakespeare's London, 1576–1642* (Princeton, N.J.: Princeton University Press, 1981), esp. pp. 52–96.

28. Laura Yungblut, *Strangers Settled Here Amongst Us: Policies, Perceptions, and the Presence of Aliens in Elizabethan England* (London: Routledge, 1996), p. 96. For more detailed scholarship on particular stranger communities in the city see in particular Robin Gwynn, *Huguenot Heritage: The History and Contribution of Huguenots in Britain* (London: Routledge, 1985); Andrew Pettegree's *Foreign Protestant Communities in Sixteenth-Century London* (Oxford: Clarenedon, 1986), and T. H. Lloyd, *England and the German Hanse, 1157–1611* (Cambridge: Cambridge University Press, 1991).

29. Yungblut, *Strangers Settled Here Amongst Us*, pp. 66–67.

30. Ibid., p. 14. See also Deborah Harkness, "'Strange' Ideas and 'English' Knowledge: Natural Science Exchange in Elizabethan London," in *Merchants and Marvels: Commerce, Science, and Art in Early Modern Europe*, ed. Pamela H. Smith and Paula Findlen (New York: Routledge, 2002), pp. 137–60. Harkness describes the many natural science practitioners from abroad who clustered in certain neighborhoods, including that around the Royal Exchange, but also in Bishops Gate and a number of liberties within and without the walls. These skilled strangers, who interacted with the English natural science community, included instrument makers, surgeons, midwives, alchemists, and distillers, among others (p. 137).

31. Yungblut, *Strangers Settled Here Amongst Us*, p. 16, and A. J. Hoenselaars, *Images of Englishmen and Foreigners in the Drama of Shakespeare and His Contemporaries: A Study of Stage Characters and National Identity in English Renaissance Drama 1558–1642* (London: Associated University Presses, 1992), p. 27. See also Richard Marienstrass, *New Perspectives on the Shakespearean World* (Cambridge: Cambridge University Press, 1985).

32. The paradoxes of mercantilist policies are very intelligently explored by Jonathan Gil Harris, *Sick Economies: Drama, Mercantilism, and Disease in Shakespeare's England* (Philadelphia: University of Pennsylvania Press, 2004).

33. Yungblut, *Strangers Settled Here Amongst Us*, p. 3, argues that xenophobia and asylum were the twin ideals, often in conflict, that motivated English Protestant reaction to Flemish and Dutch immigrants, in particular.

34. On this point I am indebted to conversations with Margaret Jacobs of the History Department at UCLA.

35. In a parallel fashion, Harris points out that nation-based mercantilist discourse, ironically, arose at the very time that England's economy was

increasingly implicated in long-distance markets. England simply could not be a self-contained economic entity, though the rhetoric of mercantilism often expressed that as a goal and figured the incursion of foreign products and foreign merchants as a contagion overtaking England. See "The Pathological Drama of National Economy," *Sick Economies*, chap. 1, pp. 1–28.

36. I am indebted for this information to Professor Alison Games who kindly let me read, in manuscript, her chapter, "Merchants and Factors," dealing with English factor culture in Lisbon, Istanbul, and Japan in the early seventeenth century. It forms part of her forthcoming book, *Agents of Empire: English Cosmopolitans in an Age of Expansion*.

37. Ibid., p. 19.

38. Jacques Derrida, "On Cosmopolitanism," in *On Cosmopolitanism and Forgiveness* (London: Routledge, 2003), pp. 3–24.

39. Henry Peacham, *The Complete Gentleman and Other Works*, ed. Virgil B. Heltzel (Ithaca: Cornell University Press, 1962), p. 243. All other quotations from this essay will refer to this edition.

40. Peter Womack, "Imagining Communities: Theatres and the English Nation in the Sixteenth Century," in *Culture and History 1350–1600: Essays on English Communities, Identities and Writing*, ed. David Aers (Detroit: Wayne State University Press, 1992), pp. 91–145.

41. Sacks and Lynch stress the mutually reinforcing nature of London's economic and political centrality. "London was simultaneously a locus of political power and commercial wealth, each depending on the other." "Ports 1540–1700," p. 391. See also Fisher, "London as an Engine of Economic Growth."

42. Braudel, *The Perspective of the World*, p. 27 and following.

43. Brenner gives the best account of this process in *Merchants and Revolution*.

44. Fisher, "The Development of London as a Centre of Conspicuous Consumption."

45. Keith Wrightson, *Earthly Necessities: Economic Lives in Early Modern Britian* (New Haven: Yale University Press, 2000) explores the many tensions that accompanied Britain's gradual but inexorable shift to a capitalist market economy. If for many their buying power rose and their material lives improved, this was not universally so, nor was increased wealth easily or unproblematically absorbed into the value systems of those whose fortunes were improving.

46. Jean-Christophe Agnew, *Worlds Apart: The Market and the Theater in Anglo-American Thought, 1550–1750* (Cambridge: Cambridge University Press, 1986), p. 41.

47. A world economy, according to world systems theorists such as Immanuel Wallerstein, is an economically autonomous sector of the globe that is larger than a nationstate and has a dominant city at its core and involves a division of labor between core, periphery, and semi-periphery. See Immanuel Wallerstein. *The Modern World System*, vol. 1, *Capitalist Agriculture and the Origins of the European World-Economy in the Sixteenth Century* (New York: Academic Press, 1974). He argues that in the sixteenth century northern European nations, especially England, begun to emerge as the core area in a world economy that would increasingly draw resources from the Americas to enable development at home and commercial transactions with Eastern economies. Wallerstein has been criticized for, among other things, the rigidity of his division of world economies into core, semi-peripheral and peripheral regions and, most recently, for a Eurocentric bias that supposedly blocks understanding of the

dominance of Eastern world economies, especially that of China, up to 1800. See Andre Gunder Frank, *ReOrient: Global Economy in the Asian Age* (Berkeley: University of California Press, 1998). I agree with many of the criticisms of Wallerstein's work, but I continue to find useful his broad historical discussion of the many factors (including a centralizing state that actively supported overseas trading ventures and the rapid development of capitalist agricultural practices) that allowed England to begin to take shape as a commercial power by the seventeenth century.

48. For the idea of England as for centuries a country on the periphery of the Mediterranean world system see Samir Amin's *Eurocentrism* (New York: Monthly Review Press, 1989). Much contemporary scholarship on England's relationship to the Ottoman world throughout the early modern period stresses English anxiety before both the military and commercial might of the Turks. See, for example, Nabil Matar, *Turks, Moors, and Englishmen in the Age of Discovery* (New York: Columbia University Press, 1999); Barbara Fuchs, *Mimesis and Empire: The New World, Islam, and European Identities* (Cambridge: Cambridge University Press, 2001); Jean-Pierre Maquerlot and Michele Willems, ed. *Travel and Drama in Shakespeare's Time* (Cambridge: Cambridge University Press, 1996); John Michael Archer, *Old Worlds: Egypt, Southwest Asia, India, and Russia in Early Modern English Writing* (Stanford, California: Stanford University Press, 2001) and Daniel Vitkus, *Turning Turk: English Theater and the Multicultural Mediterranean, 1570–1630* (New York: Palgrave Macmillan, 2003).

49. Recent scholarship has pointed to the Red Lion in Whitechapel, built in 1567, as the very first commercial public playhouse in London, but almost nothing is known about it. John Brayne, its owner, joined with James Burbage nine years later to build the more successful Theatre. See E. K. Chambers, *The Elizabethan Stage*, vol. 2 (Oxford: Clarendon Press, 1923), pp. 379–80, and William Ingram, *The Business of Playing: The Beginning of the Adult Professional Theater in Elizabethan London* (Ithaca: Cornell University Press, 1992), pp. 92–113.

50. For the existence of traveling troupes of professional players and their activities in towns, court, and the houses of noblemen before 1576, see W. R. Streitberger, "Personnel and Professionalization," in *A New History of Early English Drama*, ed. John D. Cox and David Kastan (New York: Columbia University Press, 1997), pp. 337–55.

51. Gurr, *The Shakespearean Stage 1574–1642*, pp. 115–21.

52. See Peter H. Greenfield, "Touring" in *A New History of Early English Drama*, ed. Cox and Kastan, pp. 251–68.

53. Walter Cohen, *Drama of a Nation: Public Theater in Renaissance England and Spain* (Ithaca: Cornell University Press, 1985), p. 163.

54. For a discussion of the day-to-day finances of a company such as the Chamberlain's Men see Peter Thomson, "Balancing the Books," in *Shakespeare's Theatre* (London: Routledge and Kegan Paul, 1983), pp. 19–35.

55. Some theater historians, such as Rosalyn Knutson, believe that the theater companies not only resembled guilds structurally but that they acted like guilds in working together to preserve the profitability of all members of the profession. See her *Playing Companies and Commerce in Shakespeare's Time* (Cambridge: Cambridge University Press, 2001). I believe she overestimates the resemblances between guild and theater troupe and underestimates the degree of capitalist competition between various companies.

56. For the fullest account of the theater audiences in Shakespeare's day see Andrew Gurr, *Playgoing in Shakespeare's London*.

57. Thomas Heywood, *An Apology for Actors* (London, 1612), ed. Richard H. Perkinson (reprint, New York: Scholars' Facsimilies and Reprints, 1941); all future quotations will be to this edition.

58. For representative critical works see L. C. Knights, *Drama and Society in the Age of Jonson* (1936, reprint, London: George W. Stewart, 1951); Brian Gibbons, *Jacobean City Comedy: A Study of Satiric Plays by Jonson, Marston, and Middleton* (Cambridge, Mass.: Harvard University Press, 1968); Alexander Leggatt, *Citizen Comedy in the Age of Shakespeare* (Toronto: University of Toronto Press, 1973); Theodore Leinwand, *The City Staged: Jacobean City Comedy, 1603–1613* (Madison: University of Wisconsin Press, 1986); Douglas Bruster, *Drama and the Market in the Age of Shakespeare* (Cambridge: Cambridge University Press, 1992); Lawrence Manley, *Literature and Culture in Early Modern London* (Cambridge: Cambridge University Press, 1995), esp. pp. 431–77; and Gail Kern Paster, *The Idea of the City in the Age of Shakespeare* (Athens: University of Georgia Press, 1985).

59. Jean E. Howard, "Shakespeare and Genre" in *A Companion to Shakespeare*, ed. David Scott Kastan (Oxford: Blackwell Publishing, 2000), pp. 297–310. For a lively discussion of how thoroughly Renaissance writers drew upon a language of genres or kinds, see Rosalie Colie's *The Resources of Kind: Genre Theory in the Renaissance* (Berkeley: University of California Press, 1973). See also Alistair Fowler's *Kinds of Literature: An Introduction to the Theory of Genres and Modes* (Cambridge, Mass: Harvard University Press, 1982).

60. Barbara Mowat, "'What's in a Name?' Tragicomedy, Romance, or Late Comedy," in *A Companion to Shakespeare's Works*, vol. 4, *The Poems, Problem Comedies, Late Plays*, ed. Richard Dutton and Jean E. Howard (Oxford: Blackwell Publishing, 2003), pp. 129–49, at 134.

61. For discussions of Caroline drama's use of specific places to anchor its fictions see Richard H. Perkinson's "Topographical Comedy in the 17th Century," *ELH* 3 (1936): 270–90 and Theodore Miles's "Place-Realism in a Group of Caroline Plays," *The Review of English Studies* 18 (1942): 428–40.

62. For an excellent discussion of 3.1, the Paul's Walk scene, in *Every Man Out* see "Introduction," in *Every Man Out of His Humour*, ed. Helen Ostovich (Manchester: Manchester University Press, 2001), pp. 59–68.

63. For an excellent investigation of the gendering of urban spaces see Doreen Massey, *Space, Place, and Gender* (Minneapolis: University of Minnesota Press, 1994), esp. pt. 3, "Space, Place and Gender," pp. 175–272.

64. For a discussion of performative masculinity in Shakespeare's later history plays, see Jean E. Howard, *The Stage and Social Struggle in Early Modern England*, esp. Chap. 6, "Kings and Pretenders: Monarchical Theatricality in the Shakespearean History Play," pp. 129–62.

Chapter 1. Staging Commercial London

1. Ann Saunders, "The Building of the Royal Exchange," in *The Royal Exchange*, ed. Ann Saunders, Publication No. 152 (London: The London Topographical Society, 1997), pp. 36–47, at 36.

2. In the early modern period, people born outside England were typically designated as aliens or strangers. Foreigners, as I will explain further below, was the term reserved for English persons not born in London or who lived in the city but were not freemen. See Steven Rappaport, *Worlds Within Worlds: Structures of Life in Sixteenth-Century London* (Cambridge: Cambridge University Press,

1989), p. 42, and Roger Finlay, *Population and Metropolis: The Demography of London, 1580–1650* (Cambridge: Cambridge University Press, 1981), p. 68.

3. John Stow, *A Survey of London*, 2 vols., ed. Charles Lethbridge Kingsford (Oxford: The Clarendon Press, 1908), vol. 1, p. 201.

4. Saunders, "The Building of the Royal Exchange," p. 45, notes some of the foreign visitors who commented on the Exchange in its first decades of operation. These included L. Grenade, a French Protestant, who visited the Exchange in 1576 (I will discuss his remarks below), the German Paul Hentzner in 1598, the Swiss traveler Thomas Platter in 1599, and Baron Waldstein from Bohemia in 1600.

5. Saunders, "The Building of the Royal Exchange," p. 40.

6. Ibid., p. 43.

7. Thomas Dekker and John Webster, *Westward Ho*, in *The Dramatic Works of Thomas Dekker*, vol. 2, ed. Fredson Bowers (Cambridge: Cambridge University Press, 1955), I.ii.25–35, pp. 326–27; all future references to the play will be to this edition.

8. Ibid., II.i.214–18.

9. Thomas Middleton, *A Chaste Maid in Cheapside*, ed. Alan Brissenden (London: Ernest Benn, 1968), p. 16; all future quotations from the play will be taken from this edition. These lines have been taken to refer to the lavish lying-in of the Countess of Salisbury, wife of William Cecil. For an interesting discussion of the play in relationship to lying-in practices, see Janelle Day Jenstad, "Lying-in Like a Countess: The *Lisle Letters*, the Cecil Family, and *A Chaste Maid in Cheapside*," *The Journal of Medieval and Early Modern Studies* 34 (2004): 373–403.

10. Ben Jonson, *The Staple of News*, ed. Devra Rowland Kifer (Lincoln: University of Nebraska Press, 1975), I.ii.70–71; all further references to the play will be to this edition.

11. For a discussion of the role of stage fictions in providing imagined resolutions to real social problems, see my book, *The Stage and Social Struggle in Early Modern England* (London: Routledge, 1994).

12. L. Grenade, *"Les Singularitez de Londres, 1576,"* in *The Royal Exchange*, ed. Saunders, p. 48.

13. John Eliot, *The Parlement of Pratlers* (1593; reprint, London: The Fanfrolico Press, 1928), pp. 28–30.

14. For the idea of a world economy, that is, an economic unit larger than the nation-state and depending on divisions of labor that link a core arena to semiperipheral and peripheral regions, see Immanuel Wallerstein, *The Modern World System*, vol. 1, *Capitalist Agriculture and the Origins of the European World-Economy in the Sixteenth Century* (New York: Academic Press, 1974), esp. pp. 15–129.

15. Trevor Tibbett, "Early Insurance and the Royal Exchange," in *The Royal Exchange*, ed. Saunders, pp. 76–84. Marine insurance developed early, due in part to the magnitude of the risks involved in overseas trade. In the sixteenth century such insurance was often undertaken by speculators who gambled on turning a profit from the large insurance premiums. By the end of the seventeenth century more modern insurance companies had been formed in both Holland and England. They calculated risks based on the probability of misadventure. See *The Cambridge Economic History*, vol. 5, ed. E. E. Rich (Cambridge: Cambridge University Press, 1977), esp. Herman Der Wee, "Monetary, Credit and Banking Systems," chap. 5, pp. 290–392.

16. Fernand Braudel, *The Wheels of Commerce*, vol. 2 of *Civilization and Capitalism, 15th–18th Century*, trans. Sian Reynolds (France, 1979; reprint, New York: Harper and Row, 1982), esp. pp. 73–100.

17. Saunders, "The Building of the Exchange," p. 41.

18. Ibid., p. 39.

19. In this regard, see Deborah Harkness's interesting discussion of the mixed emotions surrounding natural science practitioners of foreign origin in London in the late sixteenth century. She argues that many of these aliens lived in the area around the Royal Exchange, and she sees the building as a symbol of the blending of alien and native ideas and practices in both the economic realm and that of the natural sciences. Such blending did not occur without tension. See "'Strange' Ideas and 'English' Knowledge: Natural Science Exchange in Elizabethan London," in *Merchants and Marvels: Commerce, Science, and Art in Early Modern Europe*, ed. Pamela H. Smith and Paula Findlen (New York: Routledge, 2002), pp. 137–60.

20. Lawrence Worms, "The Book Trade at the Royal Exchange," in *The Royal Exchange*, ed. Saunders, pp. 209–26.

21. Grenade, "*Les Singularitez de Londres, 1576*," p. 48.

22. Ann Saunders, "The Organization of the Exchange," in *The Royal Exchange*, ed. Saunders, pp. 85–98, at 89.

23. Ibid., pp. 91–92.

24. See Karen Newman, *Fashioning Femininity and English Renaissance Drama* (Chicago: Chicago University Press, 1991), esp. pp. 109–43, for an important discussion of women in early modern England's commodity culture. See also Natasha Korda, *Shakespeare's Domestic Economies: Gender and Property in Early Modern England* (Philadelphia: University of Pennsylvania Press, 2002), esp. pp. 1–51, for an acute analysis of how the expanding market in consumer goods affected women's relationship to household property in the late sixteenth and early seventeenth centuries.

25. Laura Gowing, "'The Freedom of the Streets': Women and Social Space, 1560–1640," in *Londinopolis: Essays in the Cultural and Social History of Early Modern London*, ed. Paul Griffiths and Mark S. R. Jenner (Manchester: Manchester University Press, 2000), pp. 130–51, esp. 140–47.

26. See Jonathan Haynes, *The Social Relations of Jonson's Theater* (Cambridge: Cambridge University Press, 1992), pp. 28–30.

27. William Haughton, *Englishmen for My Money or A Woman Will Have Her Will*, ed., Albert Croll Baugh (Philadelphia: University of Pennsylvania, 1913), I.iii.382–722. All further references will be to this edition, in which line numbers are continuous rather than starting over at each new scene. I have also been fortunate to consult in typescript Lloyd Edward Kermode's edition of the play, forthcoming from Manchester University Press.

28. As the theater industry developed, particular theaters may eventually have interpellated specific subgroups of Londoners and differentiated them from Londoners attracted to other theaters. See, for example, Mary Bly's important study of the short-lived Whitefriars boys' company and the way the particular linguistic practices of the plays produced by that company solicited a particular kind of audience (*Queer Virgins and Virgin Queans on the Early Modern Stage* [Oxford: Oxford University Press, 2000]). However, this is simply a refinement of the more general principle I am addressing here, which is to point to the active role the theater played in constituting both the city as an intelligible entity and Londoners as a social body.

29. For a concise summary of the massive growth in London's population from the later half of the sixteenth century into the eighteenth century, and the role of migration into the capital as a factor in that growth, see Roger Finlay and Beatrice Shearer, "Population Growth and Suburban Expansion," in *The Making of the Metropolis: London 1500–1700*, ed. A. L. Beier and Roger Finlay (London: Longman, 1986), pp. 37–59.

30. In this regard, see John Gillies's interesting discussion of Venice as a site of dangerous intermixture in *Shakespeare and the Geography of Difference* (Cambridge: Cambridge University Press, 1994), pp. 122–40, and Daniel Vitkus's important discussion of Mediterranean trading cities such as Malta and Tunis in *Turning Turk: English Theater and the Multicultural Mediterranean, 1570–1630* (New York: Palgrave Macmillan, 2003), pp. 163–98.

31. Laura Yungblut, *Strangers Settled Here Amongst Us: Policies, Perceptions, and the Presence of Aliens in Elizabethan England* (London: Routledge, 1996), p. 98. For an important discussion of the paradoxes of early modern economic thought whereby a national market, though clearly dependent on the global flow of trade, stigmatized both the outflow of bullion from the nation and the influx of foreign goods, see Jonathan Gil Harris, *Sick Economies: Drama, Mercantilism, and Disease in Shakespeare's England* (Philadelphia: University of Pennsylvania Press, 2004), esp. pp. 1–28. Also Joan Thirsk, *Economic Policy and Projects: The Development of a Consumer Society in Early Modern England* (Oxford: Clarendon Press, 1978), esp. pp. 133–38. The classic discussion of mercantilist thought is Joyce Oldham Appleby's *Economic Thought and Ideology in Seventeenth-Century England* (Princeton, N.J.: Princeton University Press, 1978).

32. Fernand Braudel, *The Perspective of the World*, vol. 3 of *Civilization and Capitalism, 15th–18th Century*. trans. Reynolds (France, 1979; reprint, Berkeley: University of California Press, 1992), p. 40.

33. See Theodore K. Rabb, *Enterprise and Empire: Merchant and Gentry Investment in the Expansion of England, 1575–1630* (Cambridge, Mass.: Harvard University Press, 1967), p. 1, pp. 50–51.

34. T. H. Lloyd, *England and the German Hanse, 1157–1611* (Cambridge, Mass.: Cambridge University Press, 1991), esp. pp. 292–362.

35. Rabb, *Enterprise and Empire*, p. 2.

36. Yungblut, *Strangers Settled Here Amongst Us*, pp. 95–113.

37. In *The City Staged: Jacobean Comedy, 1603–1613* (Madison: University of Wisconsin Press, 1986), Theodore Leinwand focuses on the opposition between the social types he calls "merchant-citizens" and those he designates as "gentlemen-gallants." Often the conflict between these two groups is played out through a contest over women, with gallants often seducing, or attempting to seduce, city wives or woo the daughters of rich citizens.

38. For a discussion of Pisaro's role as usurer and Jew, see the Introduction to Lloyd Kermode's edition of the play; also Alan Stewart, "Portingale Women and Politics in Late Elizabethan London," in *Rethinking Women and Politics in Early Modern England*, ed. James Daybell (Ashgate, 2003), pp. 85–100; and Edmund Valentine Campos, "Jews, Spaniards, and Portingales; Ambiguous Identities of Portuguese *Marranos* in Elizabethan England," *ELH* 69, no. 3 (2002): 599–616.

39. Campos, "Jews, Spaniards, and Portingales," p. 610.

40. Jonathan Gil Harris, *Foreign Bodies and the Body Politic* (Cambridge: Cambridge University Press, 1998), pp. 79–106.

41. The status of denizens is a fraught issue, partly because the statutes governing denizens changed frequently in the sixteenth century and partly

because these statutes either were not uniformly enforced or were evaded by many alien merchants and artisans who illegally plied their trades within London without obtaining denizen status. In general, denizens could practice their trades in London but could not take strangers as apprentices and could have only two foreign journeymen. Their ability to own land was curtailed, and they paid an alien tax. For brief discussions of denizen rights and restrictions, see Yungblut, *Strangers Settled Here Amongst Us*, p. 78; Andrew Pettegree, *Foreign Protestant Communities in Sixteenth-Century London* (Oxford: Clarendon Press, 1986), pp. 15–16; and Ian Archer, *Pursuit of Stability: Social Relations in Elizabethan London* (Cambridge: Cambridge University Press, 1991), pp. 132–40. For a discussion of Pisaro as denizen, see Alan Stewart's "'Every Soyle to Mee Is Naturall': Figuring Denization in William Haughton's *Englishmen for My Money*," *Renaissance Drama* 35 (2006): 55–81.

42. Campos, "Jews, Spaniards, and Portingales," pp. 601–2.

43. Ibid., p. 607.

44. Stewart, "Portingale Women and Politics in Late Elizabethan London," p. 93.

45. In *Shakespeare and the Jews* (New York: Columbia University Press, 1996), esp. pp. 13–42, James Shapiro argues that the arrival in England in the late sixteenth century of Jews who had supposedly converted to Christianity raised urgent questions about who was a Jew and how a Jew was to be distinguished from a Christian. In *Englishmen for My Money* Pisaro's Jewishness is fairly transparent, but he is also assimilated to the English context to a degree not common in other cultural productions of the time.

46. Harris in *Foreign Bodies and the Body Politic*, esp. pp. 85–86, points out that Jews, condemned as poisoners and anal infiltrators, were also often selected to be physicians to monarchs. Paradoxically, they were seen as both destroyers and healers.

47. A. J. Hoenselaars, *Images of Englishmen and Foreigners in the Drama of Shakespeare and His Contemporaries: A Study of Stage Characters and National Identity in English Renaissance Drama 1558–1642* (London: Associated University Press, 1992), pp. 53–58. Hoenselaars finds this linguistic ridicule merely comic and not a sign of xenophobia. I find it less lighthearted than he, the comic, as we know from Freud, being one of the registers in which aggression finds expression. See also Emma Smith, "'So Much English by the Mother': Gender, Foreigners, and the Mother Tongue in William Haughton's *Englishmen for My Money*," *MARDIE* 13 (2001): 165–81.

48. This is one of the places where the neat ideological closure achieved by the play could be deconstructed. Frisco seems to assume that the daughters' complete assimilation to English and to Englishness might be undone by marriage to strangers, an undoing that would manifest itself in the reemergnce of linguistic difference among the women's children. The power of the alien to overcome and to swallow up Englishness is thus never entirely expunged in the play.

49. Crystal Bartolovich, "'Baseless Fabric': London as a 'World City," in *'The Tempest' and Its Travels*, ed. Peter Hulme and William H. Sherman (London: Reaktion Books, 2000), pp. 13–26.

50. For Gascoigne's account, see "The Spoyle of Antwerpe," app. 2 in *The Complete Works of George Gascoigne*, 2 vols., vol. 2, ed. John W. Cunliffe (Cambridge: Cambridge University Press, 1910), pp. 587–99. William E. Sheidley in "George Gascoigne and *The Spoyle of Antwerpe*," *Literature and the Arts* (spring/summer

1996): 48–64, discusses what he sees as Gascoigne's confused attempts to moralize the events he describes.

51. For a concise account of these events, see *The New Cambridge Modern History*, vol. 3, *The Counter-Reformation and Price Revolution 1559–1610*, ed. R. B. Wernham (Cambridge: Cambridge University Press, 1968), pp. 264–80. Fuller treatment is given by Martin van Gelderen in *The Political Thought of the Dutch Revolt 1555–1590* (Cambridge: Cambridge University Press, 1992) and in *The Origins and Development of the Dutch Revolt*, ed. Graham Darby (London: Routledge, 2001). See especially Graham Darby's opening essay, "Narrative of Events," pp. 8–28, and Henk Van Nierop's "*Alva's Throne*–Making Sense of the Revolt of the Netherlands," pp. 29–37. For a brief account from the Spanish perspective, see Henry Kamen, *Spain 1469–1714*, 2d ed. (London: Longman, 1991), pp. 131–33.

52. *Alarum for London* (1602), Old English Drama Facsimile Edition (Amersham, England: Tudor Facsimile Texts, 1912), p. D2 and F2; all references to the play will be to this edition. In Gascoigne's account of the sacking of the city, he writes "And the notable Bowrce which was wont to be a safe assemblie for Marchaunts, and men of all honest trades, had nowe none other marchaundize therein, but as many dycing tables as might be placed round about it al the day long" (p. 597).

53. The Armada scenes that comprise Act 5 of the play may once have been part of another play; perhaps they formed the end of *If You Know Not Me You Know Nobody, Part I*, a much shorter play than *Part II* depicting the life of Elizabeth as an endangered Princess before she became Queen. In the version of *Part II* that has come down to us, however, the presence of the Armada events in Act 5 heightens the sense that the building of the Exchange is a monumental event on the order of the naval defeat of England's great rival, Spain.

54. See Stephen Mullaney, *The Place of the Stage: License, Play, and Power in Renaissance England* (Chicago: University of Chicago Press, 1988), pp. 10–20; Ian Archer, "The Nostalgia of John Stow," in *The Theatrical City: Culture, Theatre and Politics in London 1576–1649*, ed. David L. Smith, Richard Strier, and David Bevington (Cambridge: Cambridge University Press, 1995), pp. 17–34; Lawrence Manley, "Of Sites and Rites," in *The Theatrical City*, ed. Smith, Strier, and Bevington, pp. 35–54; and Patrick Collinson, "John Stow and Nostalgic Antiquarianism," in *Imagining Early Modern London: Perceptions and Portrayals of the City from Stow to Strype, 1598–1720*, ed. J. F. Merritt (Cambridge: Cambridge University Press, 2001), pp. 27–51.

55. Portions of my analysis of *If You Know Not Me You Know Nobody, Part II* derive from a longer essay I wrote entitled "Competing Ideologies of Commerce in Thomas Heywood's *If You Know Not Me, You Know Nobody, Part II*" included in *The Culture of Capital: Property, Cities, and Knowledge in Early Modern England*, ed. Henry S. Turner (New York: Routledge, 2002), pp.163–82.

56. Manley, "Of Sites and Rites," p. 51, argues that Stow's Catholic leanings made him cling to an imagined ideal of an integrated social order as opposed to the acquisitive individualism he associated with the Reformation and the rise of the secular bureaucratic state.

57. For the social effects of changing patterns of poor relief, see Keith Thomas, *Religion and the Decline of Magic* (New York: Charles Scribner's Sons, 1971), esp. pp. 563–65 and 581–83. For a useful consideration of the effects of increasing overseas trade on the city, see Brian Dietz, "Overseas Trade and Metropolitan Growth," in *The Making of the Metropolis: London 1500–1700*, ed. Beier and Finlay, pp. 115–40. For changes in trades involved in production,

see A. L. Beier, "Engine of Manufacture: The Trades of London," in *The Making of the Metropolis*, pp. 141–67, while Robert Brenner, *Merchants and Revolution: Commercial Change, Political Conflict, and London's Overseas Traders, 1550–1653* (Princeton, N.J.: Princeton University Press, 1993), offers the best account of the rise of the joint stock companies and their effects on the city's fabric.

58. This phrase Stow attributes to Fitzstephen, one of his chief antecedents in the writing of London history. *The Survey of London*, vol. 1, p. 104.

59. Ibid., pp. 113–14.

60. Saunders, "The Building of the Royal Exchange," pp. 46–47.

61. Thomas Heywood, *If You Know Not Me You Know Nobody, Part II* (Oxford University Press: The Malone Society Reprints, 1934), lines 791–97; all further references will be to this edition of the play by line numbers only.

62. Vanessa Harding, "Citizen and Mercer: Sir Thomas Gresham and the Social and Political World of the City of London," in *Sir Thomas Gresham and Gresham College*, ed. Francis Ames-Lewis (Aldershot: Ashgate, 1999), pp. 24–37.

63. See introduction, pp. 29–30.

64. Edward Bonahue, Jr. "Social Control, the City, and the Market: Heywood's *If You Know Not Me, You Know Nobody, Part II*," *Renaissance Papers* (1993): 75–90, at 81–82.

65. See F. R. Salter, *Sir Thomas Gresham* (London: Leonard Parsons, 1925), esp. pp. 46–85, and Ian Blanchard, "Sir Thomas Gresham c. 1518–1599," in *The Royal Exchange*, ed. Saunders, pp. 11–19.

66. Brenner, *Merchants and Revolution*, pp. 3–50.

67. Janette Dillon in *Theatre, Court and City, 1595–1610: Drama and Social Space in London* (Cambridge: Cambridge University Press, 2000), p. 29, makes the point that the Royal Exchange had ambitions to rival a court. "It represented the city's expression of its own status in the same way as palace building expressed the court's power and magnificence." Here Gresham seems to be acting out those ambitions.

68. For the concept of the refunctioning of cultural materials associated with one class for use by another, see Michael Nerlich, *Ideology of Adventure: Studies in Modern Consciousness, 1100–1750*, vol. 1 (Minneapolis: University of Minnesota Press, 1987), pp. 60–63.

69. That this scene evokes the eucharist was first proposed by my student, Tiffany Alkan, in a seminar paper, "Piety or Prodigality? Gresham's Pearl in Thomas Heywood's *If You Know Not Me You Know Nobody, Part II*" (Columbia University graduate seminar, "Writing London," fall 2000).

70. Valerie Traub in *The Renaissance of Lesbianism in Early Modern England* (Cambridge: Cambridge University Press, 2004) provocatively discusses the appropriation of the pearl to signify Queen Elizabeth's erotic power in the "Armada portrait" (pp. 126–33).

71. In *The History of the World* Pliny the Elder gave the account of this event probably best known to Elizabethan and Jacobean writers. Describing the excesses to which many Romans were prone, Pliny described how Antony wooed Cleopatra with rich gifts and splendid feasts. In her turn, Cleopatra bet Antony that at one feast she could spend more than all he had lavished on wooing her. After they had eaten the main banquet, a servant put a cup of sharp vinegar in front of Cleopatra. She dropped one of her two pearl earrings into this cup, and the vinegar dissolved it. Then she drank it down. The two

pearls in Cleopatra's possession Pliny described as "the fairest and richest that ever have beene knowne in the world: and those possessed at one time by Cleopatra, the last queen of Egypt; which came into her hands by means of the great kings of the East, and were left unto her by descent." According to Pliny, the other pearl was taken from Cleopatra at her fall, split in half, and hung at "the eares of Venus in Rome, in the temple of Pantheon." See *The Historie of the World*, trans. Philemon Holland (London, 1601), bk. IX.c35, vol. 1, p. 257.

72. Pearls powdered and dissolved in wine were also thought to be a remedy for melancholy. See, for example, Thomas Elyot's *The Castel of Health* (1541) where pearls are listed among those substances that will heat the cold heart of the melancholic (D3). Gresham's drinking of the pearl may therefore also be considered a cure for the unhappiness occasioned by his loss of the sugar monopoly. The other famous stage example of a pearl dropped in wine was the poisoned cup offered to Hamlet by Claudius in which, ironically, the cure for melancholy was mingled with a fatal poison. See Anna K. Nardo, "'Here's to Thy Health': The Pearl in Hamlet's Wine," *English Language Notes* 23, no. 2 (December 1985): 36–42.

73. Laura Stevenson in *Praise and Paradox: Merchants and Craftsmen in Elizabethan Popular Literature* (Cambridge: Cambridge University Press, 1984), p. 145, argues that Gresham is linked through his extravagant gestures to the practice of aristocratic conspicuous expenditure.

74. For an interesting discussion of the complex handling of charity in this play, see Anita Sherman, "The Status of Charity in Thomas Heywood's *If You Know Not Me You Know Nobody, Part II*," *MARDIE* (1999): 99–120. She argues, for example, that Hobson's charity is truer than Gresham's and that Tawneycoat's poverty calls in question the legitimacy of Gresham's extreme wealth.

75. Brenner, *Merchants and Revolution*, pp. 83–91.

76. Dympna Callaghan, "Looking Well to Linens: Women and Cultural Production in *Othello* and Shakespeare's England," in *Marxist Shakespeares*, ed. Jean E. Howard and Scott Shershow (London: Routledge, 2000), pp. 53–81.

77. Eliot, *The Parlement of Pratlers*, pp. 31–33.

78. The *OED* gives the first meaning of "Moll" as "a female personal name" and the second as "a prostitute" (first use, 1604, by Thomas Middleton).

79. Thomas Heywood (?)(1607), *The Fair Maid of the Exchange* (Oxford: The Malone Society Reprints, 1962), 57–58; all further references to the play will be to this edition by line numbers only.

80. Juana Green, "The Sempster's Wares; Merchandising and Marrying in *The Fair Maid of the Exchange (1607)*," *Renaissance Drama* 53, no. 4 (2000): 1084–118.

81. "Introduction," *The Fair Maid of the Exchange*, ed. Field Barron, printed for the Shakespeare Society (London, 1846), p. v.

82. Natasha Glaisyer, "Merchants at the Royal Exchange, 1660–1720," in *The Royal Exchange*, ed. Saunders, pp. 198–202, at 199.

83. The exact location of Cripple's shop is another enigma. Field Barron in his 1846 edition of the play simply assumed that it was in another part of the Exchange from the shop where Phyllis works. This is possible. But at one point he says to Bowdler about the Exchange: "I have walkt with thee there, before the visitation of my legges, and my expence in timber, at the least a hundred times" (ll. 676–78). This might imply that his lameness now prevents him from climbing the stairs to the pawn. If so, it is quite possible that his shop is right outside the door of the Exchange in one of the surrounding streets.

84. Shapiro, *Shakespeare and the Jews*, esp. pp. 43–111.

Chapter 2. Credit, Incarceration, and Performance

1. Richard Jones published both this book and Whitney's first, *Copy of a Letter*, a series of four complaint poems modeled on Ovid's *Heroides*. He had a shop in St. Paul's yard to which Whitney refers her readers in the final poem of *The Sweet Nosegay*. Lynette McGrath has speculated that Jones felt it worth taking the chance that the novelty of a gentlewoman writing "in metre" could attract a readership, and he seems to have developed a minor specialization in books by, about, and geared toward women. Besides Whitney's book, for example, he published the pamphlet attributed to Jane Anger, and with Whitney's *Copy of a Letter* he appears to have been cashing in on the fashion for female complaint poems such as the extremely popular complaint of Jane Shore that had been added to *The Mirror for Magistrates* in 1563, just four years before Whitney's book appeared. See Lynette McGrath, *Subjectivity and Women's Poetry in Early Modern England* (Aldershot, England: Ashgate Publishing Company, 2002).

2. For a brief discussion of the rich paradoxes of Whitney's "will," see Lorna Hutson, *The Usurer's Daughter: Male Friendship and Fictions of Woman in Sixteenth-Century England* (London: Routledge, 1994), pp. 126–28.

3. All quotations from the poem refer to the edition prepared by Betty Travitsky that was published in *ELR* 10 (1980): 76–95.

4. In *Forms of Nationhood: The Elizabethan Writing of England* (Chicago: University of Chicago Press, 1992), esp. pp. 105–47, Richard Helgerson discusses the importance of both rural and urban chorographies in sixteenth- and seventeenth-century England. A mode of writing attentive to the physical landmarks, the streets, fields, and local histories of particular regions, chorography implicitly ties subjects to the land—to place broadly conceived—as much as to the monarch. By its complex delineation of urban geography, Whitney's poem sutures urban subjects to the city of London.

5. See Patricia Brace, "Teaching Class: Whitney's 'Wyll and Testament' and Nashe's 'Litany in Time of Plague,'" in *Teaching Tudor and Stuart Women Writers*, ed. Susanne Woods and Margaret Hannay (New York: The Modern Language Association, 2000), pp. 270–82.

6. For good introductions to London's prisons, see Clifford Dobb, "London's Prisons," *Shakespeare Survey* 17 (1964): 87–100 and E. D. Pendry, *Elizabethan Prisons and Prison Scenes*, Salzburg Studies in English Literature 17, 2 vols. (Salzburg, Austria: Institut für Englische Sprache und Literatur, 1974).

7. Ann Rosalind Jones, "Apostrophes to Cities: Urban Rhetorics in Isabella Whitney and Moderata Fonte," in *Attending to Early Modern Women*, ed. Susan D. Amussen and Adele Seeff (Newark: University of Delaware Press, 1998), pp. 155–75, at 157.

8. By 1662, the word "credit" also meant the actual money one borrowed (*OED* 10), as well as the reputation for probity that allowed one to borrow it. The dual meanings of the word are still in play today, and the intense focus on "credit" in the plays I examine in this chapter reveals the process by which the link between credit as reputation and credit as money borrowed emerged.

9. For the most complete listing of prison scenes in the drama of the period, see Pendry, *Elizabethan Prisons and Prison Scenes*.

10. For a brief account of Dekker's prison writings, see E. D. Pendry, ed., *Thomas Dekker: Selected Writings* (London: Edward Arnold, 1967), pp. 4–8, also Philip Shaw, "The Position of Thomas Dekker in Jacobean Prison Literature,"

PMLA 62 (1947): 366–91, and John Twyning, *London Dispossessed: Literature and Social Space in the Early Modern City* (London: Macmillan, 1998).

11. See my "Prostitutes, Shopkeepers, and the Shaping of Urban Subjects in *The Honest Whore*," in *The Elizabethan Theatre* XV, ed. C. E. McGee and A. L. Magnusson (Toronto: P. D. Meany, 2002), pp. 161–79.

12. Pendry, *Elizabethan Prisons and Prisons Scenes*, p. 285.

13. Thomas Middleton and Thomas Dekker, *The Roaring Girl*, ed. Andor Gomme (New York: W. W. Norton, 1976), p. 78; all further references to the play will be to this edition.

14. In Thomas Nashe's *Strange News, Of the intercepting certaine letters, and a Convoy of Verses, as they were going Privilie to victuall the Low Countries* (London, 1592), he, for example, makes light of the fact of having been in the Counter, saying,

> . . . I yeeld that I have dealt upon spare commodities of wine and capons in my daies, I have sung *George Gascoignes* Counter-tenor; what then? Wilt thou peremptorily define that it is a place where no honest man, or Gentleman of credit ever came?

> Heare what I say; a Gentleman is never throughly entred into credit till he hath beene there; & that Poet or novice, be hee what he will, ought to suspect his wit, and remaine halfe in a doubt that it is not authenticall, till it hath beene seene and allowed in unthrifts consistory.

> *Grande doloris ingenium.* Let fooles dwell in no stronger houses than their Fathers built them, but I protest I should never have writ passion well, or beene a peece of a Poet, if I had not arriv'd in those quarters.

> Trace the gallantest youthes and bravest revellers about Towne in all the by-paths of their expence, and you shall unfallibly find, that once in their life time they have visited that melancholy habitation.

> Come, come, if you will goe to the sound truth of it, there is no place of the earth like it to make a man wise.

> Cambridge and Oxford may stande under the elbowe of it.

> I vow, if I had a sonne, I would sooner send him to one of the Counters to learne lawe, than to the Innes of Court or Chauncery. (I–Iv)

15. For a versified list of eighteen of London's prisons, as well as mention of sixty whipping posts, stocks, and cages, see John Taylor, "The Praise and Vertue of a Jayle, and Jaylers" (London, 1623).

16. G. Mynshul, *Essays and Characters of a Prison and Prisoners* (London, 1618).

17. Pendry, *Elizabethan Prisons and Prisons Scenes*, p. 167.

18. Ibid., p. 59.

19. William Fenner, *The Compters Commonwealth* (London, 1616), p. 69. One cannot accept all of Fenner's assertions at face value, but many of the details of Counter life he provides are corroborated by other sources. His figure of 5,000 probably is best taken as an indication of the widespread perception that many poor souls passed through this institution at one time or another in their city lives.

20. Craig Muldrew, *The Economy of Obligation: The Culture of Credit and Social Relations in Early Modern England* (London: St. Martin's, 1998), p. 257.

21. Ibid., p. 264. Muldrew argues that in actuality few fraudulent suits were brought because if the suit failed, the bringer's own credit was damaged. In the drama, however, the fear of fraudulent suits is prevalent, and in the 1606 Orders regulating abuses within the Counters, there is specific mention that keepers are not to profit from malicious or vexatious suits, presumably ones

that involve extortion from innocent people with appropriate kickbacks for the jailers. See Pendry, *Elizabethan Prisons and Prison Scenes*, pp. 323–24.

22. Pendry, *Elizabethan Prisons and Prison Scenes*, pp. 25–27.

23. Fenner, *The Compters Commonwealth*, p. 57.

24. Pendry, *Elizabethan Prisons and Prison Scenes*, p. 29. See also Paul Slack, *The English Poor Law 1531–1782* (London: Macmillan, 1990).

25. W. K. Jordan, *The Charities of London, 1480–1600: The Aspirations and the Achievements of the Urban Society* (Hamden, Conn.: Archon Books, 1974), p. 180, reports that a penny a day was in many cases all that was allotted for the maintenance of any individual prisoner.

26. Ibid., p. 181.

27. "Many Local Officials Now Make Inmates Pay Their Own Way," *New York Times*, Friday, 13 August 2004, p. 1, col. 6.

28. Dobb, "London's Prisons," p. 94.

29. Fenner, *The Compters Commonwealth*, pp. 5–9.

30. Thomas Dekker, "Lanthorne and Candle-light," in *Thomas Dekker: Selected Writings*, ed. Pendry, p. 257.

31. Dobb, "London's Prisons," p. 96.

32. These Orders are reprinted in their entirety in Pendry, *Elizabethan Prisons and Prison Scenes*, pp. 320–36.

33. Fenner, *The Compters Commonwealth*, p. 62.

34. For excellent studies of the expansion of basic consumer goods in early modern England, see Carole Shammas, *The Pre-industrial Consumer in England and America* (Oxford: Clarendon Press, 1990) and Joan Thirsk, *Economic Policy and Projects: The Development of a Consumer Society in Early Modern England* (Oxford: Oxford University Press, 1978). For luxury consumption, see in particular F. J. Fisher, "The Development of London as a Center of Conspicuous Consumption in the Sixteenth and Seventeenth Centuries," in *London and the English Economy, 1500–1700*, ed. P. J. Corfield and N. B. Harte (London and Ronceverte: Hambledon Press, 1990), pp. 105–18.

35. Richard Grassby, *The Business Community of Seventeenth-Century England* (Cambridge: Cambridge University Press, 1995), p. 83.

36. Ibid., pp. 82–83.

37. Muldrew, *The Economy of Obligation*, esp. pp. 60–119.

38. Ibid., p. 107.

39. Ibid., pp. 106–15.

40. Ibid., pp. 148–72; Grassby, *The Business Community of Seventeenth-Century England*, pp. 297–301.

41. For a very interesting reading of the affective responses to debt in the period, see Theodore Leinwand's *Theatre, Finance and Society in Early Modern England* (Cambridge: Cambridge University Press, 1999). He deals with Easy's initial obliviousness to the dangers of debt, and the attentiveness that accompanies his recovery of his lands and reputation. See esp. pp. 55–60.

42. Thomas Middleton, *Michaelmas Term*, ed. Gail Kern Paster (Manchester: Manchester University Press, 2000), p. 111; all further references to the play will be to this edition.

43. Muldrew, *The Economy of Obligation*, pp. 272–312.

44. Ben Jonson, introduction to *Every Man Out of His Humour*, ed. Helen Ostovich (Manchester: Manchester University Press, 2001), p. 4. For Ostovich's larger argument about the popularity of the play, see pp. 31–40; all references to the play will be to this edition, which is based on the first quarto.

45. For a discussion of this figure, see Mario DiGangi's *The Homoerotics of Early Modern Drama* (Cambridge: Cambridge University Press, 1997), pp. 67–72. He quotes Florio at p. 70.

46. This is Ostovich's assumption. See Jonson, *Every Man Out of His Humour*, p. 43.

47. See Ostovich's excellent discussion of this scene in ibid., pp. 59–68.

48. Craig Muldrew estimates that in London, where a woman could trade as a *feme sole* even when married, 26 percent of debtors in prison were female. See his "'A Mutual Assent of her Mind'? Women, Debt, Litigation and Contract in Early Modern England," *History Workshop Journal* 55 (2003): 47–71, at 56. Alexandra Shepard argues, also, that married women were often involved in credit networks, alone or with their husbands, and that in slander cases, while women were most concerned to defend their chastity, a quarter of the cases brought by women concerned allegations of theft or dealing in stolen goods. See her *Meanings of Manhood in Early Modern England* (Oxford: University of Oxford Press, 2003), pp. 197 and 167. This makes it more interesting that the plays focus so insistently in stories of the Counter on men's fall from economic prosperity and the consequences of that fall for their social identity.

49. See, in particular, the work of Laura Gowing, *Domestic Dangers: Women, Words, and Sex in Early Modern London* (Oxford: Clarendon Press, 1996), p. 2. Although Shepard in *Meanings of Manhood* questions Gowing's exclusive emphasis on sexual chastity as a sign of woman's honor, pointing among other things to women's concern with economic honesty, Shepard nonetheless concludes that there were significant differences in how the two sexes viewed what comprised their honor and that women did indeed seem to display the greatest concern about their sexual reputations. What is interesting is her finding that men, too, expressed more concern about their sexual honesty than prior research had indicated and that above all men were concerned about attacks on their social status (pp. 152–85).

50. Amanda Bailey, "'Monstrous Manner': Style and the Early Modern Theater," *Criticism* 43 (2001): 249–84.

51. Introduction to Samuel Rowley's *When You See Me, You Know Me*, gen. ed. F. P. Wilson, The Malone Society Reprints, vol. 88 (Oxford: Oxford University Press, 1952), p. x; all references to the play will be to this edition.

52. I consider the consequences of the mixed genre of monarchical history and urban domestic tragedy in my essay, "Other Englands: The View from the Non-Shakespearean History Play," in *Other Voices, Other Views: Expanding the Canon in English Renaissance Studies*, ed. Helen Ostovich, Mary V. Silcox, and Graham Roebuck (Newark: University of Delaware Press, 1999), pp. 135–53.

53. For the Protestant politics of the play, see G. M. Pinciss, *Forbidden Matter: Religion in the Drama of Shakespeare and His Contemporaries* (Newark: University of Delaware Press, 2000), pp. 58–62; Faith M. Nostbakken, "Rowley's *When You See Me You Know Me*: Political Drama in Transition," *Cahiers Elisabethains* 45 (April 1995): 71–78; and Marsha S. Robinson, *Writing the Reformation:* Actes and Monuments *and the Jacobean History Play* (Aldershot, England: Aldergate, 2002), esp. pp. 14–18. Several critics have suggested that the play's portrayal of Prince Edward was a compliment to James's son, Prince Henry. See Pinciss, p. 59, and Kim Noling, "Women's Wit and Women's Will in *When You See Me, You Know Me*," *Studies in English Literature, 1500–1800* 33 (spring 1993): 327–42, at 333.

54. The date of *A New Wonder* is unclear. It was first printed in 1632 and was written sometime between 1611 and the death of William Rowley, its probable

author, in 1625/26. I am convinced by the arguments of George Cheatham that its probable date is 1611–14. See the introduction to Rowley's *A New Wonder, a Woman Never Vext*, ed. George Cheatham (New York: Peter Lang, 1993), pp. 19–23; all quotations from the play will be to this edition.

55. For a discussion of the theme of charity in the play, see the introduction to Rowley's *A New Wonder*, pp. 23–26.

56. Ibid., p. 30. Cheatham discusses the parallels between the two forms of risk that the brothers undertake.

57. John Stow, *A Survey of London*, ed. Charles Lethbridge Kingsford, 2 vols. (Oxford: The Clarendon Press, 1908), I, p. 39.

58. Pendry, *Elizabethan Prisons and Prison Scenes*, p. 343.

59. See Sean Shesgreen, ed., *The Criers and Hawkers of London: Engravings and Drawings by Marcellus Laroon* (Stanford, Calif.: Stanford University Press, 1990) and Charles Hindley, *A History of the Cries of London. Ancient and Modern*, 2d ed. (London: Charles Hindley, 1884).

60. Richard Dering, *The Cries of London*, ed. Denis Stevens (University Park, Pa.: The Pennsylvania State University Press, 1964), pp. 16–17 and 30–31.

61. Stow, *A Survey of London*, I, pp. 39–40.

62. Ibid., I, p. 166.

63. For this insight about the widow and her fish I am indebted to Adam Zucker who analyzes this play in his 2004 Columbia dissertation, "Comedies of Place: Space, Status, and the Social Work of Comic Form in Early Modern England."

64. For a discussion of this play's use of geography and its validation of the clever women who outwit prodigal gallants, see my essay, "Women, Foreigners, and the Regulation of Urban Space in *Westward Ho*," in *Material London, ca. 1600*, ed. Lena Orlin (Philadelphia: University of Pennsylvania Press, 2000), pp. 150–67. For an ingenious examination of how *Eastward Ho* answers and critiques the collaborative production of *Westward Ho*, see Heather Anne Hirschfield, "'Work Upon That Now': The Production of Parody on the English Renaissance Stage," *Genre* 32 (fall 1999): 175–200.

65. See Ralph Cohen, "The Function of Setting in *Eastward Ho*," in *Renaissance Papers 1973*, ed. Dennis G. Donovan and A. Leigh Deneef, Southeastern Renaissance Conference, 1974, pp. 85–96.

66. C. G. Petter, ed., *Eastward Ho!* by Ben Jonson, George Chapman, and John Marston (London: Ernest Benn Limited, 1973), p. xxiii; all references to the play will be to this edition.

67. For a reading of *Eastward Ho* as an anticolonial text, see Joseph G. Sigalas, "Sailing Against the Tide: Resistance to Pre-Colonial Constructs and Euphoria in *Eastward Ho!*" in *Renaissance Papers 1994*, ed. Barbara J. Baines and George Walton Williams, Southeastern Renaissance Conference, 1995, pp. 85–94.

68. Janet Clare in *"Art made tongue-tied by authority": Elizabethan and Jacobean Dramatic Censorship* (Manchester: Manchester University Press, 1999), pp. 140–44, discusses the censorship of this play and the possibility that it once contained even more anti-Scots material.

69. See Leinwand's discussion of Quicksilver's bravura performance in *Theatre, Finance and Society in Early Modern England*, pp. 44–55.

70. Alexandra Shepard, "Manhood, Credit and Patriarchy in Early Modern England c. 1580–1640," *Past and Present* 167 (May 2000): 75–106. Parts of this essay were incorporated into chapter 7 of her book, *Meanings of Manhood in Early Modern England*, pp. 186–213.

71. Peter Lake with Michael Questier, *The Antichrist's Lewd Hat: Protestants, Papists and Players in Post-Reformation England* (New Haven, Conn.: Yale University Press, 2002), pp. 394–407.

72. See Mynshul, *Essays and Characters of a Prison and Prisoners*, D4-F3v; Fenner, *The Compters Commonwealth*, pp. 40–53; Dekker, "Lanthorne and Candle-light," p. 280.

73. Steven Mullaney discusses the ceremonial procession route used both for royal coronations and for the Lord Mayor's annual pageants in *The Place of the Stage: License, Play, and Power in Renaissance England* (Chicago: University of Chicago Press, 1988), pp. 10–20.

74. J. Cooke, *Greene's Tu Quoque or, The Cittie Gallant*, ed. Alan J. Berman (New York: Garland Publishing, Inc., 1984), pp. vii-viii; all quotations from the play will be taken from this edition.

75. For a discussion of the similarities and differences from a somewhat similar scene in *Ram-Alley*, see the introduction to Cooke's *Greene's Tu Quoque*, pp. xv-xvii.

76. Leinwand, *Theatre, Finance and Society in Early Modern England*, pp. 73–74.

Chapter 3. (W)holesaling

1. For powerful articulations of these positions, see Craig Muldrew, *The Economy of Obligation: The Culture of Credit and Social Relations in Early Modern England* (London: St. Martin's, 1998) and Laura Gowing, *Domestic Dangers: Women, Words, and Sex in Early Modern London* (Oxford: The Clarendon Press, 1996). Alexandra Shepard, *Meanings of Manhood in Early Modern England* (Oxford: Oxford University Press, 2003) somewhat complicates this binary without entirely displacing it, arguing that neither men nor women were monolithic categories and that, in particular, there were a number of modes of masculinity in the period depending on age, status, and other variables.

2. A useful listing of many prostitution plays is given in Angela Ingram's *In the Posture of a Whore: Attitudes to "Bad" Women in Elizabethan and Jacobean Drama*, Salzburg Studies in English Literature 93 (Salzburg: Institut für Anglistik und Amerikanistik, 1984).

3. Alexander Leggatt, *Citizen Comedy in the Age of Shakespeare* (Toronto: University of Toronto Press, 1973), pp. 99–124, esp. 103–5. See also Joseph Lenz, "Base Trade: Theater as Prostitution," *ELH* 60, no. 4 (1983): 833–55. Lenz discusses prostitution not only as an emblem for commerce, but also as an emblem for the theater that uses actors' bodies to generate marketplace profits.

4. *The Oxford English Dictionary Online*, entry 2.a. for traffic, n. The word was in use after 1500, often in contexts involving overseas trade.

5. John Marston, *The Dutch Courtesan*, ed. M. L. Wine (Lincoln: University of Nebraska Press, 1965); all quotations from the play will be taken from this edition.

6. Nicholas Goodman, *Hollands Leaguer: A Critical Edition*, ed. Dean Stanton Barnard, Jr. (The Hague: Mouton, 1970), p. 67; all other quotations from this pamphlet will refer to this edition.

7. Gervase Markham, "The Famous Whore or Noble Cortizan" (London, 1609); all quotations from this poem will refer to this edition.

8. This quotation is taken from Shackerley Marmion's *Hollands Leaguer* (London, 1632), H3v, which I will discuss further below.

9. Older criticism of city plays often focused on identifying the moral attitudes of their creators. My view is that in general these dramas differ from prescriptive literature or sermons in their playful or skeptical attitude toward moral absolutes. I cannot agree, for example, with Paul Griffiths' claim that literary depictions of prostitution are moralizing and conservative ["The Structure of Prostitution in Elizabethan London," *Continuity and Change* 8, no. 1 (1993): 36–63, at 40]. As I hope this chapter will show, the drama in particular constructed prostitution plots that thoroughly destabilized the opposition between the whore and other categories of women or between the practices of the whore and those of other commercial entrepreneurs.

10. John Taylor, *A Common Whore* (London, 1635), A4v.

11. Fredson Bowers, ed., *The Dramatic Works of Thomas Dekker*, 4 vols., vol. 2 (Cambridge: Cambridge University Press, 1953–61), p. 1.

12. William Scott, *An Essay of Drapery* (London, 1635), p. 36. Theodore Leinwand, *The City Staged: Jacobean Comedies 1603–1613* (Madison: University of Wisconsin Press, 1986) p. 71, first noted Candido's resemblance to the historical figure of William Scott, though Scott's treatise postdates *The Honest Whore* by nearly thirty years.

13. R. A. Foakes and R. T. Rickert, eds., *Henslowe's Diary* (Cambridge: Cambridge University Press, 1961), p. 209.

14. I am grateful to Professor Mulholland for letting me see his edition of *The Patient Man and the Honest Whore* before its publication as part of the forthcoming Oxford edition of Middleton. His discussion of the title occurs on pp. 1–2 of his introduction.

15. For a fuller reading of the gender politics of this play, and the relationship of Candido both to Bellafront and to aristocratic masculinity, see my essay, "Prostitutes, Shopkeepers, and the Shaping of Urban Subjects in *The Honest Whore*," in *The Elizabethan Theatre* XV, ed. C. E. McGee and A. L. Magnusson (Toronto: P. D. Meany, 2002), pp. 161–79.

16. See E. J. Burford, *Bawds and Lodgings: A History of the London Bankside Brothels c. 100–1675* (London: Peter Owen, 1976). This book, while unreliable in details and often maddeningly underdocumented, still provides the closest thing we have to a continuous historical account of prostitution in the area south of London. See also Ruth Mazzo Karras, "The Regulation of Brothels in Late Medieval England," *Signs: Journal of Women in Culture and Society* 14, no. 2 (1989): 399–433; Wallace Shugg, "Prostitution in Shakespeare's London," *Shakespeare Studies* 10 (1977): 291–313, and Griffiths, "The Structure of Prostitution in Elizabethan London."

17. Gordon Williams, *A Dictionary of Sexual Language and Imagery in Shakespearean and Stuart Literature*, vol. 3 (London: The Athalone Press, 1994), pp. 1538–39.

18. Ian Archer, *The Pursuit of Stability: Social Relations in Elizabethan London* (Cambridge: Cambridge University Press, 1991), p. 212.

19. See also John L. McMullan, *The Canting Crew: London's Criminal Underworld 1550–1700* (New Brunswick: Rutgers University Press, 1984), esp. chap. 4, "Criminal Areas," in which he discusses the many areas in which prostitution and other forms of vice could be found, and Shugg, "Prostitution in Shakespeare's London," esp. pp. 296–301.

20. James F. Larkin and Paul L. Hughes, eds., *Stuart Royal Proclamations*, vol. 1 (Oxford: The Clarendon Press, 1973), p. 47. This is part of the September 16, 1603 proclamation entitled "A Proclamation against Inmates and multitudes of

dwellers in strait Roomes and places in and about the Citie of London: And for the rasing and pulling downe of certaine new erected buildings."

21. *The Norton Shakespeare*, ed. Stephen Greenblatt, Walter Cohen, Jean Howard, and Katharine Eisaman Maus (New York: Norton, 1997), p. 2033; all references to Shakespeare's plays will be to this edition of his works. For the link between the play and the proclamation, see Shugg, "Prostitution in Shakespeare's London," p. 303.

22. Archer argues from admittedly limited Bridewell records that by the end of the sixteenth century vagrancy was perceived as a more pressing urban problem than sexual vice. While the mid-century reformers had dreamed of creating a godly commonwealth, civic leaders in 1600 were focused on the problem of the growing legions of poor people who had to be brought to conform their behavior to the strictures of the new Elizabethan Poor Laws (*The Pursuit of Stability*, pp. 255–56). Nonetheless, the control of prostitution remained a preoccupation of both the Bridewell officials and the ecclesiastical bawdy courts throughout the Stuart period.

23. For a fuller discussion of this play and the significance of its opposition between Brainford and London proper, see my essay, "Women, Foreigners, and Urban Space in *Westward Ho*," in *Material London, ca. 1600*, ed. Lena Orlin (Philadelphia: University of Pennsylvania Press, 2000), pp. 150–73.

24. Thomas Dekker and John Webster, *Westward Ho*, in *The Dramatic Works of Thomas Dekker*, vol. 2, ed. Bowers, p. 319; all further reference to this play will be to this edition.

25. Thomas Dekker and John Webster, *Northward Ho*, in *The Dramatic Works of Thomas Dekker*, vol. 2, ed. Bowers, p. 411; all future references will be to this edition of the play.

26. See Burford, *Bawds and Lodgings*, p. 125, for evidence that the stews were painted white and Karras, "The Regulation of Brothels in Late Medieval England," p. 421, for a discussion of the distinctive clothing that whores were in some cities required to wear.

27. Ann Rosalind Jones and Peter Stallybrass, *Renaissance Clothing and the Materials of Memory* (Cambridge: Cambridge University Press, 2001), passim.

28. Thomas Dekker, "Lantern and Candle-light," in *Rogues, Vagabonds, Sturdy Beggars*, ed. Arthur Kinney (Barre, Mass.: Imprint Society, 1973), p. 247.

29. McMullan, *The Canting Crew*, p. 33. See also Jyotsna Singh's convincing argument that early modern prostitution was materially connected to women's poverty. "The Interventions of History: Narratives of Sexuality," in *The Weyward Sisters: Shakespeare and Feminist Politics*, ed. Dympna Callaghan, Lorraine Helms, and Jyotsna Singh (Oxford: Blackwell, 1994), pp. 7–58.

30. Gowing, *Domestic Dangers: Women, Words, and Sex in Early Modern London*, p. 17.

31. McMullan, *The Canting Crew*, p. 24.

32. Shugg, "Prostitution in Shakespeare's London," p. 296.

33. McMullan, *The Canting Crew*, p. 139.

34. John Wheeler, *A Treatise of Commerce*, ed. George Hotchkiss (New York: New York University Press, 1931), p. 316.

35. Ibid., pp. 316–17.

36. F. J. Fisher, "The Development of London as a Centre of Conspicuous Consumption in the Sixteenth and Seventeenth Centuries," in *London and the Economy, 1500–1700*, ed. P. J. Corfield and N. B. Harte (London and Ronceverte: Hambledon, 1990), pp. 105–18.

37. See Karen Newman, *Fashioning Femininity and English Renaissance Drama* (Chicago: University of Chicago Press, 1991), pp. 111–43 and Jean E. Howard, "The Evidence of Fiction: Women's Relationship to Goods in London City Drama," in *Culture and Change: Attending to Early Modern Women*, ed. Margaret Mikesell and Adele Seeff (Newark: University of Delaware Press, 2003), pp. 161–76.

38. For a discussion of women's role in retailing and in the provisioning industries, see Sara Mendelson and Patricia Crawford, *Women in Early Modern England 1550–1720* (Oxford: Clarendon, 1998), pp. 333–36. For more on the provisioning trades. see Sara Pennell, " 'Great quantities of goosberry pye and baked clod of beef': Victualling and Eating Out in Early Modern London," in *Londinopolis: Essays in the Cultural and Social History of Early Modern London*, ed. Paul Griffiths and Mark S. R. Jenner (Manchester: Manchester University Press, 2000), pp. 228–49.

39. See Gowing, *Domestic Dangers: Women, Words, and Sex in Early Modern London*, p. 15.

40. Emanuel Van Meteren, "Pictures of the English in Queen Elizabeth's Reign," in *England as Seen by Foreigners*, ed. William Brenchley Rye (London: John Russell Smith, 1865), pp. 72–73.

41. Hugh Alley's *Caveat: The Markets of London in 1598*, Folger Ms V.a.318, ed. Ian Archer, Caroline Barron, and Vanessa Harding, Publication No. 137 (London Topographical Society, 1988). Of course, Alley's drawings are stylized and push his own political agenda, which was to promote tighter regulations to govern market practices and to prevent offenses such as forestalling, that is buying goods before the official market day, or regrating, buying goods in one market and selling them in another at a higher price (Introduction, p. 5). Alley's market sketches show orderly social interactions and prominently feature pillars on which lists of market offenses could be posted. Nonetheless, women are prominent both as vendors and as buyers in many of his sketches, and in this regard Alley seems to have captured a salient fact of London market life.

42. Ian Archer, "Material Londoners?" in *Material London, ca. 1600*, ed. Orlin, pp. 174–92, at 184–85.

43. Thomas Heywood, "The Wise-woman of Hogsdon," in *The Dramatic Works of Thomas Heywood*, vol. 5 (London: John Pearson, 1874), act 1, scene 2 , p. 285 (no lineation given); all further references to the play will be to this edition and will be given by act, scene, and page numbers.

44. Dekker, "Lantern and Candlelight," p. 347.

45. Thomas Heywood, *The First Part of King Edward the Fourth*, in *The Dramatic Works of Thomas Heywood*, vol. 1, pp. 64–66; all further references to the play will be to this edition and will be given by page numbers only (no act, scene, or lineation given).

46. See, for example, act 2, scene 1 in which the gallants circulate among the shops of Mr. and Mrs. Tiltyard, Openwork, and Gallipot. Thomas Middleton and Thomas Dekker, *The Roaring Girl*, ed. Andor Gomme (New York: W. W. Norton, 1976), pp. 26–45; all future references to the play will be this edition.

47. Critics who address this topic include Dan Vitkus, *Turning Turk: English Theater and the Multicultural Mediterranean, 1570–1630* (New York: Palgrave, 2003); Nabil Matar, *Islam in Britain 1558–1685* (Cambridge: Cambridge University Press, 1998) and *Turks, Moors, and Englishmen in the Age of Discovery* (New York: Columbia

University Press, 1999); Barbara Fuchs, *Mimesis and Empire: The New World, Islam, and European Identities* (Cambridge: Cambridge University Press, 2001); and Ania Loomba, " 'Delicious traffick': Racial and Religious Difference on Early Modern Stages," in *Shakespeare and Race*, ed. Catherine M. S. Alexander and Stanley Wells (Cambridge: Cambridge University Press, 2000), pp. 203–24.

48. Goodman, *Hollands Leaguer*, p. 60.

49. Ibid., p. 66.

50. For an incisive consideration of the role of clothing in constructing urban identities and in shifting the basis of identity from birth to appearance and performance, see Mathew Martin, "'[B]egot between tirewomen and tailors': Commodified Self-Fashioning in *Michaelmas Term*," *Early Modern Literary Studies* 5, no. 1 (May 1999): 21–36. See also Gail Kern Paster's wide-ranging discussion of clothing in the play in the introduction to her edition of *Michaelmas Term* (Manchester: Manchester University Press, 2000), esp. pp. 20–32; all references will be to this edition.

51. James Shapiro, *Shakespeare and the Jews* (New York: Columbia University Press, 1996), esp. pp. 131–65.

52. For an excellent discussion of the quandaries of legibility posed by converted Catholics in early modern English Protestant culture, see Fran Dolan, *Whores of Babylon: Catholicism, Gender, and Seventeenth-Century Print Culture* (Ithaca, N.Y.: Cornell University Press, 1999).

53. For an important discussion of anal sex in a number of early modern English plays, including *Michaelmas Term*, see Celia Daileader, "Back Door Sex: Renaissance Gyno-Sodomy, Aretino, and the Exotic," *ELH* 69 (2002): 303–34.

54. Leggatt, *Citizen Comedy in the Age of Shakespeare*, p. 117, shrewdly notes that while mistakes of identity are common in city plays, *Michaelmas Term* is unusual in the fact that the play ends with the father and his daughter still unknown to one another.

55. Williams, *A Dictionary of Sexual Language and Imagery in Shakespearean and Stuart Literature*, vol. 3, pp. 1525–26, says that the "wholesale" pun is particularly apt for describing mercenary sex and lists *Michaelmas Term* as just one of a number of dramas that play with its possibilities.

56. For a brilliant discussion of the role of clothing in the many renditions of the Griselda story, see Jones and Stallybrass, *Renaissance Clothing and the Materials of Memory*, pp. 220–44.

57. Faramerz Dabhoiwala, "The Pattern of Sexual Immorality in Seventeenth and Eighteenth Century London," in *Londinopolis*, ed. Griffiths and Jenner, pp. 86–106, at 88.

58. Gowing, *Domestic Dangers; Women, Words, and Sex in Early Modern London*, esp. chap. 3, "The Language of Insult," pp. 59–110.

59. Dabhoiwala, "The Pattern of Sexual Immorality in Seventeenth and Eighteenth Century London," p. 93.

60. See John Schofield's *The Building of London from the Conquest to the Great Fire*, 3d ed. (Phoenix Mill: Sutton Publishing, 1999), esp. chap. 7, "To the Great Fire 1600–1666," pp. 157–77.

61. Steven Mullaney, *The Place of the Stage: License, Play, and Power in Renaissance England* (Chicago: University of Chicago Press, 1988), pp. 1–25, discusses what he calls the "ceremonial city" defined by events such as the monarch's or the lord mayor's carefully choreographed movement through London on ritual occasions. Both the monarch's entry procession and the annual lord mayor's pageant invariably moved along Cheapside.

62. Thomas Platter, *Travels in England,* reprint in *London in the Age of Shakespeare: An Anthology,* ed. Lawrence Manley (University Park: The Pennsylvania State University Press, 1986), pp. 38–39.

63. John Stow, *A Survey of London.* 2 vols., vol. 1, ed. Charles Lethbridge Kingsford (Oxford: The Clarendon Press, 1908), pp. 345–46.

64. Paul Griffiths, "Politics Made Visible: Order, Residence and Uniformity in Cheapside, 1600–45," in *Londinopolis,* ed. Griffiths and Jenner, pp. 176–96.

65. Pier Frassinelli, "Realism, Desire and Reification: Thomas Middleton's *A Chaste Maid in Cheapside,*" *Early Modern Literary Studies* 8, no. 3 (January 2003): 1–26.

66. Joanne Altieri, "Against Moralizing Jacobean Comedy: Middleton's *Chaste Maid in Cheapside,*" *Criticism* 30 (spring 1988): 171–87.

67. Edward Sharpham, *The Fleire* (London, 1607), Bv; all further references to the play will be to this edition.

68. Stow, *Survey of London,* vol. 2, p. 55.

69. Burford, *Bawds and Lodgings,* pp. 142–46. See also Karras, "The Regulation of Brothels in Late Medieval England," p. 415.

70. Qtd. in Burford, *Bawds and Lodgings,* p. 125. "Countries," of course, could refer to "counties" as well as foreign lands, so the whores to which Henry refers could either have been strangers or those from other parts of England. That said, the tradition of thinking of Bankside whores as Flemish has a long discursive history.

71. By the time of the famous siege of Hollands Leaguer in 1631/32, the trope had swollen to nearly parodic proportions. In a popular ballad entitled, "Newes from *Hollands Leager,*" one verse gaily proclaims:

The flaunting Spaniard,
    and boone Cavillera,
The bragging Dutchman
    though cost him deare a:
Wallouns and *Switzer,*
    both *Jewes, Turke* and *Neager,*
Scots, Danes and *French,*
    have been at *Hollands Leager.* (Goodman, *Hollands Leaguer,* p. 109)

72. See Archer, *The Pursuit of Stability,* pp. 211–33 and Griffiths, "The Structure of Prostitution in Elizabethan London," esp. p. 45. In the same article Griffiths provides a breakdown of 219 brothel clients whose status can be determined; 11.4 percent were foreign merchants and 7.8 percent were in ambassadors' retinues (see p. 55). Although the sample is limited, it is significant that nearly one fifth of identifiable clients were in some way connected to the alien communities in London. See also Duncan Salkeld, "Black Luce and the Curtizans of Shakespeare's London," *Signatures* 2 (2000): 1–10. Salkeld explores the mixed evidence for black prostitutes in Elizabethan London, and in the process turns up records of prostitutes accused of serving "ingraunt strangers" (p. 3).

73. Archer, *The Pursuit of Stability,* esp. pp. 231–33.

74. Ibid., p. 213.

75. McMullan, *The Canting Crew,* esp. pp. 56–66.

76. Stephen Gosson, *Pleasant Quippes for Upstart Newfangled Gentlewomen,* ed. Edwin Johnston Howard (Oxford, Ohio: The Anchor Press, 1942), p. vii; further quotations from this pamphlet will refer to this edition. The quotation cited here is from the original title of the tract—*A Glasse, to view the Pride of*

vainglorious women, Containing, A Pleasant Invective against the Fantastical Forreigne Toyes, daylie used in Womens Apparell—which seems to have been changed at the last minute before publication.

77. See Jonathan Gil Harris, *Sick Economies; Drama, Mercantilism, and Disease in Shakespeare's England* (Philadelphia: University of Pennsylvania Press, 2004), pp. 1–24.

78. Robert Greene, *A Disputation Betweene a Hee Conny-catcher, and a Shee Conny-catcher*, C3v.

79. J. M. Cowper, ed., *Times' Whistle: or A Newe Daunce of Seven Satires, and other Poems*, Early English Text Society 48 (London: N. Trubner and Company, 1871), satire 6, "Against Lasciviousness," p. 80.

80. For an excellent discussion of the way in which women, especially whores, were blamed for the spread of diseases, particularly the pox, see Lewis F. Qualtiere and William W. E. Slights, "Contagion and Blame in Early Modern England: The Case of the French Pox," *Literature and Medicine* 22, no. 1 (spring 2003): 1–24.

81. Taylor, *A Common Whore*, A4v.

82. For the play's comic use of Bedlam, see Ken Jackson, "Bethlem and Bridewell in *The Honest Whore* Plays," *SEL* 43, no. 2 (spring 2003): 395–413, at 405.

83. Thomas Coryat, *Coryat's Crudities*, 2 vols., vol. 1 (Glasgow: James MacLehose and Sons, 1905), p. 401.

84. Markham, *The Famous Whore*, D3v–E.

85. Mary Floyd-Wilson, in *English Ethnicity and Race in Early Modern Drama* (Cambridge: Cambridge University Press, 2003), esp. pp. 1–66, outlines the ways in which England's geographical position as a northern nation was thought to make Englishmen more sluggish and less suited to bear the imprint of civility than people of southern nations. In the first chapter I dealt with the ways in which England felt itself a latecomer to the kinds of economic and territorial expansion that Mediterranean nations, in particular, had undertaken well before 1600.

86. Philip J. Finkelpearl, *John Marston of the Middle Temple: An Elizabethan Dramatist in His Social Setting* (Cambridge, Mass.: Harvard University Press, 1969).

87. George L. Geckle, *John Marston's Drama: Themes, Images, Sources* (Cranbury, N.J.: Associated University Presses, 1980), p. 157.

88. Anthony Caputi, *John Marston: Satirist.* (Ithaca, N.Y.: Cornell University Press, 1961), p. 238.

89. Richard Horwich discusses the divide between Beatrice, who is placed outside market relations, and Franceschina, who embodies them. See his "Wives, Courtesans, and the Economics of Love in Jacobean City Comedy," in *Drama in the Renaissance: Comparative and Critical Essays*, ed. Clifford Davidson and John H. Stroupe (New York: AMS Press, 1986), pp. 255–73.

90. The definitive book on the English members of the Family of Love is Christopher W. Marsh's *The Family of Love in English Society, 1550–1630* (Cambridge: Cambridge University Press, 1994). Marsh queries the truth of the stereotypes that came to surround English Familists, but acknowledges their currency. See also Simon Shepherd, *Amazons and Warrior Women: Varieties of Feminism in Seventeenth-Century Drama* (New York: St. Martin's Press, 1982), p. 9.

91. A. J. Hoenselaars, *Images of Englishmen and Foreigners in the Drama of Shakespeare and His Contemporaries* (Toronto: Associated University Press, 1992), p. 115.

92. Donna Hamilton, "Language as Theme in *The Dutch Courtesan.*" *Renaissance Drama* 5 (1972): 75–87, at 85.

93. Finkelpearl, *John Marston of the Middle Temple*, pp. 195–96.

94. From the Interregnum to the nineteenth century the Mulligrub-Cocledemoy subplot formed the basis for most stage performances of the play. The 1950s saw the first revivals of the whole drama since the early seventeenth century. See Wine, ed., *The Dutch Courtesan*, p. xiii.

95. Some information about Hollands Leaguer comes from the ballad, play, and pamphlet written about it during the several months following the siege of 1631–32, and I will deal with those below. Details on Elizabeth Holland and on the Manor House in Paris Gardens can be found in the introduction to Goodman's *Hollands Leaguer* and in E. J. Burford, *Queen of the Bawds or The True Story of Madame Britannica Hollandia and Her House of Obsenitie, Hollands Leaguer* (London: Neville Spearman, 1973). Burford speculates that there may have been a whole family of brothel keepers named Holland in London at the end of the sixteenth century and the beginning of the seventeenth. He has found court records involving an Elizabeth, an Amy, a Henry, and a Richard Holland (pp. 97–103).

96. Burford, *Queen of the Bawds*, pp. 112–14.

Chapter 4. Ballrooms and Academies

1. "Complement," meaning "observance of ceremony in social relations: ceremoniousness; formal civility, politeness, or courtesy" (*OED* 8b) or "a ceremonious or formal tribute of (mere) courtesay paid to any one" (*OED* 9) was replaced with the French word "compliment" sometime between 1655 and 1725 (*OED* headnote to "Complement"). This linguistic shift supports one of the things this chapter argues, namely, that by the Caroline period, polite society increasingly derived its ideas of mannerly conduct from France, and the adoption of the French form of the word in midcentury seems to acknowledge that link. In this chapter, however, I retain the older spelling since most of the documents I discuss predate this shift.

2. All work on the rise of mannerly behavior in Western societies relies in part on the pioneering book by Norbert Elias, *The History of Manners* (1939), vol. 1 of *The Civilizing Process*, trans. Edmund Jephcott (New York: Urizen, 1978). My focus is more narrow and particular than his, however, looking as I do at a span of fifteen years in English culture when a concern with bodily decorum and a regime of manners came to define a particular segment of urban culture. For related work on earlier decades in the English context, see, in particular, Gail Kern Paster, *The Body Embarrassed: Drama and the Disciplines of Shame in Early Modern England* (Ithaca, N.Y.: Cornell University Press, 1993).

3. Along with Shirley's name, that of George Chapman appeared on the title page to the first edition of *The Ball*, which was printed together with the *Tragedy of Chabot Admiral of France*, a definite Shirley–Chapman collaboration. Scholars disagree as to whether Chapman had a hand in *The Ball* or whether, as G. E. Bentley argued, the attribution on the original title page is simply a mistake caused by the printer using the same setting of type for the authors of both *Chabot* and *The Ball* (*The Jacobean and Caroline Stage*, 7 vols., vol. 5 [Oxford: Clarendon Press, 1948–61], pp. 1077–78). Gifford, the play's nineteenth-century editor, assumes that the largest portion of the play is by Chapman. See *The Dramatic Works and Poems of James Shirley*, vol. 3 (reprint, New York: Russell and Russell, 1966), B2. Hanson T. Parlin, in *A Study in Shirley's Comedies of London*

Life (reprint from the *Bulletin of the University of Texas*, No. 317, November 15, 1914), p. iii, argues that Shirley was its sole author, a view echoed by Thomas Parrott, the editor of Chapman's plays, in *The Poems and Plays of George Chapman, The Comedies* (London: George Routledge and Sons, 1914), pp. 869–75. Robert Forsythe, in *The Relations of Shirley's Plays to the Elizabethan Drama* (New York: Columbia University Press, 1914), p. 408, puts forward the idea that the play was originally written by Shirley but revised by Chapman when it was censored for supposedly too closely personating lords and others of the court. I agree with Bentley, finding in *The Ball* all the hallmarks of Shirley's style and preoccupations. The parallels between *The Ball* and *Hyde Park*, also written in 1632, suggest that in both these plays Shirley was experimenting with ways to dramatize the fashionable life of London's growing West End culture.

4. All quotations from *The Ball* will refer to the edition included in Parrott's edition of Chapman noted above.

5. William Prynne, *Histrio-mastix* (London, 1633), table. The first entry under *Women-Actors* is "notorious whores." Several biographies of Henrietta Maria devote attention to her cultural enthusiasms. See Quentin Bone, *Henrietta Maria: Queen of the Cavaliers* (Urbana: University of Illinois Press, 1972) and Alison Plowden, *Henrietta Maria: Charles I's Indomitable Queen* (Phoenix Mill, England: Sutton Publishing, 2001). For a consideration of the full range of the Queen's cultural life at court, see Erica Veevers, *Images of Love and Religion: Queen Henrietta Maria and Court Entertainments* (Cambridge: Cambridge University Press, 1989). For discussion of the Prynne affair, see the important article by Sophie Tomlinson, "She that Plays the King: Henrietta Maria and the Threat of the Actress in Caroline Culture," in *The Politics of Tragicomedy: Shakespeare and After*, ed. Gordon McMullan and Jonathan Hope (New York: Routledge, 1992), pp. 189–207 and that by Kim Walker, "*New Prison*: Representing the Female Actor in Shirley's *The Bird in a Cage* (1633)," *ELR* 21 (1991): 385–400. Prynne's book was in press before the first performance of Montague's pastoral in January of 1633, but rehearsals had been going on throughout the fall. Moreover, her part in *The Shepherd's Paradise* was not Henrietta Maria's first theatrical venture. In 1626 she and some of her court ladies acted in a French pastoral in which she had a speaking part and in which some of the women performed the parts of men and wore male attire. Shirley's *Bird in a Cage*, which shows women performing a play, is famously prefaced by a satirical dedication to Prynne, who was by this time in prison.

6. Prynne, *Histrio-mastix*, table. Under *Dancing*, Prynne includes the following entries: "Delight and skil in Dancing, a badge of lewde, lascivious women & strumpets"; "The Devill danceth in dancing women"; "effeminate, mixt, lascivious dancing condemned by Scriptures, Councels, Fathers, Pagan and moderne Christian Authors, of all sorts, as an occasion of much sin and lewdness."

7. For his discussion of the development of wit and taste as markers of cultural status in West End London plays, I am especially indebted to the work of my student, Adam Zucker, whose Columbia dissertation, "Comedies of Place: Space, Status and the Social Work of Comic Form in Early Modern England," was completed in spring of 2004.

8. A number of historians have written about the development of town culture in West End London. They include Lawrence Stone, *The Crisis of the Aristocracy 1558–1641* (Oxford: Clarendon, 1965), esp. pp. 357–63 and 385–98; Martin Butler, *Theatre and Crisis 1632–1642* (Cambridge: Cambridge University Press, 1984), esp. pp. 141–80; and F. J. Fisher, "The Development of London as

a Centre of Conspicuous Consumption in the Sixteenth and Seventeenth Centuries," in *London and the English Economy, 1500–1700,* ed. P. J. Corfield and N. B. Harte (London: The Hambledon Press, 1990), pp. 105–16. Most stress the area's connection to the influx of aristocrats and gentry coming into the city in the early seventeenth century to be near the court or to take part in "the season" that increasingly dominated the elite social scene from fall to spring of each year. R. Malcolm Smuts, in "The Court and Its Neighborhood: Royal Policy and Urban Growth in the Early Stuart West End," *Journal of British Studies* 30 (April 1991): 117–49, provides a useful corrective to the emphasis on the elite nature of West End residents. While acknowledging the upscale building projects that characterized the West End and the number of gentry and peers who began to live there, he also demonstrates that the population of the area remained very mixed, with many tradesmen and day laborers residing in cramped, far-from-luxurious housing. They would not have been, however, members of "the town," a cultural construct alluding only to those who met certain standards of fashionability.

9. Two of the earliest articles to take note of Caroline comedy's use of specific locations to examine the manners of particular social groups were Richard H. Perkinson's "Topographical Comedy in the 17th Century," *ELH* 3 (1936): 270–90 and Theodore Miles's "Place-Realism in a Group of Caroline Plays," *The Review of English Studies* 18 (1942): 428–40. Perkinson is particularly good at making connections between Caroline and Restoration plays set in parks, gardens, and fairs. Miles discusses only six Caroline plays: *Holland's Leaguer, Hyde Park, Covent Garden Weeded, Covent Garden, Tottenham Court,* and *Sparagus Garden.* His emphasis on "photographic realism" (p. 431) in these plays ignores the selective nature of their representation of particular venues and the drama's role in constructing the audience's understanding of their significance.

10. Julie Sanders, *Caroline Drama: The Plays of Massinger, Ford, Shirley and Brome* (Plymouth, England: Northcote House Publishers, 1999), pp. 43–45.

11. The idea of cultural capital is perhaps best developed by Pierre Bourdieu, who in *Distinction: A Social Critique of the Judgement of Taste* (Cambridge, Mass.: Harvard University Press, 1984), discusses the role of the French educational system in producing those who belong to elite status groups and who possess that distance from economic necessity that allows them to develop aesthetic judgement and develop "taste."

12. See Janette Dillon, "The Place of Accommodation: The Royal Entertainment at the New Exchange," chap. 6 of *Theatre, Court, and City 1595–1610: Drama and Social Space in London* (Cambridge: Cambridge University Press, 2000), pp. 109–23 for descriptions of the goods advertised as in the china shop.

13. For a thorough discussion of Bedford's Covent Garden undertaking, see F. H. W. Sheppard, gen. ed., *Survey of London,* vol. XXXVI, *Parish of St. Paul Covent Garden* (London: Athalone Press, 1970), esp. pp. 19–150.

14. For information on these places of resort, see Sir Walter Besant, *London in the Time of the Stuarts* (London: Adam and Charles Black, 1903), esp. pp. 311–17 and G. H. Gater, ed., *Survey of London,* vol. XVI, *Charing Cross: The Parish of St. Martin-in-the-Fields, Part I* (London: Country Life Ltd., 1935), esp. pp. 46, 47, 52, 53, 71, and 72. Eventually the functions of the Spring Gardens were transferred in the eighteenth century to the Vauxhall Gardens south of the Thames. For an important discussion of the significance of the Vauxhall Gardens to eighteenth-century London, see Miles Ogborn, "The Pleasure Garden," in *Spaces of Modernity:*

London's Geographies, 1680–1780 (New York: The Guilford Press, 1998), pp. 116–57.

15. James Shirley, *The Lady of Pleasure*, ed. Ronald Huebert (Manchester: Manchester University Press, 1986), p. 145; all future references to the play will be to this edition.

16. Dana G. McKinnen, "A Description of a Restoration Promptbook of Shirley's *The Ball*," *Restoration and 18th Century Theatre Research* X (1971): 25–28, at 25. That McKinnen found a Restoration promptbook of Shirley's play supports earlier speculation that it might be the work to which Pepys refers, though there were a number of other plays from the 1630s that also contained comic dancing masters, some of which I examine in this chapter.

17. Wilfrid R. Prest, *The Inns of Court under Elizabeth I and the Early Stuarts, 1590–1640* (London: Longman, 1972), esp. pp. 24 and 154.

18. Sandra Burner, *James Shirley: A Study of Literary Coteries and Patronage in Seventeenth-Century England* (New York: University Press of America, 1988), esp. chap. 2, "The Gray's Inn Circle and the Professional Dramatists," pp. 41–84.

19. See B. Ravelhofer's introduction to *Louange de la Danse*, by B. De Montagut, Renaissance Texts from Manuscript, No. 3 (Cambridge, England: RTM Publishers, 2000), pp. 11–13.

20. Ibid., pp. 1–9 and p. 21.

21. John Playford, "To the Ingenious Reader," in *The English Dancing Master: or, Plaine and Easie Rules for the Dancing of Country Dances, with the Tune to each Dance* (London, 1651).

22. Anna Bryson, *From Courtesy to Civility: Changing Codes of Conduct in Early Modern England* (Oxford: Clarendon, 1998) and Jorge Arditi, *A Genealogy of Manners: Transformations of Social Relations in France and England from the Fourteenth to the Eighteenth Century* (Chicago: University of Chicago Press, 1998). The foundational text for understanding the origins of the European revolution in manners is Elias's *The History of Manners*.

23. Henry Peacham's *Compleat Gentleman*, first published in 1622, shows in the English context the adaptation of the courtesy manual to the needs of an urbane, but not necessarily a courtly, class. See Peacham's *Compleat Gentleman* (1634), with introduction by G. S. Gordon (Oxford: The Clarendon Press, 1906). Peacham argues that nobility consists more in actions than in blood and devotes a great deal of his time to explaining how a gentleman should be educated. Beyond the traditional university subjects, gentlemen should attain a wide knowledge of poetry, music, antiquities, statuary, coins, paintings, and drawings. Using the Italian term *virtuosi* (p. 105) to refer to gentlemen properly conversant with such things, he urges English readers to travel to France, Spain, and Italy where the "Gardens and Galleries of great men are beautified and set forth to admiration with these kinds of ornaments" (p. 104). While travelers are to be keen observers of men and manners, they are also to learn how to converse knowledgeably about such matters or be taken for "idiots or rakehels," just as they must understand heraldry and be proficient in all the physical exercises (running, riding, wrestling) that lead to graceful carriage and bodily health. Peacham's book does not primarily prepare courtiers to serve a prince; rather, it shows how even merchants and doctors can attain the skills that will allow them to take part in an urbane society in which standards of civil conduct obtain and cultural "idiots" are excluded.

24. Bryson, *From Courtesy to Civility*, esp. pp. 113–15 and 129–31.

25. At one point Frisk, praising Lord Rainbow's skills at dancing, says "Oh, he dance finely, begar, he deserve the Ball of de world" (II.iii.25). This could mean that he deserves to *give* or *be present at* the best dancing occasion. It could also mean that he deserves to receive the literal golden ball that eventually features in the masque that precedes the general dancing at the ball itself.

26. Robert Dallington, *A Method for Travell. Shewed by Taking the view of France As it stoode in the yeare of our Lord 1598* (London, 1605), p. B4v.

27. Montagut, *Louange de La Danse*, p. 155.

28. Dallington, in *A Method for Travell*, says that there are infinite numbers of tennis courts throughout France, in fact, twice as many as there are churches, Sig. V. See also Gordon Williams, *A Dictionary of Sexual Language and Imagery in Shakespearean and Stuart Literature*, vol. 3 (London: The Athlone Press, 1994), p. 1372.

29. Butler, *Theatre and Crisis*, pp. 110–11.

30. See, in particular, Alan Brissenden, *Shakespeare and the Dance* (Atlantic Highlands, N.J.: Humanities Press, 1981) and Skiles Howard, *The Politics of Courtly Dancing in Early Modern England* (Amherst: University of Massachusetts Press), 1998.

31. Howard in *The Politics of Courtly Dancing in Early Modern England* convincingly argues that courtly dancing had long been distinguished from country dancing by its emphasis on erect posture and regular movement. See esp. pp. 1–25. What I find interesting in the 1630s is that paradigms for courtliness, as I will discuss, are being translated to contexts outside the direct influence of the court.

32. Ibid., pp. 114–15.

33. Ibid., p. 2. A good example of the difference between country and courtly dances occurs in the first act of Heywood's *A Woman Killed with Kindness* in which two kinds of class–specific dancing follow the wedding of Anne and John Frankfurt. The servants in the hall boisterously dance "their country measures, rounds, and jigs" (I.i.84) while the friends of Anne and John retire to another room presumably to undertake more courtly dances. See *A Woman Killed with Kindness*, ed. R. W. Van Fossen (London: Methuen, 1961), pp. 6–7.

34. Frank Whigham in *Ambition and Privilege: The Social Tropes of Elizabethan Courtesy Theory* (Berkeley: University of California Press, 1984) argues that courtesy literature made aristocratic skills accessible to men of lower rank and paradoxically made imitable what was supposedly the inherent qualities of a privileged class. In *The Ball* graceful deportment in the dance marks out privileged members of town society, but the play makes very clear that such skills are teachable. It nonetheless, as I am arguing, wants to cling to the idea that some people cannot learn them.

35. See, for example, Ira Clark's view in *Professional Playwrights: Massinger, Ford, Shirley, and Brome* (Lexington: University of Kentucky Press, 1992) that Shirley consistently praises the court and its effects on town culture, admitting criticism of court ways only to contain it.

36. Butler, *Theatre and Crisis*, esp. pp. 166–80. I differ from Butler in that I do not feel the plays are political allegories or are constantly commenting on court politics. I am, in general, more interested than Butler in the cultural issues being negotiated in these town comedies. Nonetheless, I agree with him when he argues that Caroline comedies written for the public stage are perfectly capable of indirectly criticizing the court and courtly ways.

37. Introduction to *The Ball* in Parrott's *The Plays and Poems of George Chapman*, p. 869.

38. Several characters' names were changed sometime during the composition or printing of the play, and this may have been a response to censorship. Rainbow, for example, is also suggestively called Loveall in parts of the original 1639 edition of the text, while Sir Ambrose Lamount and Sir Marmaduke Travers (two of Lucina's unsuccessful suitors) were also designated as Lionell and Ambrose. See Dana Gene McKinnon's discussion of inconsistencies in the deployment of these names in stage directions and speech headings, especially in acts 4 and 5, in "The Ball by George Chapman and James Shirley: A Critical Edition" (Ph.D. diss., University of Illinois, Urbana, 1965), pp. xxiv–xxxi. Burner has proposed that another set of characters—Rainbow, certainly, but also Barker, Frisk, and Bostock, the cowardly, boasting "cousin" of Rainbow—were the likely objects of Herbert's remarks. See her *James Shirley*, p. 63.

39. The best introduction to seventeenth-century English travel abroad is John Stoye's *English Travellers Abroad 1604–1667*, rev. ed. (New Haven, Conn.: Yale University Press, 1989). See also Alison Games, "Before the Grand Tour: The Domestication of Global Travel," chap. 1 of her forthcoming book, *Agents of Empire: English Cosmopolitans in an Age of Expansion*, who argues that travel nearly always was justified as preparation for service to the monarch or to further state interests in the realms of trade and diplomacy.

40. Burner, *James Shirley*, p. 86.

41. See in particular Veevers's discussion of the royal pair's evolving sense of the importance of their chaste conjugal union in *Images of Love and Religion*, esp. pp. 14–47.

42. Williams, *A Dictionary of Sexual Language and Imagery*, pp. 1372–73.

43. For the English understanding of Aretino's work and its sexual and political significance, see Ian Frederick Moulton's *Before Pornography: Erotic Writing in Early Modern England* (Oxford: Oxford University Press, 2000), esp. pp. 119–221.

44. Mark Motley, *Becoming a French Aristocrat: The Education of the Court Nobility 1580–1715* (Princeton, N.J.: Princeton University Press, 1990), pp. 124–26.

45. Stone, *The Crisis of the Aristocracy 1558–1641*, p. 695.

46. Motley, *Becoming a French Aristocrat*, pp. 142–50.

47. Ben Jonson, *The Devil Is an Ass and Other Plays*, ed. Margaret Jane Kidnie (Oxford: Oxford University Press, 2000); all other references to the play will be to this edition.

48. James Shirley, *Love Tricks, or, The School of Complement*, vol. 1 of *The Dramatic Works and Poems of James Shirley*, ed. William Gifford, p. 49; all other references to the play will be to this edition that gives act and scene, but not line numbers.

49. For information on the historical Museum Minervae, see the account in Sheppard, gen. ed., *The Survey of London*, vol. xxxvi, *Parish of St. Paul Covent Garden*. pp. 254–58.

50. Francis Kynaston, preface to *The Constitutions of the Museum Minervae* (London, 1636), 3v.

51. Beaumont et al., *Comedies and Tragedies Written by Francis Beaumont and John Fletcher* (London, 1647), A4. *Early English Books Online*, available from http://eebo.chadwyck.com.

52. Peacham, *The Compleat Gentleman*, with introduction by Gordon, p. 238.

53. Clark, *Professional Playwrights*, p. 157, places the play in 1635, and internal evidence makes me think this date is right. The play was not published until 1658.

54. Richard Brome, "The New Academy, Or The New Exchange," in *The Dramatic Works of Richard Brome Containing Fifteen Comedies Now First Collected in Three Volumes*, vol. 2 (London: John Pearson, 1873), III.i.p.50; all future references to the play will be to this edition, which lacks line numbers.

55. This text, printed in London for Humphrey Mosley, is a compendium of dialogues, letters, salutations, greetings, and other speech acts useful in addressing others in polite society, especially one's beloved. It may have been authored by John Gough. The inclusion at the end of "A Table for the understanding of the hard *English* words contained in this Book" and another table listing the names and attributes of Greek and Roman gods and goddesses and key figures in classical history and myth suggest that the book's imagined readers were seeking self-improvement of many sorts.

56. William Cavendish, *The Variety* (London, 1649), p. 35; all further references to the play will be to this edition, which lacks line numbers.

57. The best modern edition of Aretino's poems and the woodcuts that in the 1527 edition came to replace Raimondi's engravings is Lynne Lawner's *I Modi: The Sixteen Pleasures: An Erotic Album of the Italian Renaissance*, trans. Lynne Lawner (Evanston, Ill.: Northwestern University Press, 1988).

58. Moulton, *Before Pornography*, p. 5.

59. Jasper Mayne, *The Citye Match* (Oxford, 1939), V.ii.p.59 (no lineation given).

60. Richard Brome, *The City Wit, or, The Woman Wears the Breeches*, in *The Dramatic Works of Richard Brome*, vol. 1, p. 335; all future references to the play will be to this edition.

61. Qtd. in Butler, *Theatre and Crisis*, p. 195. See pp. 195–98 for Butler's important discussion of Cavendish's politics as evident in the two plays he wrote.

62. Montagut, *Louange de la Danse*, p. 109.

63. See the Ravelhofer, introduction to *Louange de la Danse*, by Montagut, pp. 25–40.

64. Anne Barton in "Harking Back to Elizabeth: Ben Jonson and Caroline Nostalgia," *ELH* 48 (winter 1981): 706–31 argues that this is an example of Elizabethan nostalgia that was increasingly prevalent in 1630s' drama, including in the work of Ben Jonson. In this particular case, however, this nostalgia has a pointedly political valence.

65. A number of critics have noted Cavendish's debt to Jonson in this play, including Barton in "Harking Back to Elizabeth," pp. 706–10, and Butler, *Theatre and Crisis*, p. 197.

66. For women's link with consumption in city comedy, in general, see Karen Newman, *Fashioning Femininity and English Renaissance Drama* (Chicago: University of Chicago Press, 1991), esp. pp. 111–43 and my essay, "The Evidence of Fiction: Women's Relationship to Goods in London City Drama," in *Culture and Change: Attending to Early Modern Women*, ed. Margaret Mikesell and Adele Seeff (Newark: University of Delaware Press, 2003), pp. 161–76. For the cultural implications of women's use of cosmetics, see Annette Drew-Bear, *Painted Faces on the Renaissance Stage: The Moral Significance of Face-Painting Conventions* (Lewisburg: Bucknell University Press, 1994).

67. In "'Ignoring the Men': Female Speech and Male Anxiety in Cavendish's *The Female Academy* and Jonson's *Epicoene*" (*In-Between: Essays and Studies in Literary Criticism* 9, nos. 1–2 [2000]: 243–60) Rebecca Merrens argues that Cavendish's play is directly influenced by Jonson's much earlier drama. I want to suggest that while Jonson's Collegians serve as important

forerunners to the many female academicians of ensuing London comedies, Cavendish is responding to the whole tradition, not just to one Jonson play, and perhaps is responding most directly to her husband's work, *The Variety*.

68. Margaret Cavendish, *The Female Academy*, in *Playes* (London, 1662), I.ii.p.653; all further references to the play will be to this edition, which lacks line numbers.

69. In "Margaret Cavendish's Dramatic Utopias and the Politics of Gender," (*SEL* 40 [2000]: 339–54), Erin Lang Bonin comments on the originality of Cavendish's decision to depict what had not been imagined before: "an advanced educational institution for women" (p. 340).

70. Merrens, in "'Ignoring the Men': Female Speech and Male Anxiety in Cavendish's *the Female Academy* and Jonson's *Epicoene*" (pp. 247–53), usefully analyzes how the women's self-sufficiency and indifference to the men's academy enrage the men who listen at the grate.

Epilogue

1. Two excellent studies of place in Restoration and eighteenth-century London and the literature about the city are Cynthia Wall's *The Literary and Cultural Spaces of Restoration London* (Cambridge: Cambridge University Press, 1998) and Miles Ogborn's *Spaces of Modernity: London's Geographies 1680–1780* (New York: Guilford Press, 1998).

2. William Wycherley, *The Country Wife*, in *Restoration Plays*, ed. Brice Harris (New York: Modern Library, 1953), p. 73.

3. Andrew Gurr, *The Shakespearian Playing Companies* (Oxford: Clarendon Press, 1996), pp. 432–33.

Bibliography

Aers, David, ed. *Culture and History 1350–1600: Essays on English Communities, Identities and Writing.* Detroit: Wayne State University Press, 1992.

Agnew, Jean-Christophe. *Worlds Apart: The Market and the Theater in Anglo-American Thought, 1550–1750.* Cambridge: Cambridge University Press, 1986.

Alexander, Catharine M. S., and Stanley Wells, eds. *Shakespeare and Race.* Cambridge: Cambridge University Press, 2000.

Alkan, Tiffany. "Piety or Prodigality? Gresham's Pearl in Thomas Heywood's *2 If You Know Not Me You Know Nobody.*" Unpublished paper.

Altieri, Joanne. "Against Moralizing Jacobean Comedy: Middleton's *Chaste Maid in Cheapside.*" *Criticism* 30 (spring 1988): 171–87.

Ames-Lewis, Francis, ed. *Sir Thomas Gresham and Gresham College.* Aldershot: Ashgate, 1999.

Amin, Samir. *Eurocentrism.* New York: Monthly Review Press, 1989.

Amussen, Susan D., and Adele Seeff, eds. *Attending to Early Modern Women.* Newark: University of Delaware Press, 1998.

Andrews, K. R. *Trade, Plunder, and Settlement: Maritime Enterprise and the Genesis of the British Empire, 1480–1630.* Cambridge: Cambridge University Press, 1984.

Anonymous. *The Academy of Complements.* London, 1650.

Anonymous. *Alarum for London.* London, 1602. Old English Drama Facsimile Edition. Amersham, England: Tudor Facsimile Texts, 1912.

Appleby, Joyce Oldham. *Economic Thought and Ideology in Seventeenth-Century England.* Princeton, N.J.: Princeton University Press, 1978.

Archer, Ian. *The Pursuit of Stability: Social Relations in Elizabethan London.* Cambridge: Cambridge University Press, 1991.

Archer, Ian, Caroline Barron, and Vanessa Harding, eds. *Hugh Alley's Caveat: The Markets of London in 1598.* Folger MS V.a.318. Publication No. 137. London: Topographical Society, 1988.

Archer, John Michael. *Old Worlds: Egypt, Southwest Asia, India, and Russia in Early Modern English Writing.* Stanford, Calif.: Stanford University Press, 2001.

Arditi, Jorge. *A Genealogy of Manners: Transformations of Social Relations in France and England from the Fourteenth to the Eighteenth Century.* Chicago: University of Chicago Press, 1998.

Astington, John H. *English Court Theatre 1558–1642.* Cambridge: Cambridge University Press, 1999.

Bailey, Amanda. " 'Monstrous Manner': Style and the Early Modern Theater." *Criticism* 43 (2001): 249–84.

Baines, Barbara J., and George Walton Williams, eds. *Renaissance Papers 1994.* Southeastern Renaissance Conference, 1995.

Barton, Anne. "Harking Back to Elizabeth: Ben Jonson and Caroline Nostalgia." *ELH* 48 (winter 1981): 706–31.

Beaumont, Francis, John Fletcher, and James Shirley. *Comedies and Tragedies Written by Francis Beaumont and John Fletcher.* London, 1647.

Beier, A. L., and Roger Finlay, eds. *London 1500–1700: The Making of the Metropolis.* London: Longman, 1986.

Bentley, G. E. *The Jacobean and Caroline Stage.* 7 vols. Oxford: Clarendon Press, 1948–61.

Besant, Sir Walter. *London in the Time of the Stuarts.* London: Adam and Charles Black, 1903.

Bly, Mary. *Queer Virgins and Virgin Queans on the Early Modern Stage.* Oxford: Oxford University Press, 2000.

Bonahue, Edward, Jr. "Social Control, the City, and the Market: Heywood's *2 If You Know Not Me, You Know Nobody.*" *Renaissance Papers* (1993): 75–90.

Bone, Quentin. *Henrietta Maria: Queen of the Cavaliers.* Urbana: University of Illinois Press, 1972.

Bonin, Erin Lang. "Margaret Cavendish's Dramatic Utopias and the Politics of Gender." *SEL* 40 (2000): 339–54.

Boulton, Jeremy. *Neighborhood and Society: A London Suburb in the Seventeenth Century.* Cambridge: Cambridge University Press, 1987.

Bourdieu, Pierre. *Distinction: A Social Critique of the Judgment of Taste.* Cambridge, Mass.: Harvard University Press, 1984.

Braudel, Fernand. *The Wheels of Commerce.* Vol. 2 of *Civilization and Capitalism, 15th–18th Century.* Trans. Sian Reynolds. First published in France in 1979. New York: Harper and Row, 1982.

———. *The Perspective of the World.* Vol. 3 of *Civilization and Capitalism, 15th–18th Century.* Trans. Sian Reynolds. First published in France in 1979. Berkeley: University of California Press, 1992.

Brenner, Robert. *Merchants and Revolution: Commercial Change, Political Conflict, and London's Overseas Traders, 1550–1653.* Princeton, N.J.: Princeton University Press, 1993.

Brissenden, Alan. *Shakespeare and the Dance.* Atlantic Highlands, N.J.: Humanities Press, 1981.

Brome, Richard. *The Dramatic Works of Richard Brome Containing Fifteen Comedies Now First Collected in Three Volumes.* London: John Pearson, 1873.

Bruster, Douglas. *Drama and the Market in the Age of Shakespeare.* Cambridge: Cambridge University Press, 1992.

Bryson, Anna. *From Courtesy to Civility: Changing Codes of Conduct in Early Modern England.* Oxford: Clarendon Press, 1998.

Burford, E. J. *Queen of the Bawds or The True Story of Madame Britannica Hollandia and Her House of Obsenitie, Hollands Leaguer.* London: Neville Spearman, 1973.

———. *Bawds and Lodgings: A History of the London Bankside Brothels c. 100–1675.* London: Peter Owen, 1976.

Burner, Sandra A. *James Shirley: A Study of Literary Coteries and Patronage in Seventeenth-Century England.* New York: University Press of America, 1988.

Butler, Martin. *Theatre and Crisis 1632–1642.* Cambridge: Cambridge University Press, 1984.

Callaghan, Dympna, Lorraine Helms, and Jyotsna Singh, eds. *The Weyward Sisters: Shakespeare and Feminist Politics.* Oxford: Blackwell, 1994.

Campos, Edmund Valentine. "Jews, Spaniards, and Portingales: Ambiguous Identities of Portuguese *Marranos* in Elizabethan England." *ELH* 69, no. 3 (2002): 599–616.

Caputi, Anthony. *John Marston: Satirist.* Ithaca, N.Y.: Cornell University Press, 1961.

Cavendish, Margaret. *The Female Academy.* In *Playes.* London, 1662.

Cavendish, William. *The Variety.* London, 1649.

Chambers, E. K. *The Elizabethan Stage.* 4 vols. Oxford: Clarendon Press, 1923.

Clare, Janet. *"Art Made tongue-tied by authority": Elizabethan and Jacobean Dramatic Censorship.* Manchester: Manchester University Press, 1999.

Clark, Ira. *Professional Playwrights: Massinger, Ford, Shirley, and Brome.* Lexington: University of Kentucky Press, 1992.

Clark, Peter, ed. *The Cambridge Urban History of Britain.* Vol. 2. Cambridge: Cambridge University Press, 2000.

Cohen, Walter. *Drama of a Nation: Public Theater in Renaissance England and Spain.* Ithaca, N.Y.: Cornell University Press, 1985.

Colie, Rosalie. *The Resources of Kind: Genre Theory in the Renaissance.* Berkeley: University of California Press, 1973.

Cook, Ann Jennalie. *The Privileged Playgoers of Shakespeare's London, 1576–1642.* Princeton, N.J.: Princeton University Press, 1981.

Cooke, John. *Greene's Tu Quoque or, The Cittie Gallant.* Ed. Alan J. Berman. New York: Garland Publishing, 1984.

Coryat, Thomas. *Coryat's Crudities.* 2 vols. Glasgow: James MacLehose and Sons, 1905.

Cowper, J. M, ed. *Times' Whistle: or A Newe Daunce of Seven Satires, and other Poems.* Early English Text Society 48. London: N. Trubner and Company, 1871.

Cox, John D., and David Kastan, eds. *A New History of Early English Drama.* New York: Columbia University Press, 1997.

Daileader, Celia. "Back Door Sex: Renaissance Gyno-Sodomy, Aretino, and the Exotic." *ELH* 69 (2002): 303–34.

Dallington, Robert. *A Method for Travell: Shewed by Taking the view of France As it stoode in the yeare of our Lord 1598.* London, 1605.

Darby, Graham, ed. *The Origins and Development of the Dutch Revolt.* London: Routledge, 2001.

Davidson, Clifford, and John H. Stroupe, eds. *Drama in the Renaissance: Comparative and Critical Essays.* New York: AMS Press, 1986.

Daybell, James, ed. *Rethinking Women and Politics in Early Modern England.* Aldershot: Ashgate, 2003.

de Certeau, Michel. *The Practices of Everyday Life.* Trans. Steven Rendall. Berkeley: University of California Press, 1984.

Dekker, Thomas. *The Dramatic Works of Thomas Dekker.* Ed. Fredson Bowers. 4 vols. Cambridge: Cambridge University Press, 1953–61.

———. *Thomas Dekker: Selected Writings.* Ed. E. D. Pendry. London: Edward Arnold, 1967.

———. *Lantern and Candle-light. Rogues, Vagabonds, Sturdy Beggars.* Ed. Arthur Kinney. Barre, Mass.: Imprint Society, 1973.

De Montagut, B. *Louange de la Danse.* Ed. R. Ravelhofer. Renaissance Texts from Manuscript 3. Cambridge, England: RTM Publishers, 2000.

Dering, Richard. *The Cries of London.* Ed. Denis Stevens. University Park, Pa.: The Pennsylvania State University Press, 1964.

Derrida, Jacques. *On Cosmopolitanism and Forgiveness.* Trans. Mark Dooley and Michael Hughes. London: Routledge, 2001.

DiGangi, Mario. *The Homoerotics of Early Modern Drama*. Cambridge: Cambridge University Press, 1997.

Dillon, Janette. *Theatre, Court and City, 1595–1610: Drama and Social Space in London*. Cambridge: Cambridge University Press, 2000.

Dobb, Clifford. "London's Prisons." *Shakespeare Survey* 17 (1964): 87–100.

Dolan, Fran. *Whores of Babylon: Catholicism, Gender, and Seventeenth-Century Print Culture*. Ithaca, N.Y.: Cornell University Press, 1999.

Donovan, Dennis G., and A. Leigh Deneef, eds. *Renaissance Papers 1973*. Southeastern Renaissance Conference, 1974.

Drew-Bear, Annette. *Painted Faces on the Renaissance Stage: The Moral Significance of Face-Painting Conventions*. Lewisburg, Pa.: Bucknell University Press, 1994.

Dutton, Richard, and Jean E. Howard, ed. *A Companion to Shakespeare's Works*. Vol. 4, *The Poems, Problem Comedies, Late Plays*. Oxford: Blackwell Publishing, 2003.

Earle, John. *Microcosmography: or, A Piece of the World Discovered in Essays and Characters*. 1628. Reprint, London: Simpkin, Marshall, Hamilton, Kent and Co., 1897.

Elias, Norbert. *The History of Manners*. 1939. Vol. 1 of *The Civilizing Process*. Trans. Edmund Jephcott. New York: Urizon Books, 1978.

Eliot, John. *The Parlement of Pratlers*. 1593. Reprint, London: The Fanfrolico Press, 1928.

Elyot, Thomas. *The Castel of Health*. London, 1541.

Fenner, William. *The Compters Commonwealth*. London, 1616.

Finkelpearl, Philip J. *John Marston of the Middle Temple: An Elizabethan Dramatist in His Social Setting*. Cambridge, Mass.: Harvard University Press, 1969.

Finlay, Roger. *Population and Metropolis: The Demography of London, 1580–1650*. Cambridge: Cambridge University Press, 1981.

Fisher, F. J. *London and the English Economy, 1500–1700*. Ed. P. J. Corfield and N. B. Harte. London and Ronceverte: Hambledon Press, 1990.

Floyd-Wilson, Mary. *English Ethnicity and Race in Early Modern Drama*. Cambridge: Cambridge University Press, 2003.

Forsythe, Robert. *The Relations of Shirley's Plays to the Elizabethan Drama*. New York: Columbia University Press, 1914.

Fowler, Alistair. *Kinds of Literature: An Introduction to the Theory of Genres and Modes*. Cambridge, Mass.: Harvard University Press, 1982.

Frank, Andre Gunder. *ReOrient: Global Economy in the Asian Age*. Berkeley: University of California Press, 1998.

Frassinelli, Pier. "Realism, Desire and Reification: Thomas Middleton's *A Chaste Maid in Cheapside*." *Early Modern Literary Studies* 8, no. 3 (January 2003): 1–26.

Fuchs, Barbara. *Mimesis and Empire: The New World, Islam, and European Identities*. Cambridge: Cambridge University Press, 2001.

Gainsford, Thomas. *The Rich Cabinet*. London, 1616.

Games, Alison. *Agents of Empire: English Cosmopolitans in an Age of Expansion*. Forthcoming.

Gascoigne, George. *The Complete Works of George Gascoigne*. Ed. John W. Cunliffe. 2 vols. Cambridge: Cambridge University Press, 1910.

Gater, G.H., ed, *Charing Cross: The Parish of St. Martin-in-the-Fields*. Vol 16 of *Survey of London*. London: Country Life Ltd., 1935 .

Geckle, George L. *John Marston's Drama: Themes, Images, Sources*. Cranbury, N.J.: Associated University Press, 1980.

Gibbons, Brian. *Jacobean City Comedy: A Study of Satiric Plays by Jonson, Marston, and Middleton*. Cambridge, Mass.: Harvard University Press, 1968.

Gillies, John. *Shakespeare and the Geography of Difference.* Cambridge: Cambridge University Press, 1994.

Goodman, Nicholas. *Hollands Leaguer: A Critical Edition.* Ed. Dean Stanton Barnard, Jr. The Hague: Mouton, 1970.

Gosson, Stephen. *Pleasant Quippes for Upstart Newfangled Gentlewomen.* Ed. Edwin Johnston Howard. Oxford, Ohio: The Anchor Press, 1942.

Gowing, Laura. *Domestic Dangers: Women, Words, and Sex in Early Modern London.* Oxford: Clarendon Press, 1996.

Grassby, Richard. *The Business Community of Seventeenth-Century England.* Cambridge: Cambridge University Press, 1995.

Green, Juana. "The Sempster's Wares; Merchandising and Marrying in *The Fair Maid of the Exchange (1607)*." *Renaissance Drama* 53, no. 4 (2000): 1084–118.

Greenblatt, Stephen, Walter Cohen, Jean E. Howard, and Katharine Eisaman Maus, eds. *The Norton Shakespeare.* New York: Norton, 1997.

Greene, Robert. *A Disputation Betweene a Hee Conny-catcher, and a Shee Conny-catcher.* London, 1592.

Griffiths, Paul. "The Structure of Prostitution in Elizabethan London." *Continuity and Change* 8, no. 1 (1993): 36–63.

Griffiths, Paul, and Mark S. R. Jenner, eds. *Londinopolis: Essays in the Cultural and Social History of Early Modern London.* Manchester: Manchester University Press, 2000.

Gurr, Andrew. *Playgoing in Shakespeare's London.* Cambridge: Cambridge University Press, 1987.

———. *The Shakespearean Stage, 1574–1642.* 3d ed. Cambridge: Cambridge University Press, 1992.

———. *The Shakespearian Playing Companies.* Oxford: Clarendon Press, 1996.

Gwynn, Robin. *Huguenot Heritage: The History and Contribution of Huguenots in Britain.* London: Routledge, 1985.

Hamilton, Donna. "Language as Theme in *The Dutch Courtesan*." *Renaissance Drama* 5 (1972): 75–87.

Harding, Vanessa. "The population of London, 1550–1700: A Review of the Published Evidence." *London Journal* 15 (1990): 111–28.

Harris, Jonathan Gil. *Foreign Bodies and the Body Politic.* Cambridge: Cambridge University Press, 1998.

———. *Sick Economies: Drama, Merchantilism, and Disease in Shakespeare's England.* Philadelphia: University of Pennsylvania Press, 2004.

Haughton, William. *Englishmen for My Money or A Woman Will Have Her Will.* Ed. Lloyd Edward Kermode. Manchester: Manchester University Press. Forthcoming.

Haughton, William. *Englishmen for My Money or A Woman Will Have Her Way.* Ed. Albert Croll Baugh. Philadelphia: University of Pennsylvania Press, 1913.

Haynes, Jonathan. *The Social Relations of Jonson's Theater.* Cambridge: Cambridge University Press, 1992.

Helgerson, Richard. *Forms of Nationhood: The Elizabethan Writing of England.* Chicago: University of Chicago Press, 1992.

Henslowe, Philip. *Henslowe's Diary.* Ed. R. A. Foakes and R. T. Rickert. Cambridge: Cambridge University Press, 1961.

Heywood, Thomas. *The Dramatic Works of Thomas Heywood.* 6 vols. London: John Pearson, 1874.

———. *If You Know Not Me You Know Nobody, Part II.* Oxford University Press: The Malone Society Reprints, 1934.

————. *An Apology for Actors.* Ed. Richard H. Perkinson. London, 1612. Reprint, New York: Scholars' Facsimiles and Reprints, 1941.

———— (?). *The Fair Maid of the Exchange.* Ed. Field Barron. London: Printed for the Shakespeare Society, 1846.

———— (?). *The Fair Maid of the Exchange.* Oxford: The Malone Society Reprints, 1962.

————. *A Woman Killed with Kindness.* Ed. R. W. Van Fossen. London: Methuen, 1961.

Hindley, Charles. *A History of the Cries of London: Ancient and Modern.* 2d ed. London: Charles Hindley, 1884.

Hirschfield, Heather Anne. "'Work Upon That Now': The Production of Parody on the English Renaissance Stage." *Genre* 32 (fall 1999): 175–200.

Hoenselaars, A. J. *Images of Englishmen and Foreigners in the Drama of Shakespeare and His Contemporaries: A Study of Stage Characters and National Identity in English Renaissance Drama 1558–1642.* London: Associated University Press, 1992.

Howard, Jean E. *The Stage and Social Struggle in Early Modern England.* London: Routledge, 1994.

Howard, Jean E., and Scott Shershow, eds. *Marxist Shakespeares.* London: Routledge, 2000.

Howard, Skiles. *The Politics of Courtly Dancing in Early Modern England.* Amherst: University of Massachusetts Press, 1998.

Hulme, Peter, and William H. Sherman, eds. *"The Tempest" and Its Travels.* London: Reaktion Books, 2000.

Hutson, Lorna. *The Usurer's Daughter: Male Friendship and Fictions of Woman in Sixteenth-Century England.* London: Routledge, 1994.

Ingram, Angela. *In the Posture of a Whore: Attitudes to "Bad" Women in Elizabethan and Jacobean Drama.* Salzburg Studies in English Literature 93. Salzburg: Institut für Anglistik und Amerikanistik, 1984.

Ingram, William. *The Business of Playing: The Beginning of the Adult Professional Theater in Elizabethan London.* Ithaca, N.Y.: Cornell University Press, 1992.

Jackson, Ken. "Bethlem and Bridewell in *The Honest Whore* Plays." *SEL* 43, no. 2 (spring 2003): 395–413.

Jenstad, Janelle Day. "Lying-in Like a Countess: The *Lisle Letters*, the Cecil Family, and *A Chaste Maid in Cheapside.*" *The Journal of Medieval and Early Modern Studies* 34 (2004): 373–403.

Jones, Ann Rosalind, and Peter Stallybrass. *Renaissance Clothing and the Materials of Memory.* Cambridge: Cambridge University Press, 2001.

Jonson, Ben. *The Devil Is an Ass and Other Plays.* Ed. Margaret Jane Kidnie. Oxford: Oxford University Press, 2000.

————. *Every Man Out of His Humour.* Ed. Helen Ostovich. Manchester: Manchester University Press, 2001.

————. *The Staple of News.* Ed. Devra Rowland Kifer. Lincoln: University of Nebraska Press, 1975.

Jonson, Ben, George Chapman, and John Marston. *Eastward Ho!* Ed. C. G. Petter. London: Ernest Benn Limited, 1973.

Jordan, W. K. *The Charities of London, 1480–1600: The Aspirations and the Achievements of the Urban Society.* Hamden, Conn.: Archon Books, 1974.

Kamen, Henry. *Spain 1469–1714.* 2d ed. London: Longman, 1991.

Karras, Ruth Mazzo. "The Regulation of Brothels in Late Medieval England." *Signs: Journal of Women in Culture and Society* 14, no. 2 (1989): 399–433.

Kastan, David Scott, ed. *A Companion to Shakespeare*. Oxford: Blackwell Publishing, 2000.

Kerridge, Eric. *Trade and Banking in Early Modern England*. Manchester: Manchester University Press, 1988.

Knights, L. C. *Drama and Society in the Age of Jonson*. 1936. Reprint, London: George W. Stewart, 1951.

Knutson, Rosalyn. *Playing Companies and Commerce in Shakespeare's Time*. Cambridge: Cambridge University Press, 2001.

Korda, Natasha. *Shakespeare's Domestic Economies: Gender and Property in Early Modern England*. Philadelphia: University of Pennsylvania Press, 2002.

Kynaston, Thomas. *The Constitutions of the Museum Minervae*. London, 1636.

Lake, Peter, with Michael Questier. *The Antichrist's Lewd Hat: Protestants, Papists and Players in Post-Reformation England*. New Haven, Conn.: Yale University Press, 2002.

Larkin, James F., and Paul L. Hughes, eds. *Stuart Royal Proclamations*. Vol. 1. Oxford: Clarendon Press, 1973.

Lawner, Lynne, trans. *I Modi: The Sixteen Pleasures: An Erotic Album of the Italian Renaissance*. Evanston, Ill.: Northwestern University Press, 1988.

Leggatt, Alexander. *Citizen Comedy in the Age of Shakespeare*. Toronto: University of Toronto Press, 1973.

Leinwand, Theodore. *The City Staged: Jacobean Comedy, 1603–1613*. Madison: University of Wisconsin Press, 1986.

———. *Theatre, Finance and Society in Early Modern England*. Cambridge: Cambridge University Press, 1999.

Lenz, Joseph. "Base Trade: Theater as Prostitution." *ELH* 60, no. 4 (winter 1983): 833–55.

Lloyd, T. H. *England and the German Hanse, 1157–1611*. Cambridge: Cambridge University Press, 1991.

Manley, Lawrence. *Literature and Culture in Early Modern London*. Cambridge: Cambridge University Press, 1995.

"Many Local Officials Now Make Inmates Pay Their Own Way." *New York Times* 13 August 2004: p. 1, col. 6.

Maquerlot, Jean-Pierre, and Michele Willems, eds. *Travel and Drama in Shakespeare's Time*. Cambridge: Cambridge University Press, 1996.

Marienstrass, Richard. *New Perspectives on the Shakespearean World*. Cambridge: Cambridge University Press, 1985.

Markham, Gervase. "The Famous Whore or Noble Cortizan." London, 1609.

Marmion, Shackerley. *Hollands Leaguer*. London, 1632.

Marsh, Christopher W. *The Family of Love in English Society, 1550–1630*. Cambridge: Cambridge University Press, 1994.

Marston, John. *The Dutch Courtesan*. Ed. M. L. Wine. Lincoln: University of Nebraska Press, 1965.

Martin, Matthew. "'[B]egot between tirewomen and tailors': Commodified Self-Fashioning in *Michaelmas Term*." *Early Modern Literary Studies* 5, no. 1 (May 1999): 21–36.

Massey, Doreen. *Space, Place, and Gender*. Minneapolis: University of Minnesota Press, 1994.

Matar, Nabil. *Islam in Britain 1558–1685*. Cambridge: Cambridge University Press, 1998.

———. *Turks, Moors, and Englishmen in the Age of Discovery*. New York: Columbia University Press, 1999.

Mayne, Jasper. *The Citye Match.* Oxford, 1939.

McGee, C. E., and A. L. Magnusson, eds. *The Elizabethan Theatre XV.* Toronto: P. D. Meany, 2002.

McGrath, Lynette. *Subjectivity and Women's Poetry in Early Modern England.* Aldershot, England: Ashgate Publishing Company, 2002.

McKinnen, Dana G. "A Description of a Restoration Promptbook of Shirley's *The Ball.*" *Restoration and 18th Century Theatre Research* 10 (1971): 25–28.

McKinnon, Dana Gene. "*The Ball* by George Chapman and James Shirley: A Critical Edition." Diss., University of Illinois at Urbana, 1965.

McMullan, Gordon, and Jonathan Hope, eds. *The Politics of Tragicomedy: Shakespeare and After.* New York: Routledge, 1992.

McMullan, John L. *The Canting Crew: London's Criminal Underworld 1550–1700.* New Brunswick: Rutgers University Press, 1984.

Mendelson, Sara, and Patricia Crawford. *Women in Early Modern England 1550–1720.* Oxford: Clarendon, 1998.

Merrens, Rebecca. "'Ignoring the Men': Female Speech and Male Anxiety in Cavendish's *The Female Academy* and Jonson's *Epicoene.*" *In-Between: Essays and Studies in Literary Criticism* 9, no. 1–2 (2000): 243–60.

Merritt, J. F., ed. *Imagining Early Modern London: Perceptions and Portrayals of the City from Stow to Strype, 1598–1720.* Cambridge: Cambridge University Press, 2001.

Middleton, Thomas. *A Chaste Maid in Cheapside.* Ed. Alan Brissenden. London: Ernest Benn, 1968.

———. *Michaelmas Term.* Ed. Gail Kern Paster. Manchester: Manchester University Press, 2000.

Middleton, Thomas, and Thomas Dekker. *The Roaring Girl.* Ed. Andor Gomme. New York: W. W. Norton, 1976.

Mikesell, Margaret, and Adele Seeff, eds. *Culture and Change: Attending to Early Modern Women.* Newark: University of Delaware Press, 2003.

Miles, Theodore. "Place-Realism in a Group of Caroline Plays." *The Review of English Studies* 18 (1942): 428–40.

Motley, Mark. *Becoming a French Aristocrat: The Education of the Court Nobility 1580–1715.* Princeton, N.J.: Princeton University Press, 1990.

Moulton, Ian Frederick. *Before Pornography: Erotic Writing in Early Modern England.* Oxford: Oxford University Press, 2000.

Muldrew, Craig. *The Economy of Obligation: The Culture of Credit and Social Relations in Early Modern England.* London: St. Martin's, 1998.

———. "'A Mutual Assent of her Mind'? Women, Debt, Litigation and Contract in Early Modern England." *History Workshop Journal* 55 (2003): 47–71.

Mulholland, Paul, ed. *The Patient Man and the Honest Whore.* Oxford: Oxford University Press. Forthcoming.

Mullaney, Stephen. *The Place of the Stage: License, Play, and Power in Renaissance England.* Chicago: University of Chicago Press, 1988.

Mynshul, G. *Essays and Characters of a Prison and Prisoners.* London, 1618.

Nardo, Anna K. "'Here's to Thy Health': The Pearl in Hamlet's Wine." *English Language Notes* 23, no. 2 (December 1985): 36–42.

Nashe, Thomas. *Strange News, Of the intercepting certaine letters, and a Convoy of Verses, as they were going Privilie to victuall the Low Countries.* London, 1592.

Nerlich, Michael. *Ideology of Adventure: Studies in Modern Consciousness, 1100–1750.* Vol. 1. Minneapolis: University of Minnesota Press, 1987.

Newman, Karen. *Fashioning Femininity and English Renaissance Drama.* Chicago: Chicago University Press, 1991.

Noling, Kim. "Women's Wit and Women's Will in *When You See Me, You Know Me.*" *Studies in English Literature, 1500–1800* 33 (spring 1993): 327–42.

Nostbakken, Faith M. "Rowley's *When You See Me You Know Me*: Political Drama in Transition." *Cahiers Elisabethains* 45 (April 1995): 71–78.

Ogborn, Miles. *Spaces of Modernity: London's Geographies, 1680–1780.* New York: Guilford Press, 1998.

Orlin, Lena, ed. *Material London, ca. 1600.* Philadelphia: University of Pennsylvania Press, 2000.

Ostovich, Helen, ed. *Every Man Out of His Humour.* Manchester: Manchester University Press, 2001.

Ostovich, Helen, Mary V. Silcox, and Graham Roebuck, eds. *Other Voices, Other Views: Expanding the Canon in English Renaissance Studies.* Newark: University of Delaware Press, 1999.

Palliser, D. M. *The Age of Elizabeth: England under the Later Tudors 1547–1603.* London: Longman, 1983.

Parlin, Hanson T. *A Study in Shirley's Comedies of London Life.* Reprint from *Bulletin of the University of Texas,* no. 317. November 15, 1914.

Parrott, Thomas, ed. *The Poems and Plays of George Chapman, The Comedies.* London: George Routledge and Sons, 1914.

Paster, Gail Kern. *The Idea of the City in the Age of Shakespeare.* Athens: University of Georgia Press, 1985.

———. *The Body Embarrassed: Drama and the Disciplines of Shame in Early Modern England.* Ithaca, N.Y.: Cornell University Press, 1993.

Peacham, Henry. *Peacham's Compleat Gentleman 1634.* Ed. G. S. Gordon. Oxford: Clarendon Press, 1906.

———. *The Complete Gentleman and Other Works.* Ed. Virgil B. Heltzel. Ithaca, N.Y.: Cornell University Press, 1962.

Pendry, E. D. *Elizabethan Prisons and Prison Scenes.* Salzburg Studies in English Literature 17. 2 vols. Salzburg, Austria: Institut für Englische Sprache und Literatur, 1974.

Perkinson, Richard H. "Topographical Comedy in the 17th Century." *ELH* 3 (1936): 270–90.

Pettegree, Andrew. *Foreign Protestant Communities in Sixteenth-Century London.* Oxford: Clarendon Press, 1986.

Pinciss, G. M. *Forbidden Matter: Religion in the Drama of Shakespeare and His Contemporaries.* Newark: University of Delaware Press, 2000.

Platter, Thomas. *Travels in England.* Reprint in *London in the Age of Shakespeare: An Anthology.* Ed. Lawrence Manley. University Park: The Pennsylvania State University Press, 1986.

Playford, John. *The English Dancing Master: or, Plaine and Easie Rules for Dancing of Country Dances, with the Tune to each Dance.* London, 1651.

Pliny the Elder. *The Historie of the World.* Trans. Philemon Holland. London, 1601.

Plowden, Alison. *Henrietta Maria: Charles I's Indomitable Queen.* Phoenix Mill, England: Sutton Publishing, 2001.

Prest, Wilfrid R. *The Inns of Court under Elizabeth I and the Early Stuarts, 1590–1640.* London: Longman, 1972.

Prynne, William. *Histrio-mastix.* London, 1633.

Qualtiere, Lewis F., and William W. E. Slights. "Contagion and Blame in Early Modern England: The Case of the French Pox." *Literature and Medicine* 22, no. 1 (spring 2003): 1–24.

Rabb, Theodore K. *Enterprise and Empire: Merchant and Gentry Investment in the Expansion of England, 1575–1630.* Cambridge, Mass.: Harvard University Press, 1967.

Rappaport, Steve. *Worlds Within Worlds: Structures of Life in Sixteenth-Century London.* Cambridge: Cambridge University Press, 1989.

Rich, E. E., ed. *The Cambridge Economic History.* Vol. 5. Cambridge: Cambridge University Press, 1977.

Robinson, Marsha S. *Writing the Reformation:* Actes and Monuments *and the Jacobean History Play.* Aldershot, England: Aldergate, 2002.

Rowley, Samuel. *When You See Me, You Know Me.* Gen. ed. F. P. Wilson. The Malone Society Reprints 88. Oxford: Oxford University Press, 1952.

Rowley, William. *A New Wonder, A Woman Never Vext.* Ed. George Cheatham. New York: Peter Lang, 1993.

Rye, William Brenchley, ed. *England as Seen by Foreigners.* London: John Russell Smith, 1865.

Salkeld, Duncan. "Black Luce and the Curtizans of Shakespeare's London." *Signatures* 2 (2000): 1–10.

Salter, F. R. *Sir Thomas Gresham.* London: Leonard Parsons, 1925.

Sanders, Julie. *Caroline Drama: The Plays of Massinger, Ford, Shirley and Brome.* Plymouth, England: Northcote House Publishers, 1999.

Saunders, Ann, ed. *The Royal Exchange.* Publication No. 152. London: The London Topographical Society, 1997.

Schofield, John. *The Building of London from the Conquest to the Great Fire.* 3d ed. Phoenix Mill: Sutton Publishing, 1999.

Scott, William. *An Essay of Drapery.* London, 1635.

Shammas, Carole. *The Pre-Industrial Consumer in England and America.* Oxford: Clarendon Press, 1990.

Shapiro, James. *Shakespeare and the Jews.* New York: Columbia University Press, 1996.

Sharpham, Edward. *The Fleire.* London, 1607.

Shaw, Philip. "The Position of Thomas Dekker in Jacobean Prison Literature." *PMLA* 22 (1947): 366–91.

Sheidley, William E. "George Gascoigne and *The Spoyle of Antwerpe.*" *Literature and the Arts* (spring/summer 1996): 48–64.

Shepard, Alexandra. "Manhood, Credit and Patriarchy in Early Modern England c. 1580–1640." *Past and Present* 167 (May 2000): 75–106.

———. *Meanings of Manhood in Early Modern England.* Oxford: Oxford University Press, 2003.

Shepherd, Simon. *Amazons and Warrior Women: Varieties of Feminism in Seventeenth-Century Drama.* New York: St. Martin's Press, 1982.

Sheppard, F. H. W., gen. ed. *Survey of London.* London: Athalone Press, 1970.

Sherman, Anita. "The Status of Charity in Thomas Heywood's *If You Know Not Me You Know Nobody II.*" *MARDIE* (1999): 99–120.

Shesgreen, Sean, ed. *The Criers and Hawkers of London: Engravings and Drawings by Marcellus Laroon.* Stanford, Calif.: Stanford University Press, 1990.

Shirley, James. *The Dramatic Works and Poems of James Shirley.* Ed. William Gifford and Alexander Dyce. 6 vols. London, 1833. Reprint, New York: Russell and Russell, 1966.

———. *The Lady of Pleasure*. Ed. Ronald Huebert. Manchester: Manchester University Press, 1986.

Shugg, Wallace. "Prostitution in Shakespeare's London." *Shakespeare Studies* 10 (1977): 291–313.

Slack, Paul. *The English Poor Law 1531–1782*. London: Macmillan, 1990.

Smith, David L., Richard Strier, and David Bevington, eds. *The Theatrical City: Culture, Theatre and Politics in London 1576–1649*. Cambridge: Cambridge University Press, 1995.

Smith, Emma. " 'So Much English by the Mother': Gender, Foreigners, and the Mother Tongue in William Haughton's *Englishmen for My Money*." *MARDIE* 13 (2001): 165–81.

Smith, Pamela H., and Paula Findlen, eds. *Merchants and Marvels: Commerce, Science, and Art in Early Modern Europe*. New York: Routledge, 2002.

Smuts, R. Malcolm. "The Court and Its Neighborhood: Royal Policy and Urban Growth in the Early Stuart West End." *Journal of British Studies* 30 (April 1991): 117–49.

Stevenson, Laura. *Praise and Paradox: Merchants and Craftsmen in Elizabethan Popular Literature*. Cambridge: Cambridge University Press, 1984.

Stewart, Alan. " 'Every Soyle to Mee is Natural': Figuring Denization in William Haughton's *Englishmen for My Money*." *Renaissance Drama* 35 (2006): 55–81.

Stone, Lawrence. *The Crisis of the Aristocracy, 1558–1641*. Oxford: Clarendon, 1965.

Stow, John. *A Survey of London*. Ed. Charles Lethbridge Kingsford. 2 vols. Oxford: Clarendon Press, 1908.

Stoye, John. *English Travellers Abroad 1604–1667*. Rev. ed. New Haven, Conn.: Yale University Press, 1989.

Taylor, John. "The Praise and Vertue of a Jayle, and Jaylers." London, 1623.

———. *A Common Whore*. London, 1635.

Thirsk, Joan. *Economic Policy and Projects: The Development of a Consumer Society in Early Modern England*. Oxford: Clarendon Press, 1978.

Thomas, Keith. *Religion and the Decline of Magic*. New York: Charles Scribner's Sons, 1971.

Thomson, Peter. *Shakespeare's Theatre*. London: Routledge and Kegan Paul, 1983.

Traub, Valerie. *The Renaissance of Lesbianism in Early Modern England*. Cambridge: Cambridge University Press, 2004.

Turner, Henry S., ed. *The Culture of Capital: Property, Cities, and Knowledge in Early Modern England*. New York: Routledge, 2002.

Twyning, John. *London Dispossessed: Literature and Social Space in the Early Modern City*. London: Macmillan, 1998.

Van Gelderen, Martin. *The Political Thought of the Dutch Revolt 1555–1590*. Cambridge: Cambridge University Press, 1992.

Van Meteren, Emanuel. "Pictures of the English in Queen Elizabeth's Reign." In *England as Seen by Foreigners*. Ed. William Brenchley Rye. London: John Russell Smith, 1865.

Veevers, Erica. *Images of Love and Religion: Queen Henrietta Maria and Court Entertainments*. Cambridge: Cambridge University Press, 1989.

Vitkus, Daniel. *Turning Turk: English Theater and the Multicultural Mediterranean, 1570–1630*. New York: Palgrave Macmillan, 2003.

Walker, Kim. "*New Prison*: Representing the Female Actor in Shirley's *The Bird in a Cage* (1633)." *ELR* 21 (1991): 385–400.

Wall, Cynthia. *The Literary and Cultural Spaces of Restoration London.* Cambridge: Cambridge University Press, 1998.

Wallerstein, Immanuel. *The Modern World System.* Vol. 1, *Capitalist Agriculture and the Origins of the European World-Economy in the Sixteenth Century.* New York: Academic Press, 1974.

Wernham, R. B., ed. *The New Cambridge Modern History.* Vol. 3, *The Counter-Reformation and Price Revolution 1559–1610.* Cambridge: Cambridge University Press, 1968.

Wheeler, John. *A Treatise of Commerce.* Ed. George Hotchkiss. New York: New York University Press, 1931.

Whigham, Frank. *Ambition and Privilege: The Social Tropes of Elizabethan Courtesy Theory.* Berkeley: University of California Press, 1984.

White, Paul Whitfield, and Suzanne R. Westfall, eds. *Shakespeare and Theatrical Patronage in Early Modern England.* Cambridge: Cambridge University Press, 2002.

Whitney, Isabella. "Wyll and Testament." Ed. Betty Travitsky. *ELR* 10 (1980): 76–95.

Williams, Gordon. *A Dictionary of Sexual Language and Imagery in Shakespearean and Stuart Literature.* 3 vols. London: The Athalone Press, 1994.

Woods, Suzanne, and Margaret Hannay. Ed. *Teaching Tudor and Stuart Women Writers.* New York: The Modern Language Association, 2000.

Wrightson, Keith. *Earthly Necessities: Economic Lives in Early Modern Britain.* New Haven: Yale University Press, 2000.

Wycherley. *The Country Wife.* In *Restoration Plays.* Ed. Brice Harris. New York: Modern Library, 1973.

Yungblut, Laura. *Strangers Settled Here Amongst Us: Policies, Perceptions, and the Presence of Aliens in Elizabethan England.* London: Routledge, 1996.

Zucker, Adam. "Comedies of Place: Space, Status, and the Social Work of Comic Form in Early Modern England." Diss., Columbia University, 2004.

Index

Acknowledgments

More than most of my books, this one grows directly from my teaching. For several years I gave a graduate seminar at Columbia called "Writing London Circa 1600," and it was in those courses that I developed many of the ideas, and taught many of the obscure plays that appear in this book. I remain deeply grateful to the several classes of Columbia's superb graduate students who cheerfully made their way with me through this material. They contributed to the making of this book in countless ways, and they made it fun.

Many colleagues and friends gave crucial help along the way. Phyllis Rackin, as usual, read every word and gave the manuscript the generous critique for which she is famous. So did my colleague Ann Douglas whose interest in things outside her "field" never ceases to amaze me. I also benefitted from the expert advice of Alan Stewart, Julie Crawford, and David Kastan, fellow inhabitants of Philosophy Hall, and from conversations with Felicity Nussbaum, Crystal Bartolovich, Vanessa Harding, Constance Jordan, Jonathan Gil Harris, Mary Beth Rose, Margaret Ferguson, Fran Dolan, Deborah Harkness, Karen Newman, Alison Games, David Cressy, Dympna Callaghan, Don Wayne, Louis Montrose, Cynthia Herrup, Judith Bennett, Chris Kyle, Heather James, Lena Orlin, Martha Howell, Elaine Comb-Shilling, Ania Loomba, Peter Stallybrass, Margreta DeGrazia, John Archer, and Kate McLuskie.

To an unusual degree this book owes its final birthing to the generosity of Roy Ritchie who at a crucial time gave me a yearlong fellowship at the Huntington Library. There I discovered just how pleasant it is to write a book surrounded by the wonderful resources of a great research library and the finest gardens in Southern California. I am grateful to the expert staff of the Huntington for the many kinds of help they gave me that year and to a wonderful group of fellow scholars, but especially to Louise and Roy, the most gracious hosts I know.

A portion of Chapter 1 of this book was published as "Competing Ideologies of Commerce in Thomas Heywood's *If You Know Not Me You Know Nobody, Part II*," copyright © 2002, from *The Culture of Capital: Property, Cities, and Knowledge in Early Modern England*, edited by Henry Turner, reproduced by permission of Routledge/Taylor & Francis,

Group, LLC. Portions of Chapter 3 appeared as "Mastering Difference in *The Dutch Courtesan,*" *Shakespeare Studies* 24 (1996): 105–17; as "Prostitutes, Shopkeepers, and the Shaping of Urban Subjects in *The Honest Whore,*" in *The Elizabethan Theatre XV,* edited by C. E. McGee and A. L Magnussen (Toronto: P. D. Meany, 2002), all rights reserved, reproduced by permission; and as "Sex and the Early Modern City: Staging the Bawdy Houses of London," in *The Impact of Feminism in English Renaissance Studies,* edited by Dympna Callaghan (New York: Palgrave, 2006), reproduced by permission of Palgrave Macmillan. Part of Chapter 4 appears in an essay entitled "Dancing Masters and the Production of Cosmopolitan Bodies in Caroline Town Comedy," in *Localizing Caroline Drama, 1625–1642,* edited by Alan Zucker and Alan Farmer (New York: Palgrave, 2006), reproduced by permission of Palgrave Macmillan. I am grateful for permission to reprint these materials as part of this book.

My family knows, I think, how much pleasure they bring me and how much I rely on them to put work in its place. Nonetheless, I want to tell them. Thanks and much more to Jim, Katie, Caleb, Barb, Dan, Woody, Gib, and Mom.